CHAPTER 3 Writing with Sentence Variety

CHAPTER 4 Writing Well-Structured Paragraphs

CHAPTER 5 Writing Effective Compositions

Achieving Writer's Purpose

CHAPTER 6 **Personal Writing:**
Self-Expression and Reflection

CHAPTER 9 Writing to Inform and Explain

CHAPTER 10 Writing to Persuade

Applying Communication Skills

⬤ CHAPTER 14 ⬤ Directions and Speeches

Communication Resource

CHAPTER 15 Vocabulary

CHAPTER 16 Dictionary

CHAPTER 17 Library and Media Center

COMPOSITION

e firs
nd almo
oped for so
hless. The ho
miraculo
o fe

Using Your Writing Process

Good writing is easy to read. It may be so smooth and flowing that it seems as though the writer simply sat down and wrote it all out in complete form. Chances are, however, that the writing took time and effort. Good writing only appears effortless.

Think about your own writing. Do you spend time thinking of a good subject to write about? Do you plan, scratch out, erase, start over, and sometimes just give up for a while? If so, you are like most writers. Writing is a back-and-forth process of thinking, writing, rewriting, thinking again, and always improving.

Although the order of the stages may vary, most writers go through five main stages during the writing process. These are prewriting, drafting, revising, editing, and publishing. In this chapter, you will see how other writers go through the five stages and then apply them in your own writing.

Reading with a Writer's Eye

In the following selection, Graham Salisbury describes places, people, and things that have inspired him to write his books for young readers. Read the selection first to appreciate how the author turns the events of his life into ideas for his books. Reread the narrative to understand how Salisbury uses the first, or prewriting, stage of the writing process to develop these ideas into stories.

FROM

EIGHTH BOOK
of Junior Authors and Illustrators

Graham Salisbury

The most significant element of my life is the fact that I was raised, essentially, without a father. Although I had three of them, I knew none of them. My real father was killed in World War II; my first step father died when I was ten; my second step father was inaccessible. My stories often explore friendship, loyalty, courage, honor, and the relationship between fathers and sons. That last part is for me; it's what I do to fill the fatherless void in my life.

My stories come from the far corners of my mind, and if I'm lucky, from my deepest heart. "Blue Skin of the Sea" captured pieces of my adolescence on the Big Island of Hawaii. "Under the Blood-Red Sun" explored a question I'd grown up with: what was it like in Honolulu on the day Pearl Harbor was bombed? "Shark Bait" was based on a good friend of mine, a kid who loved to fight, something I wanted no part of. But he had this magnetic pull on me. I really liked the guy.

"Jungle Dogs" grew out of a phrase that came to me one day as I was driving to the gym: "My hero is my dog." Weird, how that phrase just popped up like that. But it made me think of heroes, the people we look up to in our lives. What makes them stand out? What makes them such extraordinary human beings? What is a hero? The story began (quite unexpectedly, actually) as I was working on something else. That weird phrase wouldn't let go: my hero is my dog.

I day dreamed. I considered possibilities.

I began to write: Far out on the ocean a small reef of clouds. . . .

And I was gone. Slipped away into another world.

I love that part, that entering into new worlds.

I drew on my experiences delivering the morning paper in Kailua with the bats swooshing just overhead. I drew on friendships I had, on places I explored. I drew on my respect for strong father-son and strong sibling relationships. I drew on my gut feelings, looking for a heartbeat.

Which is where all good stories must begin.

When it comes to writing, I believe in magic. Generally, I have in mind a glimpse of where I want to go when I begin a novel. I try to sketch out a premise and possible storyline before I begin. It's all extremely nebulous at this point, trying to create something out of nothing. The magic comes, really, in the writing. Something happens between my fingertips and the keyboard. I don't understand it, but it's absolutely the most fabulous and surely the most mysterious part of the writing process: write, and things happen.

Thinking as a Writer

Analyzing a Writer's Process

Much of Salisbury's narrative is about his prewriting process, or the events, feelings, and thoughts that inspire his stories. Young writers are often told to write only about what they know. Notice that Salisbury, however, also finds inspiration by daydreaming about what he wishes he knew.

- What events in Salisbury's life inspired some of his books?
- How do you think Salisbury is able to write about things he does not know, such as "what it was like in Honolulu when Pearl Harbor was bombed"?

Following a Writer's Train of Thought

Oral Expression Read the third paragraph of the selection aloud. Notice that Salisbury is writing as he might have been thinking at the time.

- Read the paragraph aloud again. This time, put yourself in Salisbury's shoes and free your imagination. Plan your own story beginning with the sentence "My hero is my dog."
- Tell your story to a friend. Feel free to add details.

Developing a Sense of Place

Viewing Places that capture a writer's imagination can be powerful raw material for the writing process. Observe these photographs. How might living in Hawaii have influenced Salisbury's work?

- What kinds of stories do you think a big city would have inspired Salisbury to write?

Refining Your Writing Process

No two writers follow the same steps in putting their thoughts into writing, but there is a general process that they use to develop ideas and communicate them effectively. Mastering this process will help you improve your writing at your own pace.

Your **writing process** is the series of stages that you go through when you are developing your ideas and discovering the best way to express them.

You may begin with a prewriting stage, when you jot down notes or brainstorm, and end when you give the finished piece to someone to read, but you probably do not proceed in a straight line through the stages in between. You may like to revise as you are drafting, for example, or you may prefer to revise after you have written a draft that you feel is complete. However you proceed, in time you will develop a writing process that works for you.

This icon will remind you to save your work in a convenient place as you work through the stages of writing. You may wish to store it in a manila folder or a binder. If you usually work on a computer, you will probably want to create a folder on your hard drive, along with some kind of backup copy on a removable storage disk. Then you can easily return to the piece you are writing and continue to work on it, or use it later for inspiration.

COMPUTER TIP

Your computer is like the world's biggest filing cabinet with an unlimited supply of folders. From the File menu, choose New Folder. Then Save your composition in the folder. Be sure to give your folder a title so you can find it later.

Process of Writing

The following diagram illustrates the stages writers go through as they create. Notice that the diagram loops back and forth. This looping shows how you often move back and forth among various stages of writing instead of going step-by-step from beginning to end. You can go back to any stage at any point until you are satisfied with the quality of your writing.

Prewriting includes the invention you do before writing your first draft. During prewriting you find and develop a subject, purpose, and audience, collect ideas and details, and make a basic plan for presenting them.

Prewriting

Drafting

Revising

Publishing

Editing

Drafting is expressing your ideas in sentences and paragraphs following your plan, as well as incorporating new ideas you discover while writing. Drafting includes forming a beginning, a middle, and an end—an introduction, a body, and a conclusion.

Revising means rethinking what you have written and reworking it to increase its clarity, smoothness, and power.

Editing involves checking and reworking sentences and sentence structure. It also includes looking for, and correcting, errors in grammar, usage, and mechanics and proofreading your final version before making it public.

Publishing is sharing your work with an audience.

Your Writer's Portfolio

As you begin your writing, think of yourself as an apprentice learning a craft. With each new composition you write, you can come a step closer to developing your own composing process. A good way to track your progress is to keep a **portfolio**—a collection of your work that represents various types of writing and your progress in them.

PORTFOLIO
This icon represents a reminder throughout the book to place your work in your writing portfolio.

Checklists at the end of each chapter will also remind you to consider including the composition you have been working on in your portfolio. When you add a piece to your portfolio, be sure to date it. Then you will have a record of when you wrote each piece.

As you work through the writing assignments in your class, you will be asked to do many kinds of writing—sharing a story from your own life, writing a poem, describing a scene, researching a complex topic, writing a letter, and many more. No single assignment could show all your skill as a writer, but collecting various works along the way can demonstrate the range of your growing skills.

You may be asked to write evaluations of your progress throughout the year. Include these evaluations in your portfolio along with your writing. This will help you examine both your success as a writer and the areas of your work that could be stronger. At year's end, you may be asked to write a "cover letter" for your portfolio in which you summarize its contents, explain why you included each piece, and evaluate your overall progress

Throughout the writing activities, you will be asked to take "Time Out to Reflect." Reflecting on your experience as a writer will give you an opportunity to develop your process even further. You can keep your written reflections in your portfolio as well.

> ## Guidelines for Including Work in Your Portfolio
> - To trace your progress, write the date on each piece of writing.
> - Attach a brief note to the piece of writing about why you decided to place it in your portfolio.
> - Include unfinished work if you feel that it was an important effort for you.

Prewriting ◄ Writing Process

During prewriting you let your mind bubble and brew with ideas. You develop a plan for your composition. After a while, you settle on a good choice of subject. You think of interesting details to back up your ideas. You organize your ideas and put them into a form that will make sense to readers.

Prewriting actually means "before writing." Yet most prewriting strategies, or techniques, involve writing. Sometimes the writing is as simple as jotting down notes. At other times you may make lists or even draw diagrams to organize your thoughts. If you keep a writing folder to store all of your work—even your notes—you will have a ready source of ideas whenever the urge to write strikes you.

Strategies for Finding a Subject

Your first goal during prewriting is to think of a worthwhile subject. Much of what you write will come from your own interests.

Taking Inventory of Your Interests Make lists of what you like, things you know about, even things you want to know more about. You may discover new things about yourself.

PRACTICE YOUR SKILLS

● *Taking an Interest Inventory*

Complete the following personal profile. List as many items as you can think of. Save your writing for future use.

My Favorites
Subjects in school:
Books:
Animals:

My Experiences
Funniest:
Proudest:
Most embarrassing:

People in My Life
Most unusual:
Oldest:
Role model:

Interests
Lessons I've taken:
Lessons I'd like
    to take:

Opinions
About school:
About my generation:
About the media:

Freewriting   Writing freely without stopping can also help you think of ideas. Do not worry about spelling or grammar. If you stop and feel unable to think of anything, write, "I don't know what to say" until you think of another idea. Your ideas will flow again.

MODEL: Freewriting from Scratch

What should I write about? I can't think of anything to say. I can think of some things to say but nothing interesting. Just boring. Boring thoughts. So here I am typing away at my computer. I like my computer. I can do research, write, play games, or go on the Internet. I wonder what computers will be able to do in the future. Maybe they'll be able to clean my room! I wonder if the people who invented the computer ever imagined all the things they'd be doing today.

As the student wrote, the subject of computers and their possible future applications began to emerge. Freewriting can result in different ideas that can be related to one another, or lead to distinct subjects or ideas.

> I'm supposed to write about my summer vacation, but I didn't go anywhere. I didn't do anything exciting. I'm trying to think of something interesting to write about, but nothing really happened. I saw a few movies with my friends. I watched some television but it was all reruns. It was kind of boring. Watching those birds outside my window was more exciting than seeing the same programs over and over. Hey, maybe I could write about that—the birds. My whole family thought it was interesting. We spent a lot of time this summer gathered around the window looking at the nest. It makes me smile when I think about it.

PRACTICE YOUR SKILLS

Freewriting

Write freely for five minutes. Write everything that comes to mind. Allow your writing to follow wherever your imagination leads you. When you have finished, review your work. Underline any ideas that seem interesting and could be further developed into a story or poem.

Freewriting with a Focus

Freewrite again, but this time concentrate on any of the subjects or passages you underlined from the preceding exercise. Try to include as many details as you can to develop your subject. Afterward, compare your two freewriting exercises and determine which one worked better for you.

Keeping a Journal Journal writing will also help you discover ideas. You can write about anything you want in your journal: the day's events, your worries, your hopes and dreams for the future. Your journal should be a place where you always feel free to write about what interests you. As you record thoughts, be sure to write in your journal every day and date each entry. You will find many journal writing activities in this book. Read the following journal excerpts to understand just a few of the kinds of writing that can be done in a journal.

I keep a small sheath of 3 x 5 cards in my billfold. If I think of a good sentence, I'll write it down. Occasionally, there's one that sings so perfectly the first time that it stays, like "My boy has stopped speaking to me and I don't think I can bear it." I wrote that down on a 3 x 5 card, perhaps on a bus, or after walking the dog. I store them in filing cabinets.

—*Joseph Heller,* The Writer's Chapbook

May 7, 1988

From time to time when we're driving in the country, Abdelouahaid recounts something that happened or is said to have happened in a village we're passing through. Some of the stories are of the sort that it would never occur to me to invent.

—*Paul Bowles*, Journal, Tangier 1987–1988

1942

I can shake off everything if I write. My sorrows disappear, my courage is reborn. I can capture everything when I write, my thoughts, my ideals and my fantasies.

—*Anne Frank,* The Diary of Anne Frank

April 15, 1912

I was awakened by a steward with a message from the Marconi Operator of my ship to the effect that the Titanic was sending out the C.O.D. call.

—*Edgar Parks*, Journal

PRACTICE YOUR SKILLS

● *Writing in Your Journal*

You encounter words and images that make impressions on you everyday. Advertisements, conversations, or dialogue in a movie or book may lead you to reflect on a topic or new ideas. Write in your journal anything that you have heard or read that made an impression. Include particular words that caused you to wonder or stirred an intellectual or emotional response.

Keeping a Learning Log   A **Learning Log** is a section of your journal that can be used as space for writing your reflections on topics that intrigue you. One purpose of the Learning Log is to help you discover what you already know about a topic and what you still need to learn. For example, suppose you were interested in learning more about future computer technology. Your entry might look like this.

MODEL: Learning Log Entry

> I can't imagine life without computers. I've heard that computer chips will control almost every machine people use. I wonder if a computer can even read my brain waves some day and write down what I'm thinking! Scary thought! I can do some research on the Internet and at the library on what computers will be able to do in the future.

Creating a Personalized Editing Checklist   A **Personalized Editing Checklist** is a section of your **journal** where you can keep track of the errors that you make in your writing, such as misspellings, usage mistakes, and mechanical errors. When you are editing your writing, you should refer to this checklist.

Choosing and Limiting a Subject

A good way to find a subject is to review everything you have written to see if any ideas or subjects appear more than once. As you read the following guidelines for choosing a good subject, remember that the most important guideline is your genuine interest in exploring a subject more fully in writing.

> ### Guidelines for Choosing a Subject
>
> - Choose a subject that genuinely interests you.
> - Choose a subject that will interest your readers.
> - Choose a subject that you know something about or can research with reasonable effort.

PRACTICE YOUR SKILLS

Making Connections Between Subjects

Write freely for five minutes to connect these two seemingly unrelated subjects: earthquakes and teenagers. Follow your hunches and do not be afraid to write something that may at first seem silly.

Limiting a Subject   Avoid choosing general topics, such as "sports" or "current events." Such subjects are too broad and often result in compositions that are poorly organized and over-generalized. Your next step is to limit your subject to one you can cover in the time and space you have.

> ### Guidelines for Limiting a Subject
>
> Limit your subject to:
> - One person or example that represents the subject.
> - A specific time or place.
> - A specific event.
> - A specific condition, purpose, or procedure.

Creative Thinking

The best time for planning a book," said Agatha Christie, the famous mystery writer, "is while you're doing the dishes." Have you ever noticed that some of your best ideas come to you when you are doing a mindless task? When you are not concentrating, your mind is free to wander where it will. In the process, it sometimes comes up with ideas that forced, concentrated thought would have missed. This kind of loose, relaxed thinking is called **creative thinking.** During prewriting, creative thinking helps you think of ideas.

A loose, relaxed mind is the most important requirement for thinking creatively. All of the following habits will help you achieve the best possible results from creative thinking.

- **Be open to new approaches and viewpoints.** Look at the familiar sport of baseball, for example, as if you came from another culture—or another planet! Better yet, think about baseball from the bat's point of view.
- **Take risks.** Creative thinking may at first result in thoughts that are unfamiliar, silly, or seem wrong. Explore them anyway. However, many good, sound ideas started as "silly" thoughts.
- **Follow your hunches.** If you have a feeling that something is worthwhile, explore it. If your hunch is wrong, you will still have learned something.
- **Make connections.** Whenever possible, look for ways to connect your sometimes scattered ideas. Look for unusual or surprising connections between thoughts that may at first seem unrelated.

Considering Your Purpose

Much of the writing you encounter has been written for a specific audience and purpose. For example, a political speechwriter may compose a speech intended to convince legislators to pass a law. Here are some purposes for writing and appropriate types of writing for each purpose.

> ### Writing Purposes
> - to inform (a nonfiction book or article)
> - to entertain (a humorous story in a magazine)
> - to persuade (an advertisement or editorial)
> - to express your feelings (a diary or journal)
> - to create a story, play, or poem (fiction, drama, poetry)

Once you have determined your purpose and the type of writing, you can begin to gather details that are appropriate to your purpose. If your purpose is to create a story, for example, you might develop your subject with events and descriptions. If your purpose is to persuade the reader to buy a product, you could gather together facts, examples, and reasons why the reader should buy the product.

PRACTICE YOUR SKILLS

● *Identifying Purpose*

Identify one possible writing purpose behind each of the following composition subjects. Be prepared to explain your answers.

1. the time I stumbled onto a big secret

2. why people should vote for Tania Martin for class president

3. why the sky changes colors during a sunset

4. what every student should know about the school's rules

Considering Your Audience

Understanding the needs of the people who will be reading your work will also help you choose the best details for your composition. Ask yourself the following questions.

> ## Audience Profile Questions
> - Are my readers adults, teens, or children?
> - What do they already know about my subject?
> - What opinions or attitudes are they likely to have about my subject?
> - What terms, if any, might I need to define for my readers?

For most of the writing you do in school, your teacher and classmates will be your audience. From time to time, though, you might want to write for a different audience: a friend, a relative, a newspaper editor. Always ask yourself questions about your audience to understand how best to address its needs.

PRACTICE YOUR SKILLS

● *Considering Audience*

Suppose you are writing a composition explaining how to start a campfire. Read each statement below about the needs and interests of different audiences. Write "True" or "False" for each statement. Explain your reasoning for each answer.

1. If you were writing for fourth graders, you would need to stress the importance of following safety rules more than if you were writing for adults.

2. If you were writing for teens who had spent a number of years in a scout troop, you would need to spell out every step in its simplest form.

3. If you were writing for third graders, you could use such words as *ignite, fuel,* and *combustion.*

Developing a Subject

Once you have determined your subject, audience, and purpose, you have formed the frame of your composition. However, you still need to fill in that frame with facts, examples, events, reasons, or descriptions. The following strategies will help you develop your subject.

Brainstorming for Details Now that you know what kinds of details you need in order to develop your subject well, you can use brainstorming to help you think of appropriate ideas and details.

Brainstorming means writing down everything that comes to mind when you think of a subject. One idea will lead to another, and then to still another. Before long, you will have a list of ideas, such as the following list on the subject of a mother cardinal caring for her young.

MODEL: Brainstorming List

- nest in vine outside window
- saw eggs
- saw tiny birds with heads up waiting to be fed
- mother sat on eggs to hatch them
- mother would feed hungry birds
- babies looked pink and bare

Writing Tip

Do not worry about neatness when you brainstorm. List ideas as quickly as you can write them. You will be able to rearrange, eliminate, and add later. Try to write as many details as you can.

Practice Your Skills

● *Brainstorming*

Choose one of the following subjects, and brainstorm a list of ideas and details.

- favorite hobby
- favorite book
- favorite TV show
- favorite (or least favorite) public figure

Clustering   One way to think of ideas and details is to make a cluster diagram. When you create a cluster, you group related ideas together. These groupings often lead to new ideas. Cluster diagrams also help organize your ideas for the drafting stage of writing.

To begin, write your subject in the middle of a blank sheet of paper and draw a circle around it. This circled subject is like the hub of a wheel. All the ideas that come to mind about that subject become the spokes of the wheel. The circled "spokes" can form new hubs as well.

MODEL: Clustering

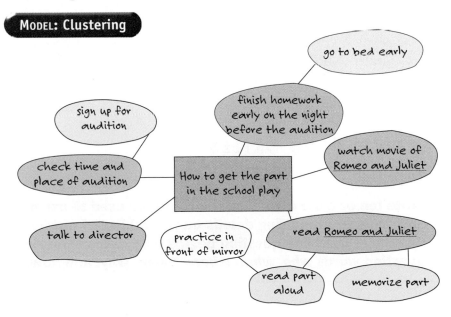

PRACTICE YOUR SKILLS

● *Clustering*

Choose one of the subjects below or think of one of your own and create a cluster diagram. You may narrow or focus the subject before you cluster.

1. television   **3.** amusement parks   **5.** music

2. pets   **4.** "in" clothes   **6.** computers

Inquiring   Another way to explore a subject is to ask who, what, where, when, why, and how. By answering these questions, you should be able to examine your subject completely and develop vivid and precise details. The following model shows how one writer used this inquiring to find details on the subject of Internet Websites. Notice that a number of questions can emerge from each word.

MODEL: **Inquiring to Develop Supporting Details**

Subject: Internet Websites
Who creates Websites?
Who regulates the creation and use of Websites?
What is a Website?
Where does one learn how to create a Website?
Why do people use Websites?
How does someone access a Website?

PRACTICE YOUR SKILLS

● *Inquiring*

Write ten or more questions that could be used to examine and develop supporting details on the subject of movies. Be sure at least one question begins with each of the six question words *who, what, where, when, why,* and *how.*

Organizing Your Ideas

When you freewrite or brainstorm, you write ideas as you think of them. Once you have written your ideas, you need to organize them so that you can present them logically to your readers.

The following strategies will help you create an organizing plan for your writing.

> ## Strategies for Organizing Ideas
>
> - Ask yourself, "What do my readers need to know first, next, last?"
> - If your subject is a story, ask yourself, "What happened first, next, then, finally?"
> - If your purpose is to explain, ask yourself how best to group the details you have chosen to help your reader understand.
> - If your purpose is to persuade, ask yourself, "Which ideas are least important, more important, and most important?" Arrange them in order from least to most or most to least important.

The following model shows how ideas from a cluster diagram on a mother cardinal and her young have been organized.

MODEL: Organizing Ideas

- First: Mother cardinal made nest in vine outside window.
- Second: I saw eggs.
- Third: Mother cardinal sat on eggs to hatch them.
- Fourth: I saw tiny birds with heads up waiting to be fed.
- Last: Mother fed hungry birds.

PRACTICE YOUR SKILLS

● *Using Logical Order*

Think about organizing logically as you answer each question.

1. If you were describing your three best friends, in which order would you describe them? Why?

2. If you were describing a graceful skyscraper from ground level all the way to the top, how would you group and present your ideas? Why?

3. If you were telling the story of your first piano lesson, in what order would you present the ideas?

Drafting
Writing Process

During this stage of your writing process, put your ideas down on paper as quickly as you can think of them. Later you can go back and improve your work until it satisfies you. The following strategies will help.

> ## Strategies for Drafting
>
> - Write an introduction that will capture the reader's interest.
> - Use your organized prewriting notes as a guide, but feel free to include new ideas as they occur to you.
> - Write fairly quickly. Do not stop to worry over how a word is spelled or how a phrase sounds. You can always go back and polish your work later.
> - Read what you have written aloud. This practice will help you get a "running start" on your next idea and keep your thoughts flowing smoothly
> - Write a conclusion that drives home the main point of your composition.

The first draft below was written from the notes about how the cardinal cares for her young. Notice that the writer did not take the time to correct mistakes. That work will be done later.

MODEL: A First Draft

A cardinal built a nest in a vine right outside our window. Soon we noticed three egg in the nest right outside our window. They were visible only when the bird left the nest. It was summertime. She sat on the eggs. To help them hatch. Finally the time came. One morning we seen three little birds with their heads back waiting for food. Their mother returned write a way and fed her babies. As they grow, our family spent more time watching out that window then watching television.

PRACTICE YOUR SKILLS

● *Writing a First Draft from Notes*

Use the notes that follow to write the first draft of a paragraph. The first and last sentences are given.

FIRST SENTENCE: Sometimes you can't tell a golden opportunity from a chore.

- at the beach last summer
- brother started building a huge sand castle
- wanted me to help
- too busy playing catch
- after a couple of hours he was done
- suddenly a cameraperson was taking pictures
- his picture in the city paper next day

LAST SENTENCE: That'll teach me to pass up a chance to lend a hand.

Television

The filming of a television show requires a process that can be broken down into stages similar to those of the writing process: planning (prewriting), development (drafting), production (revising), editing, and broadcasting (publishing). Of course, while making a video usually involves writing, most of the work involves filming and editing. Much effort in TV production goes into editing, not only the script, but also the many hours of film. A great deal more video footage is shot than is eventually used. Sometimes, in order to get it right, filmmakers will shoot a scene several times.

Media Activity

Studying a TV show—whether it is a comedy or a drama, a variety special, a newsmagazine, or a weekly talk show—is a good way to see the importance of process in the creative effort. Divide your class into teams. Agree as a team on a particular program as your subject. Then follow these steps to study the production process.

Steps for Studying Video Production

- Watch the program several times. If possible, tape the program and watch it as a team.
- As you watch, take notes on the way the director uses the camera, lighting, and music. How do these affect the overall impact of the show?
- How well does the script convey information or tell a story? Is the dialogue realistic and natural? Are there scenes that interrupt the flow of the show?
- Decide on ways to present your findings to the class. You may wish to prepare and deliver a final report about what you learned. If you have video equipment, you can create a short documentary on your findings. For information on making a video, refer to **A Writer's Guide to Electronic Publishing**.

Using Your Writing Process

In general, first drafts leave much room for improvement. As you improve your draft, you are revising it. During the revising stage, you rewrite your composition, fixing and improving whatever parts seem weak or disorderly.

Revising on Your Own

When you have finished writing your first draft, set it aside for as long as possible—a few days, a few hours, even a few minutes. Setting your work aside helps you gain perspective. When you reread it, you will be able to see what is strong and what needs work. Use the following strategies to help you revise.

Strategies for Revising

1. Add details and information. Does your composition seem thin or empty? If so, you probably need to add more specific details. Brainstorm or cluster to think of additional details to fill out the missing parts.

2. Rearrange words, sentences, or ideas. Rearrange any words, sentences, or ideas that seem out of place in a more logical order.

3. Delete unnecessary words or ideas. *Delete* means remove. In the flurry of drafting, you may unintentionally repeat yourself. You may also include an idea that does not belong. When you revise, look for unnecessary words and ideas.

4. Substitute better words and improve sentences. Your ear can help you revise. Read your composition aloud. Do any words or sentences sound lifeless or monotonous? Try to make every word sparkle with meaning. Try to make every sentence as rhythmic as music.

PRACTICE YOUR SKILLS

● *Studying a Revision*

Study the following revision of the paragraph on the cardinal's nest. (Errors will be corrected in the editing stage.) Identify which revision strategy the writer used to make each change.

Last summer   honeysuckle

∧ A cardinal built a nest in a vine right

outside our window. Soon we noticed three ∧ speckled

egg in the nest ~~right outside our window.~~ They

were visible only when the ~~bird~~ mother cardinal left the nest.

~~It was summertime.~~ During most of the day, She sat on the eggs∧ To warming them with her body

help them hatch. Finally the time came. One

morning we ~~seen~~ saw three little birds with their tilted straight and there beaks wide open

heads∧back∧waiting for food. Their mother

returned ~~right~~ a way and fed her∧ babies. As write tiny, help less

they grow, our family spent more time ~~watching~~ looking

out that window than watching television.

🖱 **COMPUTER TIP** ◄

Use the Cut and Paste features of your word-processing program to change the order of sentences. Adding, deleting, substituting, and rearranging—common activities in revising—are greatly aided by word-processing programs.

Conferencing

If you work alone on revising, you may miss ideas that are unclear or confusing. For this reason, it is a good idea to have someone else read your draft. This practice is called **conferencing.** You can conference with a classmate, friend, or family member. You can then use your reader's comments to make improvements. When you are reading someone else's work, always remember to comment about both strong and weak points. Follow the guidelines below.

> **Guidelines for Conferencing**
>
> **1.** Read your partner's work carefully.
>
> **2.** Start your comments by saying something positive. For example, you might say, "Your beginning really caught my attention."
>
> **3.** Be specific. Refer to a particular word, sentence, or section of the composition where you see a problem.
>
> **4.** Try to phrase your criticisms as questions. For example, if you think the composition lacked enough details, try asking, "Can you think of any other good details to back up your main idea?"

Editing   Writing Process

Finding ideas and drafting sentences requires concentration. For this reason, writers usually wait until the editing stage to correct errors in grammar, usage, capitalization, punctuation, and spelling.

Using an Editing Checklist

The best way to use an editing checklist is to go over your paper several times, each time looking for a different kind of error. In this way, you can work on one correction at a time.

Using Proofreading Symbols

When you edit, you may want to use proofreading symbols as a shorthand way of showing corrections. Below are some commonly used proofreading symbols.

> ## Proofreading Symbols

∧	insert	We completed an journey. (went on / a eventful)
⌄	insert comma	Meg enjoys hiking, skiing, and skating.
⊙	insert period	Gary took the bus to Atlanta.
ℯ	delete	Refer back to your notes.
¶	new paragraph	¶ Finally Balboa saw the Pacific.
no ¶	no paragraph	no ¶ The dachshund trotted away.
. . . .	let it stand	I appreciated her sincere honesty.
#	add space	She will be be back in a moment.
⌒	close up	The airplane waited on the run way.
∿	transpose	They only have two dollars left.
≡	capital letter	We later moved to the south.
/	lowercase letter	His favorite subject was Science.
(SP)	spell out	I ate 2 oranges.
⌄⌄	insert quotes	I hope you can join us, said my brother.
=	insert hyphen	I attended a school related event.
⌄	insert apostrophe	The ravenous dog ate the cats food.
⌒	move copy	I usually on Fridays go to the movies.

Prewriting Workshop
Drafting Workshop
Revising Workshop
Editing Workshop ▶
Publishing Workshop

Sentences

Written communication can break down if sentences contain errors. As you review different language skills in each composition chapter, you may want to write them in your writer's **journal** for future reference. When you have completed the composition chapters, you will have covered the major language skills you need.

Subject and Verb Agreement

Faulty subject and verb agreement is among the most common grammatical errors, even among experienced writers. A verb must agree with its subject in **number**. In other words, a singular ("one") subject takes a singular verb, and a plural ("more than one") subject takes a plural verb. To make a verb agree with its subject, ask yourself two questions: *Who or what is doing the action? Is the action being done by one or more than one?* In the following examples, the subject is underlined and the verb is underlined twice.

SINGULAR   This <u>story</u> <u>comes</u> from the far corners of my mind.

PLURAL   These <u>stories</u> <u>come</u> from the far corners of my mind.

Editing Checklist

✔ Are your sentences free of errors in grammar and usage?
✔ Did you spell each word correctly?
✔ Did you use capital letters where needed?
✔ Did you punctuate your sentences correctly?
✔ Did you indent your paragraph?
✔ Is your handwriting clear and neat?

PRACTICE YOUR SKILLS

● *Editing with Proofreading Symbols*

List each type of correction the writer has made in the paragraph below.

Last summer a cardinal built a nest in ⌃(1) a

honeysuckle vine right outside our window.

Soon we noticed three speckled egg⌃(2)s in the nest.

(3) they were visible only when the mother

cardinal left the nest. During most of the day,

she sat on the eggs, warming them with her

body to help ~~it~~ (4) them hatch. Finally the time came. One

morning we saw three little birds with their

heads t(5)ilited straight back and ~~there~~ (6)their beaks wide

open,⌃(7) waiting for food. Their mother returned

~~write~~ (8)right away and fed her tiny,(9) help‿(10)less babies. As

they gr(11)ew, our family spent more time looking

out that window th(12)an watching television.

COMPUTER TIP ➤

If you are using a word-processing program, you can
check your spelling with the spell-check feature.

> One morning we saw three little birds with their heads
> **tlited** straight back and **there** beaks wide open,
> waiting for food.

Some words sound the same but have different spellings
and meanings. Be sure to use the correct spelling.

The final stage in the writing process is **publishing**, or sharing your work with your reader in an appropriate way. The most common way to publish your composition is to hand in a neat copy of it to your teacher as error-free as possible. Be sure to follow your teacher's guidelines for headings, margins, and paper type.

Sometimes, however, you will wish to publish your writing in a different way. Sending a letter of protest to a magazine or submitting a story to a school newspaper might lead to a formal publication. You might also give a speech, produce a newsletter using desktop publishing, create a Web page, film a TV show, put on a play, or create a banner announcing the school science fair. Any public communication of your writing is a publication. Use graphics and desktop publishing technology to find new ways to publish your ideas.

Using Standard Manuscript Form   The appearance of your composition may be almost as important as its content. A marked-up paper with inconsistent margins is difficult to read. A neat, legible paper, however, makes a positive impression on your reader. When you are using a word-processing program to prepare your final draft, it's important to know how to lay out the page and how to choose a typeface and type size. Use the following guidelines for standard manuscript form to help you prepare your final draft.

> **Standard Manuscript Form**
>
> - Use standard-sized 8½-by-11-inch white paper. Use one side of the paper only.
> - If handwriting, use black or blue ink. If using a word-processing program or typing, use a black ink cartridge or black typewriter ribbon and double-space the lines.

- Leave a 1.25-inch margin at the left and right. The left margin must be even. The right margin should be as even as possible.
- Put your name, the course title, the name of your teacher, and the date in the upper right-hand corner of the first page. Follow your teacher's specific guidelines for headings and margins.
- Center the title of your essay two lines below the date. Do not underline or put quotation marks around your title.
- If using a word-processing program or typing, skip four lines between the title and the first paragraph. If handwriting, skip two lines.
- If using a word-processing program or typing, indent the first line of each paragraph five spaces. If handwriting, indent the first line of each paragraph 1 inch.
- Leave a 1-inch margin at the bottom of all pages.
- Starting on page 2, number each page in the upper right-hand corner. Begin the first line 1 inch from the top. Word-processing programs allow you to insert page numbers.

Time Out to Reflect What have you learned about your own writing process as a result of going through this chapter? What stages of your writing process do you find particularly easy and enjoyable? What stages are more difficult? Record your thoughts in the Learning Log section of your **journal.**

Using Your Writing Process

Remember that writing is a back-and-forth process. You can move among the stages to improve your writing. For example, as you draft, you can move back to the prewriting stage to think of more details.

PREWRITING

- Find a subject to write about by taking an inventory of your interests, freewriting, or keeping a journal. *(pages C9–C13)*
- Choose a subject that interests you, keeping in mind your audience and purpose. *(pages C14–C17)*
- Use various strategies to develop your subject. Brainstorm and create a cluster diagram. Keep in mind your audience and purpose. *(pages C18–C20)*
- Arrange your ideas in a logical order. *(pages C21–C22)*

DRAFTING

- Write an introduction that captures your reader's attention.
- Use your prewriting notes to help you write paragraphs and fill in ideas and details. *(pages C22–C23)*
- Write a conclusion that drives home your main point. *(pages C22–C23)*

REVISING

- Look at your first draft with a fresh eye. Use the <u>Strategies for Revising</u> to improve your work. *(page C25)*
- Conference by sharing your work with a reader. Use your reader's comments to make further improvements. *(page C27)*
- Revise your draft as often as needed to make your subject clear and interesting to readers. *(page C25)*

EDITING

- Polish your work by correcting any errors in grammar, usage, capitalization, punctuation, and spelling. Use the <u>Editing Checklist</u> and proofreading symbols. *(page C28)*

PUBLISHING

- Prepare a neat final copy of your work. Find an appropriate way to share it with readers. *(pages C31–C32)*

CHAPTER 2

Using Words Powerfully

The difference between the right word and the almost right word is the difference between lightning and the lightning bug," said the writer Mark Twain. He knew that the right words not only convey precisely what you mean but also make your ideas come alive for the reader.

You can experiment with choosing vivid, powerful words at any stage of the writing process. When you prewrite, you may jot down specific words that come to mind. As you begin to write a first draft, you can pick and choose the best words to express your ideas. While revising, you might add, delete, or substitute words to strengthen your writing. In this chapter you will learn how to select the right words for your purposes at any stage of your writing process.

Reading with a Writer's Eye

In the following selection, the novelist Julia Alvarez recalls how she acquired English as a second language when her family moved to the United States from the Dominican Republic. As you read the essay, think about how powerless Alvarez must have felt when she could not understand or speak English. Then reread the essay to trace her mastery of the English language and her discovery of the mastery of words.

FROM

LEARNING ENGLISH:
My New Found Land

Julia Alvarez

When I was 10, we immigrated to New York. How astonishing, a country where everyone spoke English! These people must be smarter, I thought. Maids, waiters, taxi drivers, doormen, bums on the street, garbage-men, all spoke this difficult language. It took some time before I understood that Americans were not necessarily a smarter, superior race. It was as natural for them to learn their mother tongue as it was for a little Dominican baby to learn Spanish. . . .

Soon it wasn't so strange that everyone was speaking in English instead of Spanish. I learned not to hear it as English, but as sense. I no longer strained to understand; I understood. I relaxed in this second language. Only when someone with a heavy Southern or British accent spoke in a movie or when the priest droned his sermon—only then did I experience that little catch of anxiety. I worried that I would not be able to "keep up" with the voice speaking in this second language. I would be like those people from the Bible we had studied in religion class, at the foot of an enormous tower that looked just like the skyscrapers all around me. They had been punished for their pride by being made to speak some slightly different version of the same language so that they didn't understand what anyone was saying.

But at the foot of those towering New York sky-scrapers, I began to understand more and more —not less and less— English. In sixth grade, I had one of the first of a lucky line of great teachers who began to nurture a love of the language, a love that had been there since childhood of listening closely to words. Sister Bernadette did not make our class interminably[1] diagram sentences from a workbook or learn a catechism[2] of grammar rules. Instead, she asked us to write little stories imagining we were snowflakes, birds, pianos, a stone in the pavement, a star in the sky. What would it feel like to be a flower with roots in the ground? If the clouds could talk, what would they say? She had an expressive, dreamy look that was accentuated by her face being framed in a wimple.[3] Supposing, just supposing . . . My mind would take off, soaring into possibilities: a flower with roots, a star in the sky, a cloud full of sad, sad tears, a piano crying out each time its back was tapped, music only to our ears.

Sister Bernadette stood at the chalkboard. Her chalk was always snapping in two because she wrote with so much energy, her

---

[1]**interminably:** (ĭn tûr´mə nə blē) Endlessly.
[2]**catechism:** (kăt ĭ kĭz´ əm) Summary of religious doctrine in the form of questions and answers.
[3]**wimple:** A piece of cloth worn around the head, framing the face, by some nuns.

whole habit[4] shaking with the swing of her arm, her hand tap tap tapping on the board. "Here's a simple sentence: *The snow fell.*" Sister Bernadette pointed with her chalk, her eyebrows lifted, her wimple poked up. "But watch what happens if we put an adverb at the beginning and a prepositional phrase at the end: *Gently the snow fell on the bare hills.*"

I thought about the snow. I saw how it might fall on the hills, tapping lightly on the bare branches of trees. Softly it would fall on the cold, cold fields. On toys children had left out in the cold, and on cars and on little birds and on people out late walking on the streets. Sister Bernadette filled the chalkboard with snowy print, on and on, handling and shaping and moving language, scribbling all over the board until English, those little bricks of meaning, those little fixed units and counters, became a charged, fluid mass that carried me in its great fluent waves, rolling and moving onward, to deposit me on the shores of the only homeland. I was no longer a foreigner with no ground to stand on. I had landed in language.

I had come into my English.

---

[4]**habit:** Distinctive clothing worn my members of a religious order.

Thinking as a Writer

Analyzing Word Choice

Julia Alvarez writes about her growing awareness of the power of words and language.

- What words does the author use to appeal to the senses of sight, touch, and hearing?
- At what point in her story does Alvarez's use of language become especially descriptive and lyrical? What do you think she is trying to show by using more expressive words?

Appreciating Vivid Words and Phrases

Oral Expression • With one or more partners, take turns reading the last three paragraphs of the story aloud. As you listen to your classmates read, close your eyes.

- Are there particular words or phrases that you especially appreciate?
- What experiences of your own do they recall for you?

Describing the Impact of a Place

Viewing This photograph was taken at an intersection in New York City. Imagine Julia Alvarez "standing at the foot of the towering skyscrapers" as a young girl.

- What does she see? Describe the scene in vivid detail.
- How might she feel as she looks up at the skyscrapers? Choose powerful words to convey her feelings.

Developing Word Choice Skills

Precise words provide the charge that lights up good writing. In the paragraph below, notice how the colorful words enliven Whitecloud's scene.

MODEL: Vivid Words

VIVID SIGHTS

VIVID SOUNDS

VIVID COLORS

> In the woods there are tracks of deer and snowshoe rabbits and long streaks where partridges slide to alight. Chipmunks make tiny footprints on the limbs, and one can hear squirrels busy in hollow trees, sorting acorns. Soft lake waves wash the shores, and sunsets burst each evening over the lakes and make them look as if they were afire.
>
> —*Thomas S. Whitecloud, "Blue Winds Dancing"*

This chapter will show you how to choose words that make your writing bright and clear.

Your Writer's Journal

The writer Evelyn Waugh said, "Words should be an intense pleasure to a writer just as leather should be to a shoemaker." In your journal write about words that give *you* pleasure. You may like some words for the things they call to mind: "birthday," "holiday," "vacation." However, you may like other words just for their sound: "rambunctious," "humongous," "awesome." Think of as many words as you can that please you, and write about why they give you pleasure.

Using Specific Words

Weak, vague words, like those in the following sentence, make writing dull and provide little information.

> **WEAK** Near the water stood a tree, some flowers, and a stone.

The sentence springs to life with specific, colorful words.

> **SPECIFIC** Near the waterfall stood a crooked birch, daffodils in bloom, and a boulder the size of a bear.

The chart below shows general and specific words for different parts of speech. When you write, always choose precise nouns, lively verbs, colorful adjectives, and specific adverbs.

	GENERAL	**SPECIFIC**	
NOUNS	road	path lane trail alley	avenue boulevard highway turnpike
VERBS	said	mumbled muttered urged whispered	boasted demanded snapped blurted
ADJECTIVES	big	lofty thick bulky roomy	bottomless towering massive important
ADVERBS	slowly	gradually cautiously hesitantly leisurely	gently lazily reluctantly sluggishly

PRACTICE YOUR SKILLS

● **Using Specific Words**

In the following fable, twenty general words and phrases have been underlined. Write a specific noun, verb, adjective, or adverb to replace each general word or phrase.

The Grasshopper and the Ants

A grasshopper lived in a (1) <u>place</u> near an anthill. Every day the ants worked (2) <u>without stopping</u>. They built (3) <u>things</u>, and they collected (4) <u>things</u>. They were preparing for winter. The grasshopper, on the other hand, said, "I'd rather (5) <u>have fun</u>."

One day the ants (6) <u>said</u>, "What will you eat and where will you sleep when the (7) <u>bad weather</u> comes in (8) <u>a few months</u> and you have no (9) <u>place to go</u>?"

The grasshopper laughed and said, "I'd rather (10) <u>have fun</u>."

In (11) "<u>a few months</u>," the wind brought snow and cold. The ants lived (12) <u>well</u> inside their (13) <u>nice</u> (14) <u>place</u>, but the grasshopper was outside, hungry, and cold.

"Please let me share your (15) <u>warm</u> (16) <u>place</u>," (17) <u>said</u> the grasshopper.

"We (18) <u>were busy</u> while you played," said the ants. "Now you are hungry and cold, but we have food and a (19) <u>nice</u> (20) <u>place</u>. You must learn to plan ahead."

Communicate Your Ideas

PREWRITING *Specific Words and Details*

Write freely about the picture of the beach on the next page. Use as many specific words as possible. Refer back to the list of words you created in your **journal** at the beginning of this chapter. Save your work for later use.

SAVE YOUR WORK

Finding Synonyms

When you substitute a precise, specific word for a more general one, you are using a synonym. **Synonyms** are words that have the same or similar meanings.

> GENERAL WORD   Suddenly Ben **saw** his sister in the crowd.
>
> SPECIFIC WORD   Suddenly Ben **spotted** his sister in the crowd.

In this sentence, *saw* and *spotted* are synonyms because they have similar meanings. *Spotted*, however, is more precise, and it carries an extra shade of meaning. *Spotted* suggests that Ben noticed his sister suddenly, maybe after looking for her for a while. The more general *saw*, in contrast, gives no extra meaning.

Using a Thesaurus

As you write and revise, you will use synonyms that you already know. At other times, however, you may wish to look up the general word in a reference work called a **thesaurus**. This tool lets you look up synonyms for words you know. You then choose which of the synonyms best conveys the meaning you intend.

COMPUTER TIP

The thesaurus feature of a word-processing program comes in handy as you search for words to improve your draft. Click on Tools in the Menu bar, and then on Language, to find the Thesaurus. Click on general words to find more specific and powerful alternatives.

PRACTICE YOUR SKILLS

● *Using Synonyms*

Revise the following paragraph, substituting more precise synonyms for the underlined words. Write your answers on a separate sheet of paper. Use a thesaurus for at least two words so that you can add new vocabulary.

Jumping Beans

The Mexican jumping bean is <u>famous</u> for its quick, jumping movements. These <u>movements</u> are caused by tiny caterpillars inside the seeds. The caterpillars make the seed <u>move</u> by grasping the web they have made on the inner wall of the seed and <u>snapping</u> their bodies. The <u>movements</u> are believed to <u>scare</u> birds who might otherwise eat the seeds. In this way, the tiny caterpillars <u>protect</u> themselves from harm until they have turned into moths. At that time, they <u>leave</u> the seed through a hole in the seed wall.

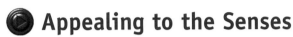

PREWRITING *Synonyms*

Look over the freewriting that you have done so far in your writing folder. Are there places where you could use livelier, more specific words? Use a thesaurus, a book of synonyms, or your dictionary to improve your word choice in your description of the beach scene.

Appealing to the Senses

You experience the world mainly through your five senses—sight, hearing, touch, smell, and taste. You can share your experiences with readers and create vivid pictures by using words that appeal to the five senses.

Sight

Writers try to capture the mood and feeling of a subject by painting a picture with words. Here are some words you can use to help your readers see what you see.

SIGHT WORDS			
Colors	**Movements**	**Shapes**	**Sizes**
beige	twisted	round	tiny
rust	raced	craggy	large
tawny	sauntered	curved	enormous
drab	sped	pointed	deep
scarlet	bent	angled	high
brilliant	jogged	zigzag	miniscule
magenta	stretched	rectangular	gigantic

PRACTICE YOUR SKILLS

● Describing Sights

Answer each question about the photograph below.

1. What colors do you see in this picture?

2. What objects do you see?

3. What shapes do you see?

4. What words describe the movements you see?

5. How would you describe the sizes in this picture?

● Writing Sentences with Sight Words

Write five sentences describing the scene in the photograph above. Use the words you thought of in the exercise above to paint a vivid picture of the scene.

Sound

All the details in the following paragraph are sounds and appeal to the sense of hearing. Notice how well they can help you imagine the scene.

SOUND OF
GLIDER

SOUND OF
CRICKETS

SOUND OF
FARAWAY TRUCK

> The glider on the front porch creaked to the slow rhythm of my grandmother's rocking. From all around the farm came the sounds of the crickets in a faster tempo. *"Chick chuck, chick chuck,"* they sang in metallic voices. Every now and then the muffled roar of a distant truck would break the soothing monotony of those summer nights.

The following words will help you to communicate what you hear to your reader. They are grouped according to the category with which we usually associate the sound.

SOUND WORDS

Objects	People	Nature	Animals
clang	moan	drip	purr
ring	murmur	splash	roar
tap	laugh	swish	cluck
bang	sigh	crackle	bark
thump	giggle	thud	hiss
crack	whisper	sizzle	whinny
squish	twitter	rustle	howl
snap	whistle	rumble	quack
sprung	sneeze	crash	chirp
crush	scream	patter	screech
	mumble		

Sometimes mixing the categories—applying a nature sound to a person, for example—can freshen and enliven your image. The sound word *sizzle* in the sentence *His voice sizzled with anger* makes the emotion come alive.

Writing Tip

Before you can write about the sounds in a scene, you must be able to hear or imagine them yourself. Practice listening to whatever is around you. If possible, close your eyes to help you concentrate.

PRACTICE YOUR SKILLS

● *Describing Sounds*

Try to imagine yourself in the picture below. Then write ten sounds that you might hear from the marching bands.

● *Writing Sentences with Sound Words*

Write five sentences describing the sounds you might hear in the picture of the marching band. Use the sound words that you listed to bring the picture to life.

Touch

Your sense of touch tells you many things. It can tell you whether something is smooth or rough, hot or cold. It can also tell you about things that your hands themselves cannot touch. When your skin feels clammy, for example, your sense of touch is recording dampness and cold. When your cheeks feel flushed, you may be embarrassed or you might have a fever. All of these sensations come under the sense of touch.

The following words will help you appeal to your reader's sense of touch.

TOUCH WORDS

silky	furry	windy	gooey
smooth	downy	gusty	oozy
cool	soft	coarse	sticky
gritty	clammy	glassy	frozen
rough	arid	wiry	steamy
grainy	damp	sandy	glossy

Notice all of the details of touch in the following paragraph.

MODEL: Touch Words

FEEL OF SUN'S WARMTH

FEEL OF COLD WATER

FEEL OF SPLASHING

FEEL OF MUD

One warm afternoon, Fern and Avery put on bathing suits and went down to the brook for a swim. Wilbur tagged along at Fern's heels. When she waded in the brook, Wilbur waded in with her. He found the water quite cold—too cold for his liking. So while the children swam and played and splashed water at each other, Wilbur amused himself in the mud along the edge of the brook, where it was warm and moist and delightfully sticky and oozy.

—*E. B. White*, Charlotte's Web

PRACTICE YOUR SKILLS

● *Writing Sentences with Touch Words*

Try to imagine yourself in the picture below. Write five sentences describing this scene. Be sure to use words that appeal to the sense of touch.

● *Describing with Touch Words*

Think of a favorite place. It could be a garden, a park bench, your bedroom, or a friend's backyard. Then write five sentences describing that place. Instead of describing its appearance, however, use details that will appeal to your reader's sense of touch.

Smell

A smell will sometimes bring back a flood of memories. Your sense of smell can help you re-create a scene in writing. The following words will appeal to your reader's sense of smell.

SMELL WORDS			
musty	fishy	fragrant	piney
burnt	stale	pungent	smoky
fruity	fresh	moldy	mildewed
stuffy	lemony	sour	floral
sharp	sweet	fresh	minty

PRACTICE YOUR SKILLS

● *Sharpening Your Sense of Smell*

Write ten words that describe smells you might experience in the scene pictured below.

● *Describing with Smell Words*

Write five sentences describing the scene in the picture. Use at least two smell words from the list above.

Taste

The following paragraph was written by Laura Ingalls Wilder about an experience in her childhood. How many different things can you taste as you read?

MODEL: Taste Words

> When they had eaten the soft maple candy until they could eat no more of it, then they helped themselves from the long table loaded with pumpkin pies and dried berry pies and cookies and cakes. There was salt-rising bread, too, and cold boiled pork, and pickles. Oo, how sour the pickles were!
>
> —*Laura Ingalls Wilder*, Little House in the Big Woods

Besides naming specific foods, you can also use any of the following taste words to whet your reader's appetite.

TASTE WORDS			
spicy	bland	sharp	savory
bitter	caramel	smooth	lumpy
tart	sugary	creamy	chewy
doughy	tender	gooey	moist
sweet	sour	dry	crisp
salty	hot	flakey	sticky
juicy	crunchy	tangy	creamy

PRACTICE YOUR SKILLS

● *Describing with Taste Words*

Write five sentences describing your favorite food. Help your reader really taste it by using precise taste words.

Elaborating

You can use your skill in appealing to a reader's senses to flesh out your writing and make it richer in detail. When you add details to your writing, you are **elaborating**.

How do you elaborate? The best way is to reread what you have written carefully. Then ask yourself the following questions: "What exactly did I mean by that? What specific examples can I think of to show what I meant by that?" The answers to those questions will be the specific details you can use to elaborate on your more general ideas.

Consider the following paragraph. As it stands, it lacks detail, giving the reader little to hold on to.

> Every season has its sights, smells, tastes, and sounds. Autumn has its own special sights. The sights and sounds of winter are different from those of fall. Spring is the time of bright colors. Summer is a time capsule full of happy moments.

Notice how the first two sentences can be elaborated into a whole paragraph by providing specific details that appeal to the senses.

> Every season has its sights, smells, tastes, and sounds. In the autumn you can see deep brown fields of grass and golden trees. If you listen carefully, you'll hear the far-off roar of football cheers and gentle, rustling leaves. Close your eyes and imagine tasting the favorite fruit of autumn lovers: the crisp tang of a ruby-red apple.

PRACTICE YOUR SKILLS

● **Elaborating**

Complete the paragraph below by writing specific details that appeal to the senses.

The sights and sounds of winter are different from those of fall. In winter I see (1) ■ , (2) ■ , and (3) ■. The winter sounds of (4) ■ and (5) ■ are everywhere. The sky looks like (6) ■ , and the air feels like (7) ■ . Spring is the time of bright colors. The flowers are (8) ■ , (9) ■ , and (10) ■ . The blue sky looks like (11) ■ . The breeze feels like (12) ■ . The sounds of (13) ■ remind me that summer will soon be here. Summer is a time capsule full of happy moments. It smells like (14) ■ and tastes like (15) ■ . The days pass quickly. The signs of autumn return.

Communicate Your Ideas

DRAFTING *Elaboration, Sensory Words*

Review your prewriting for this chapter. Use it to help you draft a composition about the beach scene. In your composition, be sure to elaborate by including details that appeal to all five senses.

Looping Back to Prewriting

As you draft, you may find specific sensory words popping into your mind. If a word does not fit immediately into the sentence you are writing, return to prewriting. Jot the word down on a brainstorming list. See if you can fit the word in elsewhere in your paragraph, and then redraft that sentence. Remember that writing is a back-and-forth process. As ideas flow during drafting, take advantage of them and treat them as prewriting ideas.

Prewriting Workshop
Drafting Workshop
Revising Workshop
Editing Workshop
Publishing Workshop

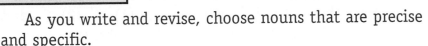

Common Nouns and Proper Nouns

As you write and revise, choose nouns that are precise and specific.

A **common noun** names any person, animal, place, or thing.

> EXAMPLES   boy, woman; dog, cat; city, state;
> store, statue

A **proper noun** names a particular person, animal, place, or thing.

Remember that proper nouns begin with a capital letter.

> EXAMPLES   José, Mrs. Lopez; Buddy, Tabby; Dallas,
> Texas; Best Computers, Statue of Liberty

Use proper nouns to make colorless sentences precise and specific.

> SENTENCES WITH   The **woman** took the **children** to
> COMMON NOUNS   see the **statue**.
>
> The **man** bought **food** for his **dog**
> at the **store**

> SENTENCES WITH   **Mrs. Lopez** took **José** and **Maria**
> PROPER NOUNS   to see the **Statue of Liberty.**
>
> **Jordan** bought **Puppy Biscuits** for
> **Buddy** at **Fresh Food Mart.**

REVISING *Specific Words and Sensory Words*

Reread your draft. Revise it carefully for word choice. Using a thesaurus, find alternative words for any you feel are vague or too general. Ask a classmate to illustrate the location you have described using the specific and sense words you have provided. If the illustration generally resembles the location, you will know that you have used effective specific and sensory words.

PORTFOLIO

Time Out to Reflect

How can you use your reading, observations, and everyday experiences to help you develop a collection of powerful words you can use in your writing? Make notes in your **journal.**

Advertising

Advertisers take the power of words and use them to convince people to buy products. They do this so well that you may find yourself reaching for a cup of hot chocolate in the middle of a summer day.

Creating ads that have just the right words is not easy. Advertisers gather a whole team of people together to brainstorm and find word combinations that will have an impact. Good advertising teams want you to remember their slogans and to have an automatic response when you hear them. "Just for the taste of it!" is one example. Try to develop a catchy slogan yourself.

Media Activity

Working in teams of three or four students, come up with a slogan to sell that cup of hot chocolate during July. Follow these steps.

- Think of a reason to drink hot chocolate on a warm day. Your reason may be serious or silly, or it may appeal to the emotions of your audience.

- Your slogan should be short and to the point. Do not include ideas or thoughts unless they express just what you want to say.

- Present your slogan to classmates, who must evaluate the slogans to decide which is the most persuasive.

Discuss with your classmates why some slogans are particularly memorable. How does the power of words contribute to their effectiveness.

Using Words Powerfully

A Writer Writes
A Character Description

Purpose: to entertain
Audience: your classmates

All of the following were actual last names of people, as recorded in the census of 1790. Choose one name that has special appeal. Think of a first name to go with it. Then write a character description of the person who had that name. Use your imagination and your five senses for ideas.

Grog	Toogood
Pancake	Buttery
Gravy	Fryover
Pettyfool	Potstoggle

Prewriting

After choosing the name you wish to write about, freewrite, brainstorm, or create a cluster diagram to develop details you could use to describe your character. When you have a number of vivid details to use, decide which order to present them in. Make a simple list showing that order.

Drafting

Using your list of details, write a first draft of your description. Try to make your character seem lifelike, as if he or she were standing right in front of you.

Revising

Review your first draft. Look for places where you could replace general words with more specific, precise words.

Also look for places where you could elaborate on your description with details that appeal to the five senses. Make any changes that will improve your description.

Editing and Publishing

Use the <u>Editing Checklist</u> and <u>Proofreading Symbols</u> on page C28 to edit your work. After catching and correcting all the errors, prepare a neat, final copy of your description. Draw a picture to go along with it. If your teacher permits, display your composition and drawing on the bulletin board.

Connection Collection

Representing in Different Ways

From Print . . .

. . . to Visuals

In his letter Ernesto contrasts two versions of the same objects. Notice how the different, specific descriptive adjectives bring to mind two different images of the object. With each pair of phrases, sketch the object, trying to incorporate into your drawings the differences between the two versions.

221 Old Eagle Lake Rd.
El Paso, TX 79901

Dear Ximena,

What a day! At the cafeteria I asked for a juicy, plump orange, but they gave me a mushy orange. After school, I stopped at the appliance store to buy my mother a toaster. I asked for a sparkling new toaster, but I received a old scratched toaster! I ran home because I was eager to be greeted by my perky puppy, but my puppy wasn't perky. My poor puppy was sluggish! What do I do?

Sincerely,
Ernesto

From Visuals . . .

. . . to Print

Write a letter to a friend describing the meal in the photograph above. Use specific details. Try to make your friend hungry just from reading your letter.

- Which strategies can be used for creating both written and visual representations? Which strategies apply to one, not both? Which type of representation is more effective?
- Draw a conclusion and write briefly about the differences between written ideas and visual representations.

Writing in the World of Work
Bulletin Board Message

The company where you work provides a break room for employees that contains tables and chairs, a microwave oven, vending machines, and a refrigerator where people store their lunches and leftovers. Unfortunately, for weeks at a time, people frequently forget the food they have put in the fridge. As a result, the refrigerator is filled with spoiled food, making it an unpleasant place for employees to store their lunches.

Write a message to your fellow employees to be posted on the bulletin board in the break room. Use specific details to vividly describe the mess in the refrigerator. Appeal to all five of the readers' senses: sight, sound, taste, smell, and touch.

What strategies did you use to make the mess in the refrigerator vivid to your fellow employees?

Writing in Academic Areas
Letter to the Curator

You are a composer who writes symphonies for non-traditional orchestras. Your symphonies include parts written for instruments such as garbage can lids, lead pipes, and half-filled soda bottles. Your symphonies also include recorded noises, such as cat meows and car engines. Next week your latest symphony will premiere for the opening of an important new art show at the Museum of Modern Art in New York City. As the orchestra plays, slides of paintings from the show will be projected onto a huge screen behind the musicians.

Write a letter to the curator of the museum describing the slides that you will project while the music is played. Be sure to use specific nouns, verbs, adjectives, and adverbs in your letter.

What strategies did you use to describe the slide show to the curator?

> *You can find information on writing business letters on pages C411–C416.*

Assess Your Learning

<u>Several</u> of us were sitting in a <u>part</u> of the <u>restaurant</u>. There was <u>food</u> on the plates in front of us, most of it uneaten, and we were trying to decide what to do. Outside the weather was <u>terrible</u>. First we went to <u>Joe's place</u>. We had some <u>fun</u> there. Then the <u>weather</u> got better so we <u>went out</u>. We <u>did</u> a lot of <u>things</u>. Miriam <u>did</u> one especially <u>funny thing</u>. Then we <u>saw</u> Trudy across the street. She <u>came</u> over and <u>we</u> did some more <u>fun things</u>.

▶ **Seventeen general words and phrases have been underlined in the passage above. Rewrite the passage using a specific noun, verb, adjective, or adverb to replace each general word or phrase.**

▶ **In revising this passage, you will be elaborating on it by providing more details. For each word or phrase you replace, ask yourself the following questions: What specific examples can I think of to show what I meant by that? What more specific noun or verb or adverb or adjective would make this detail more precise?**

🔘 *Before You Write* Consider the following questions:
What is the *subject?*
What is the *occasion?*
Who is the *audience?*
What is the *purpose?*

🔘 *After You Write* Evaluate your work using the following criteria:
- Have you gone beyond common words to find distinctive and interesting replacements?
- Have you provided specific details to illustrate the general words and phrases?
- Have you appealed to all of the reader's senses— sight, smell, hearing, touch, and taste?
- Have you written in a voice and style appropriate to your audience and purpose?
- Have you proofread for spelling, capitalization, and punctuation errors?
- Have you written in complete sentences?

Write briefly on how well you did. Point out your strengths and areas for improvement.

CHAPTER 3

Writing with Sentence Variety

Good writing can be compared to a good sports match. Think of the volleys across the net before a point; the passing of the ball before a goal; the plays before a touchdown. Some passes are lightning quick. Some plays are more complicated and take longer to complete. The combination of short and long plays makes a game exciting to watch. In the same way, you can make your writing vivid and compelling by varying the length and structure of your sentences.

Reading with a Writer's Eye

The following excerpt is from the novel *Hatchet*. In the story, a thirteen-year-old boy struggles to survive in the Canadian wilderness after an airplane crash. Read the excerpt first for enjoyment. Put yourself into the scene. Then on rereading, notice the way the author has constructed his sentences to build the tension and suspense.

FROM

Hatchet

Gary Paulsen

At first he thought it was a growl. In the still darkness of the shelter in the middle of the night his eyes came open and he was awake and he thought there was a growl. But it was the wind, a medium wind in the pines had made some sound that brought him up, brought him awake. He sat up and was hit with the smell.

It terrified him. The smell was one of rot, some musty rot that made him think only of graves with cobwebs and dust and old death. His nostrils widened and he opened his eyes wider but he could see nothing. It was too dark, too hard dark with clouds covering even the small light from the stars, and he could not see. But the smell was alive, alive and full and in the shelter. He thought of the bear, thought of Bigfoot and every monster he had ever seen in every fright movie he had ever watched, and his heart hammered in his throat.

Then he heard the slithering. A brushing sound, a slithering brushing sound near his feet—and he kicked out as hard as he could, kicked out and threw the hatchet at the sound, a noise coming from his throat. But the hatchet missed, sailed into the wall where it hit the rocks with a shower of sparks, and his leg was instantly torn with pain, as if a hundred needles had been driven into it. "Unnnngh!"

Now he screamed, with the pain and fear, and skittered on his backside up into the corner of the shelter, breathing through his mouth, straining to see, to hear.

The slithering moved again, he thought toward him at first, and terror took him, stopping his breath. He felt he could see a low dark form, a bulk in the darkness, a shadow that lived, but now it moved away, slithering and scraping it moved away and he saw or thought he saw it go out of the door opening.

He lay on his side for a moment, then pulled a rasping breath in and held it, listening for the attacker to return. When it was apparent that the shadow wasn't coming back he felt the calf of his leg, where the pain was centered and spreading to fill the whole leg.

His fingers gingerly touched a group of needles that had been driven through his pants and into the fleshy part of his calf. They were stiff and very sharp on the ends that stuck out, and he knew then what the attacker had been. A porcupine had stumbled into his shelter and when he had kicked it the thing had slapped him with its tail of quills.

Thinking as a Writer

Evaluating Sentence Structure

Notice that the author of *Hatchet* keeps you in suspense about the identity of "it" until the character has discovered it. Think about how the author builds suspense through sentence variety.

- Reread the first three paragraphs of the selection. Where does the author place short sentences?
- In sequence, write the sentences that are five words or shorter. Then read them aloud. What do you notice?
- How do the long sentences help to build suspense?

Using Dramatic Expression to Reflect Style

Oral Expression
- Choose any paragraph from the selection. Divide each long sentence into two or more short sentences.
- Read your paragraph aloud to a partner. Have your partner read it back to you. How do the shorter sentences affect the tone of the piece?

Translating an Image into Words

Viewing **Sound bites** are attention-grabbing short utterances that sum up a sentiment.

- How might you describe this scene in a short "bite"? Create a longer sentence by saying more about the image. Now compare them. In your opinion, when is it effective to use each type of sentence?

Developing Your Skills in Writing with Sentence Variety

American writer Mary Heaton Vorse writes, "The art of writing is the art of applying the seat of the pants to the seat of the chair." By that she means that writing requires discipline. The more you write, the better a writer you will become.

The hardest part of writing is looking at a blank sheet of paper. Think about writing as a process of making choices. Choosing words carefully is one secret to good writing. Arranging those words into varied and concise sentences is another. This chapter will help you improve your sentences. Filling up those blank sheets of paper will become easier and enjoyable.

Your Writer's Journal

Memories of childhood are good sources for writing ideas. Read the following childhood memory by Lorraine Hansberry. Over the next several days, write a childhood memory of your own in your journal. Try to record sights, sounds, and other sensory impressions that you remember from the events.

MODEL: Sentence Variety

Memories

Evenings were spent mainly on the back porches where screen doors slammed in the darkness with those really very special summertime sounds. And, sometimes, when Chicago nights got too steamy, the whole family got into the car and went to the park to sleep out in the open on blankets. Those were, of course, the best times of all because the grownups were invariably reminded of having been children in the South and told the best stories then. It was also cool and sweet to be on the grass, and there was usually the scent of freshly cut lemons or melons in the air.

—Lorraine Hansberry,
To Be Young, Gifted, and Black

Sentence Combining

One short sentence is clear and forceful. Too many short sentences in a row, however, sound choppy and clipped and are hard to read. Sentence combining is one way to vary the length of your sentences and add interest to your writing.

Writing Tip

Combine short sentences into longer, more interesting ones.

Combining Specific Details

Specific details help readers picture exactly what you are explaining or describing. Often the details in several separate sentences can be combined to form one longer sentence. Read the following short, choppy sentences.

CHOPPY SENTENCES   The kite bobbed.
The kite was **huge.**

It bobbed **gently.**
It moved **in the wind.**

These four sentences can be combined into one sentence by adding the descriptive words and a phrase to the first sentence. Notice how the sentence flows and the image becomes easier to picture.

COMBINED SENTENCE   The **huge** kite **bobbed gently in the wind.**

When you combine sentences to include two or more adjectives in a row, a comma is often needed to separate them. Study the following example.

CHOPPY SENTENCES   The **long** string tugged against my hand. The string was **thin**.

COMBINED SENTENCE   The **long, thin** string tugged against my hand.

PRACTICE YOUR SKILLS

● *Combining with Specific Details*

Combine each group of short sentences into one longer one.

1. Popeye is a character. He is in a comic strip. He is strong. He is also odd-looking.

2. He eats spinach. He eats it from the can. He eats it often.

3. This vegetable always gives him strength. It gives him strength immediately. It gives him tremendous strength.

4. Olive Oyl is his girlfriend. She is tall. She is thin.

5. Popeye has adventures. Olive Oyl has adventures with him.

6. Another superhero is a visitor. He is not from earth. The visitor is powerful. He comes from a distant planet.

7. Superman arrived on Earth after the destruction of the planet Krypton. Superman arrived mysteriously. Krypton is an imaginary planet.

8. He pretends to be a newspaper reporter. The reporter is timid. The reporter is mild-mannered.

9. In this disguise Superman can investigate crimes. His disguise is clever. He investigates crimes openly.

10. At the last moment, the hero stops the criminals. They are dangerous. He stops them effortlessly.

Combining Sentence Parts

Another way to combine sentences is to join equal sentence parts to form compounds. Use *and, but,* or *or* to form compound subjects and compound verbs.

COMPOUND SUBJECT	The **fish** was fresh. The **vegetables** were fresh.
	The **fish** and **vegetables** were fresh.
COMPOUND VERB	I **can bake** the chicken. I **can barbecue** the chicken.
	I **can bake** or **barbecue** the chicken.

If you combine three or more subjects and verbs, remember to use commas.

| COMPOUND VERB | On our vacation in Wyoming, we **hiked**. We **swam**. We also **canoed**. |
| | On our vacation in Wyoming, we **hiked, swam,** and **canoed**. |

PRACTICE YOUR SKILLS

● *Combining Sentence Parts*

Combine each group of sentences, using a compound subject or a compound verb. Use the conjunction *and, but,* or *or.* Use commas where needed.

EXAMPLE   Frank left his locker key at home yesterday. He forgot it again today.

ANSWER   Frank left his locker key at home yesterday **and** forgot it again today.

1. Keisha can have my extra ticket to the concert. Gary can have it.

2. We'll broil the hamburgers in the oven. We'll barbecue them on the grill.

3. José finished his science project on time. He left it at home.

4. Phil and Sarah ran a road race on Saturday. They couldn't finish it.

5. Gerard's surprise party will be on Saturday. My first soccer game will be on Saturday too.

6. Kathy skates during the winter. She runs five miles a day in the spring.

7. Willie was named Rookie of the Year. He became a basketball star.

8. Over the weekend I mowed the lawn. I weeded the garden. I also planted some vegetables.

9. The terrier growled at the visitors. He bared his teeth.

10. Penguins cannot fly. They can swim very well, even in ice-cold water.

Combining Simple Sentences

You have learned that a **simple sentence** is a sentence that has one subject and one verb.

SIMPLE SENTENCES   A **bolt** of lightning **flashed.**
The **tree exploded** into flames.

If two simple sentences contain related ideas, they can be combined to form a **compound sentence**. The two simple sentences above may be combined by using the conjunction *and* preceded by a comma.

COMPOUND SENTENCE   A **bolt** of lightning **flashed, and** the **tree exploded** into flames.

In addition to *and,* the conjunctions *but* and *or* may be used to form compound sentences.

PRACTICE YOUR SKILLS

● *Combining with Compound Sentences*

Use the conjunctions in parentheses to combine each pair of sentences into one compound sentence. Use commas.

1. Many people dream about outer space. These dreams become a reality for students at Space Camp. (but)

2. Space Camp is located in Huntsville, Alabama, at the Space and Rocket Center. The staff runs programs there from March to September. (and)

3. Students can request information by letter. The staff at Space Camp will send them an application form and brochures. (and)

4. Many students from across the United States apply to Space Camp. Each year only three thousand are accepted. (but)

5. Students in grades five through seven are in the Level I program. Students in grades eight through ten are placed in Level II. (and)

6. The students take imitation flights. Information about previous NASA missions is provided. (and)

7. NASA donates equipment to the program. Real astronauts visit and talk with the campers. (and)

8. After Space Camp some students may want careers as scientists. Perhaps others would like to work for NASA as engineers. (or)

9. Space Camp lasts for only one week. The campers will remember the experience for a lifetime. (but)

10. Three-day programs are now available for adults. Two-week advanced courses are being developed for college students. (and)

Communicate Your Ideas

PREWRITING, DRAFTING *Sentence Beginnings*

Refer back to "Memories" (pages C66–C67), written by Lorraine Hansberry, and the childhood memories you have been writing in your **journal.** Write ten simple sentences (one subject, one verb) about a summer evening you remember from your childhood. Then combine those sentences that are related. Save your work for later use.

SAVE YOUR WORK

Seeing Relationships

When you combine sentences in your own writing, you need to choose the conjunction—*and, but,* or *or*—that makes the relationship clear.

When the ideas expressed are similar or of equal importance, use *and* to combine them.

SIMILAR IDEAS	Anthony was elected class president. His twin brother was elected treasurer.
COMBINED	Anthony was elected class president, **and** his twin brother was elected treasurer.

When the ideas are contrasting, use *but*.

CONTRASTING IDEAS	Dana hit two home runs. Her team still lost the game.
COMBINED	Dana hit two home runs, **but** her team still lost the game.

When the ideas offer a choice, use *or*.

CHOICE BETWEEN IDEAS	I can finish the posters after school today. Nate can finish them on Saturday afternoon.
COMBINED	I can finish the posters after school today, **or** Nate can finish them on Saturday afternoon.

When you combine sentences, you must use a comma as well as a conjunction.

THINKING PRACTICE

Write three sentences about your day, using *and, but,* and *or*.

Writing Tip

When combining simple sentences into compound sentences, let the relationship between the ideas expressed in the two sentences determine which conjunction you use.

Sentence Variety

When all of the sentences in a passage sound the same, the writing seems dull and difficult to read. Study the example below.

> LACK OF
> SENTENCE VARIETY
>
> Sailboats rocked in the cove. Bell buoys bobbed up and down. There were flags on the boats. They fluttered in the breeze. Children were on the beach. They called to the sailors. The wind carried their voices.
>
> (The sentences are about the same length and have almost the same structure.)

Add variety to your writing by varying the length and structure of your sentences. Notice that the passage below is more interesting and easier to read.

> SENTENCE VARIETY
>
> Sailboats rocked in the cove, and bell buoys bobbed up and down. The flags on the boats fluttered in the breeze. On the beach children called to the sailors, and the wind carried their voices.

Varying Sentence Beginnings

Another way to add variety to your sentences is to begin them in different ways. Instead of starting all of your sentences with a subject, start some of them with an adverb or a prepositional phrase.

SUBJECT	The **raft** floated slowly down the river.
ADVERB	**Slowly** the raft floated down the river.
SUBJECT	A souvenir **banner** hung on the wall.
PREPOSITIONAL PHRASE	**On the wall** hung a souvenir banner.

PRACTICE YOUR SKILLS

● *Varying Sentence Beginnings*

Rewrite the following paragraph. Add variety to each sentence by moving either an adverb or a prepositional phrase to the beginning of the sentence.

Hot Spots

Volcanoes have frightened people for centuries. Smoke and steam escape during active times. The liquid rock and gases below the earth's surface gain strength. Liquid rock suddenly pours out. The liquid rock becomes lava after the eruption. The clouds above the volcano turn red. The lava slowly chokes the opening. The fiery blasts gradually die down. The liquid rock and gases again begin to build pressure. The sleeping giant will repeat its cycle soon.

Writing Sentence Beginnings

Write a sentence beginning for each of the following. Use either an adverb or a prepositional phrase as shown in parentheses.

1. ■ the lights in the house went out. (adverb)
2. ■ the field was too muddy for the soccer game. (prepositional phrase)
3. ■ Jim slammed the door to his room. (adverb)
4. ■ Angela asked us to turn down the stereo. (adverb)
5. ■ there was bumper-to-bumper traffic. (prepositional phrase)
6. ■ Maria sent me a joke in an E-mail. (prepositional phrase)
7. ■ Dad and I went to see the new dinosaur exhibit. (adverb)
8. ■ the kite sailed over the tree tops. (adverb)
9. ■ Lee and Kim will visit their grandmother. (prepositional phrase)
10. ■ Juan picked up the tiny kitten. (adverb)

Communicate Your Ideas

REVISING *Sentence Beginnings*

Read over the sentences you wrote about your childhood memory. Study the sentence beginnings you used. How many times did you start the sentence with the subject? If you started more than two sentences in the same way, revise your writing to add variety. Save your work for later use.

Television Nightly News

When we see images on television, we usually assume that the events are portrayed accurately. Although much of the information on television is certainly reliable, there is always a bias of some kind in determining what images and text to include—or exclude.

All commercial television stations are supported by advertising. Even programs such as the nightly news try to grab a viewer's attention and keep it in order to have better ratings and attract advertisers.

Sound bites (brief statements that capture an idea), compelling graphics, and live coverage of current events are a few of the techniques that television news programs use to interest viewers.

Understanding the different ways in which information is presented in this visual medium can help you evaluate what you see and hear. It may also help you become a better communicator as you try to capture in your writing what television can do so easily—combine powerful images with words.

Media Activity

Watch the local and national news on any television station, and tape the programs if possible. What do you notice about the way the stories are presented? How long is each story? Is there a difference between the type of news story on the local news and the type covered on the national news?

Choose a story that interests you and present it in a paragraph, using vivid words to capture any images that may have been used. How does the type of story influence your writing style—that is, your word choice and sentence structure?

Concise Sentences

Gymnasts always watch their weight and trim off extra pounds before a meet. When you write, trim off extra words that add no meaning to your sentences. Try to express your meaning in as few words as possible.

Rambling Sentences

Overly long sentences are as hard to read as short, choppy ones. In this paragraph, too many ideas are strung together.

RAMBLING SENTENCES

Our ball landed on the Marshalls' roof, **and** Ted climbed the tree beside the house **and** jumped onto the roof. He picked up the ball, **but** then he was afraid to climb back down, **and** I got a tall ladder from the house next door, **but** Ted still wouldn't budge. I decided to ask Mr. Marshall to help us. He climbed the ladder, **and** soon Ted was safely on the ground, **and** we smiled with relief, **but** then we realized Ted had left the ball on the roof!

NON-RAMBLING SENTENCES

Our ball landed on the Marshalls' roof. Ted climbed the tree beside the house and jumped onto the roof. He picked up the ball, but then he was afraid to climb back down. I got a tall ladder from the house next door, but Ted still wouldn't budge. I decided to ask Mr. Marshall to help us. He climbed the ladder, and soon Ted was safely on the ground. We smiled with relief. Then we realized Ted had left the ball on the roof!

A paragraph is easier to read if you break up rambling sentences by removing some of the conjunctions.

● *Revising Rambling Sentences*

Revise the paragraph to eliminate rambling sentences.

Babe Hauls the Lumber

Paul Bunyan had a mighty blue ox named Babe, and Babe often hauled logs to the lumber camp for Paul, but one rainy morning Babe arrived in camp without the logs. The rain had soaked into the leather straps of the harness, and the straps had been stretching for miles, and the lumber was somewhere back in the forest, but Paul wasn't worried. Soon the sun came out, and the leather straps started to shrink, and in no time at all, the shrinking straps pulled the load of logs right into camp.

Repetition

When you write, make every word count. Avoid wordiness, or unnecessary repetition of words or ideas.

WORDY	Because of the storm, the principal dismissed us at noon and said we could go home.
	(*Dismissed us* and *said we could go home* mean the same thing.)
CONCISE	Because of the storm, the principal dismissed us at noon.
WORDY	Tired, the weary travelers returned home.
	(*Tired* and *weary* mean the same thing.)
CONCISE	The weary travelers returned home.

Sentence Fragments

When looking over your writing, check for sentence fragments. A **sentence fragment** is a group of words that does not express a complete thought. Most fragments are missing a subject or a verb. The following examples from *Hatchet* show you how to repair sentence fragments.

No Subject	was instantly torn with pain, as if a hundred needles had been driven into it. (What was torn with pain?)
Complete Sentence	His leg was instantly torn with pain, as if a hundred needles had been driven into it. (Words have been added to make a complete thought.)
No Verb	The hatchet. (What did the hatchet do?)
Complete Sentence	The hatchet missed and sailed into the wall where it hit the rocks with a shower of sparks. (Adding a verb completes the sentence.)
No Subject or Verb	Into his shelter. (Who or what came into the shelter?)
Complete Sentence	A porcupine stumbled into his shelter. (A subject and averb have been added to complete the thought.)

Editing Checklist

✔ Have you checked your composition for sentence fragments?

✔ Do all your sentences have a subject and a verb?

PRACTICE YOUR SKILLS

● *Eliminating Repetition*

Revise each sentence by taking out words that repeat ideas.

1. She whispered to me quietly.
2. Through the mist, we could see the sight of the runway.
3. Stay in the surrounding area near the school.
4. I looked around in the bakery called Abe's Bakery.
5. I have a tiny little scar on my arm.
6. The teacher has an extra book that he doesn't need.
7. Ron lost more than 50 pounds in weight.
8. Some deadly diseases are fatal.
9. A great big bridge crosses into Canada.
10. They ate every single apple and didn't leave any.

Empty Expressions

Empty expressions are another kind of wordiness. They add nothing to the meaning of a sentence, and they slow the reader down.

WORDY   As a matter of fact, the bus left an hour ago.

CONCISE   The bus left an hour ago.

WORDY   Because of the fact that I jumped into the pile of leaves, I had to rake them again.

CONCISE   Because I jumped into the pile of leaves, I had to rake them again.

Following is a list of common empty expressions.

EMPTY EXPRESSIONS	
I think that	the thing that
on account of	what I mean is
the point is that	there is/there was
the reason is that	as a matter of fact
the reason being	because of the fact that

PRACTICE YOUR SKILLS

● *Eliminating Empty Expressions*

Revise each sentence by taking out the empty expression.

1. There was a dirt road that led to our house in Montana.

2. As a matter of fact, I'd like to join the swim team.

3. I think that whales are an endangered species.

4. The thing that everyone noticed was how tall he was.

5. There were four long tables set up for the banquet.

6. It is a fact that bikers should wear safety helmets.

7. I stayed after school because of the fact that I had band practice.

8. There was a great wave that came crashing down on the boardwalk in Seaside Heights.

9. What I mean is I would like to go to the going-away party.

10. The reason that many people visit Yellowstone National Park is to see the geysers.

Communicate Your Ideas

EDITING, PUBLISHING
Rambling Sentences, Repetition, Empty Expressions

Once again, look over your writing about a summertime memory. Check it carefully for concise sentences. Eliminate any rambling sentences, repetition, and empty expressions you may have used. Check your spelling, punctuation, and grammar. Then create a clean copy to share.

PORTFOLIO

COMPUTER TIP

If you are using a computer, look for the squiggly green lines under your sentences. The lines mean that your sentence might be a fragment. The lines might also show that the sentence is a run-on. You may want to fix the rambling sentence and it will make your writing more concise and the sentence will make better sense when you read it back. By using Spelling and Grammar in the Tools menu, the computer will help you make these decisions. Be aware that, although it is a helpful tool, the computer is not always right. You must make the final determination about what to change in your writing.

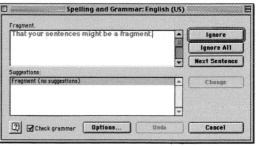

Time Out to Reflect

Write your thoughts about the work you did in this chapter in the Learning Log of your **journal**. Try to use what you have learned in this chapter to write concisely.

Process of Writing with Sentence Variety

Remember that the writing process is recursive. You can move back and forth among all the stages of the writing process. For example, if you forget a detail while drafting and are now at editing, you can return to the revising stage and add the information. The numbers in parentheses refer you to the pages where you can get help with your writing.

SENTENCE COMBINING

- Combine short sentences into longer, more interesting ones. *(pages C67–C69)*
- Use the conjunctions *and, but,* or *or* to join sentence parts. *(pages C69–C70)*
- Use the conjunctions *and, but,* or *or* to join simple sentences. Use a comma before each conjunction. *(pages C71–C74)*

SENTENCE VARIETY

- Use sentence combining to vary the lengths of your sentences. *(page C74)*
- Vary the beginnings of your sentences. *(pages C75–C76)*

CONCISE SENTENCES

- Break up long, rambling sentences into shorter ones. *(page C78)*
- Avoid unnecessary repetition or wordiness. *(page C79)*
- Eliminate empty expressions. *(pages C81–C82)*

▷ A Writer Writes

A Sportscast

Purpose: to tell what happened during a sports event
Audience: people who know and like the sport

Prewriting

When sportscasters report on the day's sporting events, they do not tell every detail about every match. Instead, they tell about the highlights—the most dramatic moments of each game.

Choose your favorite sport and write your own sportscast. Think of a real game you saw, or make up one if you do not remember a real one well enough. Identify the most dramatic moments of the match and jot those down in the order in which they happened.

Drafting

Use your notes to help you draft your sportscast. Since you will not be using film highlights to accompany your report, your words and sentences must carry all the excitement. Try hard to capture that excitement in well-chosen words and varied, concise sentences.

Revising

After getting your ideas down on paper, look back over what you have written. Read it once, looking just for places where you can combine sentences that are too short and choppy as they are. Then read it a second time, looking for places where you can vary the length or beginnings of your sentences to achieve greater interest. Revise your highlights report a third time, this

time concentrating on making your sentences as concise as possible. Strive to eliminate rambling sentences, repetition, and empty expressions.

Editing

When you are satisfied that you have written the most exciting and varied sentences you can, use the **Editing Checklist** and proofreading symbols on pages C28 and C80 to check your work for errors.

Publishing

After making all corrections, prepare a neat final copy of your highlights report and share it with an interested reader.

Connection Collection

Representing in Different Ways

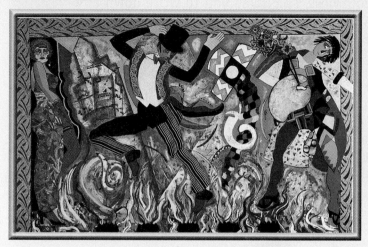

Miriam Schapiro. *Master of Ceremonies,* 1985.
Acrylic and fabric on canvas, 90 by 144 inches. Collection of Elaine and Stephen Wynn.
Courtesy Steinbaum Krauss Gallery, New York. © Miriam Schapiro.

From Print . . .

When she recalled the events of last summer, she could almost feel the soft morning breeze, the hot noonday sun, the chill of a soda can in her hands, and the thunder from an afternoon storm, making the house rattle and shake like a frightened animal.

—*Jack Clusters*

. . . to Visuals

Using the writing sample above, draw a picture, take a photograph, or find an image from a magazine or the Internet that reflects the author's style of writing.

. . . to Print

Create a written description of the painting shown above.

- Which strategies can be used for creating both written and visual representations? Which strategies apply to one, not both? Which type of representation is more effective?
- Draw a conclusion and write briefly about the differences between written ideas and visual representations.

Writing in Academic Areas

Business Memo

You are a scientist at the Carbon8 Soft Drink Factory, and recently you noticed that there is no recycling program for paper. Rachel Bubblesipper, your boss, has asked you to write down any questions or concerns in a note. Ms. Bubblesipper is in Switzerland doing research on soft drinks made from snow, and she will read your note when she returns.

> Write a one-paragraph memo to your boss explaining why you need a recycling program at the factory. In your note, be sure to use a variety of sentence structures and beginnings. This will make your note stand out from the others. Suggest a location for the recycling containers and edit the paragraph for correct spelling and grammar.

> **What strategies did you use to persuade your boss?**

Writing for Oral Communication

Presentation

You work for the advertising agency of Huntpeck and Diskette. Your boss, Dianne Diskette, has asked you to come up with a tagline or catchy slogan for CheezeBreeze, a new cheese spread made by PeopleSnax. Although you think CheezeBreeze tastes bland, you are scheduled to make a speech to Ms. Diskette about your ideas.

> Prepare a presentation for Ms. Diskette about your ideas for selling CheezeBreeze. Create at least two slogans for the product, and express them in complete sentences. Read or listen to advertisements in magazines, on TV, the radio, or on the Internet to help you brainstorm for slogans. With your teacher's permission, you may present the speech to your class.

> **What strategies did you use to present your ideas to your boss?**

You can find information on speeches and presentations on pages C433–C443.

Assess Your Learning

The popular magazine *UmpTeen* is holding a writing contest, and your teacher, Mr. Filterfunnels, wants you to enter. Outside school, your favorite activities are soccer and video games. However, you have to write on one of *UmpTeen*'s topics—Fashion, Movie Stars, or TV Trivia. You decide to write something you like first, then change it to match one of the three subjects. If you win the contest, Mr. Filterfunnels will throw a class party in your honor!

▶ **Prewrite some notes on your favorite class, sport, or other activity. Using the notes, draft a paragraph explaining what you like most about this activity, and why. Be sure to combine some of your sentences for variety. Avoid wordiness and use conjunctions to help your writing make sense.**

▶ **Now replace your topic with one of *UmpTeen*'s topics. Vary your sentence beginnings, and check for concise sentences. Notice how your sentences must change to fit the new subject. Revise and edit your draft to make a clean copy without mistakes. This is the copy you will send to *UmpTeen* and Mr. Filterfunnels.**

▶ *Before You Write* **Consider the following questions:**
What is the *subject?*
What is the *occasion?*
Who is the *audience?*
What is the *purpose?*

▶ *After You Write* **Evaluate your work using the following criteria:**
- Did you keep your audience in mind while drafting and revising your paragraph?
- Have you used several different sentence beginnings?
- Do your sentences have subjects and verbs?
- Have you combined short, choppy sentences for variety?
- Have you checked your writing for proper spelling, grammar, sense, and sentences that are concise?
- Did you correct wordy or rambling sentences by breaking them into smaller sentences?
- Have you organized your ideas in writing to help your reader understand them?

Write briefly on how well you did. Point out your strengths and areas for improvement.

CHAPTER 4

Writing Well-Structured Paragraphs

A paragraph is a block of thought. Writers present their thoughts in blocks so that readers can easily follow their ideas. The indented line at the beginning of a paragraph tells the reader that a new idea is being presented.

The simple structure of a typical paragraph—one main idea support-ed by details and examples, and a strong concluding sentence—allows ideas to flow. Understanding how these parts of a paragraph work together will help you parcel out your ideas as you write.

Reading with a Writer's Eye

Before you read the following story by Esmeralda Santiago, consider its title: "When I Was Puerto Rican." Does it offer you a clue about the story? Does the title capture your imagi-nation? What images immediately come to mind? Read the selection first for enjoyment. Then reread it and think about why the author chose this title.

FROM

When I Was Puerto Rican

Esmeralda Santiago

There are guavas at the Shop & Save. I pick one the size of a tennis ball and finger the prickly stem end. It feels familiarly bumpy and firm. The guava is not quite ripe; the skin is still a dark green. I smell it and imagine a pale pink center, the seeds tightly embedded in the flesh.

A ripe guava is yellow, although some varieties have a pink tinge. The skin is thick, firm, and sweet. Its heart is bright pink and almost solid with seeds. The most delicious part of the guava surrounds the tiny seeds. If you don't know how to eat a guava, the seeds end up in the crevices between your teeth.

When you bite into a ripe guava, your teeth must grip the bumpy surface and sink into the thick edible skin without hitting the center. It takes experience to do this, as it's quite tricky to determine how far beyond the skin the seeds begin.

Some years, when the rains have been plentiful and the nights cool, you can bite into a guava and not find many seeds. The guava bushes grow close to the ground, their branches laden with green then yellow fruit that seem to ripen overnight. These guavas are large and juicy, almost seedless, their roundness enticing you to have one more, just one more, because next year the rains may not come.

As children, we didn't always wait for the fruit to ripen. We raided the bushes as soon as the guavas were large enough to bend the branch.

A green guava is sour and hard. You bite into it at its widest point, because it's easier to grasp with your teeth. Your hear the skin, meat, and seeds crunching inside your head, while the inside of your mouth explodes in little spurts of sour.

You grimace, your eyes water, and your cheeks disappear as your lips purse into a tight O. But you have another and then another, enjoying the crunchy sounds, the acid taste, the gritty texture of the unripe center. At night, your mother makes you drink castor oil,[1] which she says tastes better than a green guava. That's when you know for sure that you're a child and she has stopped being one.

I had my last guava the day we left Puerto Rico. It was large and juicy, almost red in the center, and so fragrant that I didn't want to eat it because I would lose the smell. All the way to the airport I scratched at it with my teeth, making little dents in the skin, chewing small pieces with my front teeth, so that I could feel the texture against my tongue, the tiny pink pellets of sweet.

Today, I stand before a stack of dark green guavas, each perfectly round and hard, each $1.59. The one in my hand is tempting. It smells faintly of late summer afternoons and hopscotch under the mango tree. But this is autumn in New York, and I'm no longer a child.

The guava joins its sisters under the harsh fluorescent lights of the exotic fruit display. I push my cart away, toward the apples and pears of my adulthood, their nearly seedless ripeness predictable and bittersweet.

---

[1] **castor oil:** The oil from castor beans used as an old-fashioned remedy for stomachaches.

Thinking as a Writer

Comparing Still Life

Michel Simons, *Tulip and Flowers*, 1648-1673
Christie's, London

Fernand Léger, *Still Life With Knife* French Private Collection

Viewing The artists of these two paintings have used almost the same subject—fruit—but each has chosen a very different style to convey his ideas. The elements of art—line, shape, form, texture—are to a visual artist what words are to the writer. Principles of design—balance, proportion, pattern—are to a visual artist what sentences and paragraphs are to a writer. How does each artist use these principles to govern the

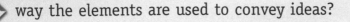

way the elements are used to convey ideas?

Evaluating Paragraphs

Childhood memories of Puerto Rico came to mind when the writer picked up a single guava fruit. The author presents her memories in a number of ways: she describes the fruit, she explains how to eat one, she tells a story, and because she clearly is enjoying her memories, she, indirectly, persuades the reader to try one.

- Although each paragraph is about the guava, the main idea of each paragraph is different. How did the author expand one memory into so many paragraphs?
- Is there anything you would change about the order of the paragraphs? Explain.

Developing a Memory

Oral Expression You just read a story about a single object that brings forth a series of memories.

- Using an item from your past, tell your class a story by weaving together your memories about it.
- Describe the object, explain its use, and tell an entertaining story about it. If you wish, persuade your listeners to share your point of view.

Developing the Skills of Well-Structured Paragraphs

"One of the most difficult things is the first paragraph. I have spent many months on a first paragraph and once I get it, the rest just comes out very easily," wrote the novelist Gabriel García Márquez.

Many writers find it difficult to write the first paragraph because they often express their main idea at the beginning of a piece. You will discover that your writing will also flow more easily once you clarify your central idea. The rest of the piece can be organized around the center.

Paragraph Structure

Most paragraphs have three kinds of sentences within them: the topic sentence, the supporting sentence or sentences, and the concluding sentence. Each type of sentence plays an important role in making a paragraph work.

A **paragraph** is a group of related sentences that present and develop one main idea.

The chart below shows the job each type of sentence performs in a paragraph.

PARAGRAPH STRUCTURE	
TOPIC SENTENCE	states the main idea
SUPPORTING SENTENCES	expand on the main idea with specific facts, examples, details, or reasons
CONCLUDING SENTENCE	provides a strong ending

The Chosen

TOPIC
SENTENCE

My dog selected me, not the other way around. As I looked carefully at the batch of Great Dane puppies, one puppy separated himself from the mob. He took several steps before his skin started moving along with the rest of him. He galloped over, sat down

SUPPORTING
SENTENCES

heavily on my feet, and looked me over carefully. He was obviously admiring me. His next step was to take my pant leg in his mouth and shake it, possibly to test the material. Then he gave several pleased body wiggles, attempted to climb on me, and washed my hand thoroughly with a salmon

CONCLUDING
SENTENCE

pink tongue. I had been chosen.

—*Jack Alan*, "How to Raise a Dog"

In the paragraph above, notice that the writer placed the topic sentence at the beginning of the paragraph and then used examples to support the main idea. The writer also provided a strong concluding sentence that restates the main idea with just a few, concise words.

Your Writer's Journal

A journal is a good place to express your thoughts and feelings. For the next week or so, write a personal message to yourself in your journal. Try to express your thoughts in paragraphs that focus on one main idea at a time. The following questions may give you ideas: What about myself would I like to change? What hopes and wishes do I have for my future? What things are hard for me to understand?

Topic Sentence

The main idea of a paragraph is stated by its topic sentence. The topic sentence is usually the first sentence. However, it may also be the last sentence of a paragraph or any middle sentence. Wherever it falls in the paragraph, its purpose is the same. Some kinds of paragraphs, like those that continue a story or narrate a series of events, do not have a topic sentence.

A **topic sentence** states the main idea of the paragraph.

The topic sentence is more general than the other sentences. Notice how the main idea of the following paragraph is expressed in the general statement at the beginning.

MODEL: Topic Sentences

TOPIC
SENTENCE

SUPPORTING
SENTENCES

CONCLUDING
SENTENCE

Pelé

The man who made soccer an important sport in the United States is a Brazilian named Pelé. Three times Pelé was on the winning team that Brazil sent to the World Cup in Sweden. When Pelé retired from soccer in 1974, the manager of the New York Cosmos persuaded him to come to New York. Pelé signed a contract to play one hundred games in three years. He made appearances on television and was photographed with famous people. Whenever he played, the stadiums were filled. Wherever he went in the United States, he won friends for himself and for soccer.

PRACTICE YOUR SKILLS

● *Identifying the Topic Sentence*

Read each paragraph to determine the main idea. Then choose and write the topic sentence from each paragraph.

1. A Real Character

Sherlock Holmes, the fictional British detective, is one of the best-known figures in English literature. Many people used to think he was real. The London post office handled much mail addressed to him at "221B Baker Street." There is even a Sherlock Holmes fan club with members all over the world. The members, who call themselves the Baker Street Irregulars, do research on Holmes's life. When Sherlock died in "The Final Problem," the outcry was so great that Holmes's creator had to bring the famous detective back to life. Even though he never answers his mail, Sherlock Holmes is still a much-loved character.

2. Edison's Contributions

The first phonograph was invented in 1877. Thomas Edison developed it. Two years later he invented the first lightbulb for home use. Edison improved or invented hundreds of useful machines. The stock ticker, the storage battery, the cement mixer, the dictaphone, and the duplicating machine are only a few. Edison, a man of practical genius, left his mark on many items.

3. Small but Serene

The southern European country of San Marino, all 24 square miles of it, has a population of only 21,000. Its army has a grand total of 180 soldiers. With the exception of its official name, The Most Serene Republic of San Marino, nearly everything about this little country is small.

Generalizing

To write a topic sentence, you use the skill of generalizing. **Generalizing** means forming an overall idea that explains specific facts, examples, or instances.

Suppose, for example, your family signs up for the Family Swim hour at the local pool. You go on Tuesday. You notice that the pool is fairly empty. On Thursday the pool is also fairly empty. When you go on Saturday, however, the pool is packed. When the pattern repeats itself the following week, your family decides to avoid swimming on weekends.

By generalizing, you and your family have formed the overall idea that the pool is more crowded on Saturdays. Your generalization explains or clarifies the specific instances that you have experienced. Good generalizations, like good topic sentences, make meaning out of specific details and information.

THINKING PRACTICE

The following chart gives Indian place names. Read each one carefully. Then write a general statement that connects all of the names in a meaningful way.

Susquehanna (river)	means "crooked water"
Merrimack (river)	means "swift water"
Ohio (state)	means "beautiful river"
Massachusetts (state)	means "people of the great hills"
Chicago (city)	means "onion place"
Michigan (state)	means "great water"
Kentucky (state)	means "meadowland"

PRACTICE YOUR SKILLS

● *Choosing Topic Sentences*

Read each paragraph and the sentences that follow it. Then choose the best topic sentence for the paragraph.

1. Saving Energy

During the winter months, close outside doors quickly as you go in or out. Cap unused electrical outlets to keep cold air out. Seal the window frames with caulking. Every little bit helps when you're trying to keep warm.

a. A few simple rules will keep your home safer.

b. A few changes can lower your heating bills.

c. The work of a skilled professional can pay for itself.

2. Nature's Sonar

As it travels through the water, a dolphin makes high-pitched sounds. When a sound hits an object, it sends back an echo. By listening carefully to the echoes, the dolphin avoids objects in its path.

a. A dolphin is an amusing mammal.

b. A dolphin can travel tremendous distances.

c. A dolphin uses its eyes *and* its ears to "see."

3. The Dinosaur Dash

A flood in Texas uncovered the tracks of a dinosaur. A scientist studied the tracks and said the dinosaur had been running at nearly 25 miles per hour. Until then scientists believed the top speed of a dinosaur was only about 7 miles per hour. This dinosaur could have beaten the men's Olympic record for the 100-meter dash.

a. Scientists study fossils to learn about the past.

b. The fastest dinosaur on record left tracks in Texas.

c. Some old tracks show that a relative of ancient dinosaurs is still living.

PREWRITING *Topic Sentence*

Review the paragraphs you wrote in your **journal** about yourself. Now write notes for a one-paragraph description of your favorite character from a book or movie. Freewrite or cluster to think of as many details as you can to describe your character. Apply the questions you asked yourself in your **journal** to your character. Then review your ideas to come up with a strong topic sentence that paints an overall picture of your character. Write your topic sentence and save it in your writing folder for later use.

Make sure your topic sentence expresses the main idea of a paragraph.

Supporting Sentences

Supporting sentences provide specific details that back up the main idea stated in the topic sentence. The supporting sentences form the body of the paragraph.

Supporting sentences explain or prove the topic sentence with specific details, facts, examples, or reasons.

Most topic sentences raise questions in readers' minds. Consider the following topic sentence.

> TOPIC SENTENCE The number of grizzly bears has decreased so seriously that the bears may soon be wiped out.

Readers might be prodded to ask "How many grizzlies are left? What has caused the number of grizzlies to decline? Why is helping grizzly bears an urgent issue?" Supporting sentences answer those questions with specific information.

In the following paragraph, the supporting sentences provide facts to explain the topic sentence. Notice that all the supporting sentences relate directly to the main idea.

Grizzly Bears in Danger

TOPIC
SENTENCE

SUPPORTING
SENTENCES

CONCLUDING
SENTENCE

The number of grizzly bears has decreased so seriously that the bears may soon be wiped out. The number of grizzly bears that live in Yellowstone Park dropped 40 percent between the early 1970s and the early 1980s. In colonial times grizzlies west of the Mississippi numbered 50,000. Now only 1,000 remain. Land development has rapidly deprived these bears of places where they can live, roam, and find food. Grizzly bears must be helped soon if they are to be saved.

PRACTICE YOUR SKILLS

● *Identifying Supporting Details*

Read the list of details under each topic sentence. Then write the letters of the three details that directly support each topic sentence.

1. The Cost of Owning a Horse

TOPIC SENTENCE   Owning a horse is expensive.

DETAILS   **a.** Horses usually cost between $500 and $800.

b. Owners spend as much as six hours a day with their horses.

c. Riding equipment and supplies cost from $500 to $1,000 a year.

d. Horses are mature at the age of five.

e. Veterinary expenses usually range from $100 to $300 a year.

2. Cars Threaten Bicycle Riders

Topic Sentence The greatest dangers to bicycle riders are cars and their drivers.

Details **a.** Drivers may not see bicyclists.

b. Drivers may open doors and hit bicyclists.

c. Drivers must pass driving tests.

d. Cars may pull out suddenly or slam on their brakes.

e. Some of the cars on the road are new.

Developing Supporting Details

Copy and complete the following cluster diagram. Choose one of the following main ideas and write a supporting detail in each surrounding circle.

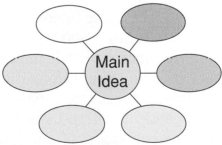

a. Being on time is a good habit.

b. Good study skills will lead to success in school.

c. Technology will change the way people work in the future.

d. Vegetables have an important place in our diets.

Across the Media: Magazines, Internet, Newspapers

At some time far in the future, how would you be able to figure out what Americans at the beginning of the twenty-first century think is important? One way would be to look at the popular culture through the media: movies, books, television, magazines, newspapers, and the Internet.

What people write about, read about, and watch reflects what they care about. Scanning the front page of several newspapers gives you a good idea of what issues are most pressing. Examining popular television programs tells you what people find entertaining. Looking at what is advertised and *how* it is advertised tells you what people are buying and why. For example, if you look through a popular magazine, you may notice many advertisements for time-saving food products. Because there are so many of these advertisements, you may conclude that many people don't have time to cook.

Media Activity

Join your classmates in contributing to a time capsule to be opened 1,000 years in the future. In one sentence sum up what is important to know about our culture. Using information gathered from the Internet, your local newspaper, and television, come up with a main idea that expresses the one aspect of our culture that you would like people of the future to know about. With your class, collect your sentences and store them in a safe place. Who knows, maybe someone in the next millennium will find and read them!

DRAFTING *Supporting Details*

 Return to the notes and the topic sentence you have written about your favorite character. Look over your collection of supporting details and decide on a logical order for them. Make a simple list or chart showing that order. Then use your list to help you draft the body of supporting sentences for your paragraph-long description. Make sure the supporting sentences support your main idea. Save your draft in your writing folder for later use.

Concluding Sentences

If someone hung up the telephone without saying good-bye, you would probably feel that you were cut off short. In the same way, a paragraph without a strong concluding sentence leaves the reader feeling cut off.

A **concluding sentence** adds a strong ending to a paragraph.

Following are several good ways to end a paragraph.

> **Guidelines for Writing Concluding Sentences**
>
> A concluding sentence may
> - summarize the paragraph.
> - state the point of the paragraph.
> - restate the main idea using different words.
> - add an insight about the main idea.

Avoid using a concluding sentence that doesn't add some meaning to the paragraph. Notice how weak the concluding sentence is in the following paragraph. It simply repeats the words in the topic sentence.

Prewriting Workshop
Drafting Workshop
Revising Workshop ▶
Editing Workshop
Publishing Workshop

Pronouns and Adjectives

Once you have written your supporting sentences, you can go back over them and improve their flow. One good way to make the sentences seem more smoothly connected is to use the pronouns *it, its, his, her, their, theirs,* as well as the adjectives *this, that, these,* and *those.* These words refer back to a word used earlier. Because they refer backwards, they force the reader to make connections between what has already been read and what is being read. These connections help create a feeling of smoothness.

In the following example, the supporting sentences sound choppy and disjointed. Notice how the revision improves the smoothness.

DISJOINTED SUPPORTING SENTENCES	The sinking of the *Titanic* was one of the biggest shipwrecks of all time. The *Titanic* was the largest ship in the world. Experts called the *Titanic* unsinkable. On the first trip of the *Titanic*, however, the *Titanic* hit an iceberg and sank.
SMOOTHER	The sinking of the *Titanic* was one of the biggest shipwrecks of all time. **This** ship was the largest in the world. Experts called the *Titanic* unsinkable. On **its** first trip, however, **this** "unsinkable" ship hit an iceberg and sank.

Jupiter's Moon

A Chinese astronomer saw one of Jupiter's moons 2,000 years before the astronomer Galileo reported it. An ancient record from 364 B.C. says, "In the year of Chan Yan, Jupiter was very large and bright. A small reddish star was attached to it." This star was most likely the moon called Ganymede.

WEAK CONCLUSION   As you can see, a Chinese astronomer reported one of Jupiter's moons before Galileo did.

The following concluding sentence is also weak. It adds new information that does not relate directly to the paragraph's main idea.

WEAK CONCLUSION   In Greek mythology Ganymede is known as the cupbearer to the gods.

The following sentence would add a strong ending. It adds real meaning that relates directly to the main idea.

STRONG CONCLUSION   After 2,400 years, the achievement of this Chinese astronomer is finally being recognized.

PRACTICE YOUR SKILLS

● *Choosing a Concluding Sentence*

Read the paragraph on the next page. Choose and write the better concluding sentence. Then write a sentence that tells why you believe your choice is better.

One Kind of Robot

Some robots have been around for hundreds of years. One kind is called an android. An android is a machine that looks and acts like a person. Most androids have been used as toys. Chinese emperors had mechanical musicians that entertained them. Japanese homes had dolls that could carry trays and serve tea. One family in Switzerland had a "boy" android that could sit at a writing desk and write messages. Today androids are being used as patients in the training of young doctors. Sim One is the name of one mechanical patient used by medical students at the University of Southern California.

a. A robot flagman has even been invented to direct traffic.

b. Modern androids, no longer playthings, can help people learn how to save lives.

Communicate Your Ideas

DRAFTING, REVISING *Concluding Sentences*

Review the supporting sentences you have written about your favorite character. Then write two possible concluding sentences that would add a strong ending to your description. Choose the one you like the best and add it to your paragraph.

As you revise, it is a good idea to reread your paragraph several times. Refer to the <u>Evaluation Checklist for Revising</u> to help you.

Looping Back to Drafting, Revising

Look over the other concluding sentence you wrote and did not use. Rewrite it to fit your paragraph.

The Copy, Cut, and Paste functions in the Edit menu on your toolbar allow you to rearrange your sentences easily. Use Copy to create a copy of your paragraph. Use Cut and Paste to rearrange sentences of the new copy. Review both old and new versions and decide which makes more sense.

Edit	View	Insert
Undo Typing		⌘Z
Redo Typing		⌘Y
Cut		⌘X
Copy		⌘C
Paste		⌘V
Paste Special...		

Evaluation Checklist for Revising

✓ Does your topic sentence introduce the subject and suggest your overall impression of it? *(pages C97–C101)*

✓ Do your supporting sentences supply specific details that bring your subject to life? *(pages C101–C105)*

✓ Did you use pronouns and adjectives to create smoothly connected sentences? *(page C106)*

✓ Does your concluding sentence summarize and add meaning to your paragraph? *(pages C105–C108)*

Communicate Your Ideas

EDITING, PUBLISHING

 Check your paragraph for spelling and punctuation errors. When you are satisfied that you have corrected all your errors, prepare a neat final copy. You can then read your paragraph aloud to your classmates. Ask them to identify your topic sentence, supporting sentences, and concluding sentence.

Time Out to Reflect Think about your classmates' comments. Do you agree with their responses? Did they understand your intention as a writer? How could you improve your paragraph from the information you received from your audience? Record your thoughts in the Learning Log section of your **journal**.

Process of Writing a Well-Structured Paragraph

PREWRITING

- Decide on a main idea for your paragraph. *(page C95)*
- List specific details—facts, examples, or reasons that support the main idea.

DRAFTING

- Write a sentence that conveys your main idea. *(page C97)*.
- Write supporting sentences that explain or prove your topic sentence. Be sure your supporting sentences are in an order that makes sense. *(pages C101–C105)*
- Write a concluding sentence that summarizes the paragraph and directly adds meaning to the main idea. Be sure your concluding sentence does not simply repeat your topic sentence. *(pages C105–C107)*

REVISING

- Put your paragraph aside for a while and do another activity, such as taking a walk or talking with a friend. Then reread your paragraph, using the <u>Evaluation Checklist for Revising</u> on page C109 to help you evaluate your work.
- Give your work to a classmate or your teacher for comments, if you wish.
- Revise your paragraph based on your own evaluation. Consider your reader's comments as you revise as well.

EDITING

- Reread your paragraph and correct any errors of grammar, usage, spelling and punctuation.

PUBLISHING

- Prepare a neat final copy and share it with an interested audience.

▶ A Writer Writes

A Contest Entry

Purpose: **to inform and to persuade**

Audience: **judges of the "Rename a Constellation" Contest**

Prewriting

All constellations, or star patterns, were named thousands of years ago. Ancient people saw pictures within these patterns. They named the star pattern shown below Orion the Hunter. They saw the three stars in the middle as the belt of Orion.

Betelgeuse

Rigel

Bellatrix

Suppose you are entering a contest to rename the constellation. What figure do you see in the star pattern called Orion? Through freewriting or clustering, explore possible shapes outlined by the stars in the constellation. Choose the one you think would be most likely to convince the judges.

Drafting

Write a topic sentence indicating your choice for the renaming of Orion. In your supporting sentences, refer to specific stars and explain how they help create the figure you see. End your

Writing Well-Structured Paragraphs

paragraph with a sentence that ties the whole paragraph together.

Revising

Review your first draft. Look for places where you could improve the flow of your sentences. Also look for opportunities to use vivid words and to vary your sentences for interest. Make any changes that would add force to your writing.

Editing

Check for errors in grammar, usage, mechanics, and spelling. Make a neat final copy of your contest entry.

Publishing

Publish a clean copy of your paragraph to share with an interested reader.

Connection Collection

Representing in Different Ways

To: a_panchez@starlabs.com (Alexandra Panchez)

From: batty@starlabs.com (Beth Thompson)

Date: 09/15/00

Subject: The Big Caving Trip

Alexandra—

The caving trip has been confirmed! Remember to bring two sets of clothes. Although it is supposed to be over 100 degrees this weekend it always remains cool underground. Bring the following clothes for our subterranean adventures: a helmet with a headlight, sturdy boots, kneepads, chinos, a heavy shirt, and plenty of drinking water. Bring the following for our adventures above ground: shorts, sandals, a tank top, a swimsuit, suntan oil, and a good book to read by the pool! We are about to experience two worlds in one weekend!

—Beth

. . . to Visuals

Using the information in the E-mail above, create a word web chart that categorizes the different types of clothes and supplies Alexandra and Beth are planning to bring on their caving trip.

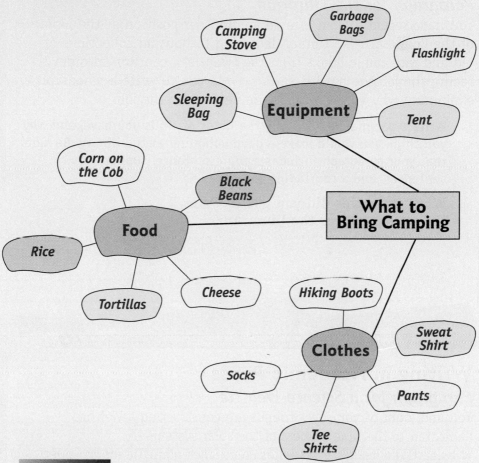

Camping Stove

Garbage Bags

Flashlight

Sleeping Bag

Equipment

Tent

Corn on the Cob

Black Beans

What to Bring Camping

Food

Rice

Cheese

Hiking Boots

Tortillas

Clothes

Sweat Shirt

Socks

Pants

Tee Shirts

. . . to Print

Using the word web above, write three paragraphs for an E-mail telling your best friend what to bring on your big weekend camping trip to the Grand Canyon. Be sure that each paragraph includes a topic sentence, supporting sentences, and a concluding sentence.

- Which strategies can be used for creating both written and visual representations? Which strategies apply to one, not both? Which type of representation is more effective?
- Draw a conclusion and write briefly about the differences between written ideas and visual representations.

Writing in the Workplace
Paragraph for the Librarian

You have recently been offered a volunteer position at the Library of the Comic Arts—a library dedicated to housing collections of old and rare comic books from the twentieth century. In order to secure the job the head librarian wants you to write a paragraph explaining why you think you are perfect for the job.

Write a paragraph describing the kinds of skills you have, and why you think you would make a good volunteer at the library. Be sure that your paragraph includes a topic sentence, supporting sentences, and a concluding sentence.

What strategies did you use to write the paragraph for the librarian?

Writing in Academic Areas
Paragraph for a Science Website

You and eight of your best friends are constructing a Website dedicated to the nine planets of the solar system— www.earthanditseightbestfriends.com. Since your friends consider you the most "far out" of the bunch, you have been assigned to write a paragraph about Pluto. Your paragraph will appear when the visitors to the Website click on the picture of the most "far out" planet.

Write a paragraph for the Website providing general information about the planet Pluto. Be sure that your paragraph includes a topic sentence, supporting sentences, and a concluding sentence.

What strategies did you use to provide information about Pluto for the Website?

Assess Your Learning

Major Filmster III, the famous movie director, has chosen you to be the subject of his next major motion picture, *A Life*. Filmster plans to film every second of your life, from now until your very last day on Earth. He estimates that the running time of the final product will be approximately 78 years. Unfortunately Filmster has missed the first eleven years of your life and he wants you to "fill him in" on some of the events that he missed. He wants you to start from the beginning.

▶ **Write two paragraphs telling Major Filmster about two of your earliest memories.**

▶ **In each paragraph include a topic sentence that states the main idea. Use supporting sentences to expand on the main idea with specific facts and details about your earliest memories. Use a concluding sentence in each paragraph to provide a strong ending. Your concluding sentence may summarize the paragraph, state the paragraph's main point, restate the main idea using different words, or add insight about the main idea.**

▶ *Before You Write* Consider the following questions:
What is the *subject?*
What is the *occasion?*
Who is the *audience?*
What is the *purpose?*

▶ *After You Write* Evaluate your work using the following criteria:
- Have you included a topic sentence that states the main idea?
- Have you included supporting sentences to expand on the main idea with specific facts or details?
- Have you included a concluding sentence that provides a strong ending?
- Have you organized your ideas in a clear and coherent manner?

Write briefly on how well you did. Point out your strengths and areas for improvement.

CHAPTER 5

Writing Effective Compositions

Many times in your schooling, you will be asked to write compositions longer than one paragraph. In social studies you may write a composition describing the landforms of Latin America. In science you may write a composition explaining how to do an experiment. Perhaps you might find yourself writing a biographical report on a historic figure. Since each of these subjects is likely to require more than one paragraph, a composition is the appropriate form.

Often in writing a composition you relate only what you already know. You have written many of this kind of composition. Just think of the "What I Did . . ." assignments. Perhaps, writing them was harder than it needed to be. As for all types of writing, the key to effective composition writing is simply learning how to organize your thoughts into a logical structure.

Reading with a Writer's Eye

The following composition is about Cleopatra, a queen of ancient Egypt. Read the composition once to learn about this famous woman in history. Then reread it, thinking about the main idea the author, William A. DeWitt, presents. Notice how he constructs sentences and paragraphs to develop his composition around one main idea.

Illustrated Minute Biographies

CLEOPATRA

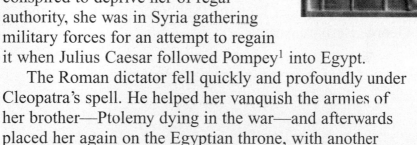

William A. DeWitt

No other woman in history has more successfully used her personal charms to further her political ambitions than Cleopatra.

Third daughter of King Ptolemy Auletes, she was born in 69 or 68 B.C. and first came to the Egyptian throne as co-ruler with her younger brother, Ptolemy Dionysus, on her father's death in 51. Three years later, Ptolemy having conspired to deprive her of regal authority, she was in Syria gathering military forces for an attempt to regain it when Julius Caesar followed Pompey[1] into Egypt.

The Roman dictator fell quickly and profoundly under Cleopatra's spell. He helped her vanquish the armies of her brother—Ptolemy dying in the war—and afterwards placed her again on the Egyptian throne, with another brother, whom she soon disposed of by poison.

Legend has it that Caesar's and Cleopatra's union produced a son, Caesarion, whom Octavian later put to death. Certainly, they lived together in Rome from 46 or

---

[1] **Pompey:** 106–48 B.C., Roman general and statesman.

45 B.C. till Caesar's assassination in 44. Then, aware of the Romans' disfavor, she fled back to Egypt.

Here Mark Anthony succumbed to her fascination and she used him as she had Caesar. Their long alliance, always unpopular in Rome, led finally to war with Octavian and their historic defeat at Actium (31 B.C.). The following year Octavian landed in Egypt and worked out with Cleopatra the plot that resulted in Anthony's suicide, committed in the mistaken belief that she, too, was taking her life.

Cleopatra then set her cap for[2] Octavian, but the man who was to be Rome's first Emperor (Augustus) proved less susceptible to her wiles[3] than Anthony or Caesar. Learning that he firmly intended taking her to Rome as a captive, Cleopatra played her dramatic last scene, killing herself (according to legend) by the bite of an asp.[4] This was in 30 B.C., and marked the end of the Ptolemies' dynasty, Egypt thereafter becoming a Roman province.

A host of writers, from her time to the present, have found inspiration in the colorful life of the Egyptian queen, among them Plutarch, Shakespeare, Dryden and George Bernard Shaw.

---

[2] **set her cap for:** Pursued.
[3] **wiles:** Playful tricks.
[4] **asp:** A venomous snake of Egypt.

▷ *Thinking as a Writer*

Analyzing the Effectiveness of a Composition

Imagine that you have been asked to give feedback to the author of Cleopatra.

- Was William A. DeWitt successful in making you understand who Cleopatra was? What details in the composition make you feel this way? Is there anything else that you would like to know about Cleopatra? What additional information would you include if you were going to write a composition about Cleopatra?

Speaking Versus Writing

Oral Expression Suppose you have been asked to appear before your class to talk about the life and times of Cleopatra.

- Prepare a short speech by writing some notes from "Cleopatra," choosing information from the composition that you think is the most important for others to know.
- Practice speaking from your notes. How is your speech different from your written notes? How are the written and spoken versions the same?

Analyzing a Visual Composition

Viewing This photograph of the pyramids in Egypt is also a composition. How is it like a written composition? How is it different?

The Power of Composing

Compositions can be long or short, serious or humorous, but usually they are informative and present facts in a logical order. Compositions may cover a wide range of subjects and take many forms at the hands of different writers.

Uses of Composition Writing

The following examples show the many different ways people use compositions in everyday life.

- **A sports reporter writes an article** on the triumph of the local football team.

- **A book reviewer writes an online review** of a popular novel for an Internet bookseller.

- **A student writes an essay about herself** to include in an application for a foreign-exchange program.

- **An actor writes an autobiography** describing his experiences in Hollywood.

- **A politician gives a speech at a rally** just before election day.

- **A popular mystery writer writes an essay** on where she gets ideas for her books.

- **A photojournalist puts together a book of photographs** on the nation's historic buildings.

Process of Writing Effective Compositions

In her book *Becoming a Writer,* Dorothea Brande writes, "The important matter is to find your own style, your own subjects, your own rhythm, so that every element in your nature can contribute to the work of making a writer of you." Compositions usually contain many facts, but that does not mean that the writing must be dry or boring. Although you must follow a structure in writing compositions, once you have learned the form, you can be as creative as you like.

A **composition** presents and develops one main idea in three or more paragraphs.

Your Writer's Journal

Ideas for compositions can come from a number of sources. Most of all, however, they come from your unique viewpoints. Nobody sees the world quite the way you do. Develop an understanding of yourself and the way you see things with the following activity for your journal.

Every day for a week, write the words to a favorite song. Then answer the following questions.

- Why do the words appeal to me? What do they say about life?
- How does the music make me feel? Do the words and music go well together?
- Of what do the music and words remind me?

Use these notes as springboards for writing ideas throughout the year.

⦿ Structure of a Composition

Paragraphs, as you have read, have three main parts: a topic sentence, a body of supporting sentences, and a concluding sentence. Compositions have three parts as well. They are (1) the introductory paragraph, which captures the reader's attention and contains sentences expressing the main idea, (2) a body of one or more supporting paragraphs that provide facts, examples, and other details, and (3) a concluding paragraph that provides a strong ending.

Each of these parts is labeled in the following composition.

MODEL: Composition

The Secrets of Handwriting

INTRODUCTION:
CAPTURES ATTENTION AND STATES THE MAIN IDEA

When you write, do your letters slant to the right? Do you write in big, bold letters with even lines, or do you write tiny letters that slant backward? However you write, you are revealing some aspects of your personality.

BODY:
PROVIDES SPECIFIC INFORMATION

Highly trained experts have been able to pinpoint some specific links between the slant of handwriting and the writer's personality. According to these experts, people who compose level lines of writing are "on the level" themselves. If a line wanders a little, the writer may be revealing the trait of carelessness. Lines that slant upward often reveal an optimistic person, while downward-slanting lines show moodiness.

Another trait of writing, size, can also reveal hidden qualities. Many people with tiny handwriting tend to be intellectual. Large writing may indicate generosity. Huge writing may mean the person is conceited but generally honest.

The way letters slant is still another indicator of personality. If letters lean far to the left, the writer may be a distrustful person. If they lean far to the right, the writer may be overly sensitive. If they lean only slightly to the right, the writer is likely to be friendly and easygoing.

CONCLUSION:

ADDS A STRONG
ENDING

In addition to these three points, experts also study the shape of individual letters, spacing between words, and other fine points of writing. In the hands of a certified expert, writing samples can be very reliable keys to personality. Studying your own handwriting can be an interesting and rewarding way to learn more about yourself.

Prewriting ▸ Writing Process

The process for writing compositions is similar to the process for writing paragraphs. The first step is to explore your own interests for writing ideas. Compositions written on subjects of real interest to the writer are usually the most effective.

Finding a Topic

At any given moment of your waking day, thoughts and ideas are rolling around through your head and words come spewing out of your mouth in conversations, but when the time comes to write a composition you are chewing on your eraser, arranging things on your desk, or looking for a snack. In other words, you are doing anything but committing thoughts to paper.

PRACTICE YOUR SKILLS

● *Thinking of Subjects by Taking Inventory*

Fold a sheet of paper in half. In the opposite direction, fold it in half again, and then again. When you open the paper, you will have eight boxes. At the top of each box, write one of the categories below. Then for each category, list the specific items that interest you most. Save your completed chart in your writing folder.

EXAMPLE   careers

POSSIBLE   animal trainer, clothing designer,
ANSWERS   pilot, dentist, teacher, architect,
              salesperson, carpenter

1. sports   **5.** animals

2. food   **6.** games

3. hobbies   **7.** history

4. music   **8.** science

Communicate Your Ideas

PREWRITING *Subject Inventory*

Brainstorm, freewrite, or cluster to complete the following statements with as many items as you can think of. When you have finished, save your work in your writing folder.

1. Scenes, objects, and people that have left a lasting impression in my mind include . . .

2. At home or with friends, I often talk about . . .

3. I could teach my friends how to . . .

4. I like to read about . . .

5. I've always wondered why . . .

SAVE YOUR WORK

Choosing and Limiting a Subject

Once you have explored your interests for writing ideas, the next step is to choose one subject that suits your purpose and audience.

Determining Your Purpose   A good composition, like a good paragraph, has a clear purpose. That purpose may be to create a story, poem, or play, to express your thoughts in a diary or **journal,** to inform or explain, or to persuade. Keeping your writing purpose in mind will help you choose a suitable subject.

Determining Your Audience   A composition must be suited to your audience. In your **journal,** for example, a composition can be personal and poetic. A composition for science class, on the other hand, needs to be more formal and informative. Sketch out an audience profile chart to help you understand your readers.

Listing Focus Points   The final step in developing a good subject is to list several possible focus points that would suit your purpose and audience. Focus points are the smaller, more limited topics contained within your general subject. If you had decided to write about gymnastics, for example, you might list the focus points below.

SUBJECT   gymnastics

PURPOSE   to explain

AUDIENCE   people who enjoy watching gymnastics but do not know much about it

FOCUS   how women's gymnastics is judged
POINTS   movements for the floor exercises
safety and training equipment
differences between men's and women's events

Any one of these four focus points would be a suitably limited subject for a short composition.

> **Steps for Limiting a Composition Subject**
> - Decide on the purpose of your composition: to create, to express, to inform or explain, or to persuade.
> - Think about who your audience (readers) will be.
> - List focus points that suit your purpose and audience.
> - Choose one focus point as your limited subject.

PRACTICE YOUR SKILLS

● *Limiting a Subject*

Write each subject. Then list three possible focus points for each one.

1. SUBJECT   victories in my life
     PURPOSE   to tell a story
     AUDIENCE   people who want to succeed

2. SUBJECT   childhood fears
     PURPOSE   to inform
     AUDIENCE   young children

3. SUBJECT   neighborhood issues
     PURPOSE   to persuade
     AUDIENCE   readers of a newspaper editorial page

4. SUBJECT   ways to earn money
     PURPOSE   to inform
     AUDIENCE   teenagers who want to earn money

5. SUBJECT   pluses and minuses of being a teenager
     PURPOSE   to express
     AUDIENCE   myself in my journal

PREWRITING *Limited Subject*

 Review your work from before. Consider your purpose and audience as you choose one subject to write about from the many you have discovered. Then list the focus points suitable for your purpose and audience. Choose one as your limited subject and circle it. Save your work for later use.

Listing Supporting Details

After you have decided on a focus point for your composition, the next step is to list the details you will use to support your main idea. Brainstorm with someone, freewrite, cluster, or use any other strategy that will help stimulate your thinking. Think of as many useful details as possible.

The kinds of details you will use to support your main idea will vary according to your writing purpose. The following chart shows the different kinds of details used for different purposes.

SUPPORTING DETAILS IN A COMPOSITION	
Purpose	**Kinds of Details**
to express	sights, sounds and other details that appeal to the senses; thoughts, feelings, reflections
to inform or explain	facts and examples, reasons, steps in a process, and directions
to create	people, places, and events that are imagined or based on real life
to persuade	reasons based on facts that support an opinion

Suppose you had decided to explain how women's gymnastics is judged to people who enjoy gymnastics but do not know much about it. If you brainstormed to come up with details, your notes might appear as follows.

LIMITED SUBJECT	how women's gymnastics is judged
BRAINSTORMING NOTES	originality and composition: 2 points
	vaulting scored separately
	perfect score: 10 points
	excellent "general impression" earns maximum of 1 point
	difficulty of routine: 5 points
	execution: 2 points
	variety of easy, medium, and hard movements: 5 points
	judging standards set by the Federation of International Gymnastics

PRACTICE YOUR SKILLS

● *Listing Supporting Details*

Brainstorm for ideas about each of the following limited subjects. List at least four supporting details for each one. Use the chart on the preceding page to help you list the kinds of details that suit the purpose. Save your work.

1. SUBJECT the first party I planned and gave
PURPOSE to create
AUDIENCE classmates

2. SUBJECT how to fall asleep if you are restless
PURPOSE to explain
AUDIENCE people who have trouble sleeping

3. SUBJECT   songs that have a special meaning for me
    PURPOSE   to express
    AUDIENCE   myself in my journal

4. SUBJECT   the first warm day of spring
    PURPOSE   to inform
    AUDIENCE   people in a different region

5. SUBJECT   the value of pets
    PURPOSE   to persuade
    AUDIENCE   people who have no pets

Communicate Your Ideas

PREWRITING *Details*

 Refer to your focused subject in your folder. Then use brainstorming or any other prewriting strategy to develop a list of details that will support your focus point. Save your work for later use.

COMPUTER TIP

Searching on the Internet is one way to discover information on almost any topic. However, just typing a one-word topic—dogs—in your search engine box can result in thousands of sites. You can learn about search techniques in **A Writer's Guide to Using the Internet on pages C566–C600**.

Developing the Main Idea

Writing is a continuous learning process. With each stage of the writing process, you discover (or at least clarify) more ideas. After brainstorming, for example, you probably have a much clearer understanding of your subject. In fact, by this time you have probably learned or rediscovered enough about your subject to formulate your **main idea statement**—the sentence that expresses the main point of your composition.

To formulate your main idea statement, look over all the brainstorming ideas you have come up with. Is any thought more important than the others as an overall idea? Or do the separate details you came up with add up to some overall idea that you can now express? Asking—and answering—these two questions for yourself will lead you to your main idea statement.

The writer who brainstormed about women's gymnastics reviewed her brainstorming notes with these questions in mind. She decided that one of the most important points she had listed was the last one—judging standards are set by the Federation of International Gymnastics. All the other details seemed to fit neatly under this main idea. So she wrote a draft of her main idea statement as follows:

MAIN IDEA   Scoring a women's gymnastic event is a matter of following the guidelines set by the Federation of International Gymnastics.

As the writer continues working, this main idea statement may change somewhat. For now, it will serve as a guide to keep all the other details in the essay anchored to a main idea.

PRACTICE YOUR SKILLS

● *Developing a Main Idea*

For each list of supporting details you developed in the activity on the preceding page, write a statement that expresses an appropriate main idea.

PREWRITING *Main Idea*

Review the details you came up with for your own subject. Ask yourself the two questions on the previous page to help you come up with a main idea statement. Write a statement expressing the main idea suggested by your details. Keep your statement in your writing folder for later use.

Selecting and Arranging Details

When you brainstorm with someone, you write down ideas in the order they occur to you. Chances are they are not in a logical order. In addition, you may have listed ideas that do not strictly relate to your subject. At this last stage of the invention, you can smooth these matters out. First look over your notes and select only those that relate directly to the main idea. Next look for a way to organize your ideas logically. This chart shows some common approaches.

TYPES OF ORDER	
CHRONOLOGICAL	Items are arranged in time order.
SPATIAL	Items are arranged in order of location.
SIZE OR IMPORTANCE	Items are arranged in order of least to most or most to least important; or by size from biggest to smallest, or smallest to biggest.
SEQUENTIAL	Items are arranged in the order in which they must be performed.

If some items do not fit neatly into the order you have chosen, save them for your introduction or conclusion.

Notice how the brainstorming notes about gymnastics have been grouped and logically arranged.

IDEAS SAVED	judging standards set by the Federation of International Gymnastics
	vaulting scored separately
LARGEST TO SMALLEST POINT VALUE	perfect score: 10 points
	difficulty of routine: 5 points
	variety of easy, medium, and hard movements: 5 points
	execution: 2 points
	originality and composition: 2 points
	excellent "general impression" earns maximum of 1 point

PRACTICE YOUR SKILLS

● *Arranging Details in Logical Order*

The following brainstorming notes are on the subject of the world's highest waterfalls. Two of the items could be used in the introduction or conclusion. Write the two items that do not fit the logical order. Then list the remaining items in logical order.

- Largest falls in the world are Angel Falls in Venezuela.
- North America has third-largest falls, in Yosemite.
- Waterfalls form when water flowing over land meets an abrupt change in the level of the land.
- Angel Falls drops 3,212 feet.
- Tugela Falls in South Africa drops 3,110 feet.
- Yosemite Falls plunges 2,425 feet.
- Because of the erosion power built into them, all waterfalls eventually disappear.

Ordering

What makes one method of organizing details "logical" and another "illogical," or hard to follow? The answer lies in the writer's skill in ordering the ideas in his or her composition. **Ordering** means placing in a sequence that makes sense and is guided by a clear principle.

As long as the details in a composition are arranged in some order guided by a principle—even an order not described—chances are they will be logical and easy for a reader to follow.

THINKING PRACTICE

The following notes for an essay are not arranged in any order. Decide how best to arrange them using your skills of ordering. Write them in an orderly list.

SUBJECT: puppy discipline

DETAILS: DO teach the meaning of *no*.

DON'T use a loud voice, or your pup will be startled.

DO follow correction with praise.

DON'T give your puppy an old shoe to chew on—it will never learn the difference between old clothes and new.

DON'T call your puppy to you to correct him—always go to him.

DO correct your puppy only when you actually catch him in the act of doing something wrong.

DO teach your puppy the command "drop it"—it could save his life.

PREWRITING *Order of Details*

Select and arrange in logical order the details you developed. Use only those details that relate directly to your main idea. Save your work for later use.

	Drafting	Writing Process	

When your notes are clearly organized, you can begin the second stage of the writing process—writing the first draft. Use your notes as you write to help you include everything you planned and to help you follow a logical order.

Drafting the Introduction

One of the most important features of a strong introduction is a sentence that states the main idea of the composition. This sentence can come first, last, or in the middle of your introductory paragraph. Following is the introductory paragraph for the composition on gymnastics. Notice that the main idea statement has been changed slightly to fit smoothly into the paragraph.

MODEL: Introduction

INTRODUCTION

Anyone who has seen a women's gymnastics match knows the excitement of waiting for the judges' scores. When the numbers finally appear, the crowd usually responds with cheers or groans. In most cases, the scores from the various judges are very close. To a casual observer, the similarity of

MAIN IDEA   the scores may seem surprising. To the judges, however, scoring a gymnastic event is a matter of following the guidelines of the Federation of International Gymnastics.

In addition to expressing the main idea, an effective introduction has several other qualities. The following guidelines will help you write strong introductions.

> ## Writing an Introduction

A strong introduction

- catches the reader's attention with an interesting fact, detail, or incident.
- gives background information if needed.
- includes a statement of the composition's main idea.
- does not include such empty expressions as "In this essay I will . . ." or "This essay will be about . . ."

PRACTICE YOUR SKILLS

● *Improving a Weak Introduction*

Revise this introduction using the guidelines above.

How to Give Medicine to a Pet

People have been keeping pets for thousands of years. The first dogs may have been wolves that early hunters tamed. Pets can be interesting and playful. Some pets have even saved lives. Sometimes, however, pets get sick. This composition will be about how to give medicine to a sick pet.

DRAFTING *Introduction*

Using all your prewriting work and the guidelines above, write an introduction to your composition. Save your work for later use.

Drafting the Body

The body of the composition is the longest part. It is where the information, examples, and facts supporting the main idea introduced in the first paragraph appear. As you write the body, try to achieve two goals. Use your notes to write complete, varied sentences with vivid words. Also use transitions as needed to connect your thoughts smoothly.

Notice how the prewriting notes about gymnastics become, with transitions, smooth sentences in the composition body. The transitions are printed in **bold** type.

MODEL: Body

All events except vaulting are scored by the same system. A perfect score is 10 points. **By far the most important** category in that score is "difficulty," which is worth 5 points. If the proper number of difficult movements is included in the routine, the gymnast earns the full 5 points. The **next** category, execution, is worth 2 points. If a gymnast fails to perform a movement properly, she may lose tenths of a point in this category. Originality and composition are **also** worth 2 points. For this category the judges look at how the movements are combined in the routine. The category with the **lowest** point value is "general impression," worth 1 point. In this category judges react to the overall performance of the gymnast.

DRAFTING *Body*

Draft the body of your composition using examples, information, and facts. Follow the order you chose in your previous writing activity. Remember to express your thoughts in complete, varied sentences with vivid words. Use transitions to show how your thoughts are connected. Save your work for later use.

Drafting the Conclusion

Some paragraphs may not need concluding sentences. All compositions, however, need a concluding paragraph that sums up the composition and makes clear to the reader that the end has come. A good conclusion often ends with a clincher—a memorable phrase or statement.

The **conclusion** completes the composition and reinforces the main idea.

Read the following conclusion to the composition about scoring in gymnastics. Notice how the writer creates tension with the statement, "all eyes turn anxiously to the scoreboard."

MODEL: Conclusion

A perfect 10 is rare. More often, gymnasts will have tenths of points taken off in one or more categories. Most gymnasts know the scoring system so well that they have a good idea of how well they did even before the judges' cards come up. Still, after the final movement or dismount, all eyes turn anxiously to the scoreboard, wondering if the perfect 10 will somehow appear.

Use the guidelines below to write strong conclusions.

 Writing a Conclusion

A strong concluding paragraph

- emphasizes the main idea without restating it exactly.
- may refer to ideas in the introduction to round out the composition.
- does not introduce a completely new idea.
- does not contain empty expressions such as "I have just told you about . . . " or "Now you know how . . . "

Writing a Title

When you have completed your first draft, add a title to your composition. The title should be short and catchy. It should suggest the main idea of your composition and invite your readers to read on.

PRACTICE YOUR SKILLS

● *Improving a Weak Conclusion*

Read the following weak conclusion to a composition about how watching television affects family life. Then revise it, using the guidelines above.

As I have shown you, watching television together has given my family members many things to talk about. In our case, at least, television viewing has not cut into family conversations. My family also goes camping together, which we enjoy very much. Spider Lake is our favorite spot.

● *Writing Titles*

Write three possible titles for the composition about women's gymnastics.

Across the Media: News Styles

Writing effectively depends on knowing for whom you are writing and why. A news reporter writing for a national newspaper is going to have a different style than a reporter writing for a radio station. Each reporter is writing for a different medium and addressing a different audience.

- A printed article can be skimmed by the viewer, picked up or put down at any time, or read in one sitting, whereas a report on the radio can only be heard in the moment.
- Television news often shows brief video clips to catch the attention of its channel-surfing audience, while newspapers and magazines might use an interesting picture or a giant headline to grab the readers' interest.
- Radio news reports are often short blurbs intended to update commuters driving to and from work.
- Because of time constraints, stories written for broadcast news are shorter, while something written for print may be longer and contain more detail. Television and radio writers both use sound bites (short bits of recorded sounds or videotaped images) to convey information that in a print article would need to be described.

Media Activity

Working in groups of three, brainstorm a list of current news stories. Choose one that is likely to be in the news for several days and read about it in a newspaper or magazine, watch coverage of it on television, and listen to it on the radio. How is the coverage different in each medium? How is it similar? Which medium presented the story in the greatest depth? Which medium gave the story the least coverage? Write a paragraph describing your findings. Share your work with classmates.

DRAFTING *Conclusion and Title*

Add a strong conclusion to the composition you have been developing. Then think of a title that would make your readers want to read on. Save your draft for revising and editing later.

Looping Back in Drafting

New Conclusion

Look at the ending you have written. Ask yourself if there is any way in which you can improve upon your original ending. Is the language strong and clear? Are there any unnecessary words or phrases? Experiment with at least three different new conclusions and choose the one you like best.

Revising — Writing Process

The first draft of any writing is a trial copy. Writing that is as good as you can make it usually requires several tries. Use the following checklist to improve the first draft of your composition.

Evaluation Checklist for Revising

Checking Your Essay

✓ Do you have an interesting introduction that includes a sentence stating the main idea of the composition? *(pages C136–C137)*

✓ Do all of your sentences relate directly to that main idea? In other words, is your composition unified? *(pages C101–C102)*

✓ Are your ideas organized logically with smooth transitions? In other words, is your composition coherent? *(page C138)*

✓ Do you have a strong conclusion? *(pages C139–C140)*

Checking Your Paragraphs

✓ Does the body of your composition contain more than one paragraph? *(page C123)*

✓ Is each paragraph unified? *(pages C101–C102)*

✓ Is each paragraph coherent?

Checking Your Sentences and Words

✓ Did you eliminate short, choppy sentences by combining related sentences? *(pages C67–C71)*

✓ Did you vary the beginnings of your sentences? *(page C75)*

✓ Did you eliminate rambling sentences? *(page C78)*

✓ Are your sentences free of repetition and empty expressions? *(pages C79–C82)*

✓ Are your words fresh and vivid? *(page C40)*

Communicate Your Ideas

REVISING *Checklist*

Use the checklist above to improve the draft of your composition. Save your work for editing and publishing.

Editing ◄ Writing Process

By the editing stage, you are satisfied with the content and style of your composition. Your main goal now is to polish it. Use the proofreading symbols on page C28 when you edit.

Prewriting Workshop
Drafting Workshop
Revising Workshop
Editing Workshop ▶
Publishing Workshop

Verb Tense

Good writers are not finished when they place the final period on a piece of paper. They always review and edit their work. One area to check is correct use of verb tense.

Notice how confusing this passage from "Cleopatra" becomes when the tense shifts.

CONFUSING TENSE SHIFTS	The Roman dictator **fell** quickly and profoundly under Cleopatra's spell. He **helps** her vanquish the armies of her brother—Ptolemy dying in the war—and afterwards **placed** her again on the Egyptian throne, with another brother, whom she soon **disposes** of by poison. (shift between present and past tense)

Now notice how the author has used verb tense consistently.

CONSISTENCY IN TENSE	The Roman dictator **fell** quickly and profoundly under Cleopatra's spell. He **helped** her vanquish the armies of her brother—Ptolemy dying in the war—and afterwards **placed** her again on the Egyptian throne, with another brother, whom she soon **disposed** of by poison. (consistent use of past tense)

Editing Checklist

✔ Have you used the correct tense?
✔ Did you avoid shifts in tense?

When you prepare to publish your composition, the appearance of it can be almost as important as its content. A paper with uneven margins and words crossed out or crowded together is difficult to read. A neat paper, however, can help you convey your message.

You can learn more about the correct form for a composition on pages C31–C32.

Communicate Your Ideas

EDITING, PUBLISHING

Use the **Editing Checklist** on the previous page to edit your composition. Then follow the guidelines on pages C31 and C32 to make a final neat copy of your revised and edited composition. Then present it to an interested reader.

PORTFOLIO

▶ Process of Writing a Composition

The writing process is recursive—you can move back and forth among the stages. For example, if you discover while editing that an important detail is missing, return to the revising stage and add the detail. Refer to the page numbers in parentheses to help you with your writing.

PREWRITING

- Explore your interests for possible subjects. *(pages C125–C126)*
- Choose one subject from your list. *(page C127)*
- Limit your subject by deciding on your purpose, audience, and focus point. *(pages C127–C128)*
- Freewrite, brainstorm, or cluster to develop a list of supporting details. *(pages C129–C130)*
- Develop a main idea that will control your whole composition. *(pages C131–C132)*
- Select the supporting details that relate directly to your main idea, and arrange them in a logical order. *(pages C133–C134)*

DRAFTING

- Write an introduction that includes a sentence stating the main idea. *(pages C136–C137)*
- Use your notes to write the body of your composition, with smooth transitions between ideas. *(page C138)*
- Add a concluding paragraph. *(pages C139–C140)*
- Add a title that will capture your reader's attention. *(page C140)*

REVISING

- Put your first draft aside for a while. Then use the <u>Evaluation Checklist for Revising</u> on pages C142 and C143 to improve your first draft. Use the revision strategies of adding, deleting, substituting, and rearranging.

EDITING

- Use the <u>Editing Checklist</u> on pages C28 and C144 to polish your work.

PUBLISHING

- Prepare a neat final copy and present it to an interested reader. *(pages C31–C32)*

A Writer Writes

A Composition

Purpose: **to convince someone of the excitement of white-water rafting**

Audience: **a person who has never been white-water rafting**

Prewriting

Look at the picture above of people white-water rafting. Then freewrite or cluster to think of as many details as you can that will create a vivid picture of the event in the minds of your readers. Add sights, sounds, and smells that you think would go along with this scene. Next look over your details and formulate a main idea statement. Finally select and arrange your details so they clearly support your main idea.

Drafting

Use your prewriting work to write a first draft of your composition, including the introduction, body, and conclusion. Be sure your introduction contains the statement of your main idea. Try to get your thoughts down on paper as smoothly as possible.

Revising

Exchange papers with a classmate. Ask whether he or she actually "feels" the details in your composition. In other words, have you succeeded in creating the excitement? Make improvements as needed, and then use the **Evaluation Checklist for Revising** on pages C142–C143 as you prepare your final revision. Go over your draft several times. Each time, look for a different kind of problem or a fresh way to improve your composition.

Editing

Use the **Editing Checklists** on pages C28 and C144 to find and correct errors in your composition. Again, go over your paper several times looking for different kinds of errors each time.

Publishing

After catching any mistakes you might have made, follow the guidelines on pages C31–C32 for the correct form for a composition. Then share your finished work with an interested reader.

Connection Collection

Representing in Different Ways

From Visuals . . .

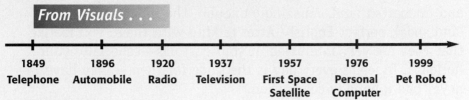

1849	1896	1920	1937	1957	1976	1999
Telephone	Automobile	Radio	Television	First Space Satellite	Personal Computer	Pet Robot

. . . to Print

Based upon the time line above, write a short composition about inventions.

From Print . . .

Today will be a very busy day for Rich. He has to walk his pet robot, Fluffy, at 7:15 A.M. He has to meet his friend on the corner at 7:45 A.M. School ends at 3:15 P.M., and he has sports practice until 5:00 P.M. His dentist appointment is at 5:30 P.M. He must return books to the library by 6:30 P.M., and get home by 7:00 P.M. to complete his homework. His mother is calling home from her business trip at exactly 7:20 P.M. Sometime in the afternoon or evening, he has to devote 45 minutes to walking, feeding, and playing with Fluffy.

To Visuals . . .

Plot Rich's day on a time line. Remember to block off appropriate amounts of time for each activity.

- Which strategies can be used for creating both written and visual representations? Which strategies apply to one, not both? Which type of representation is more effective?
- Draw a conclusion and write briefly about the differences between written ideas and visual representations.

Writing in Everyday Life
Informative Composition

While taking a shortcut home from school, you discover a new and uncharted land. Amazingly enough, the inhabitants of the land speak perfect English. After talking with them, you realize that they are very interested in your customs—especially your holidays. It seems every day is the same for them—they have never had a holiday celebration.

Write a composition about your favorite holiday to leave with the people of this new land. Tell them about the origins of the holiday, and the customs associated with it. Also tell them why it is your favorite. Give your composition a strong introduction and support it with supporting details. Finally, write a solid conclusion for your work. Remember to give your work an interesting title.

What strategies did you use to inform the people of the new land about your favorite holiday?

You can find information on writing informative compositions in on pages C266–C285.

Writing in the Workplace
Persuasive Composition

A famous talent scout, Faye Muss, is in your town searching for new talent. She is looking specifically for a young person with a fresh new face who can play a seventh grader in an upcoming movie. Unfortunately for you, the audition appointments are all taken.

Write a composition to submit to Ms. Muss persuading her to make an exception and give you an audition. Tell her why you would make an excellent seventh grader in her movie. Make your introduction attention-grabbing. When writing the body of your work, order your supporting details in a logical order. Be sure to use precise, lively words so that your composition is interesting throughout.

What strategies did you use to persuade Ms. Muss to give you an audition?

You can find information on writing persuasive compositions in on pages C301–C317.

Assess Your Learning

You own and operate Life of the Party, a well-known party planning service. You are currently organizing an event for a new client, Poochie. Poochie is a world famous movie star, who also happens to be a dainty French poodle.

▶ Write a composition describing your plan for Poochie's party to be presented to Poochie and her owner. Include descriptions of the invitations, menu, decorations, entertainment, and music.

▶ Your composition should include an introduction, a body with supporting points, and a conclusion. Use specific details and sensory words to paint a vivid picture or your party plans. Be sure to arrange your details in a logical order. Be sure all the parts of your composition work together to form one unified work.

▶ *Before You Write* Consider the following questions:
What is the *subject?*
What is the *occasion?*
Who is the *audience?*
What is the *purpose?*

▶ *After You Write* Evaluate your work using the following criteria:
- Is your topic focused?
- Did you write the composition in a voice and style appropriate to the purpose and audience?
- Does the work contain an introduction that states the main idea with vivid supporting details, body, and conclusion with a clincher sentence?
- Did you arrange your supporting details in a logical order?
- Do you use transitions to connect ideas?
- Did you use specific vocabulary and avoid wordiness?
- Is the work unified and coherent?

Write briefly on how well you did. Point out your strengths and areas for improvement.

CHAPTER 6

Personal Writing: Self-Expression and Reflection

One of the most important challenges every writer faces is that of expressing his or her own thoughts and feelings clearly. No doubt you have usually discussed your thoughts and feelings with people who know and understand you. Sometimes, however, an experience may touch you deeply enough to inspire a more thoughtful form of self-expression.

Writing a personal narrative provides an opportunity both to reflect on the experience and to share with a larger audience an event that may well have changed how you view yourself or the world. The reader may know nothing about you, yet still you may feel you have something important to share.

In this chapter you will explore and develop your skills of self-expression. Your goal will be to tie together moments of self-reflection and transform them into a vital and compelling form of communication.

Reading with a Writer's Eye

In the following passage, Graham Salisbury relates a brief, moving experience with an ending that for both him and the reader is unexpected. As you read, immerse yourself in the experience he tells. Then reread the passage thinking about how the writer reflects on his experience through the act of writing, and consider what his purpose in writing might be.

FROM

NOT YOUR NORMAL BEAST

Graham Salisbury

Yesterday I was in a huge hurry to get home, driving in slow traffic down by Portland Civic Auditorium. A man was driving in front of me with his wife in the front seat and two teenage sons in the back. Stop, go, stop, go . . . slow, slow, slow! Finally, he stopped in the right-hand turn lane at the corner of a block to let one of his sons out, blocking me and forcing me to wait. I became frustrated, but managed to keep from honking at them. The mother got out and held her seat back for one of the boys to get out. Apparently he was headed for something going on at the Civic. He was young, maybe 14, and off in the big city on his own. To say goodbye to him, his mother put her hand on his cheek and looked into his eyes with the most beautiful, loving look on her face. The moment was so tender it broke my heart down to where it should have been all along. Instantly, all my frustration left me. There is great and wonderful power in such a simple act of love, even to those of us who only manage to observe.

Thinking as a Writer

Evaluating the Author's Purpose

- What do you think Graham Salisbury's purpose was in writing this narrative? Do you think he wants others to seek out similar experiences, or did he have a goal in mind for himself? Explain your answer.
- How might the experience of writing have affected Salisbury's feelings about what happened to him?

Analyzing Narrative Techniques

Oral Expression • Discuss with a classmate an event that happened to you in the past week, one that brought up strong feelings or thoughts for you. Does telling the story bring up those feelings again? Does it change anything about how you view the event?

- Now invite your partner to tell you a story. Listen carefully as he or she speaks. How might you convey the same meanings in writing?

Recognizing the Uses of Reflection

Viewing • Look closely at this photograph. List five words that tell about the scene.

- Think back to a time when you were in a hurry to get somewhere and something prevented you. How did you react? In what ways does reflecting on the event change how you feel about it? What might you have done differently?

The Power of Personal Writing

A personal narrative tells a story. This kind of story may appear to be unimportant to anyone but the person telling it, but in fact can be profoundly moving. In personal writing you can take an experience that is completely your own and share it with others for them to understand and appreciate.

Uses of Personal Writing

Personal experiences happen every day, to every human being. Here are some of the ways in which people share those experiences with others.

- **A refugee from a war-torn country writes daily journal entries** telling about his every-day life during the chaos of war.

- **A firefighter speaks to a group of students** about saving a child from a burning apartment building and relates what the experience means to her.

- **A movie actor writes his autobiography** and reflects on his 30-year acting career.

- **Your grandmother writes you an E-mail message,** telling you how much your visit means to her.

- **Your best friend writes a postcard** while on vacation, telling you about her amazing experience of visiting the Grand Canyon.

Developing Your Skills of Personal Writing

"In many ways, writing is the act of saying *I*," wrote the author Joan Didion. This statement seems particularly true of narrative writing. Writers often use narration to express their thoughts, tell about events in their lives, and share what they have learned from an experience.

A **personal narrative** expresses the writer's personal point of view.

The following is an example of personal writing. It tells a true story about three abandoned bear cubs—Rusty, Dusty, and Scratch—and the man who adopted them. While reading, pay attention to the structure of the paragraph: the topic sentence, the body of supporting sentences, and the concluding sentence.

MODEL: Narrative Paragraph

Unspoken Friendship

TOPIC SENTENCE:
STATES THE MAIN IDEA

BODY OF SUPPORTING SENTENCES:
TELLS EVENTS IN THE ORDER THAT THEY HAPPENED

On the ninth evening, I learned what little bears require beyond food, shelter, and protection. Supper was over, dishes were put away, and I was reading in front of a crackling fire. From his rug near the hearth, Rusty looked up at me. After a while he strolled cautiously to my chair and placed both front paws on my knee. I was surprised at the roughness of his tongue when he licked my fingers. I ran my hand across his neck and shoulders. It was the first time I had touched one of the cubs. As I scratched his puppy like head, the little fellow pulled himself up into my lap, where he turned around several times and then finally lay down. Soon Dusty ambled over to the chair, climbed my leg like a monkey, and staked her claim on one third of my lap. Before long Scratch joined his siblings, knocking my book to the floor. As we studied each other's expressions, I became certain of

CONCLUDING SENTENCE:

SUMS UP THE STORY

one thing. No matter what time might bring, all of our lives were from that moment on affected by the unspoken pact of friendship that night.

—*Robert Franklin Leslie,* The Bears and I

Your Writer's Journal

Use your journal to record what happens during each day for the next week. Note anything of special interest that happens during the morning, afternoon, and evening. You may be able to turn one of these happenings into a lively narrative.

Prewriting ► Writing Process

Instead of wondering about what to write, many writers simply begin to write. They jot down any ideas that come to mind. They use freewriting, brainstorming, and clustering to unlock ideas. One idea leads to another and then to still another. Before long they have found a good subject.

As you have read, this stage in the writing process is called prewriting. It includes all the invention and planning you do before writing the first draft. The first goal of prewriting is to start your ideas flowing. The following questions will help.

PRACTICE YOUR SKILLS

● *Thinking of Subjects for Narratives*

Read each question. Think about your past experiences. Then write one or two sentences in response to each question.

1. Which birthday holds special memories for you? Why?

2. Which school vacation do you remember best? What happened?

3. Have you ever been caught in a storm? What happened?

4. What were some important experiences in your life (first time on a bicycle, first time at a computer, first day at a new school, and so on)? What happened? How did you feel?

Choosing a Subject

The next step in writing a narrative is to choose one subject from your list. The following guidelines will help you make your choice.

> **Guidelines for Choosing a Subject**
> - Choose an event that interests you.
> - Choose an event that will interest your audience.
> - Choose an event that has a high point of action and an interesting outcome.

Your own judgment will help you follow the first guideline. To follow the second guideline, think about who will be reading your narrative. Will your readers find the event interesting? To follow the third guideline, consider whether the event is unusual and dramatic or merely an everyday event. Events that are out of the ordinary often make the best stories.

PREWRITING *Subject for a Narrative*

Write three possible subjects for a personal narrative. You may use ideas from the previous practice activity or one of the events you have already recorded in your **journal**. Next review the guidelines on the previous page. Then circle the subject that comes closest to following all three guidelines. Save your work for later use.

COMPUTER TIP

If you are working on a computer, you can create a new folder for all your narrative writing and color-code the icon. It is simple to do: Choose Preferences from your Edit menu. You'll see a list of label choices. To choose a color, click the color swatch. Save all your narrative writing documents in that folder.

Limiting a Subject

Occasionally a subject is broad enough to fill an entire book. A slightly more specific subject may take up a whole chapter. A subject for a short narrative, however, must be very specific. Read the following examples.

BOOK LENGTH	CHAPTER LENGTH	SHORT NARRATIVE
my travels	one summer vacation	my first case of poison ivy
holidays	Thanksgiving	our dog eating the turkey
memories	moving to a new city	the day I forgot where I lived

Be sure to limit your subject so that it can be covered adequately in one paragraph.

PRACTICE YOUR SKILLS

● *Identifying Limited Subjects*

Decide whether each subject listed is limited enough for a one-paragraph narrative. Indicate your answer by writing either *limited* or *too broad*.

EXAMPLE   my childhood
ANSWER   too broad

1. my week at soccer camp
2. the game in which I scored the winning goal
3. the time I thought I heard a burglar
4. sixth grade
5. my week in Washington, D.C.

● *Limiting Subjects That Are Too Broad*

The following subjects are too broad for a one-paragraph narrative. Select five subjects. For each one, list two events that are limited enough to be covered in one paragraph.

EXAMPLE   playing baseball
POSSIBLE ANSWERS   my first home run
                                 quick thinking on the play

1. entering a new school   **6.** seeing old friends
2. trying something new   **7.** getting lost
3. meeting new friends   **8.** making home videos
4. belonging to a club   **9.** entering a contest
5. performing for an   **10.** receiving an award
     audience

Listing Details

Once you have chosen and limited a subject, you are ready to list the events and details that make up the story. Brainstorming is an especially good way to help you remember all the details. To prod your memory, ask yourself the following questions about your subject.

> ### Brainstorming Questions
> - Who besides you is involved in the story?
> - Where did the event take place?
> - When did the event take place?
> - How did you feel?
> - What happened to start things rolling?
> - What happened next?
> - What is the high point of the story?
> - What is the outcome?
> - What did you learn from the experience?

If you were writing about the time that you took pictures of a dog and her puppies, your notes might look like the following:

WHO IS IN THE STORY?	Rags, her puppies, and I
WHERE DID IT HAPPEN?	my neighbor's kitchen
WHEN DID IT HAPPEN?	last week
HOW DID YOU FEEL?	I was eager to get good pictures.
WHAT HAPPENED FIRST?	I went next door to take pictures of Rags and her puppies.
WHAT HAPPENED NEXT?	I walked close to get a good shot.
WHAT IS THE HIGH POINT?	Rags charged at me.
WHAT IS THE OUTCOME?	I dropped my camera and left.
WHAT DID YOU LEARN?	Rags was protective of her pups.

Is **Thinking**

Recalling

To help you come up with the details you need for your narrative paragraph, you use the skill of **recalling**. Stored somewhere in the mysterious gray mass of your brain are fragments of virtually all the experiences you have ever had. Through active recall, you can bring some of these fragments to your memory—and use them to make your writing rich and lifelike.

Different writers use different techniques to retrieve memories, but the following strategies may help you tap into some nearly forgotten parts of your past.

STRATEGIES FOR RECALLING

- Relax. Shut down the part of your mind that usually disciplines your thoughts. Let one thought lead to another as you float on top of your general memory. Before you know it, you will probably have a flood of specific memories.

- Try to recall *exactly* one aspect of the experience you wish to remember. Focus your thoughts on that one single memory. Chances are good that other details will soon come to mind as well.

- What if you were looking at a photograph or video of the event? Little by little, let your mind fill in all the details in the picture or video until you can see it as clearly as if it really existed.

THINKING PRACTICE

Think back to one of the most pleasant memories of your childhood. Use any or all of the strategies above to bring even the smallest details of that experience to mind. Jot down each detail as it occurs to you. Save your work in case you want to develop your memories into a composition later.

PRACTICE YOUR SKILLS

● *Details for a Narrative Paragraph*

Write one of the following subjects on your paper. Then under it brainstorm a list of details. Use the questions on page C161 and the skill of recalling to help you think of ideas.

1. the day I lost something valuable

2. my first dance

3. the time I met a new friend

4. the day I made a promise I could not keep

5. the way I got my first pet

● *Reflecting on an Experience*

Use the subject you chose from the activity above or one from your own personal experience to fill in the chart below. Think of as many details as you can to present a well-rounded picture of what happened and what you learned from it.

Event (what happened)	Reflection (what you learned from It)

Communicate Your Ideas

PREWRITING *Details*

Review the subject you chose for your personal narrative. Limit it so that it is suitable for a single paragraph. Then use brainstorming and recalling to develop a list of details you can use to tell your story. Keep your list of details in your writing folder for later use.

Use recalling to think of specific details that will add richness to your writing.

Arranging Details in Chronological Order

To help readers follow your story easily, you should present the events in the order in which they happened. This type of order is called **chronological order**, or time order.

Read the following narrative paragraph. Notice that several things happen in this story. The writer tells about each one in the order that it happened.

MODEL: Chronological Order

Applause from the Cabbage Patch

BEFORE RECITAL

On the day of my first piano recital, I became more and more nervous. To help me calm down, my piano teacher told me to place several heads of cabbage in the room where I practiced. If I could play for them, he said, I could play for a real audience. I was so eager to get over my nerves that I was willing to try anything. For the next few hours, I played to an audience of cabbage heads.

BEGINNING OF RECITAL

DURING RECITAL

HIGH POINT

OUTCOME

When the time of the recital finally arrived, I was still a wreck. I waited, sick with fear, for my turn. My hands felt like ice. When I finally walked across the stage, I looked out into the dark audience. I could not see anyone! All those people out there could just as easily have been cabbage heads! As I sat down to play, my hands relaxed. Before I knew it, I had played all my pieces without a mistake. For the first time, the cabbage heads applauded!

PRACTICE YOUR SKILLS

● Arranging Details in Chronological Order

Write each of the following subjects. Then write the details under each subject in chronological order.

1. SUBJECT   the surprise party for me last year

DETAILS
- turning on the lights
- noticing that lights in house were out
- everyone shouting, "Surprise!"
- opening the door carefully

2. SUBJECT   the time I won the race

DETAILS
- crossing the finish line
- gasping for breath toward the end
- lying exhausted on the grass
- crouching at the chalk line

3. SUBJECT   losing a homework assignment on the computer

DETAILS
- rewriting the whole report the night before it was due
- working for two weeks writing a report on the computer
- being careful after each day's work to remove the disk and store it carefully
- chasing my dog and seeing his foot catch on the cord and unplug the computer
- playing with my dog to celebrate having finished the report
- turning the computer back on and finding the whole report had been erased
- watching the computer screen go black

PREWRITING *Chronological Order*

Review the list of details you developed for your personal narrative. Then arrange them in chronological order. Think carefully about what occurred first, next, and so on. Save your work for later use.

Drafting Writing Process

With your prewriting notes handy, you are ready to begin the first draft of your paragraph. As you write, keep the interests of your readers in mind.

Drafting a Topic Sentence

Remember, the topic sentence states the main idea of a paragraph. In a narrative paragraph, the main idea is the event you plan to write about. The tips outlined below may help you draft your topic sentence.

Tips for Drafting a Topic Sentence
- Look over your prewriting notes.
- Try to express your main idea in one sentence.
- Rewrite that sentence until it covers all the supporting details you listed in your notes.

If you were writing a paragraph about the time you tried to take pictures of Rags and her newborn pups, you might write the following topic sentence.

TOPIC SENTENCE   Rags was a protective mother.

If you were to look over your prewriting notes again, however, you would notice that this sentence does not clearly set the stage for the story to follow. Your readers would not know who Rags is, and they would not know what to expect in the rest of the paragraph. The following topic sentence does a better job.

TOPIC SENTENCE   Photographing pets can sometimes be a dangerous and expensive hobby.

This topic sentence is strong because it focuses attention on the subject and prepares the reader for what is to follow. Avoid openings such as "This paragraph will be about . . ." or "In this paragraph I will . . ." These phrases focus attention on the writer rather than on the story.

PRACTICE YOUR SKILLS

● *Drafting Topic Sentences*

Read the three lists of details for narrative paragraphs. Then write a topic sentence for each list. Save your work.

1. • rained all day
   • lights went out
   • went to basement for candles
   • basement flooded
   • spent all evening drying things out

2. • left at 4:00 A.M. on a fishing trip
   • drove for two hours
   • rented a boat
   • rowed out into lake
   • discovered I had left fishing gear home

3. • decided to paint a picture of my dog
   • bought paints and brushes
   • spilled paint on the rug
   • thought the dog looked like a seal
   • dog ran off with picture

Television Talk Shows

One of the most popular media forms is the daytime talk show. The producers of these shows come up with a different situation for each show, a "hook" that tends to be moving, disturbing, or even shocking. Then the producers locate ordinary citizens who are willing to appear on national television to discuss their experiences. The result can be fascinating, touching, enlightening, maddening, or simply boring.

What usually makes the difference is the host. This role is one that requires a strong ability to talk through any situation, as well as a lively personality. The show's following is made up of people who find the host's personality compelling.

Media Activity

Work with several classmates. Ask your parents to help you choose a daytime talk show to watch. Videotape it, if possible, for several days. As you watch, notice the content and overall message, as well as how the message is presented.

Questions for Analyzing a Daytime Talk Show
• Who is the host? What is the best way to describe the host's personality?
• List the topic for each show you watched. How does the theme relate to the host's personality?
• How is the studio audience involved in the program? Does the host interview audience members throughout the show?
• Are there clips of background material or interviews? Are they effective?

Share your findings with your classmates.

Drafting the Paragraph Body

The supporting details that make up the body of a narrative paragraph are the specific events in the story. Presenting these ideas in chronological order will help your readers follow the events. To make sure that the order is clear, use transitionals. **Transitions** are words and phrases that show how ideas are related. In chronological order, transitions point out the passing of time.

In the following first draft about Rags and her puppies, you can see how the prewriting notes have been made into sentences. The transitions are in **bold** type.

MODEL: Transitions

TOPIC SENTENCE	Photographing pets can sometimes be a dangerous and expensive hobby. **One day last week** I went next door to take some pictures of
EVENTS IN THE ORDER THAT THEY HAPPENED	Rags and her newborn puppies. **As** I walked close to her and her pups, she charged at me, barking in a wild, high-pitched voice. **Before** I knew it, I was racing to the door, dropping my camera on the way. **Only later** did I learn that all animals are very protective of their young.

Following is a list of transitions that are often used with chronological order.

TRANSITIONS FOR CHRONOLOGICAL ORDER

before	finally	meanwhile
after	last	after a while
first	at last	later that day
next	soon	the next day
then	when	on Saturday

● *Writing the Body of a Narrative Paragraph*

Choose a topic sentence from the previous practice activity. Then use the details listed to write the body of the paragraph. Be sure to add transitions where necessary.

Drafting a Concluding Sentence

The last sentence in a narrative paragraph is as important as the punch line in a joke. A strong concluding sentence brings the event to a close and leaves the reader satisfied. A concluding sentence may serve a variety of purposes.

▷ **Tips for Drafting a Concluding Sentence**

The concluding sentence may

- restate the topic sentence in fresh words.
- summarize the paragraph.
- pull the supporting sentences together.
- state an insight or lesson learned from the experience.

Any of the following would be a strong concluding sentence for the paragraph about Rags and her pups.

CONCLUDING SENTENCES

Although my hobby has its risks, the chance to snap good pictures is worth it. (restates an idea from the topic sentence) Trying to photograph Rags and her pups was an experience I will never forget. (summarizes the paragraph) Rags may have thought her pups were in danger, but I knew I was! (pulls the supporting sentences together) Next time I will play it safe and wait till the pups are older. (states a lesson learned from the experience)

DRAFTING *Topic Sentence, Body, Concluding Sentence*

Review your prewriting work. Then write the first draft of your narrative paragraph. Include a topic sentence, a body of supporting sentences, and a concluding sentence. Save your work for later use.

Revising | Writing Process

In the revising stage of the writing process, try to read your work as if you were seeing it for the first time. In this way you can spot and correct any confusing or unclear passages.

Checking for Unity

A paragraph in which all the sentences support the topic sentence is said to have **unity**. Sentences that wander off the subject make your ideas hard to follow.

In the following paragraph, the crossed-out sentences stray from the story. Read the paragraph twice—once with the sentences that stray and once without them. Notice that the paragraph is clearer and easier to read without the sentences that wander from the main idea.

MODEL: Paragraph Unity

My Comic Book Collection

Because I am a pack rat, I may be a rich person someday. Ten years ago my aunt gave me a subscription to "The Fantastic Four." ~~I once saw a "Fantastic Four" cartoon.~~ Since I never throw anything away, I kept all the copies of the old comic books in a carton in my closet. ~~I keep my sports equipment there too.~~ Just recently I learned that those old comic books are worth money. If I keep them another ten years, they will be worth even more. Maybe I will sell them then and retire before I even start working.

A ▾ Writing Tip

Check your paragraph for **unity** by eliminating any sentences that stray from the point.

Checking for Coherence

A paragraph with **coherence** is well organized and tightly knit. The ideas are presented in a logical order with clear transitions. The writer of the following paragraph has used chronological order. Notice how the writer has improved the paragraph by revising the order and adding a transition.

MODEL: Paragraph Coherence

An Unexpected Guest

My family is large, and we're used to having neighborhood friends drop in. One summer night, a visitor surprised us all. ~~The next morning even our visitor had a good laugh.~~ We were all sitting in the living room, watching a late movie. During an especially scary moment, the door opened, and our nine-year-old neighbor Sasha, dressed in pajamas, walked in without knocking. He headed straight for the kitchen and poured himself a glass of milk. ^Then^ He left quickly and silently. My dad rushed after him to make sure he arrived home safely. Sasha had been sound asleep the whole time!

Writing Tip

Revise your paragraph for **coherence** by checking the logical order of ideas and adding transitions where needed.

PRACTICE YOUR SKILLS

● *Checking for Unity*

Two sentences in the following narrative paragraph wander off the subject. Write the sentences that break the unity of the paragraph.

Skiing Ups and Downs

All skis should read: "Skiing may be hazardous to your health." I should know, because I tried skiing for the first time yesterday. Many of my friends know how to ski. I fell getting onto the chair lift, and I fell getting off the chair lift. Then as soon as I started skiing, my skis crossed. I fell forward, lost my skis, and rolled halfway down the hill. We were skiing in the Green Mountains. Then I had to climb back up again to pick up my skis. After falling several more times and running into another skier, I finally reached the bottom of the hill.

● *Adding Transitions*

The paragraph on the following page lacks transitions. Write the paragraph adding a transition each time you see a blank space. Choose the transitions from the list below.

the following day   the next day
later that afternoon   by the third day

An Unusual Passenger

When the wood for our fireplace was delivered one afternoon, I stacked it in the garage. Dad noticed the wood and asked me to move it. "If you leave it in the garage," he said, "we will have mice in the garage and in the house too. Stack it between the two birch trees and cover it with plastic." ▪ I was too busy with homework to move the wood. ▪ our class had a car wash, and the wood still remained in the garage. ▪ , Dad had waited long enough. "Move that wood!" he commanded. "This morning a mouse tried to catch a ride with me on the hood of the car."

Looping Back to Drafting

Concluding Sentence

Review the concluding sentence you wrote for your paragraph. Does your concluding sentence state what you have learned from the experience you wrote about?

Time Out to Reflect What have you learned from the experience you wrote about? Use these reflections to help you add details that will make your narrative more interesting to a reader.

Communicate Your Ideas

REVISING

Revise your paragraph using the **Evaluation Checklist for Revising** on page C176. Save your work in case you want to polish it to share it with someone later.

Prewriting Workshop
Drafting Workshop
Revising Workshop ▶
Editing Workshop
Publishing Workshop

Adverbs

An **adverb** is a word that modifies a verb, an adjective, or another adverb. Adverbs show *how* an action was done. Also, many of the transitions you use with chronological order are adverbs. They modify the verb in the sentence and answer the question *when?* All of the following transitional words are adverbs that tell *when* something happened.

now	finally	then	last
first	soon	next	later

Notice how Graham Salisbury uses the adverbs, shown in **bold** type, in "Not Your Normal Beast."

> **Yesterday** I was in a huge hurry to get home . . .
> (*Yesterday* tells when—in the past.)
>
> Stop, go, stop, go . . . slow, slow, slow! **Finally** he stopped in the right-hand turn lane . . .
> (*Finally* also tells when—after a long period of time.)
>
> **Instantly** all my frustration left me.
> (*Instantly* tells when—almost immediately.)

The adverbs Salisbury uses tell us *when*, but they also convey *how long*. When you revise your draft of a narrative paragraph, pay special attention to the adverbs you use between the different events in the story. Where appropriate, use adverbs that tell how long as transitions that show the passing of time.

> ## Evaluation Checklist for Revising

Checking Your Paragraph

✓ Does your topic sentence focus attention on the subject and prepare the reader for what is to follow? *(pages C166–C167)*

✓ Are your supporting details in chronological order? *(page C164)*

✓ Did you use transitions to give your paragraph coherence? *(page C172–C173)*

✓ Does your paragraph have unity? *(page C171)*

✓ Does your concluding sentence bring the event to a close? *(page C170)*

Checking Your Sentences

✓ Did you combine related sentences to avoid too many short, choppy sentences in a row? *(pages C67–C68)*

✓ Did you vary the beginnings of your sentences? *(page C75)*

✓ Did you avoid rambling sentences? *(page C78)*

✓ Did you avoid repetition? *(page C79)*

✓ Did you avoid empty expressions and unnecessary wordiness? *(pages C81–C82)*

Checking Your Words

✓ Did you use specific, lively words? *(page C40)*

✓ Did you use words that appeal to the senses? *(pages C44–C51)*

Process of Writing a Personal Narrative

Remember that you can move back and forth among the stages of the writing process to achieve your purpose. For example, during editing you may wish to return to the drafting stage to add details that have occurred to you while editing. The page numbers in parentheses refer to pages where you can get help with your writing.

PREWRITING

- Think about your purpose in writing and consider your audience. *(pages C16–C18)*
- Make a list of subjects by freewriting or simply jotting down ideas. *(page C157)*
- Choose one subject and limit it. *(pages C158–C160)*
- Brainstorm a list of supporting details. *(pages C161–C163)*
- Arrange your details in chronological order. *(pages C164–C165)*

DRAFTING

- Draft a topic sentence. *(pages C166–C167)*
- Draft a body of supporting sentences telling the story event by event. Use transitions. *(page C169)*
- Add a concluding sentence. *(page C170)*

REVISING

- Using the Evaluation Checklist for Revising on page C176, check your paragraph structure, sentences, and word choice.

A Writer Writes

A Memoir

Purpose: to reflect on entering the seventh grade
Audience: your sixth-grade schoolmates

Prewriting

The start of a new school year, a time when you are introduced to new teachers and subjects, can be a time of
worry as well as excitement. Take time to reflect on your
experiences and feelings when you started the seventh
grade. Use freewriting or brainstorming to recall the
experiences and reflect on their meaning for you.

Drafting

Write a topic sentence that explains your main idea, a
body of supporting sentences with details, and a conclusion that shows what you have learned.

Revising

Review your personal narrative looking for ways to improve it. Does it have unity? Coherence? Did you use
transitions? Keep working on your memoir until you are
satisfied you have done the best you can.

Editing

Correct any errors in spelling, grammar, and usage that
you may have made while drafting.

Publishing

Make a copy of your reflection for a sixth grader you know.

Connection Collection

Representing in Different Ways

From Visuals . . .

N. C. Wyeth. *Jim Hawkins Leaves Home*, 1911.
Brandywine Museum, Chadds Ford, Pennsylvania.

. . . to Print

What story does the painting above suggest to you? Write a letter to a friend, telling that person the "story" of this painting. Be sure to put your narrative in chronological order.

From Print . . .

> 7 Bowden Street
> Burnt Hills, NY 12005
> June 20, 2000
>
> Dear Francine,
>
> The latest news here is that Joey ruined Mrs. Simm's birdbath. Joey and Zelda were playing a series of seven croquet games. The loser had to buy ice cream for the winner every Saturday afternoon for the rest of the summer.
>
> The croquet course wound all over the neighborhood and ended in Mrs. Simm's backyard. It was the final match. Everybody in the neighborhood was watching— including Mrs. Simm. Joey knocked Zelda's ball away from the final wicket. The ball flew across the lawn, skipped off a rock, and broke the cherub statue off the top of the birdbath. Joey was so scared that he dropped his mallet and ran toward the birdbath, but he slipped in the wet grass and could not stop without grabbing hold of the birdbath and breaking it in two.
>
> For the rest of the summer, Joey has to buy Zelda ice cream on Saturdays and mow Mrs. Simm's lawn on Sundays to pay for the birdbath. Don't tell Joey, but Mrs. Simm told me she never liked the birdbath anyway!
>
> Sincerely,
> Susie

. . . to Visuals

Draw a picture that represents the events of Susie's story.

- Which strategies can be used for creating both written and visual representations? Which strategies apply to one, not both? Which type of repre-sentation is more effective?
- Draw a conclusion, and write briefly about the differences between written ideas and visual representations.

Writing in the Workplace
Bulletin Board Message

You are the owner of a goat farm. Recently, a group of seventh graders visited your farm on a field trip. You showed them the shelters and hay barns, the equipment for milking goats, and the pastures where the goats graze. At the end of the morning, your dairy provided the students with a lunch that included goat cheese and goat milk.

> **Write a message to be posted on an electronic bulletin board for other small farmers. In your message, include a personal narrative describing the field trip. Reflect on why the experience was important to you and the seventh graders. Revise the message to check for unity and coherence.**
>
> **What strategies did you use to order and unify your narrative?**

You can learn more about communicating on the Internet on pages C578–C52.

Writing for Oral Communication
Personal Speech

You are a member of the seventh grade Travel Club. Your group has recently been invited to speak to a group of fourth graders about your travel experiences. Each of you decided to speak about a different aspect of travel, and you have chosen to discuss the topic of transportation.

> **Write a speech describing the first time you were ever on a train, plane, or bus. Narrate the events of that day and what you felt about the experience. Put your narrative in chronological order and include a topic sentence and concluding sentence. Check that you use transitions to help guide your listeners through the story.**
>
> **What strategies did you use to help the fourth graders follow your story clearly?**

You can find information on speeches in on pages C433–C443.

Assess Your Learning

Mr. and Mrs. Peabody are an elderly couple who live in your hometown. Many of their neighbors consider them "peculiar"—after all, their house is painted bright orange, and both husband and wife make frequent trips to the local junkyard to decorate their lawn. But on a recent sunny day, you stopped to speak to the Peabodys while they were working on their lawn, and you found them to be quite interesting and extremely nice. They showed you their many unusual and interesting possessions—old comic books, antique dolls, and world coins collection—and even baked you a chocolate cake!

▶ **Write a letter to a friend describing an afternoon you spent at the Peabodys' house. Put your narrative in chronological order. Tell your friend what happened that afternoon, and be sure to include reflections on what the experience meant to you. Remember to use specific and colorful details in describing the Peabodys and their home.**

▶ *Before You Write* **Consider the following questions:**
What is the *subject?*
What is the *occasion?*
Who is the *audience?*
What is the *purpose?*

▶ *After You Write* **Evaluate your work using the following criteria:**
- Is your narrative about your afternoon at the Peabodys' home in chronological order?
- Have you reflected on what meeting Mr. and Mrs. Peabody meant to you?
- Are your paragraphs unified and coherent?

Write briefly on how well you did. Point out your strengths and areas for improvement.

CHAPTER 7

Using Description: Observation

Every day, all kinds of pictures—or images—surround us. Movies, television, advertisements, games, and computers present real and imaginary places, people, events, and objects in vivid color and stereo surround sound.

How can words compete with the awesome power of images that can be seen and heard?

An astronaut describes with awe the beauty of "the blue planet" Earth from high in orbit. A sports reporter describes the winning team's jubilation at the moment of victory. A relief worker describes the destruction left behind by a blazing fire.

Their descriptions make you feel as if you are there—looking down on Earth, hearing the roar of the crowd, smelling the charred remains of grass and trees. Their words make you see, hear, smell, taste, and touch "the blue planet," the victory, and the fire.

Reading with a Writer's Eye

The following selection is from *Julie of the Wolves*, a novel by Jean Craighead George. The story describes the experiences of a girl lost on the Alaskan tundra, with only wolves for company. Read it once to immerse yourself in her experience. What from the story can you see? hear? smell? taste? touch? Read the selection again. Notice words that create mental images. Why do you think the writer uses these words?

FROM

JULIE OF THE WOLVES

Jean Craighead George

Miyax pushed back the hood of her sealskin parka and looked at the Arctic sun. It was a yellow disc in a lime-green sky, the colors of six o'clock in the evening and the time when the wolves awoke. Quietly she put down her cooking pot and crept to the top of a dome-shaped frost heave, one of the many earth buckles that rise and fall in the crackling cold of the Arctic winter. Lying on her stomach, she looked across a vast lawn of grass and moss and focused her attention on the wolves she had come upon two sleeps ago. They were wagging their tails as they awoke and saw each other.

Her hands trembled and her heart-beat quickened, for she was frightened, not so much of the wolves, who were shy and many harpoon-shots away, but because of her desperate predicament. Miyax was lost. She had been lost without food for many sleeps on the North Slope of Alaska. The barren slope stretches for three hundred miles from the Brooks Range to the Arctic Ocean, and for more than eight hundred miles from the Chukchi to the Beaufort Sea. No roads cross it; ponds and lakes freckle its immensity. Winds scream across it, and the view in every direction is exactly the same. Somewhere in this cosmos was Miyax; and the very life in her body, its spark and warmth, depended upon these wolves for survival. And she was not so sure they would help.

Miyax stared hard at the regal black wolf, hoping to catch his eye. She must somehow tell him that she was starving and ask him for food. This could be done she knew, for her father, an Eskimo hunter, had done so. One year he had camped near a wolf den while on a hunt. When a month had passed and her father had seen no game, he told the leader of the wolves that he was hungry and needed food. The next night the wolf called him from far away and her father went to him and found a freshly killed caribou. Unfortunately, Miyax's father never explained to her how he had told the wolf of his needs. And not long afterwards he paddled his kayak into the Bering Sea to hunt for seal, and he never returned.

She had been watching the wolves for two days, trying to discern which of their sounds and movements expressed goodwill and friendship. Most animals had such signals. The little Arctic ground squirrels flicked their tails sideways to notify others of their kind that they were friendly. By imitating this signal with her forefinger, Miyax had lured many a squirrel to her hand. If she could discover such a gesture for the wolves she would be able to make friends with them and share their food, like a bird or a fox.

Propped on her elbows with her chin in her fists, she stared at the black wolf, trying to catch his eye. She had chosen him because he was much larger than the others, and because he walked like her father, Kapugen, with his head high and his chest out. The black wolf also possessed wisdom, she had observed. The pack looked to him when the wind carried strange scents or the birds cried nervously. If he was alarmed, they were alarmed. If he was calm, they were calm.

Using Description: Observation

Long minutes passed, and the black wolf did not look at her. He had ignored her since she first came upon them, two sleeps ago. True, she moved slowly and quietly, so as not to alarm him; yet she did wish he would see the kindness in her eyes. Many animals could tell the difference between hostile hunters and friendly people by merely looking at them. But the big black wolf would not even glance her way.

A bird stretched in the grass. The wolf looked at it. A flower twisted in the wind. He glanced at that. Then the breeze rippled the wolverine ruff on Miyax's parka and it glistened in the light. He did not look at that. She waited. Patience with the ways of nature had been instilled in her by her father. And so she knew better than to move or shout. Yet she must get food or die. Her hands shook slightly and she swallowed hard to keep calm.

Miyax was a classic Eskimo beauty, small of bone and delicately wired with strong muscles. Her face was pearl-round and her nose was flat. Her black eyes, which slanted gracefully, were moist and sparkling. Like the beautifully formed polar bears and foxes of the north, she was slightly short-limbed. The frigid environment of the Arctic has sculptured life into compact shapes. Unlike the long-limbed, long-bodied animals of the south that are cooled by dispensing heat on extended surfaces, all live things in the Arctic tend toward compactness, to conserve heat.

The length of her limbs and the beauty of her face were of no use to Miyax as she lay on the lichen-speckled frost heave in the midst of the bleak tundra. Her stomach ached and the royal black wolf was carefully ignoring her.

"*Amaroq, ilaya,* wolf, my friend," she finally called. "Look at me. Look at me."

She spoke half in Eskimo and half in English, as if the instincts of her father and the science of the *gussaks*, the white-faced, might evoke some magical combination that would help her get her message through to the wolf.

Amaroq glanced at his paw and slowly turned his head her way without lifting his eyes. He licked his shoulder. A few matted hairs sprang apart and twinkled individually. Then his eyes sped to each of the three adult wolves that made up his pack and finally to the five pups who were sleeping in a fuzzy mass near the den entrance. The great wolf's eyes softened at the sight of the little wolves, then quickly hardened into brittle yellow jewels as he scanned the flat tundra.

Not a tree grew anywhere to break the monotony of the gold-green plain, for the soils of the tundra are permanently frozen. Only moss, grass, lichens, and a few hardy flowers take root in the thin upper layer that thaws briefly in summer. Nor do many species of animals live in this rigorous land, but those creatures that do dwell here exist in bountiful numbers. Amaroq watched a large cloud of Lapland longspurs wheel up into the sky, then alight in the grasses. Swarms of crane flies, one of the few insects that can survive the cold, darkened the tips of the mosses. Birds wheeled, turned, and called. Thousands sprang up from the ground like leaves in a wind.

The wolf's ears cupped forward and tuned in on some distant message from the tundra. Miyax tensed and listened too. Did he hear some brewing storm, some approaching enemy? Apparently not. His ears relaxed and he rolled to his side. She sighed, glanced at the vaulting sky, and was painfully aware of her predicament.

Here she was, watching wolves—she, Miyax, daughter of Kapugen, adopted child of Martha, citizen of the United States, pupil at the Bureau of Indian Affairs School in Barrow, Alaska, and thirteen-year-old wife of the boy Daniel. She shivered at the thought of Daniel, for it was he who had driven her to this fate. She had run away from him exactly seven sleeps ago, and because of this she had one more title by gussak standards—the child divorcée.

The wolf rolled to his belly.

"Amaroq," she whispered. "I am lost and the sun will not set for a month. There is no North Star to guide me."

Amaroq did not stir.

"And there are no berry bushes here to bend under the polar wind and point to the south. Nor are there any birds I can follow." She looked up. "Here the birds are buntings and longspurs. They do not fly to the sea twice a day like the puffins and sandpipers that my father followed."

The wolf groomed his chest with his tongue.

"I never dreamed I could get lost, Amaroq," she went on, talking out loud to ease her fear. "At home on Nunivak Island where I was born, the plants and birds pointed the way for wanderers. I thought they did so everywhere . . . and so, great black Amaroq, I'm without a compass."

It had been a frightening moment when two days ago she realized that the tundra was an ocean of grass on which she was circling around and around. Now as that fear overcame her again she closed her eyes. When she opened them her heart skipped excitedly. Amaroq was looking at her!

Thinking as a Writer

Evaluating Descriptive Language

- Which words does the author use to create images in your mind? Which of her words or images make the strongest impression on you?
- In what ways do these sensory details contribute to the story? Do they contribute to the action? to the setting? to a feeling or mood? How are they important to the story?

Matching Voice to Mood

Oral Expression
- What is the tone of the first paragraph? Is it sad? happy? frightening? suspenseful? Is this tone consistent throughout the selection? Does it change? If so, where?
- Choose two or three paragraphs to read aloud with a partner. Take turns reading. Try to use a manner of expression that reflects the tone or mood of the piece. Are some parts particularly satisfying to read?

Putting an Image into Words

Viewing
- Look closely at this image. How does it appeal to the five senses? What words describe the mood or feeling this picture evokes in you?

The Power of Description

The author of *Julie of the Wolves*, Jean Craighead George, translates observations about the sights, sounds, tastes, feelings, and smells of Alaska into vivid descriptions that help the reader picture the tundra and feel the mood— and the suspense—of her gripping tale.

Uses of Description

Here are a few examples of how the power of description plays a role in everyday life.

- **You write to a pen pal in a foreign country,** describing your home, your neighborhood, and your school.

- **You describe your idea for a band T-shirt to an artist friend.** Your friend will draw the design you have imagined.

- **You write a letter to the student newspaper protesting the food served in the cafeteria.** You include a graphic description of the soggy vegetables and mystery meats.

- **You listen as a reporter describes the jubilation of people celebrating a political victory** to a television news anchor.

- **You observe an amazing shot in the last seconds of a basketball game,** and you describe the move to a group of friends who missed the game.

Developing Your Skills of Description

Descriptive writing takes the reader into a world created by words. "I am a dreamer of words, of written words. I think I am reading; a word stops me. I leave the page," states French writer Gaston Bachelard. Writers gather the sensory details that help the reader "leave the page" through observation. The descriptive writer goes out into the world with senses wide open, noticing the sharp edges of midday shadows, the scent of fresh-cut grass in the summertime, the irritating scratch of a new wool sweater, or the relentless hammering of rain on the roof. When you want your reader to see the world through your eyes, you use descriptive writing.

Descriptive writing creates a picture of a person, an object, or a scene through words.

Your Writer's Journal

You can use your journal to help you develop your power of observation. Every day for five days, choose a different place that you know well. Go to each place and observe carefully. Record different kinds of sensory impressions in your journal. Write your details under the headings *Sight, Sound, Taste, Smell, Touch.*

Descriptive Paragraph Structure

In the following descriptive paragraph, the writer's purpose is to describe a barn. As you read the paragraph, notice how each sentence works to create the picture.

The Old Barn

TOPIC
SENTENCE

SUPPORTING
DETAILS

CONCLUDING
SENTENCE

   Their barn was a marvelous, solid structure with a sense of long ago about it. There were a couple of old horse stalls in there. There were even a few oats left in the feed bins and some wisps of old, shiny hay, dark with age. With a little imagination you could hear a gentle ghostly whinny and the restless stirring of ironshod hooves on the wide-board floors. People sometimes tried to buy the barn for lumber, or to haul it away to someplace else and make a house out of it. The owners refused to sell. Barns like this, they said— once they are gone they do not come back.

   —*Mary Stolz*, The Edge of Next Year

The following chart summarizes the function of each kind of sentence in a descriptive paragraph.

Structure of a Descriptive Paragraph

- The **topic sentence** introduces the subject of the paragraph and suggests a general impression of it. The topic sentence is often the first sentence, but it does not have to be.
- The **supporting sentences** provide details that bring the subject to life.
- The **concluding sentence** summarizes the overall impression of the subject.

● *Writing Topic Sentences*

For each descriptive subject, write a topic sentence that suggests a general impression. The impression may be either positive or negative.

EXAMPLE   a cave
POSSIBLE ANSWER   The cave was dark and mysterious, full of sights from another world.

1. a porpoise
2. a city bus
3. a block party
4. a spring day
5. a seashore
6. a path in the woods
7. a pair of new shoes
8. a hockey game
9. an ice, snow, or rainstorm
10. a view from a rooftop

Communicate Your Ideas

PREWRITING *Topic Sentence*

Freewrite answers to the following questions.

• If you were moving and could take only ten objects with you, what would you take?

• If you were making a photo album of places to remember in years to come, what five places would you include?

Choose the subject that appeals to you for a descriptive paragraph, and write a topic sentence about it that expresses a general impression.   SAVE YOUR WORK

● Specific Details and Sensory Words

If a description contains only vague ideas and general words, readers will soon lose interest. Specific details and words that appear to the senses are the sparks that activate a reader's imagination.

Writing Tip

Use **specific details** and **sensory words** to bring your description to life.

Notice the sensory words used to describe the canyon in the following paragraph.

MODEL: Specific Details and Sensory Words

The Santa Elena Canyon

SUGGESTS
GENERAL
IMPRESSION

SIGHTS

    Just before dawn one day, I stood at the mouth of the majestic Santa Elena Canyon, watching the sun come up. The Rio Grande, about 50 feet wide at this point, spilled out of the canyon. As the sun rose, the coloring of the canyon walls, reflected in the slow-moving waters, gradually changed. Faint blacks, browns, and warm, rusty reds faded into grayish white. Before long the sun moved on and left the canyon in shade. I felt dwarfed by the high, massive, sheer walls.

SOUNDS

More than anything I remember the sounds. Like a symphony songs of birds and insects flowed from the lower canyon, then vibrated and echoed up and out of the sky. Looking up, following the sounds, I could see black vultures soaring up and down the canyon walls. It looked almost as if they were dancing to the songs.

    —Tor Eigeland, America's Majestic Canyons

Practice Your Skills

● *Listing Specific Details*

Under each subject list four specific details. One should appeal to the sense of sight, one to sound, one to taste or smell, and one to touch.

1. a skating rink

2. an attic

3. a costume party

4. a lake in autumn

5. a pancake breakfast

● *Developing Sensory Details by Clustering*

Clustering is a strategy for developing and grouping details. Using the following cluster diagram as a model, choose two of the following subjects, and make a new cluster diagram for each. Attach as many details as you can to each of the sensory circles.

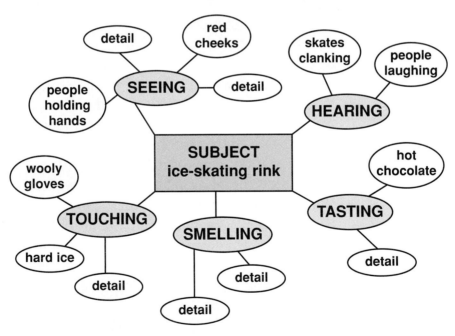

1. a windy day

2. a hayride

3. a parade

4. a locker room

5. a hospital

Visualizing

When you completed the previous activities, how did you know what details to list? Chances are you did not actually go to each place and observe the scenes. By concentrating, you were able to remember or imagine some of the specific details that stand out in each place.

The process of seeing something in your "mind's eye" is called **visualizing**. Although visualizing usually refers to seeing, it can also refer to hearing, tasting, touching, and smelling. Visualizing is an important skill for any writer of description. The better you can visualize the person, place, or object you are describing, the better you can communicate your vision to readers.

You can strengthen your visualizing skills the same way an athlete strengthens muscles. Use them often, and stretch them a little further each time. When writing, do not settle for a so-so, bland description. Let your "mind's eye" create a whole vivid scene as if you were watching a movie. Then record the details you have visualized.

THINKING PRACTICE

Choose one of the places you wrote about in your journal. Then concentrate as you let your mind's eye recreate it. As you are visualizing, jot down all the details you see. Even after you think you have enough details, close your eyes again and take a closer look: what have you left out? Then use your details to write a description of your place with plenty of specific details and words that appeal to the senses.

Spatial Order and Transitions

For readers to "see" what you are describing, your details must be arranged in a logical order. The most logical order for descriptions is usually spatial order.

Spatial order arranges details according to their location.

Transitions show the relationships between the details.

The following chart shows several types of spatial order and transitions.

SPATIAL ORDER	TRANSITIONS
near to far (or reverse)	close by, beyond, around, farther, across, behind, in the distance, near
top to bottom (or reverse)	at the top, in the middle, lower, below, at the bottom, above, higher
side to side	at the (far, near) left (right), in the middle, next to, beside, between, at one end, at the other end
inside to outside (or reverse)	within, in the center, (on the) inside, the next layer, further in/out, in between, (on the) outside

In the following paragraph, the details are arranged from bottom to top. Notice how transitional words are used to show the spatial order.

The Singing Tower

Thousands of people have listened to the music of the bells at the Singing Tower in Lake Wales, Florida. **At the base** of the tower is a clear pool that reflects the entire 205-foot structure. **Reaching from the bottom of the tower to the top** are wide stripes of pink and gray marble. Florida plants and animals are carved in these marble stripes. **At the crown-shaped top** of the tower, a set of bells plays melodies. People from all over the country come to hear the bell chimes ring out over the surrounding park.

PRACTICE YOUR SKILLS

Using Spatial Order

Look at the picture below. Based on what you see, complete the paragraph that follows with the appropriate transitions. Choose the transitions from the following list.

- in the far left corner
- by the stove
- behind the table
- inside the far room
- in the rear doorway
- near the table

Doris Lee (American, 1905–1983).
Thanksgiving, 1935.
Oil on canvas, 28 ⅒ by 40 inches (71.4 by 101.6 cm).
The Art Institute of Chicago.

This painting of a 1930s Thanksgiving shows the many uses of a single room. ■, a child is playing with a cat. ■, a woman is rolling pastry dough. Another woman is taking plates from a shelf. ■, yet another woman is bending over to check the food. A boy stands ■, smiling. ■ two babies cry for food. Through the rear door, ■, a dining table stands ready for the food. As in many homes from this period, this one room served as kitchen, dining room, workroom, and playroom.

Logical Order

Sometimes details for descriptive paragraphs do not fall neatly into spatial order. How do you order the details in such cases? Ask yourself what makes the most logical sense. Suppose you are writing about a person. You could order your details based on your first impressions of that person, then your second impressions, and finally your later impressions as you looked more closely, or got to know the person better.

Logical order should help the reader clearly and simply picture what you are trying to describe. Transitional words that work well with logical order include *first of all, most important, in addition, also, further, then, later, finally.*

PRACTICE YOUR SKILLS

Using Logical Order

Decide on a logical order for arranging the following details, and write a sentence for each one. Then arrange the sentences into a descriptive paragraph, using transitional words to show the relationship between the details.

PURPOSE   to describe water moccasins so people can recognize and avoid them

AUDIENCE   people who fish or use boats

DETAILS

- no strong pattern of colors
- between three and six feet long
- head shaped like a stone arrowhead
- brownish gray color
- often looks like a stick hanging from a tree limb
- nicknamed cottonmouth because its open mouth is white
- wide, flat body

Communicate Your Ideas

PREWRITING, DRAFTING *Details and Logical Order*

Review your work from the activity on page C194. Cluster, freewrite, or brainstorm to think of as many specific details as possible to use in describing your subject. Carefully visualize your subject so that you can clearly see it in your mind. After thinking of as many details as you can, arrange them in logical order. Then use your topic sentence and details to write a draft of your descriptive paragraph. Be sure to add a strong concluding sentence. Save your work.

Classified Advertisement

Words can paint beautiful pictures, but sometimes these pictures can be deceiving. When it comes to classified advertising, the rule is, Consumer beware! Examine the photograph below of a house that is for sale. Then read the description of the house that appears in a real-estate advertisement.

CHARMING VINTAGE VICTORIAN HOUSE FOR SALE. Brimming with character and authentic details, this bargain is a collector's item. If you believe in old-style family values, you'll be proud to own this traditional family house that will increase in value with the years. Visit us on our Website and tour the premises without leaving the comfort of your office or home. Call now to talk with one of our hospitality representatives. This offer won't be on the market long. Act today and move into the house of your dreams tomorrow!

Analyze the language of this advertisement. List the words or phrases that convey a positive image. Next to each word or phrase, write the positive words or feelings that the phrase evokes. Explain how, with a few words, the truth is slightly twisted to make an old and run-down house sound like a real steal!

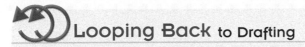

Looping Back to Drafting

Classified Advertisement

Rewrite your descriptive paragraph from page C199 as a classified advertisement for a newspaper. Describe the place or object you chose in terms that would make it attractive to potential buyers. What details do you need to include for this purpose? What details from your original paragraph are no longer relevant? Study the language of classified advertisements.

COMPUTER TIP

You can use the Thesaurus feature on your computer to find fresh and interesting synonyms for descriptive and sensory words. Pull down the Tools menu on your Tools bar. Select Language and then Thesaurus. When you substitute one word for another, check to see that the new word is the correct part of speech for your sentence.

Spelling and Grammar	
Language ▶	Set Language
Word Count	**Thesaurus**
AutoSummarize	Hyphenation
AutoCorrect	

Time Out to Reflect   In what ways have your descriptive writing skills improved so far? Have you sharpened your powers of observation? Are you more aware of the power of description? What do you feel you have learned about writing description? What do you think you still need to work on? Record your thoughts in the Learning Log section of your **journal**.

Process of Writing a Descriptive Paragraph

The power of observation is the mark of a good writer. Practice sharpening your senses. Think of yourself as a "sensitive recording device." Notice all the details of the environment around you. Look for precise words to record your observations. Your readers will savor the clarity and individuality of your perceptions.

Describing an Object

Prewriting

Look at the picture below. What does it make you think of? How would you describe it? Write freely for five minutes, answering these questions. Then study your notes and make a plan for writing a paragraph describing this sculpture.

Alexander Calder.
Flamingo, 1973.
Steel, 53 by 24 by 60 feet.
Federal Center Plaza, Chicago.

Drafting

Use your plan to write a descriptive paragraph. Be sure to include specific details that will create a clear picture in the mind of your reader.

Revising Conferencing

Exchange papers with a classmate. Read your partner's paragraph carefully. Point out the parts that you like as well as the parts that could be improved. When your paper is returned to you, make any revisions that are needed to improve your description.

PORTFOLIO

Describing a Person

Prewriting

Imagine that you are writing a science fiction story about someone living on a distant planet. Give your character a name. Then jot down answers to the following brainstorming questions. Visualize carefully to bring your character to life.

1. What does your character's face look like?

2. What do your character's hands look like?

3. What do your character's feet look like?

4. How does your character move around?

5. How does your character sound?

Use your brainstorming notes to create a plan for a descriptive paragraph.

Drafting

Use your plan to write the first draft of a paragraph describing your character.

Revising Conferencing

Exchange papers with a classmate. Draw a picture of the character described in your partner's draft. Give the picture and the draft back to your partner. Then look at the picture your partner drew. Does it accurately reflect your character? Revise your paragraph to include anything that brings your written picture into sharper focus.

PORTFOLIO

Prewriting Workshop
Drafting Workshop
Revising Workshop ▶
Editing Workshop
Publishing Workshop

Vivid Adjectives

As you read *Julie of the Wolves*, you were probably able to picture the Alaskan tundra, the wolves, and the young girl, Miyax.

> Miyax was a <u>classic</u> <u>Eskimo</u> beauty, <u>small</u> of bone and delicately wired with <u>strong</u> muscles. Her face was <u>pearl-round</u> and her nose was <u>flat</u>. Her <u>black</u> eyes, which slanted gracefully, were <u>moist</u> and <u>sparkling</u>. Like the beautifully formed <u>polar</u> bears and foxes of the north, she was slightly <u>short-limbed</u>.

The underlined words in this passage are adjectives. **Adjectives** are words that modify a noun or pronoun. Descriptive writing is an especially good place for using clear, striking adjectives to help etch a picture into the reader's mind.

Writer Anne Bernays believes readers need to be surprised now and then. "It isn't enough to have smooth and pretty language. You have to surprise the reader frequently, you can't just be nice all the time. . . . Astonish the reader. Writing that has no surprises is as bland as oatmeal. . . . Use one startling adjective per page."

Notice how the following sentence is greatly improved with vivid adjectives.

WITHOUT ADJECTIVES	The wolf curled up into a ball.
WITH VIVID ADJECTIVES	The **half-starved** wolf curled up into a **shivering** ball.

Evaluation Checklist for Revising

Checking Your Paragraph

✓ Does your topic sentence introduce the subject and suggest a general impression of it? *(pages C166–C167)*

✓ Do your supporting sentences provide details that bring your description to life? *(pages C192–C194)*

✓ Does your paragraph have unity? *(page C171)*

✓ Are your details in either spatial order or another logical order? *(pages C196-C197 and C198–C199)*

✓ Did you use transitions to give your paragraph coherence? *(pages C169 and C196)*

✓ Does your concluding sentence summarize the overall impression of the subject and provide a strong ending? *(pages C105, C107, and C191)*

Checking Sentences

✓ Did you combine related sentences to avoid too many short, choppy sentences in a row? *(pages C67–C68)*

✓ Did you vary the beginnings of your sentences? *(page C75)*

✓ Did you avoid rambling sentences? *(page C78)*

✓ Did you avoid repetition and empty expressions? *(pages C81–C82)*

Checking Words

✓ Did you use specific, lively words? *(page C40)*

✓ Did you use words that appeal to the senses? *(pages C192–C194)*

Process of Writing a Descriptive Paragraph

Remember that the writing process gives you a lot of flexibility. You can always return to an earlier step to rework your writing while continuing on a later draft. The numbers in parentheses refer to pages where you can get help with your writing.

PREWRITING

- Consider your purpose and audience. *(pages C16–C17)*
- Make a list of possible subjects, including scenes, objects, and persons. *(pages C127–C128)*
- Choose a subject that interests you and suits your purpose and audience. *(pages C127–C128)*
- Limit your subject so that it can be adequately covered in one paragraph. *(pages C159–C160)*
- Brainstorm a list of sensory details that come to mind when you think about your subject. *(pages C44–C51)*
- Arrange your notes in either spatial or some other logical order. *(pages C196–C199)*

DRAFTING

- Write a topic sentence that expresses an overall impression of your subject. *(page C191)*
- Use your prewriting notes to write supporting sentences that bring your description to life. *(pages C192–C194)*
- Add a concluding sentence that summarizes the overall impression and provides a strong ending. *(pages C105 and C191)*

REVISING

- Put your paper aside for a while. Then come back to it with a fresh eye. Use the <u>Evaluation Checklist for Revising</u> on page C205 to improve your work.

EDITING

- Edit your work and prepare a final, polished paragraph.

PUBLISHING

- Present your finished work to an interested reader.

A Writer Writes
A Description of an Object

Purpose: to describe a scarecrow using specific details

Audience: young children

Prewriting

For the picture above, brainstorm a list of details that could be used in a descriptive paragraph. What details help you capture the look and feel of the scarecrow? Look over your details and add any more that come to mind. Then arrange your details in a logical order.

Drafting

Draft a topic sentence that conveys an overall impression of the scarecrow you are describing. Then use your organized list of details to draft the supporting sentences in your paragraph. Be sure to use transitions where needed to help your ideas flow smoothly. Finally add a strong concluding sentence that summarizes the overall impression.

Revising

Carefully reread your work. Remember your purpose and especially your audience. Have you presented your description clearly enough for young children to understand? Have you used any words that might be too hard for young children? Make any necessary adjustments to your writing to make sure it suits your purpose and audience. Then use the **Evaluation Checklist for Revising** on page C205 for a thorough revision.

Editing

Check your work to polish your description.

Publishing

Prepare a neat, easy-to-read copy of your paragraph and present it to a young reader who might enjoy it.

Connection Collection

Representing in Different Ways

From Visuals . . .

Andrew Wyeth. *Christina's World*, 1948.
Tempera on gessoed panel, 32 1/4 by 47 3/4 inches.
The Museum of Modern Art, New York. Purchase
Photograph © 1996 The Museum of Modern Art, New York.

. . . to Print

A famous art collector has asked you to write a description of Andrew Wyeth's painting *Christina's World* for a catalog of all the works in his collection. Be sure to include a topic sentence that gives a general impression of the painting. In the body of your description, describe what you see in the painting. Use as many specific details and sensory words as you can. Conclude with a statement about what the painting means to you.

Connection Collection

This jazzy collage captures the feel of modern life. Looking at the bright, clashing colors, crossing lines and fragments of newspaper and magazine headlines, you almost feel as though you can hear, smell, taste, touch, and feel all the sights and sounds of the modern city: the fire engines' screech, the mariachi sounds of a street fair, the big smiling faces of children, the latest celebrity scandal, the latest world tragedy. Mixing contemporary "found" materials such as newspaper and magazine clippings, along with more traditional media such as paint and pastel, this artist has caught the pulse of modern life inside a modest frame. The only thing lacking is a title. How about it, artist?

. . . to Visual

Using pictures from old magazines and newspapers, or drawings and paintings of your own, create a collage that fits the description of the catalog entry above. When you finish your collage, give it a title that captures its mood.

- Which strategies can be used for creating both written and visual representations? Which strategies apply to one, not both? Which type of representation is more effective?
- Draw a conclusion and write briefly about the differences between written ideas and visual representations.

Assess Your Learning

You have just been reelected for a second term as President of the United States. Newspapers and magazines all over the country are calling you the most popular President ever, and the Appreciation League has announced that they have raised enough money to re-create your childhood home. Unfortunately no one but you knows what your childhood home looked like. There is a fast-food restaurant where it once stood.

▶ **Write a letter to the Appreciation League describing your childhood home. Fully describe both the outside and inside of the home so that the Appreciation League's re-creation is accurate.**

▶ **Create a vivid picture of your childhood home by using specific details and sensory words. Be sure that each paragraph of your letter includes a topic sentence that introduces the subject, supporting sentences that provide details that bring your childhood home to life, and a concluding sentence that summarizes your overall impression. Organize the details in your letter in spatial order.**

Before You Write Consider the following questions:
What is the *subject?*
What is the *occasion?*
Who is the *audience?*
What is the *purpose?*

After You Write Evaluate your work using the following criteria:
- Have you created a vivid picture of your childhood home by using specific details and sensory words?
- Does each paragraph of your letter include a topic sentence that introduces the subject?
- Do your supporting sentences provide details that bring your childhood home to life?
- Have you written a concluding sentence that sums up the general impression you wish to convey?
- Have you arranged the details in your letter in spatial order?

Write briefly on how well you did. Point out your strengths and areas for improvement.

CHAPTER 8

Creative Writing: Stories, Plays, and Poems

A writer's desire to write stories, poems, and plays is motivated by the writer's own actions, thoughts, and feelings or by observing other people and situations. While entertaining, a writer may lead a reader to wonder about the story. Why did that character do that? What will happen next? How does the story end? Why was that funny?

Think of how many times you have discussed stories you have read or seen. Because it is so compelling to read books, plays, and poems, you have probably been inspired to write in these forms already.

This chapter will give you practice in writing creatively. You will see the various parts of a story, a play, and poems at work in creating an overall effect. You will also have a chance to put your creative writing skills to work.

Reading with a Writer's Eye

Did you find it easier to draw and think up stories when you were younger? Drawing pictures and making up stories to go along with them come effortlessly and easily for most children. As people grow older, using their imaginations sometimes becomes harder. How does someone create? How do you explain the process? Read what author Julia Cunningham says about writing. How would you explain your creative writing process?

Pauses

Lee Bennett Hopkins

*Inspired by questions from his
students, the well-known poet and
teacher Lee Bennett Hopkins began
to wonder about how the people
who have shaped the world of
children's books use their inspirations to write.
In search of answers, Hopkins interviewed hundreds of
authors and illustrators. In the following excerpt, Hopkins
presents the reflections of Julia Cunningham, whose popular
novels include* The Vision of François Fox *and* Drop Dead.

W hen I am working on a book, I make a valiant
effort to sit down at my typewriter at the same time
each morning, usually nine o'clock. I am able to concentrate effectively for only about an hour and a half and am
lucky to come up with a page a day. The ideas come from
anywhere—a conversation, a turn of someone's head, a
fragrance, or simply a character walking into my imaginary life and taking over. I am not able to do much
rewriting, at least not successfully, and am mostly an
intuitive worker. The first draft must almost always be
completely right.

I never had any formal training in writing. I just began at the age of nine and continued. I did have a wonderful English teacher in high school who did not interfere but encouraged me.

I have been asked for whom I write and the answer might be expected to be "for children." But that is untrue. I believe that basically most of us write for ourselves, not egotistically to hear ourselves talk but because of that other self, the one who enters any landscape of the imagination and is suddenly and totally involved with the lives of his or her characters. They appear from nowhere and hold center stage. They lead you, follow you, haunt you, occasionally club you to death, invite you to ride dragons, imprison you in an iron cage, and all of them, even the villains, befriend you. After all, who is telling the story? If the miracle has happened and you are at the core of this other reality, then they are telling the story.

A writer is a seeker who uses a typewriter instead of a schooner.[1] He does it because he wants to. And each journey is an adventure, whether one returns with a bad cold and no money for a hot grog or, once in an inexplicable while, with a wreath of roses.

---

[1] **schooner** (sko͞o′nər): A fore-and-aft rigged sailing vessel with two or more masts.

Thinking as a Writer

Analyzing the Creative Process

Julia Cunningham writes about entering a "landscape of the imagination."

- What does she mean when she says she suddenly is totally involved with the lives of her characters? How can you enter the landscape of imagination in conceiving characters for a short story or a play?

Using Language That Reflects Characterization

- *Oral Expression* Choose a character from your favorite story, movie, or television program. Who does that character remind you of? How does he or she speak?
- In a small group, improvise a conversation among your characters. How does dialogue reflect your character's personality? How did relating the character to someone you know help you construct the dialogue?

Capturing Experience

Viewing Sculptor Glenna Goodacre made this sculpture to honor the 250,000 women who served during the Vietnam War. Many veteran women have told her, "That was me. That's how I felt."

- How has Goodacre captured the experience of the female veterans of the Vietnam War?
- Why do you think the woman who kneels, looking down at the soldier, is often considered to be the heart and soul of the sculpture?

Glenna Goodacre. Vietnam Women's Memorial, 1993.
Bronze cast, height 92 inches. National Mall, Washington, D.C.

The Power of Creative Writing

Creative writing takes many forms besides stories, such as plays, poems, songs, movie scripts, and comic strips. Creative writing may be humorous, serious, sad, suspenseful, or fantastic—if you can imagine it, you can write it.

Uses of Creative Writing

Here are a few examples of the ways in which creative writing plays a role in everyday life.

- **A lyricist writes words** to accompany a tune for a new musical.

- **A screenwriter develops a storyline for a movie** about a fantastic planet inhabited by strange creatures.

- **You engage in a humorous imaginary dialogue** with one of your friends on the telephone.

- **A group from your school drama club performs a play** about a local historical event for your town's 200-year celebration.

- **You and your classmates write some funny sketches** about school life for a talent show.

- **A comedian writes a series of one-liners** and delivers them at an awards ceremony.

Writing a Short Story

"First sentences are doors to worlds," wrote the author Ursula K. LeGuin. In other words, start your story off so well that your reader will want to read on. Your story can begin with dialogue, description, or action. You can also use humor or mystery to provoke a reader's interest.

In the process of personal writing, you have already gained practice in telling stories. Short stories usually have more details than personal narratives. They are also not true-life events. The events in a story may have actually happened to the writer or to someone the writer knows, but they are presented in an imaginative way.

A **short story** is a fictional account of characters resolving a conflict or problem.

Read the following short story by Cynthia Rylant. As you read, think about how the author has developed her characters through the use of dialogue and description.

MODEL: Short Story

Stray

—*Cynthia Rylant*

In January, a puppy wandered onto the property of Mr. Amos Lacey and his wife, Mamie, and their daughter, Doris. Icicles hung three feet or more from the eaves of houses, snowdrifts swallowed up automobiles and the birds were so fluffed up they looked comic.

The puppy had been abandoned, and it made its way down the road toward the Laceys' small house, its ears tucked, its tail between its legs, shivering.

Doris, whose school had been called off because of the snow, was out shoveling the cinderblock front steps when she spotted the pup on the road. She set down the shovel.

"Hey! Come on!" she called.

The puppy stopped in the road, wagging its tail timidly, trembling with shyness and cold.

Doris trudged through the yard, went up the shoveled drive and met the dog.

"Come on, Pooch."

"Where did *that* come from?" Mrs. Lacey asked as soon as Doris put the dog down in the kitchen.

Mr. Lacey was at the table, cleaning his fingernails with his pocketknife. The snow was keeping him home from his job at the warehouse.

"I don't know where it came from," he said mildly, "but I know for sure where it's going."

Doris hugged the puppy hard against her. She said nothing.

Because the roads would be too bad for travel for many days, Mr. Lacey couldn't get out to take the puppy to the pound in the city right away. He agreed to let it sleep in the basement while Mrs. Lacey grudgingly let Doris feed it table scraps. The woman was sensitive about throwing out food.

By the looks of it, Doris figured the puppy was about six months old, and on its way to being a big dog. She thought it might have some shepherd in it.

Four days passed and the puppy did not complain. It never cried in the night or howled at the wind. It didn't tear up everything in the basement. It wouldn't even follow Doris up the basement steps unless it was invited.

It was a good dog.

Several times Doris had opened the door in the kitchen that led to the basement and the puppy had been there, all stretched out, on the top step. Doris knew it had wanted some company and that it had lain against the door, listening to the talk in the kitchen, smelling the food, being a part of things. It always wagged its tail, eyes all sleepy, when she found it there.

Even after a week had gone by, Doris didn't name the dog. She knew her parents wouldn't let her keep it, that her father made so little money any pets were out of the question, and that the pup would definitely go to the pound when the weather cleared.

Still, she tried talking to them about the dog at dinner one night.

"She's a good dog, isn't she?" Doris said, hoping one of them would agree with her.

Her parents glanced at each other and went on eating.

"She's not much trouble," Doris added. "I like her." She smiled at them, but they continued to ignore her.

"I figure she's real smart," Doris said to her mother. "I could teach her things."

Mrs. Lacey just shook her head and stuffed a forkful of sweet potato in her mouth. Doris fell silent, praying the weather would never clear.

But on Saturday, nine days after the dog had arrived, the sun was shining and the roads were plowed. Mr. Lacey opened up the trunk of his car and came into the house.

Doris was sitting alone in the living room, hugging a pillow and rocking back and forth on the edge of a chair. She was trying not to cry but she was not strong enough. Her face was wet and red, her eyes full of distress.

Mrs. Lacey looked into the room from the doorway.

"Mama," Doris said in a small voice. "Please."

Mrs. Lacey shook her head.

"You know we can't afford a dog, Doris. You try to act more grown-up about this."

Doris pressed her face into the pillow.

Outside, she heard the trunk of the car slam shut, one of the doors open and close, the old engine cough and choke and finally start up.

"Daddy," she whispered. "Please."

She heard the car travel down the road, and, though it was early afternoon, she could do nothing but go to her bed. She cried herself to sleep, and her dreams were full of searching and searching for things lost.

It was nearly night when she finally woke up. Lying there, like stone, still exhausted, she wondered if she would ever in her life have anything. She stared at the wall for a while.

But she started feeling hungry, and she knew she'd have to make herself get out of bed and eat some dinner. She wanted not to go into the kitchen, past the basement door. She wanted not to face her parents.

But she rose up heavily.

Her parents were sitting at the table, dinner over, drinking coffee. They looked at her when she came in, but she kept her head down. No one spoke.

Doris made herself a glass of powdered milk and drank it all down. Then she picked up a cold biscuit and started out of the room.

"You'd better feed that mutt before it dies of starvation," Mr. Lacey said.

Doris turned around.

"What?"

"I said, you'd better feed your dog. I figure it's looking for you."

Doris put her hand to her mouth.

"You didn't take her?" she asked.

"Oh, I took her all right," her father answered. "Worst looking place I've ever seen. Ten dogs to a cage. Smell was enough to knock you down. And they give an animal six days to live. Then they kill it with some kind of a shot."

Doris stared at her father.

"I wouldn't leave an *ant* in that place," he said. "So I brought the dog back."

Mrs. Lacey was smiling at him and shaking her head as if she would never, ever, understand him.

Mr. Lacey sipped his coffee.

"Well," he said, "are you going to feed it or not?"

Cynthia Rylant has written a simple short story about a young girl who finds a stray puppy. Doris's wish to keep the puppy creates a problem, for her family is too poor to keep a pet. Think about times when you or someone you know wanted something you or they could not have. In your journal, list some of these thoughts for the next week.

At the end of the week, reread your journal entries. Which ones seem suitable for developing into a short story? In the margins, make notes that add an imaginative twist to your ideas.

Short Story Structure

Each short story has three main parts. The **beginning** introduces the characters and the main conflict. The **middle** tells all the events in the story. The **ending** shows how the problem was finally resolved.

ELEMENTS IN A SHORT STORY	
NARRATOR	• the person telling the story; may be first person (if he or she is in the story) or third person (if he or she is telling what happened to others)
SETTING	• the time and place in which the story takes place
CHARACTERS	• the people involved in the story
CONFLICT	• the problem at the heart of the story
TRIGGERING EVENT	• the event that starts the story rolling
CLIMAX	• the point in the story where the conflict or problem is most serious
OUTCOME	• how the problem or conflict is solved
DIALOGUE	• words spoken by the characters
DESCRIPTION	• writing that helps the reader see, hear, feel, taste, or smell what is happening

As you write your short story, try to recall other stories you have enjoyed. Ask yourself what made those stories exciting or interesting.

Were the characters special or fantastic in some way?

Were they like people you know?

Did they face problems that you have also faced?

Did you care about what happened to them?

What kept you reading?

Prewriting Writing Process

Few writers have a complete story in their heads, just waiting to be set down on paper. Most writers begin with the seed of an idea and gradually develop it into a story. Finding a good "seed" is one of the most important parts of writing a story.

Choosing a Subject

Where do you look for a good idea for a story? One good place is your **journal** where you will find recent events. Another good way to find story ideas is to search your memory for events from your past. Events with strong meaning for you are often the best to use as the basis for a story. Then asking yourself specific questions and freewriting will help you discover the best subject for your story.

The guidelines on the following page will help you as you search for an appropriate subject for a short story.

Guidelines for Choosing a Subject

- Choose an event or experience that has strong meaning for you. Ask yourself:

  What happened to me last year that I will never forget?

  From what experiences have I learned an important lesson?

  At what times in my life have I overcome a problem?

  What has been the proudest moment of my life?

  What events in my past made me especially admire a family member?

- Search your memory for events that are unusual or special. Ask yourself:

  When was the first time I felt like a grownup?

  What funny things have happened to me?

  What stories do my family members like to tell about times before I was born?

  When have I felt in danger? What happened?

  What unusual places have I been? What happened in those places?

Communicate Your Ideas

PREWRITING *Subject*

Freewrite answers to the questions in the guidelines above. Then circle the answers that seem most memorable or unusual to you. Jot down notes about why these events are memorable. Perhaps your notes will jog other memories. Write down these thoughts as well. Save your work for later use.

SAVE YOUR WORK

Sketching Characters

Once you have an idea of what your story will be about, you can plan out the cast of characters that will appear in it. One good way to make your characters lifelike is to draw a word sketch of them before you actually begin writing. First list all the characters that will play a part in your story. Then describe each one briefly in a sketch. Include both physical features and personality traits. The following character sketches are for the story you just read, "Stray."

DORIS	Timid, lonely, emotional, only child, about eleven to thirteen years old
FATHER	Not talkative, hardworking, strict but with a kind heart, clearly the head of the household
MOTHER	Not talkative, hardworking, thrifty
PUPPY	Six months old puppy, part shepherd mix, a good dog

PRACTICE YOUR SKILLS

● *Writing Character Sketches*

Write a brief character sketch of the following people.

1. yourself

2. a childhood friend

3. a cousin

4. an older relative

5. your teacher

6. a neighbor

7. someone you see often but do not know

Imagining

To create lifelike characters, you can observe people firsthand and try to capture all their characteristics in your story. You can also add your own imaginative details to your characters. The skill of imagining will help you create interesting, memorable characters. **Imagining** means creating mental pictures of something or someone you have never actually seen or experienced.

Both pretending and imagining require you to invent new places, people, things, and situations. In the process, however, you also draw on whatever related experiences you have had. Suppose, for example, you want to try to imagine what a newly discovered animal called the "frogaroocerous" looks like. Some of the sounds in the animal's name might make you think of frogs, kangaroos, and rhinoceroses. Drawing on what you know about these animals and their special characteristics, you would let your imagination put these characteristics together in a way that was all your own. You would use both your previous knowledge and your skill at imagining to create a whole new creature.

THINKING PRACTICE

Pretend that one of the characters in your story is a rich old woman. Draw on what you might already know about real-life rich old women and let your imagination create a whole new character. Use a two-column chart to organize what you already know and what you can imagine. Write a brief sketch of that character, including physical appearance, personality traits, and even gestures that the character often uses.

Creating a Setting

The process of creating a setting is similar to the process of sketching characters. You may start with a real-life setting where the events actually *did* happen. You can then expand on that setting by imagining more striking details.

When creating your setting, be clear in your own mind about when and where the story takes place. Then use your imagination to add as many striking, lively details as possible as you sketch out the specifics of your setting. Below are some details of the setting of "Stray."

MODEL: Details of a Setting

WHERE
- a semirural area
- small house of hardworking people
- a girl's room, very plain, with few toys, books, or possessions
- a simple kitchen with a kitchen table

WHEN
- January
- after a blizzard
- over the course of nine days
- anytime over the last fifty years

Writing Tip

Create a **setting** by determining the time and location of your story. Add details to bring the setting to life.

PRACTICE YOUR SKILLS

● *Creating Settings*

Use your imagination to add at least three details to the following locations and times for stories.

1. location: a desert   time: morning
2. location: a swimming pool   time: midnight
3. location: a movie set   time: noon
4. location: a state park   time: spring
5. location: a restaurant   time: evening
6. location: a beach   time: winter
7. location: a kindergarten classroom   time: noon
8. location: a museum   time: afternoon

Listing Events in Chronological Order

Most stories present the events that take place in chrono-logical order, the order in which they occur. This order helps readers follow the events as they rise to their climax and are resolved at the end. Use the following questions to help you list all the separate events in your story in the proper order.

Listing Events in Chronological Order

- What happened to start the story rolling?
- What happened next? next? next?
- What is the climax of the story?
- What finally happened to resolve the conflict?
- How does the story end?

Writing Tip

List all the events in your story in chronological order. Include the event that starts the story in motion, the climax of the story, the resolution of the conflict, and the outcome.

PRACTICE YOUR SKILLS

● *Listing Events*

Choose two of the following subjects. Then use the questions on the preceding page to list the events that might make up each story.

1. choosing your pet from an animal shelter

2. having your most embarrassing moment

3. having an encounter with a space alien

4. hunting for dinosaur bones

5. going on your first airplane ride

Communicate Your Ideas

PREWRITING *Story Sketch*

Using your work from the activity on choosing a subject, plan your story by completing the following sketch. Save your work.

- Narrator (character in story? or telling about others?):

- Characters, with brief descriptions:

- Setting, with brief description:

- Events:

Drafting ◄ Writing Process

What happens to you when you read a good story? Chances are you lose yourself in the world the writer has created. Help your readers lose themselves in your story by making your story interesting and lively. Choose details that will keep your readers involved.

Drafting the Beginning

Between all the responsibilities of school and home, sports or other activities, television or movies, the Internet, friends or pets, a reader's attention can be hard to grab. You want to draw your readers into your story and get their full attention right from the start.

The following suggestions will help you accomplish all you need to in the beginning of the story. Remember, however, that you should always try to grab the reader's attention.

Guidelines for Beginning a Story

- Set the time and place of the story, adding details that capture the reader's attention.
- Introduce the characters in the story.
- Provide any background information needed.
- Include the event that starts the story in motion.

Communicate Your Ideas

PREWRITING, DRAFTING *Story Beginning*

Review your work from the previous activity. Then use the guidelines above to write a gripping beginning for your story. Remember that you want to hook your reader's attention right away. Save your work for later use.

Drafting the Middle

As you draft the middle of your story, refer to your list of chronologically ordered events. Remember to use transitions to show how the events are related in time. The following guidelines will help you draft the events that make up the middle of your story.

> ### Drafting the Middle of a Short Story
>
> - Tell the events in chronological order, using transitions to show the passing of time.
> - Build on the conflict, or problem, until the action reaches a climax, or high point.
> - Use dialogue to show what the characters are thinking.
> - Use descriptive, colorful sensory words to bring the events to life.

PRACTICE YOUR SKILLS

● *Writing Dialogue*

Write about ten lines of dialogue between you and a friend that show a time when you disagreed about something or had an argument. Try to make the dialogue sound the way people actually talk. Have a partner read your dialogue aloud with you. Ask others to tell you if your dialogue sounds natural and interesting.

Communicate Your Ideas

PREWRITING, DRAFTING *Story Middle*

Return to your story beginning. Now write the middle of your story, telling the events in chronological order. Be sure to use transitions where needed. Also add dialogue where appropriate, and include description that brings your story to life.

Drafting the Ending

The ending of your story should bring the conflict or problem in the story to a logical resolution. In many stories, the ending is also where the reader feels the most emotion, or the most surprise. The ending of your story will probably linger in your reader's mind longer than any other part of your story, so make it as strong as possible.

Writing Tip

End your story by telling how the conflict was **resolved.** Tell the final **outcome** of the story.

Communicate Your Ideas

PREWRITING, DRAFTING *Story Resolution*

Add a strong ending to your story. Try several different endings by asking yourself questions that begin with *What if* . . . See if you can find a surprising or unexpected way to end your story. Save your work for revising and editing later.

Revising   Writing Process

Most writers agree that their first drafts are good starting points but rarely good enough ending points. Usually the effort of just getting your ideas down in a smooth, flowing form takes all your concentration when drafting. Once your draft is on paper, however, you can stand back from it and concentrate on improving your story. Maybe you will find a place where more details will help bring your characters to life. Maybe you will realize that some of the events you included in your story do not really belong. Revising is the time to squeeze out your story—to rid it of unnecessary bulk. The following checklist will help you revise your short story.

> ## Evaluation Checklist for Revising

✓ Does the beginning of your story give the setting, capture attention, introduce characters, and include the triggering event? *(pages C224–C227 and C229)*

✓ Does the middle tell the events in chronological order with transitions? *(pages C227–C228 and C229–C230)*

✓ Does your story build on the conflict until the action reaches a climax? *(pages C227–C230)*

✓ Did you use dialogue and description to bring your story to life? *(page C230)*

✓ Does the ending show how the conflict was resolved and bring the story to a close? *(pages C230–C231)*

✓ Have you given your story a title that captures the reader's attention?

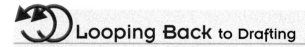

REVISING

Use the checklist above to revise your short story. Save your work in your writing folder for editing later.

Looping Back to Drafting

New Beginning

Look at the beginning of an earlier story you have written. Review the <u>Guidelines for Beginning a Story</u> on page C229 and see if your story has met these criteria. Is there any way in which you can improve your original beginning? Ask yourself if this beginning really hooks your reader right away. Experiment with using dialogue, action, humor, or mystery to improve your story's beginning.

The editing stage gives you the opportunity to catch spelling, grammar, usage, and mechanics errors in your story. Use the proofreading symbols on page C28 as a shorthand while you edit.

COMPUTER TIP

Click on Tools in your menu bar for help in checking Spelling and Grammar. You may also want to use the Thesaurus for help with word choice.

Communicate Your Ideas

EDITING *Dialogue*

Carefully edit your short story, using the editing checklists on pages C234 and C28. Pay special attention to punctuating your dialogue correctly. Use the **Editing Workshop** on the next page to help you. Use proofreading symbols to make your corrections.

Publishing ≡ Writing Process

When you are satisfied you have found all your errors, prepare a neat final copy of your story. You may also want to draw a picture to go along with it. You can then present both your story and your picture to the reader who would enjoy it the most.

Prewriting Workshop
Drafting Workshop
Revising Workshop
Editing Workshop ▶
Publishing Workshop

Dialogue Punctuation

Now that you have revised your story, you can edit it for proper dialogue form, which is meant to help your reader easily know who is speaking. The following rules will help.

- Use quotation marks to enclose a person's exact words.

- Capitalize the first word of a direct quotation.

- Use a comma to separate a direct quotation from a speaker tag, such as "he said" or "she whispered." Place the comma inside the closing quotation marks. Place a period inside closing quotation marks when the end of the quotation comes at the end of the sentence.

- When writing dialogue, begin a new paragraph each time the speaker changes.

The following example from "Stray" shows how Cynthia Rylant uses correct punctuation in dialogue.

> EXAMPLE
>
> "You'd better feed that mutt before it dies of starvation," Mr. Lacey said.
> Doris turned around.
> "What?"
> "I said, you'd better feed your dog. I figure it's looking for you."

Editing Checklist

✔ Have you used a new paragraph for each speaker?

✔ Have you enclosed exact quotes in quotation marks?

✔ Have you used commas to separate direct quotations from speaker tags?

Writing a Play

A play is a special type of creative writing because it is written to be performed by one or more actors on a stage. Plays and stories have some characteristics in common, such as characters, setting, and plot. However, unlike a story, the plot of a play develops through the actors' words and actions alone.

The playwright provides the words in a script along with information on how the characters should act. The actors then decide how they will deliver the words and carry out the actions in a way that will make a powerful performance.

The playwright also provides information about the setting—where and when the action takes place. This information becomes the basis for the set design used in the stage performance.

A **play** is a piece of writing intended to be performed on a stage by actors.

The following play script is from a scene from *The Dancers* by Horton Foote. As you read the script, notice how the combination of the characters' words and the playwright's stage directions brings the scene to life.

MODEL: Play Scene

The Dancers

The lights are brought up D.L. on the living room of Inez Stanley. HERMAN STANLEY *and his brother-in-law,* HORACE, *come in.* HERMAN *is carrying Horace's suitcase.* HERMAN *is in his middle thirties.* HORACE *is eighteen, thin, sensitive, but a likable boy.*

HERMAN: Inez. Inez. We're here. (*He puts the bag down in the living room.* INEZ *comes running in from R.*)

INEZ: You're early.

HERMAN: The bus was five minutes ahead of time.

INEZ: Is that so? Why, I never heard of that. *(She kisses her brother.)* Hello, honey.

HORACE: Hello, sis.

INEZ: You look fine.

HORACE: Thank you.

INEZ: You haven't put on a bit of weight though.

HORACE: Haven't I?

INEZ: Not a bit. I'm just going to stuff food down you and put some weight on you while you're here. How's your appetite?

HORACE: Oh, it's real good. I eat all the time.

INEZ: Then why don't you put on some weight?

HORACE: I don't know. I guess I'm just the skinny type.

INEZ: How are the folks?

HORACE: Fine.

INEZ: Mother over her cold?

HORACE: Yes, she is.

INEZ: Dad's fine?

HORACE: Just fine.

INEZ: Oh, Herman, did you ask him?

HERMAN: Ask him what?

INEZ: Ask him what? About his tux.

HERMAN: No, I didn't . . . .

INEZ: Honestly, Herman. Here we have him a date with the prettiest and most popular girl in Harrison and Herman says ask him what. You did bring it, didn't you, Bubber?

HORACE: Bring what?

INEZ: Your tux.

HORACE: Oh, sure.

INEZ: Well, guess who I've got you a date with. Aren't you curious?

HORACE: Uh. Huh.

INEZ: Well, guess . . . . *(A pause. He thinks)*

HORACE: I don't know.

INEZ: Well, just try guessing . . . .

HORACE: Well . . . uh . . . uh . . . *(He is a little embarrassed. He stands trying to think. No names come to him.)* I don't know.

INEZ: Emily Crews. Now isn't she a pretty girl?

HORACE: Yes. She is.

INEZ: And the most popular girl in this town. You know her mother is a very close friend of mine and she called me day before yesterday and she said I hear Horace is coming to town and I said yes you were and she said that the boy Emily is going with is in summer school and couldn't get away this week-end and Emily said she wouldn't go to the dance at all but her mother said that she had insisted and wondered if you'd take her . . . .

HORACE: Her mother said. Does Emily want me to take her?

INEZ: That isn't the point, Bubber. The point is that her mother doesn't approve of the boy Emily is in love with and she likes you . . .

HORACE: Who likes me?

INEZ: Emily's mother. And she thinks you would make a very nice couple.

HORACE: Oh. *(a pause)* But what does Emily think?

INEZ: Emily doesn't know what to think, honey. I'm trying to explain that to you. She's in love.

HORACE: Where am I suppposed to take her to?

INEZ: The dance.

HORACE: But, Inez, I don't dance well enough . . . . I don't like to go to dances . . . yet . . .

INEZ: Oh, Horace. Mother wrote me you were learning.

HORACE: Well . . . I am learning. But I don't dance well enough yet.

INEZ: Horace, you just make me sick. The trouble with you is that you have no confidence in yourself. I bet you can dance.

HORACE: No, I can't . . . .

INEZ: Now let's see. (INEZ *goes to the radio and turns it on. She comes back to him.*) Now, come on. Show me what you've learned . . . .

HORACE: Aw, Sis . . .

HERMAN: Inez. Why don't you let the boy alone?

INEZ: Now you keep out of this, Herman Stanley. He's my brother and he's a stick. He's missing all the fun in life and I'm not going to have him a stick. I've sat up nights thinking of social engagements to keep him busy every minute of these next two weeks—I've got three dances scheduled for him. So he cannot dance. Now come on, dance with me . . . .(*He takes her by the arm awkwardly. He begins to lead her around the room.*) Now, that's fine. That's just fine. Isn't that fine, Herman?

HERMAN: Uh. Huh.

INEZ: You see, all you need is confidence. And I want you to promise me you'll talk plenty when you're with the girl, not just sit there in silence and only answer when you're asked a question . . . .Now promise me.

HORACE: I promise.

INEZ: Fine. Why, I think he dances real well. Don't you, Herman?

HERMAN: Yes, I do. Just fine, Inez.

INEZ: Just a lovely dancer, all he needs is confidence. He is very light on his feet. And he has a fine sense of rhythm—why brother, you're a born dancer—(HORACE *is smiling over the compliments, half wanting to believe what they say, but then not so sure. He is dancing with her around the room as the lights fade. They are brought up on the area* U. R. EMILY CREWS *is in her living room. She has on her dressing gown. She is crying.* ELIZABETH, *her mother, comes in from* U. R.)

ELIZABETH: Emily.

EMILY: Yes, ma'm.

ELIZABETH: Do you know what time it is?

EMILY: Yes, ma'm.

ELIZABETH: Then why in the world aren't you dressed?

EMILY: Because I don't feel good.

ELIZABETH: Emily . . .

EMILY: I don't feel good . . . *(She begins to cry.)* Oh, Mother. I don't want to go to the dance tonight. Please, ma'm, don't make me. I'll do anything in this world for you if you promise me . . .

ELIZABETH: Emily. This is all settled. You are going to that dance. Do you understand me. You are going to that dance. That sweet, nice brother of Inez Stanley's will be here any minute . . . .

EMILY: Sweet, nice brother. He's a goon. That's what he is. A regular goon. A bore and a goon . . . .

ELIZABETH: Emily . . .

EMILY: That's all he is. Just sits and doesn't talk. Can't dance. I'm not going to any dance or any place else with him and that's final. *(She runs out R.)*

ELIZABETH: Emily . . . Emily . . . You get ready this minute . . . *(The doorbell rings. Yelling.)* Emily . . . Emily . . . Horace is here. I want you down those stairs in five minutes . . . dressed. *(She goes out L. and comes back in followed by HORACE, all dressed up. He has a corsage box in his hand.)* Hello, Horace.

HORACE: Good evening.

ELIZABETH: Sit down, won't you, Horace? Emily is a little late getting dressed. You know how girls are.

HORACE: Yes, ma'm. *(He sits down. He seems a little awkward and shy.)*

ELIZABETH: Can I get you something to drink, Horace?

HORACE: No, ma'm. *(A pause. ELIZABETH is obviously very nervous about whether Emily will behave or not.)*

ELIZABETH: How's your family?

HORACE: Just fine, thank you.

ELIZABETH: I bet your sister was glad to see you.

HORACE: Yes, she was.

ELIZABETH: How's your family? Oh, I guess I asked you that, didn't I?

HORACE: Yes you did. *(ELIZABETH keeps glancing off R., praying that Emily will put in an appearance.)*

ELIZABETH: I understand you've become quite an accomplished dancer . . . .

HORACE: Oh . . . well . . . I . . .

ELIZABETH: Inez tells me you do all the new steps.

HORACE: Well—I . . .

ELIZABETH: Excuse me. Let me see what is keeping that girl.

Your Writer's Journal

Looking at really important parts of your life, or the lives of people with whom you are close, is a good way to find possible subjects for a play scene. In addition to writing in your journal, you can make cluster diagrams, freewrite, or ask yourself questions to explore the drama of life.

Choosing a Conflict or Problem

Like stories, plays are based on conflict. A conflict may be between two or more people, as between Emily and her mother in *The Dancers*. A conflict may also exist within a single person, as within Horace. For a conflict to be interesting in a play, it must be seen and heard onstage.

Movies and Plays

What makes a performance of a live play different from a movie? When you watch a movie, you are viewing a carefully edited sequence of events, actions, and dialogue that will be the same every time it is viewed. When you watch a play, however, each performance will be different from the next. Although the characters, setting, and script remain the same, the actors will interpret the dialogue and actions and respond differently from performance to performance.

In a movie the camera controls what the audience sees. Close-ups of actors create a sense of intimacy, while long, sweeping shots of scenery suggest the larger world. In a play people in the audience see the entire stage and can choose what they want to watch. It's up to the actors and the playwright to let the audience know what is important. A monologue (in which one person speaks for a long time) is one way of helping the audience realize that what someone is saying is important. The plot, or action in the play, is another way.

Media Activity

Work with several classmates to adapt the scene from *The Dancers* into a screenplay. Use the following questions as guides.

- Is there an image you could show that would tell the story more effectively than characters can tell or show it? What character or image do you want to see in each shot?
- Would you change the setting of the stage play for the screenplay? If so, to where?

Discuss how your ideas for a screenplay are different from the ideas of others in your group. What have you learned about the differences between a stage play and a screenplay?

PRACTICE YOUR SKILLS

● *Choosing a Conflict or Problem*

Freewrite a response to each question below. Save your work.

1. What is the most dramatic conflict you have lived through, seen, or heard about?

2. What current news events have affected you strongly?

3. Who are the two most interesting people you know and why? What might happen if they had an argument?

4. What would be the most surprising thing that could happen to you today? How would you react? How would this event change you?

Sketching Characters

Characters are usually the most important element of a play. In drama, the characters are brought to life by actors— real people who use their individual movements and tones of voice to perform the playwright's words in a unique way.

PRACTICE YOUR SKILLS

● *Sketching Characters*

Choose two details from below and build a character for a play around each one. To develop additional details, use brainstorming in one case, freewriting in the second, and clustering in the third. Then sketch out each character. Save your sketches for later use.

- an extremely neat person

- a wide-brimmed hat

- large greenish-blue eyes

Deciding on a Setting

A story in a book or movie may have many scenes with different settings. One scene may take place inside a house during a rainy afternoon. Another scene may take place outside the house on a clear, starlit night. Still another scene may take place on a snowy ski slope.

Because of the difficulty in creating sets that can be changed quickly, most plays have only a few scenes with different settings. In fact, an entire play may take place in one room with the actors moving the **props**—chairs, tables, and so on—to different positions. The playwright must create an interesting, dramatic story using scenery that can be changed easily and quickly.

PRACTICE YOUR SKILLS

● *Deciding on Settings*

Write five places that would make good settings for a stage play. For each location explain why you think it would make a good setting. Be sure your settings are simple and specific enough to be shown on a stage.

Using Dialogue

Remember that plays consist of live action and the audience is not reading descriptions of what is going on. Most plays, therefore contain a great deal of dialogue. **Dialogue** is the way a playwright shows the development of the plot of a play through the characters' words.

As in a story, the dialogue in a play should seem real. Each character should have his or her own personal way of speaking. In addition, the dialogue needs to deliver information to the audience. Everything that the reader learns about the characters must be shown through action and dialogue. For example, if a character had been missing for two years and then returned home at the beginning of the play, some character in the play would probably say something like, "Where have you been for the last two years? We were so worried about you!" The need to express information and characterization at the same time makes the dialogue in plays particularly rich in content.

PRACTICE YOUR SKILLS

● *Writing Dialogue*

Write a conversation between two friends who are lost in the woods. Have one insist that they wait until someone finds them and the other that they find their own way home. Write at least five separate lines for each character. Save your work.

Using Stage Directions

Playwrights frequently supply directions in the script so the reader (and the actors and director) will know how the characters should speak and move around the stage. These **stage directions** usually appear in *italic* print.

Because the dialogue itself usually conveys almost everything the audience learns about the characters, most modern playwrights like to keep their stage directions short. For example, if a character's words convey anger, then the playwright is unlikely to include the stage direction *Angrily*.

Some stage directions are necessary, however. They indicate which character should enter or exit, or they express meaningful actions, such as one character taking another character's hand.

In addition to describing how the actors should speak or move, a playscript provides information on how the characters should look and dress. It also includes information on what the **set,** or physical design of the stage, should look like. Then the stage directions indicate which props, or physical objects, should appear within the set.

● *Writing Stage Directions*

Return to the dialogue you wrote about the two friends who are lost in the woods. Write a least two stage directions for each character. Be sure your stage directions express action or emotion.

▶ Writing a Scene from a Play

Write a scene on one of the following subjects or choose a subject of your own.

- two teenagers at a party

- a teenager and a parent on the way to school

- a foreign exchange student in an American class

Decide on the setting—the time and the location in which the action takes place. Then write the dialogue along with stage directions. To be sure that the dialogue sounds real, have two friends read it aloud to you. Also have them perform your stage directions. Are the actions easy to carry out? Do the emotions convey the feelings you want?

Revise your script. Cut or add words or lines in the dialogue. Make your stage directions more specific and descriptive.

When you are satisfied with your scene, prepare a final copy, using the script format shown on page C235. Make extra copies and give them to friends who want to portray the characters. Have them perform the scene for the class.

PORTFOLIO

Writing a Poem

Dig deeply into your feelings and experiences, and you may find that you are inspired to write a poem rather than a short story. Poetry allows you to say something in an imaginative way. In this section you will learn how to use language in special ways to express special feelings. In other words you will learn how to write a poem.

Poetry is a writing form that encourages the expression of feelings through sound and the imaginative use of language.

Poems can be sad, silly, or serious. They are an expression of you—what you feel and what you imagine. Sometimes they may express your humor. They may be silly jokes or clever plays on words, like the following poem.

MODEL: Humorous Poem

If Mary goes far out to sea,
  By wayward breezes fanned,
I'd like to know—can you tell me?
  Just where would Maryland?

Two girls were quarreling one day
  With garden tools, and so
I said, "My dears, let Mary rake
  And just let Idaho."

—*Anonymous*, Stately Verse

Notice what happens to the state names when you say them slowly—*Maryland* (Mary land) and *Idaho* (Ida hoe). Both words are similar in sound, but they take on new meaning. The poet has used a play on words. This type of play on words is called a pun. A **pun** is a humorous use of a word that suggests two or more different meanings. It may also suggest the meaning of another word similar in sound.

Look through your journal notes on your thoughts and experiences. Ask yourself questions about the events and scenes in your mind. For example, what is it like to eat spaghetti? What comes into your mind when you see something red? Jot down your impressions.

Finding Ideas for Poems

Since a poem is really about your own thoughts and feelings, you can choose any subject. For a humorous poem, your subject may be a joke you have laughed at until you cried. It may be an amusing experience you recently had. Or it may just be about something silly, like "Stately Verse."

PRACTICE YOUR SKILLS

● *Finding Ideas for a Humorous Poem*

Copy and complete the following word web. Add funny or unusual humorous examples.

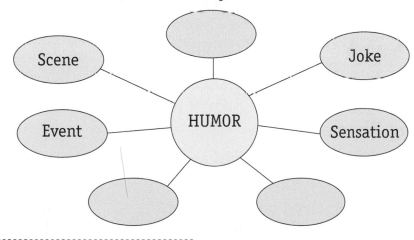

Using Sound Devices

All creative writing makes use of the way words sound, but in poetry sound is basic. In fact, the full effect of a poem comes through only when you read it aloud. In the following poem, the poet has repeated the sounds of *fl* to create humor. The repetition of consonant sounds at the beginning of a series of words is called **alliteration.**

MODEL: Alliteration

A **fl**ea and a **fl**y got caught in a **fl**ue.
Said the **fl**y, "Let us **fl**ee."
Said the **fl**ea, "Let us **fl**y."
So together they **fl**ew through a **fl**aw in the **fl**ue.

—*Anonymous,* "The Flea and the Fly"

PRACTICE YOUR SKILLS

● *Using Alliteration*

Develop a list of words with the same beginning sound for each subject below.

1. a color   **3.** a ball

2. a month   **4.** star

Using Rhyme

A rhymed poem usually has a pattern, or **rhyme scheme,** that can be shown by letters.

"Mother, may I go out to **swim?**"	*a*
"Yes, my darling **daughter,**	*b*
But hang your clothes on a hickory **limb,**	*a*
And don't go near the **water.**"	*b*

Notice that the rhyme pattern for the poem on the previous page is **ABAB.** The first line rhymes with the third, and the second line rhymes with the last. You may also write poetry with the pattern **AABB.** In this pattern the first two lines rhyme and then the next two.

● Writing a Poem

Prepare to write a poem on a subject of your choice. Your poem may be funny, sad, serious, or just plain silly. Use your **journal** and your notes from the practice activities on page C247. Then use the suggestions on page C248 to develop sound devices. Choose a rhyme scheme for your poem—ABAB or AABB—and write your poem. Read your poem aloud as you work. Finally read the final draft aloud to your classmates and friends.

PORTFOLIO

Time Out to Reflect You have had the opportunity to write a short story, a play, and a poem in this chapter. Which form do you prefer? Why? In what ways have your skills of writing stories, plays, and poems been sharpened as a result of completing this chapter? Which skills do you want to practice more?

A Writer Writes

A Humorous Story or Poem

Purpose: to entertain

Audience: your classmates

Prewriting

Brainstorm, freewrite, or cluster to think of a subject for a story or poem.

Stories and poems sometimes get their humor from exaggeration. Use your imagination to think of some possible sources of amusement, such as a practical joke that you once played on someone, or something ridiculous about an ordinary situation. Discuss with classmates whether what you want to tell could be best told in a story or a poem.

If you are writing a story, complete a sketch like the one on page C228. Sketch the characters and setting and list all of the events in chronological order. Decide whether your narrator will be a character in the story or will tell what happens to others. If you are writing a poem, decide if you will use sound devices and rhyme.

Drafting

Draft your story using your story sketch as a guide. Follow the suggestions on pages C228–C231 for drafting the beginning, the middle, and the ending of your story. For a poem, develop your sound device by writing a list of words for your subject with the same sound. Decide if you want to use the **ABAB** or the **AABB** rhyme pattern. You can refresh

your memory on rhyme patterns by looking at pages
C248–C249.

Revising

Exchange stories or poems with a classmate. Comment
on how well your partner's story or poem achieves its
purpose and suits the audience. Also comment on how
effectively the story or poem holds your interest. Did
you find it humorous? What words or phrases contribute
to the humor? How might it become even funnier? Be as
specific as possible.

    Consider your partner's comments. Use the
suggestions you find appropriate and the **Evaluation
Checklist for Revising** on page C232 to improve
your work.

Editing

Check your story or poem for possible errors, using the
Editing Checklist on page C28 as a guide. If you have
written a story, be sure you have punctuated your
dialogue correctly. If you have written a poem, be sure
you have used a capital letter at the beginning of each
new line.

Publishing

After correcting any errors you may find, make a neat
final copy of your story or poem and share it with your
classmates.

Connection Collection

Representing in Different Ways

Marc Chagall. *Birthday (L'Anniversaire)*, 1915.
Oil on canvas, 31¾ by 39 inches.

. . . *to Print*

Cursive, your school literary journal, is doing a special issue called "Birthdays." The editors have asked you to write a poem based on the famous painting by Marc Chagall. Examine the image and create an original poem from your feelings and impressions of this painting.

To: All interested students
From: Editors, <u>Cursive</u> Literary Journal
Date: May 1, 2000
Subject: Special "Birthdays" issue

Dear Students:

   We, the editors of <u>Cursive</u>, are currently finishing up our special "Birthday" issue. However, we have yet to agree on a suitable image for our cover. We are asking all interested students to search through magazines, art history books, or the World Wide Web to find a photograph or painting by a famous artist that you feel best illustrates the theme of the issue.

. . . to Visuals

From the information in the request given in the editors' note, find an image for the cover of your school's literary journal.

- Which strategies can be used for creating both written and visual representations? Which strategies apply to one, not both? Which type of representation is more effective?
- Draw a conclusion and write briefly about the differences between written ideas and visual representations.

Writing in Everyday Life
Humorous Poem

Zack, a classmate of yours, has recently fallen ill and is now re-covering at home. Your teacher has suggested that Zack would appreciate receiving original artwork, stories, or poems from his peers. You have decided to create a humorous poem for Zack to cheer him up.

Write the poem that your teacher will include in the batch of creative gifts for Zack. Begin by creating a word web to find your idea. When you have decided on a topic, write the poem, using at least one simile, one pun, and one example of alliteration in your lines. You might also want to consider an effective rhyme scheme.

What strategies did you use to create a humorous poem for your friend?

You can find information on writing poetry on pages C246-C249.

Writing for Oral Communication
Oral Presentation of a Play

You are the manager of Ziegfield's, a popular restaurant in town. Critics everywhere are raving about your expertly prepared dishes and friendly waitstaff. Later this month, you will take on many new workers. You wish to teach them about the job and familiarize them with safety tips about working in a restaurant, and you have decided to write a short play for this purpose.

Write the short play to be performed for the restaurant's new workers. Consider effective dramatic situations that could illustrate your points about safety on the job. Be sure to include vivid characters and an appropriate setting for the play.

What strategies did you use in writing an effective play about job safety?

You can find information on writing plays on pages C235-C245.

Assess Your Learning

For extra credit at school, you volunteer once a week to help the teacher of a kindergarten class. The teacher, Mrs. McKid, has heard that you are a good storyteller. She has arranged with your seventh grade teacher to give you extra credit if you can create an original story and present it to the class. Mrs. McKid has warned you, though: her five- and six-year-olds are a discriminating bunch!

▶ **Write a humorous short story for the audience of kindergartners. Mrs. McKid has told you that they like stories about animals the best, but has left you to be as creative as you like. Create characters and settings with as much colorful and vivid detail as possible. Make sure the story has a definite beginning, middle, and ending. Include a main conflict and a humorous resolution. Consider the best ways to create a story that will appeal to your audience of kindergartners.**

▶ *Before You Write* **Consider the following questions:**
What is the *subject?*
What is the *occasion?*
Who is the *audience?*
What is the *purpose?*

▶ *After You Write* **Evaluate your work using the following criteria:**
- Have you thought about your kindergarten audience, and written in a voice and style appropriate to them?
- Have you included effective details to bring the setting of your short story to life?
- Have you created vivid and lifelike characters?
- Does your short story have a clear beginning, middle, and end?
- Does the beginning of your short story introduce the main characters and central conflict? Is the conflict resolved at the end of your story?
- Have you produced legible work that shows accurate spelling and correct use of the conventions of punctuation and capitalization?

Write briefly on how well you did. Point out your strengths and areas for improvement.

CHAPTER 9

Writing to Inform and Explain

Think of an encyclopedia article, a map of directions, or the instructions used to assemble a bicycle. These are all kinds of informative writing. It is easy to see why everyone relies on this type of writing. Writing that gives information or explains how to make or do something is the most common type of writing. You will use this kind of communication throughout your life in many different situations. This chapter will help you explore and develop the skills you need to inform and explain effectively in writing.

Reading with a Writer's Eye

When writing about a subject as complicated as geology, what do you think is the best approach? You might present your information as the writers do here, informing the reader about the topic with some examples and facts. As you read, notice how the text explains the illustrations and how the illustrations clarify the text— in other words, how the two complement each other.

FROM THE AUSTIN AMERICAN-STATESMAN

Austin's archive of natural history

CARVED IN STONE

What caused the hills and terrain that make Austin, well, Austin? It all started millions of years ago, when the forces that cause the Earth's plates to move shoved ocean sediments north from what is now the Gulf of Mexico. Those mountains are now buried hundreds of feet below Austin, which has also been home to a lagoon crammed with sea life, a volcano and an earthquake-prone zone. Thankfully, things have settled down. But you can still see the results of these eons of geologic forces in the landscape around you. Here, a brief guide to our geologic past:

Loriola Texana
Rock formation: Glen Rose
Fossil size: 6/8" diameter, 2/8" thick
Estimated age: 107 million years
Location found: Travis County, near Turkey Foot

What our region looked like millions of years ago

1,150–1,120 million years

Approximate time periods

322–290 million years

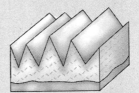

The continents collide, seas cover and then recede from the region in repeated cycles. Rocks from this period (Precambrian) can be seen in West Texas and Llano because of erosion and uplifting.

About 700 feet below present-day Austin is a mountain range that was formed when ocean sediments from the precursor of the Gulf of Mexico were shoved north and folded. Part of these ancient mountains can be seen north of Big Bend National Park.

290–115 million years

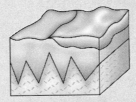

Geologists don't have much detailed evidence of what was happening in Austin. Based on information from other parts of the United States and Mexico, geologists can deduce that Austin was hilly or mountainous. The Gulf of Mexico was a newly formed ocean. Austin was about 100 miles closer to the Gulf than it is now.

115–97 million years

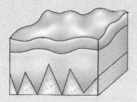

The ocean slowly flooded across Texas, forming a shallow sea. Imagine Austin as a large lagoon filled with abundant marine life and small islands with shell beaches. Rudists (see fossil) were main reef builders. During this period Glen Rose, Edwards and Georgetown formations took shape.

97–66 million years

The ocean spread inland. Sharks swam above Austin. The Del Rio, Eagle Ford, Taylor and Navarro formations took shape. Buda Limestone and Austin Chalk formed from bodies of plankton accumulated on the ocean floor. A volcano formed in what is now south Austin, now known as Pilot Knob.

24–21 million years

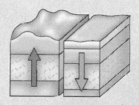

Earth's crust broke along the faults of the Balcones Fault Zone. (See map on following page.) Austin may have experienced earthquakes at this time. One thousand feet of displacement took millions of years.

11,000 years–present

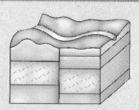

The modern Colorado River cut its valley and deposits sand and gravel in bars and terraces. You can see this and older sand near Longhorn Dam. The Balcones Fault seems to be still now. Scientists have not detected any movement in the Balcones Fault today.

Why is West Austin hilly...

The **Balcones Fault Zone** separates the inland edge of the Coastal Plain from the Hill Country. The faulting created two distinct geological environments with distinct soils, distributions of plants and animals, and land appearance.

The view looking southwest from Mount Bonnell. Surrounding hills provide prime real estate.

Balcones Fault Zone

Hill Country

● Dallas

● **Austin**

Coastal Plain

Del Rio ●

Balcones Fault Zone

Lake Travis

OLDER ROCKS

Edwards Formation

Walnut Formation

360

MoPac Blvd.

Glen Rose Formation

Sea level

Basal Cretaceous sands

Ouchata rocks, buried mountains

Direction fault slipped

. . . and East Austin so flat?

While West Austin was being pushed up, East Austin was held back by the drag of the Gulf of Mexico. The floor of the Gulf of Mexico sank because of loading by huge volumes of sediment poured into the Gulf from rivers and by cooling of the ocean floor as it ages.

Rock composition

Chalk: Made from skeletons of floating algae.

Limestone: Made from fragments of fossil shells.

Dolomite: Similar to limestone, but includes magnesium from seawater.

Altered tuff: Volcanic ash altered by sea water and air.

Basalt: Hard black rock that forms when lava cools.

The view looking south from U.S. 290 shows a different kind of landscape. Flat fields with rich soil provide for excellent farming and ranching.

Balcones Fault Zone

Buda, Georgetown, Del Rio, Eagle Ford Formations

Walter E. Long Lake

183

YOUNGER ROCKS

Taylor Marl

Austin Chalk

Edwards Formation

Walnut Formation

Glen Rose Formation

Direction fault slipped

Made in Central Texas

Common Austin area fossils

Eoradiolites (Rudists)
Rock formation: Edwards
Fossil size: 6 2/8" length, 1 2/8" wide, 1" thick
Estimated age: 105 million years
Location found: Bell County. Example shown was chosen for its size and detail. Rudists have been found in the RM 2222 and Loop 360 area.

Paracymatoceras
Rock formation: Georgetown
Fossil size: 3 4/8" longest length, 2 6/8" wide, 1 6/8" thick
Estimated age: 100 million years
Location found: East of Brodie Lane, on Oakdale Drive

Shark tooth
Rock formation: Taylor
Fossil size: 1/2" height, 1/2" across the base
Estimated age: 75 million years
Location found: Near Taylor

How fossils are formed

IMAGINE
Millions of years ago, Austin's current site was a sea filled with aquatic life.

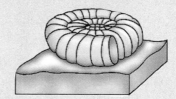

A SHELLFISH DIES
It drops to the seabed and the animal inside the shell decays.

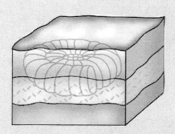

THE SHELL IS BURIED
Layers of ooze and sand fill with shell fragments. The composition of the shell slowly changes. Minerals replace organic material.

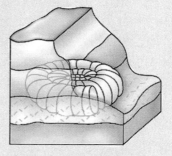

YEARS PASS
The sea recedes. Weather and water wear away the layers of sediment above the fossil, exposing the ancient fossil.

Graphics by Linda Scott/AA-S
Photos by Tom Lankes, Deborah Cannon/AA-S
Topographic map by UT Bureau of Economic Geology

Sources: UT Bureau of Economic Geology, Geological Society of America Bulletin, Down to Earth at McKinney Falls State Park, Texas, Oxford Planet Earth, Rand McNally Picture Atlas of Prehistoric Life

Thinking as a Writer

Analyzing Information in Different Media

"Carved in Stone" is an informative article that uses photographs, diagrams, maps, and text to explain how geological and fossil formations have occurred in Austin, Texas.

- How do the text and illustrations work together to provide information? Is one form easier to understand than the other? Why or why not? Are both forms together easier to understand? Explain.
- The writer could have presented the information without using maps, photographs, or illustrations. Would the article have been easier or more difficult to write? To read? Why do you say so?

Evaluating Completeness of Information

Oral Expression This article was written for a newspaper. Suppose it had been written for the radio.

- With a partner, take turns reading parts of the article on page C257 that include only text. Why can't you picture the information from your partner's reading? What additional information would your partner need to provide?

Analyzing Different Kinds of Visuals

Viewing "Carved in Stone" presents information that compares and contrasts East and West Austin.

- Study the photographs and maps on pages C260 and C261. What information do the photographs provide that the maps do not? What information does each map include that the photos do not? How do the photographs and the maps together give you a complete picture of Austin's geography?

The Power of Informative Writing

You have just read an example of informative writing—a newspaper article explaining the causes and making comparisons of the different land formations in Austin, Texas. A well-written informative article offers stimulating ideas on an interesting subject. You can find examples of informative writing everywhere—on television, in books, on the Internet, and even in your own experiences.

Uses of Informative Writing

Here are some examples that show the uses of writing that informs and explains in everyday life.

- ▶ **You write a report on the life cycle of a butterfly** for your science class.

- ▶ **A travel writer prepares copy for a brochure** describing the animals and vegetation of the Florida Everglades.

- ▶ **A theater critic provides background information** on a play to be included in the program.

- ▶ **A game developer writes instructions** on how to play a new video game.

- ▶ **A nutrition expert contributes a magazine article** reporting the latest research in healthful eating.

- ▶ **Your math teacher writes the explanations** for solving complex problems on the chalkboard.

Developing Your Informative Writing Skills

One of the most common purposes for writing is to inform. Informative writing can serve two purposes. One purpose is to provide information. Writing that tells why the moon shines gives factual information. The second purpose is to give directions. Writing that tells how to find the moon through a telescope gives step-by-step instructions.

> **Informative writing** presents information using facts and examples or explains by giving directions or listing steps in a process.

Your Writer's Journal

Over the next few days, answer the questions below in your journal to help you explore subjects for informative paragraphs.

- If I were asked to teach young children, what have I learned that I could explain to them? (List as many subjects as you can think of.)
- What do I already know about each subject?
- What more must I learn in order to explain each subject clearly?

As you investigate and read about the subjects, keep in mind your responses to the third question. Then identify what you learned, contrasting it with what you wanted to know.

Paragraph Structure

The purpose of the paragraph on the following page is to inform. Notice the clear structure of the paragraph.

Which Li Wei?

TOPIC SENTENCE:

STATES MAIN IDEA

SUPPORTING SENTENCES:

PROVIDE FACTS AND EXAMPLES

CONCLUDING SENTENCE:

ADDS STRONG ENDING

With the population of China so enormous, the authorities have great trouble keeping track of people with the same name. In one district 4,800 women were found with the same name. In one work unit ten men shared the name Li Wei. To tell one from another, they were called "Big Li Wei," "Li Wei No. 2," "Big Eyes Li Wei," and so forth. To try to reduce the confusion, one government district is supplying parents with a guide to naming babies.

—*Milton Meltzer,* A Book About Names

In the following paragraph, the writer's purpose is to explain by giving directions. The same overall structure is used.

MODEL: Paragraph That Explains

How to Lace Your Ice Skates

TOPIC SENTENCE:

STATES MAIN IDEA

SUPPORTING SENTENCES:

GIVE STEPS IN ORDER

CONCLUDING SENTENCE:

SUMMARIZES

Properly laced ice skates should be loose enough to let your toes stay warm and tight enough to support your ankles. First, remove all laces. Then, starting near the toe, thread the laces loosely through the first two eyelets. Next, slip your foot into the skate. Finally, thread the remaining eyelets securely over your instep and ankle. Skates laced this way will give your ankles support without pinching your toes.

The chart on the next page shows the role of each sentence in an informative paragraph.

> ## Structure of an Informative Paragraph
> - The topic sentence states a main idea based on fact.
> - The supporting sentences provide facts, examples, or steps in a process.
> - The concluding sentence summarizes the main idea and adds a strong ending.

PRACTICE YOUR SKILLS

● *Identifying the Purpose in Topic Sentences*

Read each topic sentence. Then write whether the sentence provides information or gives directions.

EXAMPLE   Invisible ink is easy to make.
ANSWER   gives directions

1. Releasing a bowling ball properly is the key to a high score.

2. The zodiac is made up of 12 constellations.

3. It is important to warm up before exercising.

4. Before taking a picture, follow these steps to make sure the lighting is correct.

5. Dogs and wolves are similar in many ways.

● *Writing Informative Topic Sentences*

Choose two subjects from each list below. Under each subject write a topic sentence that suits the purpose.

PROVIDING INFORMATION	GIVING DIRECTIONS
what classes you have	how to make friends
what a double play is	how to train a pet
why pets are popular	how to get to school
what ROM means	how to load a program disk

PREWRITING *Subject*

Use your **journal** responses or the following ideas to help you think of a good subject for an informative paragraph.

- List two interesting television shows you have watched recently. Next to each one, write an idea or a lesson you learned from watching the show.

- Browse through the library/media center. Check out a few books on a subject that interests you. Write down any new information that you learn from reading these books.

- Ask family members who are older than you to tell you how their youth was different from yours. Write their responses in note form.

Choose the subject that interests you the most. Then write a topic sentence that makes clear your purpose. Ask yourself what kinds of details would best answer any questions raised by your topic sentence. Brainstorm a list of details you could use to explain your subject clearly. Save your work.

SAVE YOUR WORK

Methods of Development

The purpose of your paragraph will help you decide what kind of supporting details you need. When providing information, you use facts and examples. When giving directions, your supporting details will be the steps in the process.

Facts and Examples

Read the following topic sentence. Then ask yourself what kinds of supporting details you expect the rest of the paragraph to contain.

TOPIC SENTENCE   For many years disabled athletes have set milestones.

The questions probably raised in your mind are these: *Who were these athletes? What did they do to set new milestones?* Facts and examples will answer these questions.

FACTS AND EXAMPLES

- Jack Robertson, an athlete with paralyzed legs, swam most of the English Channel.
- Bruce Jennings, an athlete with only one leg, bicycled three thousand miles across the United States.
- Two wheelchair athletes in the 1977 Boston Marathon finished in the top third.

Writing Tip

Use **facts** and **examples** to support the main idea of a paragraph that provides information.

PRACTICE YOUR SKILLS

● *Listing Facts and Examples*

Write each topic sentence. Then, under each one, list at least three facts or examples to back it up.

EXAMPLE   The Fourth of July is a holiday with many traditions.

POSSIBLE ANSWER   People usually watch firework displays.
Many people have barbecues.
Some towns have parades.

1. The parents of my friends have interesting jobs.
2. Most television comedy series have one male and one female lead character.
3. The only way to lose weight is to use up more calories than you take in.
4. Dogs express emotion in many ways.
5. The one invention I could never live without is the ▪. (Fill in your choice.)

Steps in a Process

The following topic sentence introduces a paragraph that gives directions. What are the questions it raises?

TOPIC SENTENCE You can return tennis balls hit to you if you follow a few important steps.

Readers will wonder what these steps are. The following details give the steps in the process.

STEPS IN A PROCESS
- First decide whether to use your forehand or backhand as the ball approaches.
- Then, turn your body to get into position.
- As you turn, bring your racket as far back as possible.
- Bend your knees and swing through with your whole body.
- Follow through on your stroke.

Writing Tip

Use **steps in a process** in the supporting sentences of a paragraph that gives directions.

PRACTICE YOUR SKILLS

● *Supporting Details*

Write each of the following topic sentences. Then list the steps in the process the reader will have to follow to accomplish the goal in the topic sentence.

1. Learning how to ride a bicycle requires help at first.

2. Checking a book out of the library/media center is easy.

3. A good way to get downtown from my house is by bus.

4. I have found a way to get up on time every morning.

5. Following these steps can help you prepare for a test.

● *Plotting Steps in a Process*

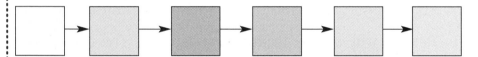

Choose one set of steps in a process you came up with from the above activity and plot it on a chart like the one above. Use as many boxes as necessary.

Communicate Your Ideas

PREWRITING *Supporting Details*

Look over your topic sentence. Brainstorm a list of at least three detailed supporting sentences that provide information or explain how to carry out your activity. Remember that the supporting sentences will be either facts and examples or steps in a process. Save your work for later use.

Analyzing

If the purpose of your informative paragraph is to give directions for performing a process, you will need to break down the process into separate, logical steps. To do so, you will use the skill of **analyzing.**

Think about the process of brushing your teeth. Analyze all your actions, and you become aware that you complete several smaller steps as part of the larger process. You start by holding the toothbrush a certain way to add toothpaste. Then you bring the toothbrush up to your mouth. After that you follow a pattern of movement to brush the teeth in different parts of your mouth. Then you probably rinse both your mouth and your toothbrush. Finally you put the toothbrush back in its holder. All these actions are the small steps that make up a larger process; here the end result is clean, sparkling teeth.

THINKING PRACTICE

Analyze the steps in the process of getting from the bus station to the stadium. Write the steps in order.

Logical Order and Transitions

Explanations that are presented in a logical order help readers understand your message. Two kinds of order often used in informative paragraphs are order of importance or size and sequential order.

Order of Importance or Size

In paragraphs that offer information, details are often arranged in the order of least to most or most to least. Transitions point out the relationships among the details.

TRANSITIONS USED WITH ORDER OF IMPORTANCE OR SIZE		
first	larger	equally important
next	even larger	more important
finally	the largest	most important

Writing Tip

To provide information, use **order of importance or size** with appropriate **transitions**. Arrange the details in order of least to most or most to least.

MODEL: Order of Importance or Size

TOPIC
SENTENCE

ORDER OF
SMALLEST TO
LARGEST

The five Great Lakes in North America vary significantly in size. The smallest is Lake Ontario, covering 7,340 square miles. Lake Erie is slightly larger, with an area of 9,910 square miles. Lake Michigan is the third largest lake. It is as big as Lake Erie and Lake Ontario combined. Next in size is Lake Huron. Its total area is 23,000 square miles. Lake

	Superior deserves its name as the largest of the Great Lakes. Its total area, in the United States and Canada, is 31,700 square miles. So important have the Great Lakes been to North Americans that even the smallest is great.

CONCLUDING SENTENCE appears to the left of the boxed text above.

PRACTICE YOUR SKILLS

● *Arranging Details in Order of Size*

Write each topic sentence. Then arrange the supporting details in the order of least to most or most to least.

1. Dogs come in many sizes.

- Mid-sized dogs, such as retrievers, hounds, setters, and huskies, usually weigh between 40 and 75 pounds.
- Small dogs, such as the Chihuahua and the Pekinese, often weigh between 10 and 40 pounds.
- Large dogs, such as the Great Dane, the Saint Bernard, and the Newfoundland, weigh up to 150 pounds.

2. Some branches of the armed services have many more people on active duty than do others.

- In March of 2000, the Air Force had 354,411 people on duty.
- The 2000 figure for the U.S. Army was 473,481.
- The Marines had 170,598 people in March 2000.
- The U.S. Navy had 368,064 in March 2000.

3. Humans have the longest life span of all mammals, living an average of about seventy years.

- A rabbit lives an average of five years.
- A leopard lives an average of twelve years.
- An opossum lives only one year.
- A lion lives an average of fifteen years.
- A gorilla lives twenty years, on average.
- A hippopotamus lives about twenty-five years.

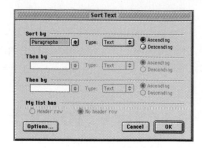
Sequential Order

In paragraphs that explain by giving directions, the supporting details must be presented in the proper sequence. This kind of order is called sequential order. In the following paragraph, the directions are clear because the steps are presented in the order that the reader would do them. The transitions are printed in **bold** type.

MODEL: Sequential Order

How to Make a Magnifying Lens

TOPIC SENTENCE

STEPS IN SEQUENTIAL ORDER

A simple magnifying lens can be made from a piece of wire and a drop of water. **First,** partly fill a container with water. **Then,** cut a piece of thin wire about six inches long. Bend one end of the wire, forming a small loop. **Next,** twist the wire at the bottom of the loop to hold it in place. **Now** you are ready to dip the loop into the water. **When** you do, a drop of the water will stay in the loop. **When** you look through the drop of water, you will see things magnified four or five times their real size. With only wire, water, and a little know-how, you have created a magnifying lens.

CONCLUDING SENTENCE

To explain by giving directions, use **sequential order** and appropriate **transitions**.

The following chart shows some useful transitions for sequential order.

TRANSITIONS FOR SEQUENTIAL ORDER			
first	before	while	finally
next	after	as soon as	as a last step
then	when	second	now

PRACTICE YOUR SKILLS

● *Listing Steps in Sequential Order*

The illustrations below show how to say in sign language, "Please write your name and address." Using the illustrations, rewrite the directions on the following page in the proper sequence.

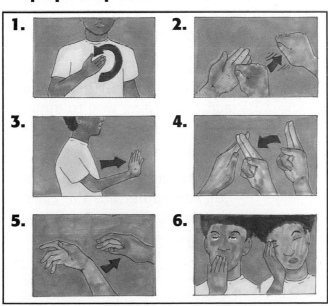

- To make the sign for *name*, extend the second and third fingers of both hands while your hands are apart. Then bring the right hand over the left to form an X.

- You can make the sign for *please* by rubbing in a circular motion on your chest with your right hand.

- The sign for *address* is a combination of two signs that indicate eating and sleeping.

- With all five fingers cupped together, bring your right hand up to your mouth.

- Make the sign for *and* by closing the fingers of your right hand as you move your hand to the left.

- The second part of the sign is the right hand over the ear, signifying sleep.

- *Your* is signed by pushing your open hand outward from the chest.

- In the sign for *write*, your left hand acts as the paper, while your right hand slides outward from your palm to your fingers as if it were holding a pencil.

Adding Transitions

Use the following sentences and your work from the previous activity to write a well-organized paragraph about sign language. Add transitions where necessary.

TOPIC SENTENCE Learning to sign the sentence "Please write your name and address" is one way to appreciate the sign language used by people who have a hearing impairment.

CONCLUDING SENTENCE By learning to sign this sentence, you can appreciate the clarity of sign language.

DRAFTING *Details, Transitions*

Review your previous work. Now arrange your supporting sentences, using transitions and details, in a logical order. Draft your paragraph and include your topic sentence, the rearranged supporting sentences, and a concluding sentence. Save your work for revising and editing in case you later decide to share it with an interested reader.

Time Out to Reflect

What have you learned about informative writing? In your **journal**, make a list of five ideas to remember when writing informatively. Add to the list or change it each time you learn more about this type of writing. Use your list the next time you write to inform or explain.

Prewriting Workshop
Drafting Workshop
Revising Workshop ▶
Editing Workshop
Publishing Workshop

Strong Verbs

As you revise your informative paragraph, pay special attention to the quality of the verbs you use. Verbs convey the action of a sentence. A dull verb may get the job done, but a strong, colorful verb will give your sentences life, vibrancy, and movement.

Careful selection of verbs will not only tell your readers what happened but also give them a sense of *how* it happened. Consider the following modified examples from "Carved in Stone."

DULL VERB	Weather and water **affect** the layers of sediment above the fossils.
COLORFUL VERB	Weather and water **wear away** the layers of sediment above the fossils.

In the first sentence, the reader gets the idea that the wind and water have done something to the earth but has no idea what has occurred.

The second sentence, however, gives the reader a more specific sense of what takes place—erosion—and conveys the sense that this is a long-term process. The verb phrase *wear away* adds to the descriptive power of the writing.

The same can be said of the verb *cuts* in the following example.

DULL VERB	The Colorado River **runs** through the land.
COLORFUL VERB	The Colorado River **cuts** through the land.

Process of Writing
Informative Paragraphs

The activities in this section of the chapter will help you write clear informative paragraphs. Use the strategies and process that work best for you. During prewriting, however, be sure to consider the needs of your audience as you plan your explanations. During drafting, put your thoughts in flowing sentences. As you revise and edit your work, look for any weaknesses or errors in your writing and correct them. The result should be an explanation that is easy for your intended readers to follow.

Explaining Symbols

Prewriting

You know what all the symbols on the American flag stand for. The white stars stand for the fifty states. The red and white stripes stand for the original thirteen colonies. Red, white, and blue are also the colors of the British flag. Each shape and color on that flag stands for something as well.

Now think about yourself. Think about the things that are important to you and that help identify you. Then make a list of some of your interests. Create symbols for these interests. When you have created a number of symbols, design your own personal flag. Draw a picture of your flag, using colors that have special meaning for you.

Drafting

Draft an informative paragraph explaining each symbol and color on your flag. Since your readers will already have a picture of your flag, you do not need to describe it in your paragraph.

Revising Conferencing

Exchange paragraphs and pictures with a classmate. Read your partner's paragraph carefully as you study the picture. Are any symbols or colors left out of the paragraph? Tell your partner about them. Make any revisions that would improve your writing. Use your partner's comments and the following checklist to help you.

> ### Evaluation Checklist for Revising
>
> **Checking Your Paragraphs**
>
> ✓ Does your topic sentence state a main idea based on fact? *(pages C267–C268)*
>
> ✓ If your paragraph provides information, do your supporting sentences uphold the main idea with facts and examples? *(pages C268–C271)*
>
> ✓ If your paragraph gives directions, do your supporting sentences provide the steps in the process? *(pages C268, C271–C273)*
>
> ✓ Are your details arranged in logical order? *(pages C274–C278)*
>
> ✓ Do you use transitions to give your paragraph coherence? *(pages C274–C278)*
>
> ✓ Does your paragraph have unity? *(pages C171–C172)*
>
> ✓ Does your concluding sentence summarize the main idea and add a strong ending? *(pages C170–C171)*
>
> **Checking Your Sentences**
>
> ✓ Did you combine related sentences to avoid too many short, choppy sentences in a row? *(pages C67–C72)*
>
> ✓ Did you vary the beginnings of your sentences? *(pages C74–C76)*
>
> ✓ Did you avoid rambling sentences? *(page C78)*
>
> ✓ Did you avoid repetition and empty expressions? *(pages C79–C82)*
>
> **Checking Your Words**
>
> ✓ Did you use clear, specific words? *(page C40–C41)*

Editing

Check over your paragraph for errors in spelling, grammar, mechanics, and usage.

Publishing

Make a neat final copy. On a separate sheet of paper, make a fresh picture of your flag. Mount your paragraph and flag on a large sheet of construction paper. Display your finished work in your classroom or at home for others to enjoy.

Giving Directions

Prewriting

Think about exercises you know. Toe touches, knee bends, and jumping jacks might be a few. Write them down. Under each one, list all the steps you follow to complete that exercise. Then choose the exercise you most like to do. Write a sentence telling why that exercise is your favorite.

Drafting

Use your notes to draft a paragraph giving directions on how to do the exercise you chose.

Revising Conferencing

Pair off with a partner. Leave room to move around. Have your partner read his or her paragraph to you. Follow the directions as your partner reads them. Let your partner know if any parts of the directions are confusing. Use your partner's comments and the <u>Evaluation Checklist for Revising</u> on the previous page to help you revise your directions.

Editing

Check over your paragraph for spelling, grammar, mechanics, and usage errors.

Publishing

Make a neat final copy using the publishing suggestions on pages C31–C32.

Across the Media: News Lead-ins

Learning the techniques of one medium can help you learn about another. Understanding the power of images on television, for example, can remind you to include strong description in your writing. Recognizing how different media present information can help you improve your informative writing.

Techniques for grabbing a reader's attention, or lead-ins, are especially useful to study and include in your work.

A newspaper story usually begins with the whole story summarized in the first sentence: *Bilco is being acquired by Zinc Enterprises for about $162 billion in stock in what would be the biggest corporate merger ever.* The rest of the story supplies the details, but the reader is drawn in by knowing the outcome.

A newsmagazine, in contrast, might begin with a descriptive paragraph setting the scene: *Surrounded by lawyers and looking weary but elated, Bilco CEO Jessica Zacks surveyed the mayhem around her. Barely two years after starting her outrageously successful Internet company, the 23-year-old executive was preparing for her biggest coup yet.*

Media Activity

Use the following guidelines to analyze different writing techniques in newspapers, newsmagazines, and the Internet. Skim through a newspaper, newsmagazine and the Internet until you find a headline that interests you. Read only the first paragraph of the story. Then ask yourself these questions.

- Does the lead-in grab my attention? How?
- How did the writer get my attention?
- What is the implied or stated message? If it is stated, where is it placed in the introduction?

When you are finished, discuss your findings with your classmates.

▶ Process of Writing to Inform or Explain

During the writing process you can move back and forth among the stages. For example, during revising you may think of a detail or step that you overlooked. You can return to the drafting stage and add the missing information. The page numbers in parentheses tell you where you can find help with your writing.

PREWRITING

- Determine your purpose and your audience.
- Choose a subject that interests you the most.
- Limit your subject so that it can be adequately covered in one paragraph.
- If your purpose is to provide information, list facts and examples. If your purpose is to give directions, list steps in the process. *(pages C268–C273)*
- Arrange your notes in a logical order. *(pages C274–C278)*

DRAFTING

- Write a topic sentence suited to your purpose. *(pages C267–C268)*
- Use your prewriting notes to write the supporting sentences. *(pages C268–C272)*
- Add a concluding sentence that summarizes the main idea and adds a strong ending. *(page C268)*

REVISING

- Use the <u>Evaluation Checklist for Revising</u> on page C282 to make it as clear as possible.

EDITING

- Polish your writing, correcting any errors in grammar, usage, spelling, and mechanics.
- Verify and correct any factual errors (dates and so on).

PUBLISHING

- Prepare a neat final copy and share your information or directions with an interested reader.

A Writer Writes

A Time Capsule Entry

Purpose: to inform others of your accomplishments

Audience: future generations

Thomas Jefferson was a president of the United States, but he wanted to be remembered for his other accomplishments as well. One was the Declaration of Independence. The second was the Statute of Virginia for Religious Freedom. The third was the founding of the University of Virginia.

Prewriting

Suppose your class is preparing a time capsule. Think about three things that you would like to be remembered for. They can be small or large accomplishments. They can be things you have already done or things you hope to do in the next five years. Brainstorm, freewrite, or cluster to develop reasons why these accomplishments would make you proud. Then arrange your three accomplishments in a logical order.

Drafting

Using your prewriting notes, write a draft of your accomplishments in the form of an informative paragraph. Be sure to include a clear topic sentence, well-ordered supporting sentences with transitions, and a strong concluding sentence.

Revising

Use the **Evaluation Checklist for Revising** on page C282 to make your entry as strong as it can be. Pay special attention to the quality of the verbs you use. Are they as lively and specific as you can make them?

Editing

Use the **Editing Checklist** on page C28 to catch any errors you may have made in your drafts.

Publishing

Make a neat, corrected copy of your entry and draw an illustration to go with it. Place your entry in a sturdy container and store it in a safe place.

Representing in Different Ways

Students for Sale

Jennifer Rowan

Commercial advertising in public schools used to be subtle and issue-oriented, like the science posters about the need for pest control sponsored by insecticide makers. But blunter commercialism has entered many classrooms, in the form of direct advertising of products and access to students for marketing surveys in return for gifts to schools like free computers. One company, for example, sponsors oral hygiene classes in elementary school in return for distributing samples of its toothpaste. Concern about using students as captive consumers has led one Washington lawmaker to introduce a bill to ban the collection of any information in school from any student under 18 for commercial purposes without first getting written permission from parents. The lawmaker sponsoring the bill mentioned the practice of one California company that has offered schools free computers with limited Internet access, but then monitors the students' Web selections to get information on what advertising would appeal to them. He also noted deals with schools in several states in which marketers held focus groups with students and had them take taste tests and fill out questionnaires. The bill, the Student Privacy Protection Act, would also order a broad Federal study of the extent and the trends of commercialism in schools, including both advertising and market research.

. . . to Visuals

Create a graphic or find a photo to accompany the above newspaper column.

. . . to Print

Write an informative newspaper article that might be accompanied by the photo above.

- **Which strategies can be used for creating both written and visual representations? Which strategies apply to one, not both? Which type of representation is more effective?**
- **Draw a conclusion and write briefly about the differences between written ideas and visual representations.**

Writing for Oral Communication
Television Presentation

You have been asked by a local cable station to appear on Mr. Klutsy's Science Safety Hour. You are to perform and explain the steps in the process of a science experiment. You have heard a rumor: the network is looking for a replacement for Mr. Klutsy, who will soon be retiring. You know that if you dazzle them, you could be king of the Bunsen burners.

Write the steps in the process of performing a science experiment that you are familiar with. Be sure the steps are in sequential order and use transitions to connect ideas. Perform your experiment for the class, who will watch as the studio audience. Explain the steps (from your written explanation) as you perform them.

What strategies did you use to explain the steps in the process of the experiment to the audience?

> You can find information on giving oral presentations on pages C433–C443.

Writing in Academic Areas
Personal History

In school it always seems that you are learning about people you do not know. In an attempt to personalize history, your social studies teacher has decided to publish a book about the history of the members of your class.

Write a short encyclopedia-like entry about yourself and your past to be published in the class book. Inform readers about yourself and explain how you came to be in this particular class. Try to avoid opinions and use only facts to construct your history. Your work should have an interesting introduction and conclusion, as well as a body of supporting details. Arrange details in a logical order.

What strategies did you use to inform your classmates about your history?

Assess Your Learning

Your older brother, Brian, often ends arguments with you by shouting, "You don't know anything!" and slamming the door. You are determined to prove him wrong. You plan to show him exactly what you know.

▶ Choose a subject you know well. Write an informative paragraph about the subject to slip under Brian's door the next time he slams it. Your informative paragraph should include a topic sentence.

▶ Use facts and examples in the body of the work to support your topic sentence. Arrange your details in a logical order that will ensure progression and coherence. Use transitions between your supporting details. Your concluding sentence should summarize the information you have presented.

Before You Write Consider the following questions:
What is the *subject?*
What is the *occasion?*
Who is the *audience?*
What is the *purpose?*

After You Write Evaluate your work using the following criteria:
- Does the topic sentence include a limited subject and focus?
- Did you use facts and examples instead of opinions to support the topic sentence?
- Did you organize supporting details into a logical order?
- Did you use transitions to connect the supporting ideas?
- Does the concluding sentence summarize the main points?
- Is your vocabulary precise?
- Did you follow the conventions of grammar, spelling, and punctuation?

Write briefly on how well you did. Point out your strengths and areas for improvement.

CHAPTER 10

Writing to Persuade

Every day people fight for your attention. They are trying to persuade you. Advertisers want you to buy their products. Television producers want you to watch their shows. Designers want you to wear their clothes, and teachers want you to do your homework. It is not any different on the home front, as family and friends take up the fight. "Come see this movie . . ." "Please keep your room clean . . ."

Language is one tool of persuasion. When you recognize the persuasive language the advertisers, designers, teachers and friends are using, you are better able to decide whether to go along with an idea or to reject it. When you understand the language of persuasion, you are better able to write persuasively.

Reading with a Writer's Eye

Following is a speech in which President John F. Kennedy tries to persuade the country—and the rest of the world—of the necessity for a manned expedition to the moon. Read it a few times. Look for phrases you think are particularly persuasive. What makes them effective? Notice how Kennedy develops his argument to suggest space exploration is inevitable.

on the NATION'S SPACE EFFORT

John F. Kennedy

Houston, Texas, September 12, 1962

We meet at a college noted for knowledge, in a city noted for progress, in a state noted for strength, and we stand in need of all three, for we meet in an hour of change and challenge, in a decade of hope and fear, in an age of both knowledge and ignorance. The greater our knowledge increases, the greater our ignorance unfolds.

Despite the striking fact that most of the scientists that the world has ever known are alive and working today, despite the fact that this nation's own scientific manpower is doubling every 12 years in a rate of growth more than three times that of our population as a whole, despite that, the vast stretches of the unknown and the unanswered and the unfinished still far outstrip our collective comprehension.

No man can fully grasp how far and how fast we have come, but condense, if you will, the 50,000 years of man's recorded history in a time span of but a half-century. Stated in these terms, we know very little about the first 40 years, except at the end of them advanced man had learned to use the skins of animals to cover them. Then about 10 years ago, under this standard, man emerged from his caves to construct other kinds of shelter. Only five years ago man learned to write and use a cart with wheels. Christianity began less than two years ago. The printing press came this year, and then less than two months ago, during this whole 50-year span of human history, the steam engine provided a new source of power.

Newton explored the meaning of gravity. Last month electric lights and telephones and automobiles and airplanes became available. Only last week did we develop penicillin and television and nuclear power, and now if America's new spacecraft succeeds in reaching Venus, we will have literally reached the stars before midnight tonight.

This is a breathtaking pace, and such a pace cannot help but create new ills as it dispels old, new ignorance, new problems, new dangers. Surely the opening vistas of space promise high costs and hardships, as well as high reward.

So it is not surprising that some would have us stay where we are a little longer to rest, to wait. But this city of Houston, this State of Texas, this country of the United States was not built by those who waited and rested and wished to look behind them. This country was conquered by those who moved forward—and so will space.

William Bradford, speaking in 1630 of the founding of the Plymouth Bay Colony, said that all great and honorable actions are accompanied with great difficulties, and both must be enterprised and overcome with answerable courage.

If this capsule history of our progress teaches us anything, it is that man, in his quest for knowledge and progress, is determined and cannot be deterred. The exploration of space will go ahead, whether we join in it or not, and it is one of the great adventures of all time, and no nation which expects to be the leader of other nations can expect to stay behind in the race for space.

Those who came before us made certain that this country rode the first waves of the industrial revolutions, the first waves of modern invention, and the first wave of nuclear power, and this generation does not intend to founder in the backwash of the coming age of space. We mean to be a part of it—we mean to lead it. For the eyes of the world now look into space, to the moon and to the planets beyond, and we have vowed that we shall not see it governed by a hostile flag of conquest, but by a banner of freedom and peace. We have vowed that we shall not see space filled with weapons of mass destruction, but with instruments of knowledge and understanding.

Yet the vows of this Nation can only be fulfilled if we in this Nation are first, and, therefore, we intend to be first. In short, our leadership in science and in industry, our hopes for peace and security, our obligations to ourselves as well as others, all require us to make this effort, to solve these mysteries, to solve them for the good of all men, and to become the world's leading space-faring nation.

We set sail on this new sea because there is new knowledge to be gained, and new rights to be won, and they must be won and used for the progress of all people. For space science, like nuclear science and all technology, has no conscience of its own. Whether it will become a force for good or ill depends on man, and only if the United States occupies a position of pre-eminence can we help decide whether this new ocean will be a sea of peace or a new terrifying theater of war. I do not say that we should or will go unprotected against the hostile misuse of space any more than we go unprotected against the hostile use of land or sea, but I do say that space can be explored and mastered without feeding the fires of war, without repeating the mistakes that man has made in extending his writ around this globe of ours.

There is no strife, no prejudice, no national conflict in outer space as yet. Its hazards are hostile to us all. Its conquest deserves the best of all mankind, and its opportunity for peaceful cooperation may never come again. But why, some say, the moon? Why choose this as our goal? And they may well ask why climb the highest mountain? Why, 35 years ago, fly the Atlantic? Why does Rice play Texas?

We choose to go to the moon. We choose to go to the moon in this decade and do the other things, not only because they are easy, but because they are hard, because that goal will serve to organize and measure the best of our energies and skills, because that challenge is one that we are willing to accept, one we are unwilling to postpone, and one which we intend to win, and the others, too.

It is for these reasons that I regard the decision last year to shift our efforts in space from low to high gear as among the most important decisions that will be made during my incumbency in the office of the Presidency. . . .

Within these last 19 months at least 45 satellites have circled the earth. Some 40 of them were "made in the United States of America" and they were far more sophisticated and supplied far more knowledge to the people of the world than those of the Soviet Union. . . .

Transit satellites are helping our ships at sea to steer a safer course. Tiros satellites have given us unprecedented warnings of hurricanes and storms, and will do the same for forest fires and icebergs.

We have had our failures, but so have others, even if they do not admit them. And they may be less public.

To be sure, we are behind, and will be behind for some time in manned flight. But we do not intend to stay behind, and in this decade, we shall make up and move ahead.

The growth of our science and education will be enriched by new knowledge of our universe and environment, by new techniques of learning and mapping and observation, by new tools and computers for industry, medicine, the home as well as the school. Technical institutions, such as Rice, will reap the harvest of these gains.

And finally, the space effort itself, while still in its infancy, has already created a great number of new companies, and tens of thousands of new jobs. . . .

To be sure, all this costs us all a good deal of money. This year's space budget is three times what it was in January 1961, and it is greater than the space budget of the previous eight years combined. . . . But if I were to say, my fellow citizens, that we shall send to the moon, 240,000 miles away from the control station in Houston, a giant rocket more than 300 feet tall, the length of this football field, made of new metal alloys, some of which have not yet been invented, capable of standing heat and stresses several times more than have ever been experienced, fitted together with a precision better than the finest watch, carrying all the equipment needed for propulsion, guidance, control, communications, food and survival, on an untried mission, to an unknown celestial body, and then return it safely to earth, re-entering the atmosphere at speeds of over 25,000 miles per hour, causing heat about half that of the temperature of the sun—almost as hot as it is here today—and do all this, and do it right, and do it first before this decade is out—then we must be bold.

I'm the one who is doing all the work, so we just want you to stay cool for a minute. [laughter]

However, I think we're going to do it, and I think that we must pay what needs to be paid. I don't think we ought to waste any money, but I think we ought to do the job. And this will be done in the decade of the sixties. It may be done while some of you are still here at school at this college and university. It will be done during the term of office of some of the people who sit here on this platform. But it will be done. And it will be done before the end of this decade. . . .

Many years ago the great British explorer George Mallory, who was to die on Mount Everest, was asked why did he want to climb it. He said, "Because it is there."

Well, space is there, and we're going to climb it, and the moon and the planets are there, and new hopes for knowledge and peace are there. And, therefore, as we set sail we ask God's blessing on the most hazardous and dangerous and greatest adventure on which man has ever embarked.

Thank you.

Thinking as a Writer

Evaluating Persuasive Evidence

- What goal is President John F. Kennedy urging the United States to pursue? How does President Kennedy use history to "prove" his argument? How does he appeal to his listener's emotions?
- Some people credit the president's speech with starting the space program as we know it. How does his speech accomplish this?

Using Persuasive Tone

Oral Expression President Kennedy was known for giving speeches with a particular style. One element of that style was repetition of key phrases.

- Find places in the speech where the president repeats a phrase or set of words. How does this repetition add to the tone of the speech?
- In small groups, take turns reading parts of the speech aloud. Why is it easy to be persuasive with the president's phrases?

Enhancing Persuasive Appeal

Viewing • Observe the two photographs below.

If you were choosing a photo to accompany President Kennedy's speech, which photo would you choose? Explain your reasoning.

The Power of Persuasion

John F. Kennedy's speech is just one example of how powerful persuasive writing can be. The President gave it at a time when the nation needed leadership, and he felt strongly about the direction in which the United States should move. That was a national issue, but there are plenty of times when persuasion can be useful in your daily life.

Uses of Persuasion

Here are just a few examples of the ways in which persuasive writing can be found in your everyday life.

- **Students write a proposal to the principal** outlining plans for a new after-school club.

- **Movie reviewers write articles** for magazines telling people why they should or should not see the newest releases.

- **Organizations protecting endangered species write pamphlets** persuading people to help out.

- **Residents write to the city council persuading** them to change their plans to pave over a playing field.

- **Advertisers write television commercials** aimed at convincing people to buy products.

Developing the Skills of Persuasion

A famous historian once said, "The aim of oratory is not truth, but persuasion." Anybody who has ever argued passionately for a particular result will probably understand this statement. People will sometimes ignore the facts that do not support their argument and emphasize the ideas an audience wants to hear. What is it, though, that makes persuasion work? Can facts actually help a case? Can emotion? How can you sharpen your skills of persuasion?

The ability to convince others of what you believe is one of the most valuable life skills you can acquire. Being truly persuasive will aid you in work, school, and the world at large. Writing persuasive compositions is one way to develop and refine this skill.

Persuasive writing states an opinion on a subject and uses facts, reasons, and examples to convince readers.

Your Writer's Journal

Do you feel the new dress code at your school is too strict? Do you know of an intersection that needs a stop sign? Is a senator from your state about to vote on an issue you care about?

Find a topic that really matters to you. Then freewrite about it in your journal, brainstorming a list of facts and arguments to support your idea of what should be done. If you are having trouble getting started, state your opinion in a single sentence, such as, "I believe the government should not count ketchup as a vegetable in school lunches."

Persuasive Paragraphs

If people always agreed with each other, there would not be a need for writing persuasive paragraphs. However, as you well know, opinions come in as wide a variety as people do. Having your own opinion is an important part of being human and sometimes means disagreeing with someone else.

When trying to persuade someone to share your views, you need to use the techniques of persuasion. A clear, logical structure, combined with carefully supported points, will help you build a strong case for your opinion.

Read the following persuasive paragraph twice. The first time you read it, decide whether or not you agree with the writer's argument. The second time, notice the structure of the paragraph. Think about the role each sentence plays in building a persuasive paragraph.

MODEL: Persuasive Paragraph

Year-round School

TOPIC
SENTENCE

SUPPORTING
SENTENCES

CONCLUDING
SENTENCE

Year-round school is a good idea. First of all, the school buildings would be put to good use during the summer instead of just lying empty. Second, students could enjoy several shorter vacations throughout the year during which they can apply their learning in everyday life. Most important, students would remember more from class to class if there were not a long summer vacation breaking the flow of learning between grades. With short breaks planned along the way, year-round school would provide real benefits economically, personally, and educationally.

Use these structural hints to build your paragraphs.

> **Structure of a Persuasive Paragraph**
> - The **topic sentence** states an opinion.
> - The **supporting sentences** use facts, examples, and reasons to back up the opinion.
> - The **concluding sentence** makes a final appeal to readers.

PRACTICE YOUR SKILLS

● *Writing Persuasive Topic Sentences*

For each of the following subjects, write a topic sentence that states an opinion.

EXAMPLE   The school newspaper

POSSIBLE ANSWER The school newspaper should include an advice-to-students column.

1. school rules

2. the Internet

3. your neighborhood

4. bad habits

5. television shows

6. telephones

7. national holidays

8. cars and driving

9. movies

10. UFOs

PREWRITING *Topic Sentence*

Review your **journal** notes about the subjects that stir strong opinions in you. Then brainstorm other ideas for a persuasive paragraph. Choose the one subject from the list that you feel most strongly about. Write a topic sentence for that subject. Save your work for later use.

Facts and Opinions

Readers who disagree with your opinion need proof before they will consider changing their minds. Facts and examples will help you prove your point. Opinions, on the other hand, will not prove anything.

A **fact** is a statement that can be proved.

An **opinion** is a belief or judgment that cannot be proved.

Advertisers know that opinions can be very persuasive. Commercials on television and advertisements in newspapers and magazines often use opinions to sell products. Advertisements are meant to convince you that one soda tastes better than another; or that the style of one car is more attractive than the style of another; or that one brand of jeans is cooler than another. If the advertisement is persuasive, you are more likely to buy the "better tasting" soda or "cooler" jeans. Try to spot all the opinions in the following advertisement.

This advertisement appeals to the emotions. It implies that owning a Windsprite will make dreams come true and will give the owner power. Although not a single fact is presented, the advertisement stirs strong feelings and could succeed in selling the Windsprite.

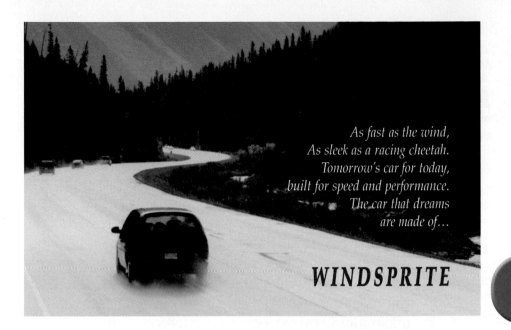

As fast as the wind,
As sleek as a racing cheetah.
Tomorrow's car for today,
built for speed and performance.
The car that dreams
are made of...

WINDSPRITE

A different approach to selling the Windsprite would be to provide some facts about the car. The facts might include its gas mileage, leg room, trunk space, warranty policy, available colors, and price. Facts like these would help a person compare the features of the Windsprite with those of other cars.

When you develop a persuasive paragraph, rely on facts to prove your point. Although opinions and emotions may often help to sell a product, they alone will not convince serious readers. Watch for words such as the following that signal an opinion.

OPINION WORDS	
should	better
must	best
ought	worst

Political Cartoons

Political cartoons appear in many newsmagazines and on the editorial pages of most major newspapers. They serve two purposes: (1) to make people think critically about current issues in politics and government, and (2) to entertain. Most political cartoons address issues that are currently in the news and on the public's mind. Unlike most cartoons in the cartoon section that use both text and pictures to tell a story or make a joke, political cartoons rely almost solely on the pictures to make their point. Political cartoonists usually assume that the readers know enough about current issues to understand the cartoon's message.

All political cartoonists use similar techniques to communicate their point: they use symbols to represent certain ideas, caricatures and exaggerations of a person's or object's physical features, and simple captions to clarify or emphasize the cartoonist's point.

Media Activity

Look through several magazines or newspapers to find examples of what you think are good political cartoons. Identify the different techniques that the cartoonists have used to make their point. Show the cartoons to the class and, for each one, explain the cartoonist's message and the techniques that the cartoonist used to communicate the message.

An argument based on opinions is like a house built on sand. Use **facts** and **examples** to convince your readers.

PRACTICE YOUR SKILLS

● *Identifying Facts and Opinions*

For each statement write *F* if it is a *fact* or *O* if it is an *opinion*.

1. The Petronas Tower in Kuala Lumpur is the world's tallest building.
2. Hawaii became a state in 1959.
3. Cats make better pets than dogs.
4. Nothing tastes better than a glass of cold milk.
5. Milk contains both protein and calcium.
6. All the best movies are comedies.
7. Robert Frost was truly a great poet.
8. Yosemite is America's most beautiful national park.
9. Nathaniel Hawthorne wrote *The Marble Faun*.
10. Weeping willow trees do not really weep.

Communicate Your Ideas

PREWRITING *Facts and Opinions*

Review the topic sentence you have chosen. Then brainstorm or freewrite to develop facts, examples, or reasons you could use to support your opinion. Save your work for later use.

Evaluating

To make your persuasive writing as forceful as possible, you should take opposing views into consideration. **Evaluate**, or judge, the facts and examples your opponents might use in their arguments. Reread the paragraph on page C302 about year-round school. The writer uses three main points to support the topic sentence.

1. Using the building all year would be good.

2. Enjoying several shorter vacations would allow students to apply their learning in everyday life.

3. Continuing school without a long break would help students better remember what they learn.

To evaluate these details, ask yourself whether any of them could also be turned around to support the opposing view. For example, keeping school open during summer might require air-conditioning, which is expensive. Or, summer vacation might provide necessary relaxation.

After evaluating each detail, you may decide that you agree with the original paragraph after all. On the other hand, you may now be convinced that schools should not remain open year round. Only by evaluating all the possible supporting details can you decide for sure.

● Order of Importance and Transitions

Ideas at the beginning or at the end of a paragraph are more likely to stay in a reader's mind than those located in the middle. For this reason, the most important point is usually placed either at the beginning or at the end of a persuasive paragraph. Transitions help to show the order of importance of the ideas presented.

TRANSITIONS FOR ORDER OF IMPORTANCE		
also	for example	moreover
another	in the first place	furthermore
besides	in the second place	in addition
finally	in the same way	more important
first	likewise	most important
second	to begin with	similarly

Notice the logical order in the following paragraph. The transitions are printed in **boldface** type.

MODEL: Order of Importance and Transitions

Preparing for the Worst

TOPIC SENTENCE:
OPINION

SUPPORTING POINTS:
IN ORDER OF LEAST TO MOST IMPORTANT

CONCLUDING SENTENCE:
FINAL APPEAL

   Communities along the San Andreas Fault should plan ahead in case an earthquake should strike. **First**, the risk of an earthquake along the fault is very high. Scientists predict a major earthquake will occur within the next 100 years. **Second**, emergency shelters, food supplies, and fire extinguishers needed for adequate planning are not expensive compared to other town or city costs. **Most important**, conducting earthquake drills, like fire drills, can help people be as calm as possible if an earthquake does occur. Perhaps thousands of lives could be saved with proper planning.

Writing Tip

Arrange your supporting points in order of importance. Use transitions to show the connections between ideas.

PRACTICE YOUR SKILLS

● *Using Transitions*

In the paragraph below, the ideas are arranged in order of least to most important. The transitions, however, are missing. Using the list on the previous page, rewrite this paragraph to include transitions.

Bicycle Lanes Are a Good Idea

The city should paint bicycle lanes along Reston Street, Tower Avenue, and Madison Street. Having a safe place to bicycle might encourage more people to take their bikes rather than their cars to work. Fewer cars would mean less pollution. Fewer people would ride their bikes on the sidewalks, where they endanger pedestrians. Bicycle lanes promote safety by keeping cyclists away from cars and by reminding drivers that cyclists are on the road. The cost of having the lanes painted is low compared to the benefits.

● *Using Index Cards to Order*

A good way to organize your ideas from least to most important is to use index cards. Write each of your ideas on a separate index card. You may even want to list supporting details under each point. Then you can move the cards around to decide the best order.

Complete the following index cards based on the paragraph on bicycle safety above.

TOPIC SENTENCE

The city should paint bicycle lanes along Reston Street, Tower Avenue, and Madison Street.

LEAST IMPORTANT POINT

NEXT MOST IMPORTANT POINT

MOST IMPORTANT POINT

CONCLUDING SENTENCE

The cost of having the lanes painted is low compared with the benefits.

PREWRITING, DRAFTING *Details, Order of Importance*

Look at the list of facts, examples, and reasons that you brainstormed. Add details to the list. Evaluate each item—is it a fact or an opinion? Can it be used to support an opposing point of view? Do the facts effectively prove your point? Then arrange the items in order of importance. You may want to use index cards like the ones on the preceding page. Use your ordered notes and index cards to write a draft of your persuasive paragraph.

COMPUTER TIP

If you are working at your computer and have an Internet connection, you can quickly find other word choices to use in persuasive writing by going to an online version of *Roget's Thesaurus*. All you have to do is type a word and press Enter. A whole list of options for synonyms is returned to you. You may want to bookmark this page as a tool you can return to time and again.

http://www.thesaurus.com

Be sure to choose a synonym that makes sense in the sentence.

Prewriting Workshop
Drafting Workshop ▶
Revising Workshop
Editing Workshop
Publishing Workshop

Adjectives and Adverbs

In persuasive writing, you may need to compare two or more things using adjectives and adverbs. John F. Kennedy used all three degrees of comparison for adjectives and adverbs, as shown in the examples below.

- Use the positive degree if no comparison is made.

  ADJECTIVE   Its hazards are **hostile** to us all.

  ADVERB   This country was conquered by those who moved **forward**—and so will space.

- Use the comparative degree to compare two people, things, or actions.

  adverbs ——— Some 40 of them were "made in the United States of America" and they were **far more**
  adjective ——— **sophisticated** and supplied **far more** knowledge . . . than those of the Soviet Union.

- Use the superlative degree when comparing two or more people, things, or actions.

  adverb——— . . . And, therefore, as we set sail we ask
  adjectives——— God's blessing on the **most hazardous** and **dangerous** and **greatest** adventure on which man has ever embarked.

Using the correct degree of comparison for adverbs and adjectives will help you as you draft and revise your persuasive paragraphs.

Process of Writing Persuasive Paragraphs

When you plan a persuasive paragraph, think about the people who disagree with you. Why do they see things differently? If you were debating with these people, what points would they probably make to support their viewpoint? Having solid arguments to counter opposing viewpoints will help you win your case.

Persuading with Examples

Prewriting

Imagine that you are having a debate with a friend about which television show is best. You think that your favorite show is best because the characters are true to life. Plan a persuasive paragraph by listing all the important characters in your show, and then arrange your list in the order of least to most important. For each character, give several examples that show how he or she is true to life.

Drafting

Use your notes and the following topic sentence to write a draft of a persuasive paragraph.

Topic Sentence	[Your favorite show] is the best show on television because its characters are true to life.

Revising Conferencing

Exchange papers with a classmate. Read your partner's paper carefully. Does it convince you that his or her choice could be considered the best show on television? Tell your partner what is good about the paragraph and what could be improved. After your paper has been returned, revise your paragraph to make it as convincing as possible.

PORTFOLIO

Persuading with Facts

Prewriting

A young boy you know often stays up late at night reading adventure stories. When he does, he seems tired and cranky the next day. Think of how to advise this boy to get to sleep at an earlier hour. The following facts will help you back up your advice. Arrange the facts in a logical order.

- Heartbeat slows down to about 56 beats per minute during sleep.

- Lungs and other organs rest during sleep.

- People who do not dream enough during the night do not perform well during the day.

Now think about how the boy might respond to your advice. Make a list of objections he might have. Prepare yourself to answer his objections with convincing solutions.

Drafting

Using your prewriting notes, draft a paragraph advising the boy on the benefits of sufficient sleep. Be sure to include answers to any objections he may have.

Revising Conferencing

Exchange papers with a classmate. As you read your partner's paper, pretend you are the boy receiving advice. Would you be convinced? Tell your partner why or why not. When your own paper is returned, revise it as needed to make it more persuasive.

PORTFOLIO

Persuading with Reasons

Prewriting

Think of a club you would like to join. Imagine that you need to write a letter requesting that the club accept you as a member. Brainstorm a list of reasons why the club should let you join its ranks. Perhaps it is a stamp club and you have a great collection. Maybe it is a skateboarding club and you have some great moves.

Drafting

Using your list of reasons, draft a letter requesting that the club grant you membership. Use compelling reasons and wording. Be sure to use logical order and transitions.

Revising   Conferencing

Exchange paragraphs with a partner. Read your partner's paper carefully. Tell your partner whether or not you agree with the order of importance given to each reason. When your own paper is returned, revise it as needed for clarity.

PORTFOLIO

Evaluation Checklist for Revising

Checking Your Paragraph

✓ Does your topic sentence state an opinion? *(pages C302–C303)*

✓ Did you use facts, examples, and reasons to support your position? *(pages C303 and C304–C308)*

✓ Are your supporting points organized in order of importance? *(pages C309–C310)*

✓ Did you use transitions to give your paragraph coherence? *(page C309)*

✓ Does your paragraph have unity? *(pages C171–C172)*

✓ Does your concluding sentence make a final appeal? *(page C303)*

Checking Your Sentences

✓ Do your sentences have varied beginnings and lengths? *(pages C66–C72)*

Checking Your Words

✓ Did you use lively, specific words? *(page C40)*

Process of Writing a Persuasive Paragraph

PREWRITING

- Use brainstorming, freewriting, or clustering to identify issues about which you have strong opinions. *(pages C9–C13)*
- Choose one subject and identify the audience you want to persuade. Write a topic sentence that accurately presents your opinion. *(pages C302–C303)*
- Brainstorm a list of supporting ideas. *(pages C304–C307)*
- Evaluate your evidence. *(page C308)*
- Develop a defensible argument by considering pros and cons, by supporting the topic sentence with facts and examples, and by acknowledging any weak points in your argument. *(pages C304–C308)*
- Organize the details of your argument into an outline in order of importance. *(pages C309–C310)*

DRAFTING

- Write an introduction that includes your topic sentence. *(pages C136–C137)*
- Use your outline to write the body of your paragraph. *(page C138)*
- Use transitions to link your thoughts. *(page C309)*
- Add a concluding statement. *(page C303)*

REVISING

- Revise your composition to make it as persuasive as possible. Use the **Evaluation Checklist for Revising**. *(page C316)*

EDITING

- Proofread and edit your work for grammar, usage, spelling, and mechanics.

PUBLISHING

- Make a neat final copy of your composition in standard manuscript form, and share it with an interested reader.

Time Out to Reflect

In what ways have your persuasive skills deepened as a result of completing this chapter? If you have written a persuasive composition earlier in the year, take it out and read it again. How does it differ from the work you just completed? What did you do better in your most recent work? Is there anything you did better before? What would you like to improve upon further? Record your thoughts in the Learning Log section of your **journal**.

A Writer Writes

An Editorial

Purpose: to convince community members to support your plan for a community project

Audience: community residents

Prewriting

President John F. Kennedy's speech *(page C293)* makes a bold case for his plan of action. Reread the speech and think about how President Kennedy made his argument appealing. What role did the persuasive writing skills you have just learned play in the effectiveness of the speech?

Think of a way in which community residents, despite their diverse backgrounds, could come together for a community project. Maybe it could be by using less money for decorations on lampposts and more money for feeding hungry children. Maybe it could be a partnership between the police department and a youth organization to go door to door with information on preventing gun violence. The possibilities are limited only by your imagination.

Before you formulate a recommendation, read some magazine and newspaper articles that describe what people in your community have already accomplished to help those in need or to make more positive changes. Then develop a plan that would be likely to work as a project in your community. Think about who would need to be persuaded for your plan to succeed. Write a working topic sentence that makes clear the purpose of your editorial and establishes your main idea.

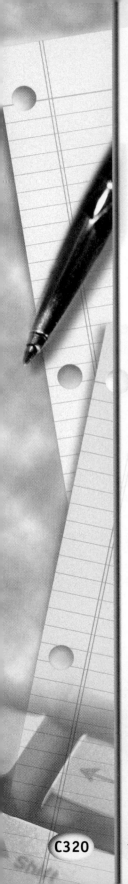

Gather more information if necessary—listing both the pros and the cons of your position. Be sure to revise your topic sentence if necessary to cover all the facts. Then choose an organizing scheme and outline the body of your editorial.

Drafting

Write the first draft of your editorial, beginning with an introduction that will capture your readers' attention. Then, after you write a strong introduction around your topic sentence, follow your outline to develop the arguments that support your opinion in the body paragraphs. You might want to use examples of similar projects that have succeeded in other communities. Remember to confront opposing arguments and show why your arguments are more reasonable. In your conclusion reaffirm your position and suggest ways that convinced readers can take action.

Revising

Set your editorial aside for a day or so and then read it over carefully. Following the <u>Evaluation Checklist for Revising</u> on page C316, revise your editorial to make it as persuasive as possible.

Editing

Proofread and edit your work for grammar, usage, spelling and mechanics.

Publishing

Prepare a final copy of your editorial and add a cover letter to it, explaining how and why you wrote it. Then send both to the editor of your local newspaper.

Representing in Different Ways

From Print . . .

. . . to Visuals

From the information in the letter, create a bar graph (with three sets of bars) that illustrates Fernando's and Juan's care of the iguana. Use different color bars for each of them and remember to label your graph.

3332 Patton Street
Birmingham, AL 35226
July 9, 2000

Dear Mom and Dad,

Thank you for my recent allowance. I really can use it. I am writing because I feel that I earn my allowance a little better than Fernando does. In fact I believe that Fernando should not get an allowance at all. Ever since we got the iguana, Fernando has only fed it 25% of the time. I have fed it 75% of the time. I clean its cage 80% of the time, while he only cleans it 20% of the time. Like the pet store suggested, I have petted and sung to it 100% of the time while Fernando has not done it once. As you can see, Fernando is not a responsible pet owner. Besides, I am your son and Fernando is only the family dog. I would like him to stop receiving an allowance right away.

Sincerely,
Juan

From Visuals . . .

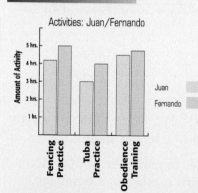

Activities: Juan/Fernando

. . . to Print

As Fernando, use the information in the above graph to write a letter to Juan's parents, convincing them that you do not have the same amount of time that Juan does to take care of the iguana.

- Which strategies can be used for creating both written and visual representations? Which strategies apply to one, not both? Which type of representation is more effective?
- Draw a conclusion and write briefly about the differences between written ideas and visual representations.

Writing For Oral Presentation
Persuasive Speech

The school water balloon team has not won a game all season. This afternoon you play the best water balloon team in the district.

Prepare a speech to give to your teammates to convince them of the importance of winning this game. Take opposing views (such as the view that with such an embarrassing record, it will not matter anyway) into consideration. Deliver your speech to your classmates who will act as the team.

What strategies did you use to persuade your teammates?

> You can find information on preparing speeches on pages C433–C443.

Writing in the Workplace
Persuasive Note

One of the houses on your paper route is the house of Ms. Robin. Ms. Robin likes her paper to be placed in her mailbox, which you are happy to do. The only problem is that Ms. Robin lives in a tree house and you have to climb the tree to get to her mailbox.

Write a note to Ms. Robin persuading her to move her mailbox down to the ground. Support your opinion with reasons and examples. Anticipate any objections she might have and address them. Be sure to organize your ideas in order from most to least important. Remember to avoid highly charged or emotional language.

What strategies did you use to persuade Ms. Robin to relocate her mailbox?

Assess Your Learning

The Recreation Commission of your town has recently established a Teen Center. You think it is a good idea, but the members of the commission have used the budget money to set up activities like Pick-up Sticks and Go Fish. They have also installed a television that only picks up one station—the all-macramé channel.

▶ Think of some ways the Teen Center could be improved. Pepare some remarks to deliver to the Recreation Commission peruading them to make the Center more interesting to teens.

▶ When preparing your remarks, be sure you create a clear, lcical structure and support your points adequately. Use polite, resonable language. Anticipate any objections they may have and addrs them without taking weight away from your own points.

▶ *Before You Write* Consider the following questions:
What is the *subject?*
What is the *occasion?*
Who is the *audience?*
What is the *purpose?*

▶ *After You Write* Evaluate your work using the following criteria:
- Does the topic sentence state an opinion?
- Were facts, examples, and reasons used to support the position?
- Are supporting points organized in order of importance?
- Are opposing possible objections anticipated and addressed?
- Are transitions used to give the work coherence?
- Does the concluding sentence make a final appeal?
- Are the conventions of grammar, spelling, and mechanics followed?

Write briefly on how well you did. Point out your strengths and areas for improvement.

a blind plunge their strategy, raw youth their protection and benediction.[2]

Now and again the boy heard a vast wind come up, that gently stirred the air. But he knew what it was, the army here, the army there, whispering to itself in the dark. Some men talking to others, others murmuring to themselves, and all so quiet it was like a natural element arisen from south or north with the motion of the earth toward dawn.

What the men whispered the boy could only guess, and he guessed that it was: Me, I'm the one, I'm the one of all the rest won't die. I'll live through it. I'll go home. The band will play. And I'll be there to hear it.

Yes, thought the boy, that's all very well for them, they can give as good as they get!

For with the careless bones of the young men harvested by night and bindled[3] around campfires were the similarly strewn steel bones of their rifles, with bayonets fixed like eternal lighting lost in the orchard grass.

Me, thought the boy, I got only a drum, two sticks to beat it, and no shield.

There wasn't a man-boy on this ground tonight did not have a shield he cast, riveted, or carved himself on his way to his first attack, compounded of remote[4] but nonetheless firm and fiery family devotion, flag-blown patriotism, and cocksure immortality strengthened by the touchstone of very real gunpowder, ramrod, minié ball,[5] and flint. But without these last the boy felt his family move yet farther off away in the dark, as if one of those great prairie-burning trains had chanted them away never to return, leaving him with this drum which was worse than a toy in the game to be played tomorrow or some day much too soon.

---

[2] **benediction** (bĕn ĭ dĭk´shən) *n*.: Blessing, especially one given at the close of a religious service.

[3] **bindled** *adj*.: Bedded.

[4] **remote** *adj*.: Located far away.

[5] **minié ball** (mĭn´ ē-ā bôl) *n*.: Cone-shaped rifle bullet that expands when fired.

The boy turned on his side. A moth brushed his face, but it was peach blossom. A peach blossom flicked him, but it was a moth. Nothing stayed put. Nothing had a name. Nothing was as it once was.

If he lay very still, when the dawn came up and the soldiers put on their bravery with their caps, perhaps they might go away, the war with them, and not notice him lying small here, no more than a toy himself.

"Well, by God, now," said a voice.

The boy shut up his eyes, to hide inside himself, but it was too late. Someone, walking by in the night, stood over him.

"Well," said the voice quietly, "here's a soldier crying *before* the fight. Good. Get it over. Won't be time once it all starts."

And the voice was about to move on when the boy, startled, touched the drum at his elbow. The man above, hearing this, stopped. The boy could feel his eyes, sense him slowly bending near. A hand must have come down out of the night, for there was a little rat-tat as the fingernails brushed and the man's breath fanned his face.

"Why, it's the drummer boy, isn't it?"

The boy nodded, not knowing if his nod was seen. "Sir, is that *you?*" he asked.

"I assume it is." The man's knees cracked as he bent still closer.

He smelled as all fathers should smell, of salt sweat, ginger tobacco, horse and boot leather, and the earth he walked upon. He had many eyes. No, not eyes, brass buttons that watched the boy.

He could only be, and was, the General.

"What's your name, boy?" he asked.

"Joby," whispered the boy, starting to sit up.

"All right, Joby, don't stir." A hand pressed his chest gently, and the boy relaxed. "How long you been with us, Joby?"

"Three weeks, sir."

"Run off from home or joined legitimately,[6] boy?"

Silence.

"Damn-fool question," said the General. "Do you shave yet, boy? Even more of a damn-fool. There's your cheek, fell right off the tree overhead. And the others here not much older. Raw, raw, damn raw, the lot of you. You ready for tomorrow or the next day, Joby?"

"I think so, sir."

"You want to cry some more, go on ahead. I did the same last night."

"*You*, sir?"

"God's truth. Thinking of everything ahead. Both sides figuring the other side will just give up, and soon, and the war done in weeks and us all home. Well, that's not how it's going to be. And maybe that's why I cried."

"Yes, sir," said Joby.

The General must have taken out a cigar now, for the dark was suddenly filled with the smell of tobacco unlit as yet, but chewed as the man thought what next to say.

"It's going to be a crazy time," said the General. "Counting both sides, there's a hundred thousand men, give or take a few thousand out there tonight, not one as can spit a sparrow off a tree, or knows a horse clod from a minié ball. Stand up, bare the breast, ask to be a target, thank them and sit down, that's us, that's them. We should turn tail and train four months, they should do the same. But here we are, taken

---

[6] **legitimately** (lə jĭt′ ə mĭt lē) *adv.*: In a lawful manner; in accordance with the law.

with spring fever, and thinking it blood lust, taking our sulfur with cannons instead of with molasses as it should be, going to be a hero, going to live forever. And I can see all of them over there nodding agreement, save the other way around. It's wrong, boy, it's wrong as a head put on hind side front and a man marching backward through life. It will be a double massacre if one of their itchy generals decides to picnic his lads on our grass. More innocents will get shot out of pure enthusiasm than ever got shot before. Owl Creek was full of boys splashing around in the noonday sun just a few hours ago. I fear it will be full of boys again, just floating, at sundown tomorrow, not caring where the tide takes them."

The General stopped and made a little pile of winter leaves and twigs in the darkness, as if he might at any moment strike fire to them to see his way through the coming days when the sun might not show its face because of what was happening here and just beyond.

The boy watched the hand stirring the leaves and opened his lips to say something, but did not say it. The General heard the boy's breath and spoke himself.

"Why am I telling you this? That's what you wanted to ask, eh? Well, when you got a bunch of wild horses on a loose rein somewhere, somehow you got to bring order, rein them in. These lads, fresh out of the milkshed, don't know what I know, and I can't tell them: men actually die, in war. So each is his own army. I got to make *one* army of them. And for that, boy, I need you."

"Me!" The boy's lips barely twitched.

"Now, boy," said the General quietly, "you are the heart of the army. Think of that. You're the heart of the army. Listen, now."

And, lying there, Joby listened.

And the General spoke on.

If he, Joby, beat slow tomorrow, the heart would beat slow in the men. They would lag by the wayside. They would drowse in the fields on their muskets. They would sleep forever, after that, in those same fields, their hearts slowed by a drummer boy and stopped by enemy lead.

But if he beat a sure, steady, ever faster rhythm, then, then their knees would come up in a long line down over that hill, one knee after the other, like a wave on the ocean shore! Had he seen the ocean ever? Seen the waves rolling in like a well-ordered cavalry charge to the sand? Well, that was it, that's what he wanted, that's what was needed! Joby was his right hand and his left. He gave the orders, but Joby set the pace!

So bring the right knee up and the right foot out and the left knee up and the left foot out. One following the other in good time, in brisk time. Move the blood up the body and make the head proud and the spine stiff and the jaw resolute.[7] Focus the eye and set the teeth, flare the nostrils and tighten the hands, put steel armor all over the men, for blood moving fast in them does indeed make men feel as if they'd put on steel. He must keep at it, at it! Long and steady, steady and long! Then, even though shot or torn, those wounds got in hot blood—in blood he'd helped stir—would feel less pain. If their blood was cold, it would be more than slaughter, it would be murderous nightmare and pain best not told and no one to guess.

The General spoke and stopped, letting his breath slack off. Then, after a moment, he said, "So there you are, that's it. Will you do that, boy? Do you know now you're general of the army when the General's left behind?"

The boy nodded mutely.

"You'll run them through for me then, boy?"

"Yes, sir."

---

[7] **resolute** (rĕz´ ə lōōt´) *adj.*: Having or showing strong determination.

"Good. And, God willing, many nights from tonight, many years from now, when you're as old or far much older than me, when they ask you what you did in this awful time, you will tell them—one part humble and one part proud—'I was the drummer boy at the battle of Owl Creek,' or the Tennessee River, or maybe they'll just name it after the church there. 'I was the drummer boy at Shiloh.' Good grief, that has a beat and sound to it fitting for Mr. Longfellow. 'I was the drummer boy at Shiloh.' Who will ever hear those words and not know you, boy, or what you thought this night, or what you'll think tomorrow or the next day when we must get up on our legs and *move!*"

The general stood up. "Well, then. God bless you, boy. Good night."

"Good night, sir."

And, tobacco, brass, boot polish, salt sweat and leather, the man moved away through the grass.

Joby lay for a moment, staring but unable to see where the man had gone.

He swallowed. He wiped his eyes. He cleared his throat. He settled himself. Then, at last, very slowly and firmly, he turned the drum so that it faced up toward the sky.

He lay next to it, his arm around it, feeling the tremor, the touch, the muted thunder as, all the rest of the April night in the year 1862, near the Tennessee River, not far from the Owl Creek, very close to the church named Shiloh, the peach blossoms fell on the drum.

Thinking as a Writer

Identifying Challenges of Writing Historical Fiction

- What challenges do you think the author of "The Drummer Boy of Shiloh" faced in writing this story?
- Was he able to make the story realistic and believable? Which details are effective? How could he add to the realism of the story?
- List three questions you have about the characters, setting, or dialogue, or about the choices the writer made in telling the story the way he did. Share your questions with your classmates and discuss your responses.

Creating a Dramatic Interpretation

Oral Expression Together with two other classmates, choose a section of the story that includes narrative and dialogue. Create a dramatic interpretation of this part of the story.

- Identify any words in the passage that you do not understand or do not know how to pronounce. Look them up in a dictionary for meaning and pronunciation.
- Decide who will read the narrative, and the other two roles. Read the passage aloud together, with the assigned roles.
- Listen carefully to each other. Do you each succeed in creating a distinct voice for your role? Brainstorm criteria for improving your readings. Experiment with elements such as rate of speaking, volume, pitch, and tone.
- Present your dramatic interpretation in front of another group, or to the whole class.

Interpreting Narrative Elements
in a Historical Image

Viewing The Civil War was one of the first conflicts to
be documented by photography, a new invention
at that time.

- Look closely at this photograph of Civil War soldiers.
  What word or words would you use to describe the
  mood of this scene? What specific details contribute
  to this mood?
- Choose one of the figures in the scene who looks
  interesting to you. How old do you think this
  person was at the time of the photograph? What do
  you imagine he was thinking when this picture
  was taken?

The Power of Writing About Literature

You have just read a work of literature—a short story. Whether you realized it or not, you have also already begun to think critically about it, by thinking about the characters' voices, generating questions about their roles, and by examining a visual portrayal of a scene.

Uses of Writing About Literature

Here are some examples of writing about literature.

- **You are taking a standardized test that** asks you to read and analyze a literary passage.

- **A political candidate uses a famous quote** from literature in a speech.

- **Critics write reviews of books, movies, and even television programs.**

- **You want to tell your friends about a book** that you think is superb.

Developing Your Skills of Writing About Literature

A good way to understand and appreciate a literary work is to write a sketch of one of the characters in the work. To back up a statement you make about the character, you use details from the story itself. To begin a character sketch, note your personal reactions to the characters in the story. Then learn to recognize the clues that the author provides to the characters' traits.

Your Writer's Journal

Discover your taste in literature. In your journal, record your responses to any work of literature you are reading. Begin with the following suggestions in response to "The Drummer Boy of Shiloh."

- Tell what you liked or disliked about what you read.
- Write about anything that left a strong impression or that puzzled you.
- Keep track of how your feelings about the characters change.
- Make predictions about what you think will happen next.

 Responding from Personal Experience

When you read a book or story for the first time, you are busy responding to it whether or not you are aware of it. For example, you are probably forming judgments about each character as you read. You are most likely rooting for the "good guys" and hoping the "bad guys" will get caught in the end.

Often there are characters in the work whom you begin to care about strongly.

Much of your response to the story is based on your own personal experiences. One character, for example, might remind you of yourself when you faced a similar problem or conflict. Another might remind you of a kind uncle who always made you feel comfortable. Still another might call to mind a friend who hurt your feelings or treated you unfairly. How you feel about characters in a work is often related to how you feel about the people they remind you of.

Strategies for Responding from Personal Experience

The following strategies will help you understand your personal responses to a literary work.

> **Personal Response Strategies**

1. In your **journal**, freewrite answers to the following questions:

   • Where in the poem, story, novel, or play do you see yourself? In other words, what character do you identify with? Do the other characters remind you of other people you know?

   • How does the main character make you feel? Why?

   • If you were a character in the work, would you have behaved differently? Whose behaviors in the story puzzle you?

   • What experiences from your own life come to mind as you read this work? How did those experiences make you feel?

2. Write a "personal response statement." In this statement, explain your feelings about the main character.

3. In small discussion groups, share your various reactions to the above questions. Feel free to adjust your reactions if your classmates suggest ideas that make good sense to you. After the discussion, write freely about how, if at all, your ideas about the work changed after talking them over with your classmates.

PRACTICE YOUR SKILLS

● *Responding from Personal Experience*

In your journal, freewrite answers to the following questions:

- What do you think of Joby? Does he remind you of anyone you know? How would you describe his personality? What do you think of the General? Does *he* remind you of anybody you know?

- When you were reading the story, did you predict the outcome? If not, why did you think it would end differently?

- Write about times in your life that came to mind when you read the story.

Communicate Your Ideas

PREWRITING *Personal Response*

Write a personal response statement. In this statement, explain your feelings about one of the main characters from the excerpt from *Julie of the Wolves* on pages C183–C187. Save your work for later use.

SAVE YOUR WORK

Responding from Literary Knowledge

To understand a literary work, you can use your knowledge of literary works in general. You know, for example, that most short stories have elements that work together. By studying these elements and their impact on the whole story, you can add to your understanding of a story.

> ## Literary Knowledge Strategies
>
> - Analyze the plot of the story. Identify the key events in the story and the meaning or significance of them to the main character. Identify the major conflict in the story.
>
> - What is the main character's motivation, or reason for behaving? How does the main character describe himself or herself? How do other characters describe the main character? How does the narrator of the story describe the main character? What do the main character's words and actions reveal about the character's personality?
>
> - What are the most important details in the setting? What overall feeling do they convey?
>
> - Express in your own words what you think the theme, or message, of the story is. Use details from the story (including the title) to help explain the theme.

Communicate Your Ideas

PREWRITING *Literary Knowledge*

Reread the excerpt from *Julie of the Wolves*. Then freewrite in your **journal** to complete all the strategies above.

Process of Writing a Character Sketch

After exploring your personal responses to a work of literature, you are ready to begin a sketch of one of the characters in the story.

Prewriting — Writing Process

You will no doubt find the greatest amount to say about the main character in a story or book. However, you may feel a closer bond with one of the minor characters and choose to write about that character. One good way to help you choose a subject is to do some prewriting about the character for whom you have the strongest feelings.

Choosing a Character

If a character has succeeded in stirring your feelings, chances are good that you will have much of genuine interest to say about that character. Another good way to choose the character for your paper is to decide which one puzzles you the most. Having to solve a puzzle about why a character behaves as he or she does will make you think (and feel) so keenly that your writing is bound to be good.

Look over your personal and literary responses for ideas that strike you as most interesting. They may help you choose the character to sketch in your composition.

PREWRITING *Character*

Reflect on your personal and literary responses to *Julie of the Wolves*. Which one of the characters did you like more? Which of them characters interests, stirs, or puzzles you more? Choose one for your character sketch. Write a sentence explaining your overall reaction to that character. Save your work for later use.

Gathering Evidence

You already have a fairly clear idea of how you feel about the character you have chosen to write about. On the basis of your personal and literary responses, you have decided whether your character is likable or unlikable, proud or humble, generous or stingy, happy or sad. Now, however, you need to put your reactions to a test. You need to gather evidence from the work itself to support your overall impression of the character.

To gather evidence for a character sketch, read the story, looking for clues about the character's personality. For each clue you come across, create an index card to record the information. Include the page number on which the clue can be found, so you can easily return to that part of the story if you need to. Make a brief note to yourself explaining what you think each clue means.

The clues to a character's personality come in various forms. The following chart summarizes where you might find clues to a character.

> ## Clues to Character Traits

External Traits

- What the character says about himself or herself
- What other characters say about the character
- What the narrator of the story says about the character
- How the character looks (physical description)
- What the character actually does—how he or she solves the main problem in the story

Internal Traits

- What the character thinks about himself or herself
- What other characters think about the character
- What the narrator thinks or implies about the character

The note cards below and on the next page show how one writer looked for clues to the internal and external traits of the character Miyax in the excerpt from *Julie of the Wolves* at the beginning of Chapter 7, Using Description: Observation.

MODEL: Gathering Evidence

Text Portions

"Her hands trembled and her heart-beat quickened, for she was frightened, not so much of the wolves, who were shy and many harpoon-shots away, but because of her desperate predicament. Miyax was lost. She had been lost without food for many sleeps on the North Slope of Alaska. The barren slope stretches for three hundred miles from the Brooks Range to the Arctic Ocean, and for

Note Cards

1. Miyax is afraid. In a desperate and life-threatening predicament, she is alone. The description of her exact geographic location explains just how alone she is: "The barren

slope stretches for three hundred miles from the Brooks Range to the Arctic Ocean, and for more than eight hundred miles from the Chukchi to the Beaufort Sea. No roads cross it;

more than eight hundred miles from the Chukchi to the Beaufort Sea. No roads cross it; ponds and lakes freckle its immensity. Winds scream across it, and the view in every direction is exactly the same. Somewhere in this cosmos was Miyax; and the very life in her body, its spark and warmth, depended upon these wolves for survival. And she was not so sure they would help."
–page C183.

"She had been watching the wolves for two days, trying to discern which of their sounds and movements expressed goodwill and friendship."–page C184.

"Propped on her elbows with her chin in her fists, she stared at the black wolf, trying to catch his eye. She had chosen him because he was much larger than the others, and because he walked like her father, Kapugen, with his head high and his chest out. The black wolf also possessed wisdom, she had observed. The pack looked to him when the wind carried strange scents or the birds cried nervously. If he was alarmed, they were alarmed. If he was calm, they were calm."–page C184.

ponds and lakes freckle its immensity. Winds scream across it, and the view in every direction is exactly the same."—page C183. Miyax is afraid that she may not be able to get the help she needs from the wolves: "...the very life in her body, its spark and warmth, depended upon these wolves for survival. And she was not so sure they would help."—page C183.

2. This passage shows that, despite her situation, Miyax has not lost her wits or panicked. She is very determined and patient. "She had been watching the wolves for two days, trying to discern which of their sounds and movements expressed goodwill and friend-ship."—page C184. She knows that to survive, she has to identify which wolf is the leader and get his help, as her father once did. She draws on past experience. She is also extremely observant. She chooses the black wolf to concentrate on because he is the largest and because "he walked like her father, Kapugen, with his head high and his chest out."—page C184.

She also chooses him because she observes that "he has wisdom"—page C184—and the rest of the wolf pack looks to him for their safety and

leadership. The action she takes, external traits, reflect her inner traits, patient and observant.

PREWRITING *Evidence*

 Look through the excerpt from *Julie of the Wolves* for details about the traits of the character you have chosen to write about. Remember to look for all the different types of clues summarized on page C341. Make note cards like the ones on pages C341–342 for each clue you find, and save your work for later use.

COMPUTER TIP

You can use the Notepad feature on your computer to take notes on clues to a character's personality. You can keep notes there that are separate from your word-processing documents. You will find the notepad feature under Desktop Accessories.

Refining Your Main Idea

Before you began to gather evidence, you had already formed an overall impression of your character. Now that you have looked the story over carefully in search of clues, has your overall impression changed any? Did you find any details that made you rethink your first impression of your character? If so, rewrite the statement explaining your overall reaction to the character until it takes into account all the evidence you uncovered. The resulting statement will serve as the main idea of your character analysis. The following examples show how one writer refined her reaction to Miyax in the excerpt from *Julie of the Wolves* after gathering evidence.

> ORIGINAL REACTION Miyax is frightened and desperate and does not have much chance for survival.

REFINED MAIN IDEA	Miyax is frightened and desperate, but she does not lose her head. She uses her considerable power of observation to take steps for her survival. She has some chance for survival.

Organizing Your Supporting Details

The final step before drafting your character sketch is to organize your supporting details in a logical order. One common approach is to present your supporting evidence in the order in which it appears in the story. Another good approach is to arrange your details in order of importance related to the main idea you are trying to make. Still another way to organize details is according to the different character traits you identify in your character. For example, your main idea may be that your character is outwardly conceited but inwardly shy. So you may wish to arrange your details in an order that first presents evidence for conceit and then presents evidence for shyness.

PRACTICE YOUR SKILLS

● *Organizing Supporting Details*

Use the herringbone organizer on the next page to organize supporting details about the character traits of Joby from "The Drummer Boy of Shiloh." On the diagonal lines, write down character traits. On the horizontal lines, list details from the story that support that trait.

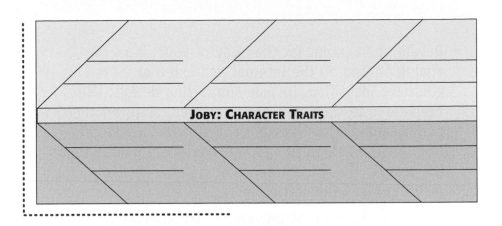

JOBY: CHARACTER TRAITS

Communicate Your Ideas

PREWRITING *Supporting Details*

 Review the writing you have done so far. Examine your evidence and refine your main idea if necessary. Use a herringbone organizer to arrange your supporting details in a logical order. Save your work for later use.

Drafting ▸ Writing Process

When you write a draft of your character sketch, you may find the following guidelines helpful.

> **Guidelines for Drafting a Character Sketch**
> - Assume your readers are familiar with the work you are writing about.
> - In your introduction, identify the title and author of the work you are discussing, and the character on which you are focusing.
> - Include your main idea somewhere in the introduction, revised if needed and worked in as smoothly as possible.

- Develop paragraphs for the body of your character analysis based on the internal and external traits you have identified. Include supporting details. Use transitions to show how one detail relates to another within paragraphs. Use transitions to move smoothly from one paragraph to another. Use direct quotes from the story if they strengthen your points. Always enclose direct quotes in quotation marks.

- Add a conclusion that provides a strong ending to your character analysis.

- Add a title that makes the focus of your character analysis clear.

- The following character sketch may give you ideas for your own. This sample has already been revised and edited, so it is probably more polished than your first draft will be. Use it, though, as a guide to the different parts of a character sketch.

MODEL: Character Analysis

TITLE:
IDENTIFIES FOCUS

INTRODUCTION:
IDENTIFIES TITLE
AND AUTHOR

MAIN IDEA

FIRST BODY PARAGRAPH:
ANALYZES MIYAX'S
TRAITS AT
BEGINNING OF
SELECTION

A Chance for Survival

At the beginning of the excerpt from *Julie of the Wolves* by Jean Craighead George, Miyax appears to be helpless, in a hopeless situation. By the end of the selection, however, Miyax has proven to be extremely resourceful, patient, and determined. She *has* a chance of survival, and it rests on her own courage and initiative.

Miyax's extreme predicament is presented in the opening paragraphs of the selection. She is lost, "lost without food for many sleeps on the North Slope of Alaska." The author's description of the landscape emphasizes just how alone Miyax is. She writes, "The barren slope stretches for three hundred miles from the Brooks Range to the Arctic Ocean, and for more than eight hundred miles from the Chukchi to the Beaufort Sea. No roads cross it; ponds and lakes freckle its immensity. Winds scream across it, and the view in every direction is exactly the same." It is not surprising then that Miyax is afraid. Her internal state of mind mirrors her external situation. She knows, however, that the wolves can help her. Her father once got help from wolves. Yet she is afraid that she may fail where her father succeeded.

SECOND BODY PARAGRAPH:
ANALYZES MIYAK'S TRAITS IN THE BODY OF THE SELECTION

Miyax's efforts to get the wolves to help her show her internal traits, namely, her patience and power of observation. She has been watching the wolves for two days, "trying to discern which of their sounds and movements expressed goodwill and friendship." She singles out the big black wolf to focus on based on careful observation. He is not only the biggest wolf, but he also walks "like her father, Kapugen, with his head high and his chest out. The black wolf also possessed wisdom, she had observed. The pack looked to him when the wind carried strange scents or the birds cried nervously. If he was alarmed, they were alarmed. If he was calm, they were calm." Miyax draws on past experience to help her in this crisis. She recalls how her father got wolves to help him. She remembers her own experiences with animals. She demonstrates courage and patience.

THIRD BODY PARAGRAPH:
ANALYZES MIYAK'S TRAITS AT END OF SELECTION

By the end of the selection, Miyax has been watching and observing the wolf for a long time. She has observed his every move and tried to get him to look at her. Finally, she begins to speak to him. She tells him how she got lost on the tundra, and how there are none of the familiar signs to guide her. She says, "I am lost and the sun will not set for a month. There is no North Star to guide me." She continues, "At home on Nunivak Island where I was born, the plants and birds pointed the way for wanderers. I thought they did so everywhere . . . and so, great black Amaroq, I'm without a compass." She remembers the moment when she realized she was lost. Fear closes in on her again and she closes her eyes.

CONCLUSION:

REINFORCES
MAIN IDEA

   Just when she thinks her efforts will never be rewarded, she opens her eyes to find the wolf finally looking at her. Her efforts have paid off and she has gained the wolf's trust. In a situation where she has no one to turn to but herself, Miyax draws on her own strengths and knowledge. It now appears that she has a chance for survival.

Communicate Your Ideas

DRAFTING *Character Sketch*

   Using the guidelines on pages C345–C346, draft your character sketch. Save your work for later use.

Evaluating Performances

Some stories can be understood better when they are performed. In fact, both the audience *and* the performer can understand the work more fully because of a performance. An audience can get visual and spoken clues that they wouldn't find by reading. The actor, in turn, can learn from the way a live audience responds to a performance. In the case of a film performance, an actor may learn from movie reviews or from how popular the movie is. In all these ways, a performance of a play, or a movie version of a book can bring the story more fully to life.

Many books are adapted for movies and television. *Stuart Little* is a recent example. The book by E. B. White was popular with children for many years before it was turned into a live-action film in 1999. The character of Stuart Little is played by a computer-generated animation mouse, which makes the performance all that much more interesting. Of course the voice is a real human being.

Media Activity

Rent or check out from your local library either *Stuart Little* or another movie based on a book. Use the following questions to help you as you watch.

- Did the film move you?
- Did the film make confusing parts of the book seem clearer?
- Did the voices give character to the animals that were not apparent in the reading of the book?
- Were camera angles, lighting, sequencing, and music used effectively? How do they contribute to the overall effect?

The following checklist will help you improve your character analysis. You may also wish to share your work with a peer reader to find out where you could strengthen your character's description. Make as many drafts as you feel necessary to refine your main idea and find the supporting details.

> **Evaluation Checklist for Revising**

Checking Your Whole Composition

✓ Do you have a strong introduction that identifies the author, work, and character you will discuss? *(page C345)*

✓ Does your introduction contain a clearly worded statement of your main idea? *(pages C343–C344)*

✓ Does the body of your essay provide ample details from the work to support your main idea? *(pages C340–C342)*

✓ Did you use quotes from the work to strengthen your points? *(page C346)*

✓ Does your conclusion add a strong ending? *(page C346)*

✓ Does your whole composition have unity and coherence? *(pages C171–C172)*

✓ Did you add a title showing the focus of your character sketch? *(page C346)*

Checking Your Paragraphs

✓ Does each paragraph have a topic sentence? *(page C97)*

✓ Is each paragraph unified and coherent? *(pages C171–C172)*

Checking Your Sentences and Words

✓ Are your sentences varied and concise? *(pages C74–C82)*

✓ Did you use lively, specific words? *(page C40)*

REVISING *Conferencing*

Exchange papers with a partner. Comment on the strengths and weaknesses your partner's paper has. Try to be as specific as possible in your suggestions. Keep your partner's comments in mind as you use the checklist to improve your draft. Save your work for later use.

Looping Back to Prewriting and Drafting

Imagine that the character you chose to write about in your character analysis is several years older than when the story took place. Consider how the character may have changed based on the events of the story. Also think about how the character may have changed since the time the story took place. Compose an analysis of this older character. Refer to specific details from the story to support your ideas.

Editing ◄ Writing Process

When you are satisfied with your character analysis, you can begin to polish it for presentation to readers.

Titles

Titles of books, magazines, magazine articles, and other works require special treatment. Some titles are italicized and others are enclosed in quotation marks. Since you cannot write in italics, you should substitute underlining in handwritten work. The following guidelines will help.

- Underline the titles of long works, including books, magazines, newspapers, full-length plays, movies, long poems, operas, symphonies, recordings, paintings, and sculptures.

  EXAMPLE   I took my brother to see <u>The Lion King</u>.

- Use quotation marks to enclose the titles of chapters, articles, stories, one-act plays, short poems, and songs.

  EXAMPLES   I am writing a poem called "The Phantom School Bus."

              I just finished reading "The Drummer Boy of Shiloh" by Ray Bradbury.

              I can play "Stars and Stripes Forever" on the kazoo.

Editing Checklist

✔ Have you enclosed titles of short poems, stories, articles, and songs in quotation marks?

✔ Have you underlined the titles of books, newspapers, movies, and long poems?

EDITING

Reread your paper carefully, looking for errors. Refer to your Personalized Editing Checklist to make sure you are not repeating errors you have made in the past. The checklist on the previous page will help you edit your work. You may also want to ask a classmate to exchange papers with you. In the process of editing your own and each other's papers, use the proofreading marks on page C28 as a quick shorthand. After checking your work in any of the ways suggested here, prepare a final draft in the standard manuscript form shown on pages C31–C32.

Publishing ◄ Writing Process

You have arrived at the final stage of the writing process. You now want to consider how to share your work with the public. Remember when you *begin* a writing assignment, one of the first things you do is consider who your audience might be. Now you want to connect with your audience, and make sure they get a chance to read what you have written. When you have caught any errors you may have made, prepare a neat final copy of your character analysis to present to readers. Some possible ways of publishing your paper are listed on the following page.

PUBLISHING

 • Publish a class anthology of critical compositions. Decide how to organize, illustrate, bind, and circulate your anthology.

• Hold a reader's roundtable. At this meeting, each participant reads his or her character sketch aloud. The rest of the group responds with questions and varying interpretations of the same character.

• Draw a picture of your character in one of the scenes from the selection. Post both your picture and your character sketch on a bulletin board.

Writing a Book Report

Writing a book report is another way for you to write about literature.

A **book report** offers a brief summary of the book and an opinion about the quality of the book.

> **Structure of a Book Report**
>
> **Introduction**
> - gives the title and the author's name
> - tells the subject of the book
> - may give background information about the author
> - identifies the time and location of the story
> - expresses its writer's opinion of the book
>
> **Body**
> - offers specific reasons and examples from the book to support the writer's opinion
> - includes highlights from the book
>
> **Conclusion**
> - restates your opinion in new words
> - adds a strong ending

When you write a book report, assume that your readers are not familiar with the book. Include a brief summary of what the book is about. Do not try to retell the whole story, however. You will soon run out of room for your opinion of the book if you give too many details.

Also, watch your writing for unnecessary shifts in tense. If you are telling what happened to a character, use the present tense and stick to it. ("The main character, Mark, *tries* to find his father and *searches* throughout the West.")

Summarizing

Although you should not try to retell the whole story in your book report, you will need to provide a clear summary of what happens in the book. **Summarizing** means selecting the most important information for a short version of the original.

When you summarize, you actually call on other thinking skills as well. Suppose, for example, you were summarizing the fairy tale "Snow White." You would call on your skill of recalling to bring the whole story to mind. Then you would call on the skill of analyzing to remember all the parts of the story. Next you might use your skill of evaluating to decide which points in each part of the story are most important and which could be left out. Finally, you might use the skill of generalizing to tell the main ideas without having to give all the details.

SUMMARY OF "SNOW WHITE"

"Snow White" is the story of a princess whose evil stepmother, the Queen, is jealous of her beauty. The Queen wants Snow White killed, but the man she hires cannot bring himself to slay the young girl. He leaves her in the forest, where she finds shelter in the home of seven friendly dwarfs. But the Queen finds out in her magic mirror that Snow White is not dead. She puts on a disguise, finds Snow White, and gives her a poisoned apple that causes her to sleep as if dead. Only the kiss of her true love can save her. A handsome prince eventually comes, fights off the forces of evil, and restores Snow White to life with a kiss.

THINKING PRACTICE

Write a brief summary of a fairy tale from your culture. Remember to tell only the most important parts of the story, leaving out most of the details.

INTRODUCTION:

IDENTIFIES TITLE
AND AUTHOR

A Wrinkle in Time by Madeleine L'Engle is a novel about a young girl's voyages through space and time to find her father. Along the way she also finds appreciation of her true self. The girl, Meg, and her brother, Charles Wallace, are accompanied by their friend, Calvin O'Keefe. They are aided by three magical spirits, Mrs. Whatsit, Mrs. Who, and Mrs. Which. These three loving spirits transport the young people through wrinkles in time, called tesseracts. The

STATES AN OPINION

suspenseful story, the variety of interesting characters, and the theme of individuality make A Wrinkle in Time a very enjoyable book.

BODY:

PROVIDES EXAMPLES
AND REASONS TO
SUPPORT OPINION

At the beginning of the book, Meg is a troubled girl. She becomes angry and belligerent in school, and she dislikes her plain appearance and her inability to control her feelings. As the story progresses, she is put to test after test. On the evil planet of Camazotz, where everyone is a carbon copy dominated by a single brain called IT, Meg learns the value of individuality, of just being herself. Later, on a gray planet called Ixchel, she learns the enormous power of love from a sightless, tentacled creature named Aunt Beast. Meg uses her power to love in a daring rescue of Charles Wallace, who is trapped by the evil power of IT on Camazotz.

The interesting characters in the book reinforce the theme of individual differences. Charles Wallace, believed to be dim-witted by some of the neighbors, is actually gifted with special mind-reading powers. Calvin, a popular boy in school, learns that he has been denying an important, different part of himself. The three spirits, Aunt Beast, and a soulful character called the Happy Medium are each unique.

CONCLUSION:

REINFORCES OPINION IN NEW WORDS

When you finish reading <u>A Wrinkle in Time</u> you feel glad that people are as different as they are from one another. You also feel that the powers of love and goodness are strong enough to keep IT and other evils in check.

Writing Tip

When writing a book report, briefly summarize the plot of the book you are writing about, but avoid retelling the whole story.

Time Out to Reflect   Use your knowledge of literary analysis to gauge how your understanding of literature has changed. Date the writing you did for this chapter. Keep a folder where you continue to take notes about books you are reading. Think about how your understanding of literature has deepened. How has this affected the way you read and write about about literature?

Communicate Your Ideas

REVISING *Conferencing*

Use the **Process for Writing a Book Report** guidelines on page C359 to write a book report on one of your favorite books.

Process of Writing a Book Report

Remember that the writing process is fluid. While you are working on drafting or even revising and editing, you can still return to earlier steps to add details or ideas.

PREWRITING

- If you are writing about a nonfiction book, briefly summarize the author's main point in your own words. If you are writing about a fiction book, briefly summarize the story in your own words. Identify the book's overall effect on you. How did you feel when reading it?
- Skim the book, jotting down specific details that lead to your overall feeling about the book.

DRAFTING

- Refer to the chart on page C355 to draft the introduction, body, and conclusion of your book report.

REVISING

- Make sure to summarize the book briefly. *(pages C355–C358)*
- Check for consistent use of present tense. *(page C355)*
- Avoid stating you liked or disliked the book. Instead, offer a specific opinion.

EDITING AND PUBLISHING

- Check your work for errors in grammar, spelling, punctuation, and capitalization.

PUBLISHING

- Make a neat final copy to share with readers. *(pages C31–C32)*

A Writer Writes

A Portrait of a Character

Purpose: **to describe and analyze a character from your favorite television show**

Audience: **a pen pal from a foreign country who may not be familiar with this show or character**

Prewriting

Some television characters are so much a part of everyday life that you might feel as if you know them personally. Imagine you have a pen pal in another country who is not familiar with this television show and your character. Write a brief character analysis of your character for your pen pal. Begin by freewriting or clustering to recall everything you can about this character's personality. What are some of his or her internal and external traits? What details can you think of from different episodes of the show to support your ideas? Also think and write about people in your own life who share some of this character's qualities. How do you feel about them? How do you feel about your character?

Now, write a statement of your main idea about your character. Then arrange the supporting details you have thought of in a logical order.

Drafting

Using your prewriting notes and the guidelines on pages C345–C346, write a draft of your character analysis. Remember you are writing for someone unfamiliar with your subject, so make sure your writing is simple and clear.

Revising

Use the <u>Evaluation Checklist for Revising</u> on page C350 to improve your character analysis as much as you can. Then, with your teacher's permission, exchange papers with a classmate. Ask your partner to pretend to be unfamiliar with the character. Would everything in your character analysis be clear? If not, fix any unclear parts as you see fit.

Editing

Polish your writing, paying special attention to grammar, usage, mechanics, and spelling.

Publishing

Print a copy of your portrait of a character so that a pen pal could read it. If you have a pen pal, send your writing to him or her.

Connection Collection

Representing in Different Ways

From Visuals . . .

Personality:
-Sassy
-Somewhat irresponsible
-Likes to play practical jokes
-Gets angry easily

12-year-old 7th grader

Character: Samantha

Appearance:
Tall
Dark Hair
Bright clothing
Unforgettable Laugh

Conflict:
With her ex-friend, Wanda, who would not let her copy her homework

. . . to Print

Write a character analysis of Samantha, based on the word web above. Use your imagination to elaborate on the clues to her personality, appearance, and conflict shown in the web. Make a prediction, based on your own prior experience, about Samantha's motivations and how she will resolve the conflict.

Wanda was glad to find a seat on the bus by herself that afternoon. She needed time to think. As the other kids chattered and talked about school, Wanda stared out the window and thought about Samantha. In some ways, their friendship had been a total mismatch from the beginning. They were complete opposites. Everything that was important to Wanda was just a joke to Samantha. Wanda cared a great deal about her schoolwork and getting good grades. She cared about the opinion of her parents and teachers. She was quiet and shy in a crowd of people, and especially with boys, while Samantha's laugh could be heard from one end of the hall to the other. Even physically, Wanda and Samantha were opposites. Wanda was short and roundish while Samantha was tall and skinny. Logically speaking, it seemed there was no way to explain their friendship, and Wanda thought that she was probably better off without Samantha. But that didn't change the fact that she felt bad about the whole mess. The truth was, she missed Samantha's friendship.

by Tayesha Morton

. . . to Visuals

Create your own word web to diagram a character analysis of Wanda. Label the web parts by character trait, and then list the specific details from the paragraph above that illustrate that trait.

- Which strategies can be used for creating both written and visual representations? Which strategies apply to one, not both? Which type of representation is more effective?
- Draw a conclusion and write briefly about the differences between written ideas and visual representations.

Writing in the Workplace
Descriptive Movie Review

Your older brother has come up with a great idea to make money: he is starting a newspaper, *The Cucumber Bulletin*, that will be distributed for free. All costs are to be paid by advertisers who are hoping to gain access to a segment of the local youth market. Your brother invites you to write the movie reviews, knowing how much time you spend in the theater on weekends.

> **Write a review of a movie you have seen recently for *The Cucumber Bulletin*. Tell whether you liked the movie or not, and why. Then summarize the plot. Be sure to support your points with descriptions of the main characters, the setting, and the main conflict.**
>
> **What strategies did you use to convey your opinion about the movie?**

Writing in Academic Areas
Character Analysis Essay

A national software company has announced an upcoming competition for seventh grade students. The guidelines state that entrants should write an essay about a character from a book who provides a good role model for students. The essay writers are to describe why this character is such a good role model. One hundred winners of the contest get a new home computer, and you really want to win!

> **Write a draft of your essay for the company's contest. Choose a character from literature, and draft a topic sentence that explains your feelings about this character. Jot down a list of admirable character traits and specific details that reveal those traits.**
>
> **What strategies did you use to analyze your character?**

For extra credit at school, you volunteer one hour a week as an assistant to Mrs. Pickles, a third grade teacher. It is often your job to read to the third graders, as well as to recommend books for them. Lately, the young students have been asking you questions such as, "If fiction isn't true, why do we have to read it?" When you posed this same question to your seventh grade teacher, he decided to assign it as the topic of your end-of-year composition.

▶ **Write the composition for your class assignment. Directly address the question posed by the third grade students, and explain your feelings about the insights you have gained from fiction. Organize your supporting details, gathering specific examples from literature to back up your points. Consider the elements of plot, character, and setting in the books you choose to answer the question.**

▶ *Before You Write* **Consider the following questions:**
What is the *subject?*
What is the *occasion?*
Who is the *audience?*
What is the *purpose?*

▶ *After You Write* **Evaluate your work using the following criteria:**
- Have you chosen a main idea for your composition and refined it to fit the topic?
- Have you accurately addressed the assignment and written the composition in a voice and style appropriate to the audience and purpose?
- Are your ideas about the importance of fiction organized in a logical and coherent manner? Have you included appropriate information to support your ideas?
- Does the body of your composition provide ample details from the books you chose to support your main idea? Have you used quotes from the books to support your ideas?
- Have you used writing to discover and support what you know and what you need to learn about the topic of the importance of fiction?

Write briefly on how well you did. Point out your strengths and areas for improvement.

CHAPTER 12

Reports

You live in an exciting world where amazing things happen every day. Exploration and learning are big parts of this world, but you may not be able to investigate, in person, all the subjects that interest you. In that case, you can turn to a report. Reports are collections of facts—information gathered under one roof. They are written storehouses of information. They are in books, magazines, E-mail messages, newspapers, newsletters, and on the Internet. The weather forecast on television is an example of an oral report.

Being able to organize information into a report is helpful in today's world. You live in a time when information is becoming increasingly available. This availability may make researching facts easier, but it also means you have to choose your facts carefully and be able to present them in a way that is logical and easy to understand. A good report does just that.

Reading with a Writer's Eye

The following selection about mummies is from nationalgeographic.com, the National Geographic Society's Website. As you read through the pages, think about what types of sources may have been used in preparing this report. How do you think the author went about organizing the information into the format you see presented?

nationalgeographic.com

SITE INDEX ▼

Mummies UNMASKED

ANCIENT EGYPTIANS BELIEVED THERE WAS LIFE AFTER DEATH. TO PREPARE FOR THE AFTERLIFE, EGYPTIANS WHO COULD AFFORD IT HAD THEIR DEAD BODIES MADE INTO MUMMIES. READ ON TO GET THE WRAP ON MUMMY MAKING.

Click

The priests who mummified King Tutankhamun 3,300 years ago placed this mask over his face. The golden portrait gives us a clue as to what the boy-king looked like.

Mask photograph by Kenneth Garrett; mummy photograph by the Metropolitan Museum of Art.

---

nationalgeographic.com

SITE INDEX ▼

Mummies UNMASKED

ANCIENT EGYPTIANS BELIEVED THERE WAS LIFE AFTER DEATH. TO PREPARE FOR THE AFTERLIFE, EGYPTIANS WHO COULD AFFORD IT HAD THEIR DEAD BODIES MADE INTO MUMMIES. READ ON TO GET THE WRAP ON MUMMY MAKING.

The priests who mummified King Tutankhamun 3,300 years ago placed this mask over his face. The golden portrait gives us a clue as to what the boy-king looked like.

Mask photograph by Kenneth Garrett; mummy photograph by the Metropolitan Museum of Art.

nationalgeographic.com

SITE INDEX ▼

Mummies UNMASKED

Sometime around 2,500 B. C. Egyptians began to mummify, or preserve, the dead bodies of kings and other important people. The practice continued for 3,000 years. The rituals of mummy-making and burial reflected the Egyptians' belief in life after death. Egyptians believed a person had not only a body but a spirit. After death a person's spirit could go on living if it had a body in which to dwell. The body, however, had to preserve the dead person's appearance. A mummified body did just that. Preparing mummies was a religious rite. A priest wearing a jackal-shaped mask—symbol of Anubis, god of embalming—directed the ritual. Other priests treated the body to protect it from decay. That process was called embalming. Priests drained the fluids and wrapped the corpse in cloth. <u>CHECK OUT A MUMMY IN THE MAKING.</u>
Photograph by Kenneth Garrett

Pharaoh Seti I had a rough journey to the afterlife 3,200 years ago. Ancient grave robbers accidentally separated his head from his body. Priests later put the mummy back together.

Click

Mummies UNMASKED

JOIN THE TALK BOARD!

In an artist's portrayal of an ancient ritual, priests put the finishing touches on a mummy. Scroll over the picture to learn what went into mummy making.

Click an item to learn more!

3

1

5

6

4

2

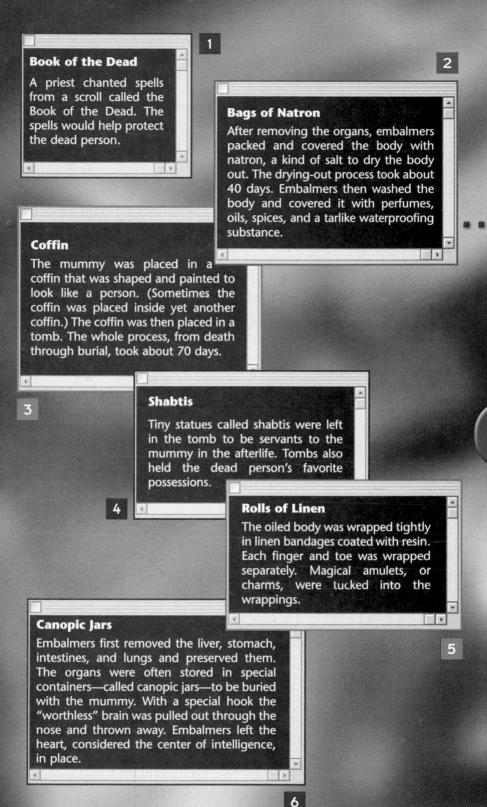

1

Book of the Dead

A priest chanted spells from a scroll called the Book of the Dead. The spells would help protect the dead person.

2

Bags of Natron

After removing the organs, embalmers packed and covered the body with natron, a kind of salt to dry the body out. The drying-out process took about 40 days. Embalmers then washed the body and covered it with perfumes, oils, spices, and a tarlike waterproofing substance.

Coffin

The mummy was placed in a coffin that was shaped and painted to look like a person. (Sometimes the coffin was placed inside yet another coffin.) The coffin was then placed in a tomb. The whole process, from death through burial, took about 70 days.

3

Shabtis

Tiny statues called shabtis were left in the tomb to be servants to the mummy in the afterlife. Tombs also held the dead person's favorite possessions.

4

Rolls of Linen

The oiled body was wrapped tightly in linen bandages coated with resin. Each finger and toe was wrapped separately. Magical amulets, or charms, were tucked into the wrappings.

Canopic Jars

Embalmers first removed the liver, stomach, intestines, and lungs and preserved them. The organs were often stored in special containers—called canopic jars—to be buried with the mummy. With a special hook the "worthless" brain was pulled out through the nose and thrown away. Embalmers left the heart, considered the center of intelligence, in place.

5

6

Thinking as a Writer

Evaluating the Effectiveness of a Report

- What types of references and resources may have been used in gathering information for this report?
- How did the author organize the information? Did this organization help make the report clear? How?
- How did the author ask questions and answer them? Were there any questions left unanswered?

Distinguishing and Complementing Tone

Oral Expression
- Take turns with a partner reading sections of the report aloud. Listen as your partner reads.
- What is the author's tone in the report? Give reasons for your answer.
- Suppose this article is to be used as a script for a television program on mummies. You are the producer of the program. With the tone of the report in mind, what type of music would you choose as a soundtrack for the program? Explain your answer.

Evaluating Purpose and Effectiveness of Images

Viewing Visual images are often included when a Website is designed.
- Reread "Mummies Unmasked" from the National Geographic Society's Website, paying special attention to how the visuals are used there.
- Do the visuals in this Website report serve the author's purpose? If so, what is that purpose?
- Would the report have been as effective without the use of visuals? Why or why not?
- Choose one of the images from the article. Suppose this picture had not been available to use in the report. How might the author have explained in words the information presented visually? Would the written version be as effective as the image?

Process of Writing a Report

When you want to give a factual summary of the research you have done on a particular subject, you write a report. Learning to research and write a report will help you develop skills that can be used in any kind of factual or objective writing and research.

A **report** is a composition based on information from books, magazines, the Internet, and other sources.

Your Writer's Journal

Subjects for reports can be found almost any place and at any time. You may come across an interesting subject while browsing through a magazine or newspaper, surfing the Internet, reading a book, watching television—even by talking with and interviewing people. You may think of an interesting subject while walking down the street. When a subject comes to mind, write it down in your journal. Also jot down anything you already know about the subject as well as any questions you have about it.

Structure of a Report

The three main parts of a report are the introduction, the body, and the conclusion. In addition, a report has a title and a page that lists your sources of information. Each part of the report has a special purpose.

STRUCTURE OF A REPORT

TITLE	• suggests the subject of the report
INTRODUCTION	• captures the reader's attention
	• provides any background information that the reader may need to know
	• contains a sentence expressing the main idea of the report
BODY	• supports the main idea stated in the introduction
	• follows the order of your outline
	• includes specific information from your sources
CONCLUSION	• brings the report to a close
	• summarizes the main idea
	• includes a comment that shows the importance of your subject
SOURCES PAGE	• lists your sources of information
	• appears at the end of the report

Prewriting Writing Process

In some ways writing a research report is like working on a puzzle. The first step in solving it is finding pieces of information from various print and electronic sources. The second step is fitting those pieces together into an organized whole. To help you keep track of all the pieces of information, gather the supplies you will need, which include a folder with pockets, index cards, paper clips, and rubber bands.

Choosing and Limiting a Subject

When you choose a subject for a personal essay, you try to find one that you know enough about to explain well. When you choose a subject for a report, however, you often choose one that requires research.

Compare the following subjects. Only those that require research are suitable for a report.

Personal Experience	Research
how to practice the piano	the history of the piano
my best Thanksgiving	the first Thanksgiving
why I like sports	televising a sports event
my experience during an earthquake	the San Francisco earthquake of 1989

Once you have several ideas for a subject, use the following guidelines to help you choose one.

Choosing a Subject

- Choose a subject you would like to know more about.
- Choose a subject your reader might like to know more about.
- Choose a subject that can be covered adequately in a short report.
- Choose a subject that you can research in the library or on the Internet.

After you have decided on a general subject that requires research, the next step is to limit it. Your subject should be limited enough to allow you to cover it completely in a short report. To limit your subject, think about the smaller parts that make up your general subject. Also consider limiting it to a specific time or place. The guidelines on the next page will help you limit a subject for a report.

WAYS TO LIMIT A SUBJECT

Divide the general subject into its smaller parts.

EXAMPLE	televising a sports event
PARTS	setting up the camera crew
	selling commercials
	choosing announcers

Limit the subject to a certain time or place.

EXAMPLE	the history of the piano
TIME	pianos in Mozart's time
PLACE	pianos made in Japan

PRACTICE YOUR SKILLS

● Limiting a Subject

For each general subject, write two limited subjects that would be suitable for a short report.

EXAMPLE:

GENERAL SUBJECT	whales
LIMITED SUBJECTS	how whales breathe
	training whales to perform

1. city life

2. Native Americans

3. games

4. television shows

5. football

6. zoos

7. computers

8. driving

PREWRITING *Choosing and Limiting a Subject*

Review your **journal** writing. Make a list of ten possible subjects for a report. Then decide which one you are most interested in, your readers will find most interesting, and you are likely to find information about. Limit your subject so that you can adequately cover it in a short report. Save your work.

Gathering Information

Once you have a limited subject, you can gather information by making a list of questions. Think of what you already know about your subject. Then write a list of questions that you need to answer in order to explain your subject in more detail.

Suppose you decide to write a report on protecting the bald eagle. You might ask the following questions.

- When did bald eagles become endangered?

- How many bald eagles are left?

- How are people trying to help the bald eagles?

The following strategies will help you find answers to your research questions.

Strategies for Gathering Information

- Begin by checking an encyclopedia in print, online, or on CD-ROM. This will give you an overview of your subject. It may also contain a list of books and other references with more information.

- Use the traditional card catalog to find more books on your subject.

- Check *The Readers' Guide to Periodical Literature (page C527)* and an index like *Facts on File* for magazine and newspaper articles.

- Look on the Internet using a search engine to find Websites related to your subject.
- Make a *source card* for each of your sources. Use a 3- by 5-inch note card to record the necessary information. For each source, record the proper information in the proper format.

The examples below show how to prepare source cards so they contain all the needed information. If you cannot find all the information for a source, include the information you have.

ENCYCLOPEDIA

William H. Drury, "Eagle," World Book Encyclopedia, 1982 ed.

BOOK

Birds of Prey by Glenys and Derek Lloyd, New York: Grosset & Dunlap, 1970, Y5982 LL

MAGAZINE

Sierra, March/April 1983, pp. 68–69, "In Celebration of Eagles" by Tupper Ansel Blake

CD-ROM

"Bald Eagles." Encarta 98 Deluxe Encyclopedia. CD-ROM. Redmond: Microsoft Corporation, 1999.

WEBSITE

"All About Eagles." National Foundation to Protect American Eagles. 26 March 1999. 23 Sept. 1999 <http://www.eagles.org>

(The last update to this Web page was March 26, 1999. The material was accessed on September 23, 1999)

Documentary

Documentaries use images, interviews, and narration to create a powerful report. Their subjects may range from coal miners to cartoonists. Documentaries can make the public more aware of a social condition. One example would be a film on terrible working conditions in another country. Such a documentary might cause people to write to government leaders, who in turn might appeal to the leaders of that country to make changes.

Media Activity

Research in your school library or media center for a documentary to watch. As you are watching, think about how a visual report is different from a written one.

Work with several classmates to think of a topic that you think is important. There may be an issue at school or in your neighborhood that you feel strongly about. Prepare an outline for the documentary. Use the following guidelines as you work.

Guidelines	for Outlining a Short Documentary

- Brainstorm with your partners about what should be included in your documentary. Identify people you would interview and live-action or background footage you would shoot.

- Use note cards to organize your ideas. Use the guidelines for preparing an outline on page C382.

- Be critical. What do you need to put your concept on film or videotape. Music? Narration? Titles? Add these elements to your outline.

Now share your outline with your class and ask for feedback. For more information on making a video, see <u>A Writer's Guide to Electronic Publishing</u>, page C548.

When you are searching the Web, different search engines may give you different results. Try using some of the specialized search engines available online. One that specializes in sights of particular interest to young adults is Yahooligans: www.yahooligans.com.

PRACTICE YOUR SKILLS

● *Using Source Cards*

Use the library or media center to find three sources for each subject. At least one source should be a magazine. Use source cards, like the ones below, to record your findings.

1. formations on Mars

"Mars, Water and Life."
NASA. 6 Dec. 1999. 7 Dec.
1999 <http://polarlander.jpl.nasa.
gov/why.html>

Uncovering the Secrets of the
Red Planet: Mars by Paul
Raeburn, Washington, D.C.:
National Geographic Society,
1998, 523.43 R

2. police dogs
3. the goals of the Police Athletic League
4. creating Web pages
5. grizzly bears in Yellowstone Park

PREWRITING *Source Cards*

 Use the <u>Strategies for Gathering Information</u> on pages C375–C376 to find the information you need for the subject you chose. Your sources should include at least one article from a magazine and one from an encyclopedia. Check your source cards to be sure you have accurately recorded the necessary information. The call number is especially important, since it will help you find your source again quickly if you need to refer to it many times. Save your source cards for future use.

Taking Notes

Before you begin taking notes, skim your sources, looking for information that will answer your research questions. When you find the part of the source that answers your questions, read it carefully, looking for the main ideas. Then write those ideas on your card in your own words. Read the following excerpt from *World Book Encyclopedia* on the subject of eagles. The sample note card that follows shows how the information can be summarized on an index card.

> Until the mid-1900s, hunters and trappers killed many bald eagles. The species has been protected by federal law since 1940 in 48 states, and since 1953 in Alaska. However, the continued loss of wilderness regions due to the growth of farms and urban areas has caused a further decline in the bald-eagle population. The number of bald eagles has also dropped because of the pollution of lakes and rivers with pesticides and industrial wastes. These pollutants build up in the bodies of fish, which are then eaten by the eagles. In most cases the pollutants do not kill the birds, but they interfere with the bird's ability to reproduce.

Sample Note Card

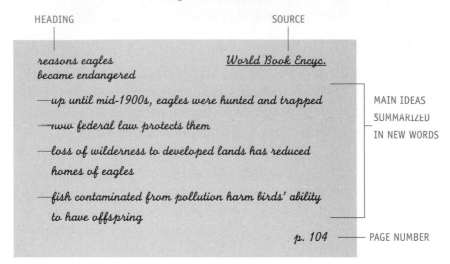

HEADING   SOURCE

reasons eagles became endangered   *World Book Encyc.*

—*up until mid-1900s, eagles were hunted and trapped*

—*now federal law protects them*

—*loss of wilderness to developed lands has reduced homes of eagles*

—*fish contaminated from pollution harm birds' ability to have offspring*

p. 104

MAIN IDEAS SUMMARIZED IN NEW WORDS

PAGE NUMBER

To help you later when you sort your notes, be sure to prepare your card according to the following guidelines.

> ### Taking Notes
>
> - Write the title of your source in the upper right-hand corner of your note card.
> - Write a heading in the upper left-hand corner of your card to identify the part of the subject being discussed.
> - Begin a new card whenever you start taking notes on a different part of your subject.
> - Summarize main points in your own words.
> - Record the page number from which your information is taken.
> - Clip together all cards from the same source. Later you will sort them into categories.

Organizing by Outlining

When you have finished your research, you are ready to organize your notes into an outline for the body of your report.

Classifying

Grouping ideas into categories is called **classifying.** When you classify, you look for ways in which items are similar enough to belong to the same category. For example, scientists classify cows, dogs, and humans as mammals. Although cows, dogs, and humans are different, they are all warm-blooded, they have backbones, and the females produce milk for their young.

By taking notes, you have already started classifying. The heading at the top of each note card shows how it fits into your subject. When you are ready to classify your note cards, you can use these headings to create categories.

THINKING PRACTICE

Imagine that you are writing a report on animal behavior. In your research you have come up with a list of notes. Give each of the following facts about amazing animals a heading suitable for a note card. Then create two categories to help you classify these details into categories.

- A cat in Lawrence, Kansas, moved all her kittens days before a cyclone came and knocked down their old home.
- In April 1961, bees from Sam Rogers's hives in England came to his funeral and sat in funeral wreaths for a half hour.
- Redsy, an Irish Setter, refused to get on a boat, saving owner, William H. Montgomery, from hurricane in 1938.
- John Gambill once nursed a wounded goose back to health; when Gambill died a flock of geese circled and honked over the hospital.

> ## Preparing an Outline

- Use the headings on your note cards to group the cards into a few categories. Save the cards that do not fit into any category for possible use in the introduction or conclusion.
- Make a list of your categories. Then, using Roman numerals (I, II, III, etc.), arrange your categories in a logical order. *(pages C274–C278)*
- Use the categories as the main topics in your outline.
- Using your note cards, list subtopics under each main topic. (Use capital letters for subtopics.)

The outline for the body of this report might appear as follows.

MODEL: Topic Outline

SUBJECT

STATEMENT OF
MAIN IDEA

MAIN TOPIC

SUBTOPICS

MAIN TOPIC

SUBTOPICS

MAIN TOPIC

SUBTOPICS

Efforts to save eagles
　　Scientists are finding creative ways to increase the population of eagles.
　　　I.　Controlled hatching
　　　　　A. Eggs taken from nest
　　　　　B. Eggs warmed by a chicken
　　　　　C. Hatchlings returned to wild
　　　　　D. Hatchlings adopted by foster eagle parents
　　　II.　Hacking
　　　　　A. Moving eaglets to tower in safe location
　　　　　B. Caring for eaglets for five or six weeks
　　　　　C. Releasing them as free birds
　　　III.　Preserving wilderness lands
　　　　　A. Importance of Alaska
　　　　　B. Protection of southeast Alaska

After you have finished your outline, use the following guidelines to check its form.

> ### Outline Form
>
> - Include a title and a statement of the main idea.
> - Use a Roman numeral and a period for each main topic.
> - Use a capital letter and a period for each subtopic.
> - Always include at least two subtopics under each main topic.
> - Indent as shown in the above model.
> - Capitalize the first word of each entry.

PRACTICE YOUR SKILLS

● *Outlining*

Use the subtopics below to complete the following outline. Place each subtopic under the proper main topic.

SUBJECT	How the movie *Titanic* was filmed without a real ship sinking
STATEMENT OF MAIN IDEA	Clever model techniques and computer technology made it appear that a real ship was sinking

I. The basic equipment

    A.

    B.

II. The backgrounds

    A.

    B.

III. The actors

    A.

    B.

SUBTOPICS	• miniatures and models of the ship
	• movement of the ocean
	• leading man, Leonardo DiCaprio, filmed in front of a blue screen
	• latest technology—specialized computer programs
	• performances in tanks of cold water
	• sunset behind the ship

Communicate Your Ideas

PREWRITING *Taking Notes, Outlining*

Review the sources you identified on your chosen subject. With your note cards handy, follow the guidelines for taking notes on page C380. Then use your note cards—and your skill at classifying—to organize your information and outline your report. Save your work.

Drafting
Writing Process

Your goal in writing the first draft of your report is to structure your information into an introduction, a body, and a conclusion. The model you will see in the pages that follow will help you structure your report. Note, however, that this model has already been revised and edited. Do not worry if your first draft is less polished than the model you will read.

You can learn more about the structure of a report on page C372.

Drafting the Introduction

A good introduction is like a promise to your readers. It focuses your readers' attention on the main idea and leads them to expect certain details in the rest of the report. Use the following guidelines to write a strong introduction for your report.

 Writing an Introduction

A strong introduction

- captures the reader's attention.
- provides any background information needed.
- contains a sentence expressing the main idea of the report.

Read the following introduction to a report on eagles. Then read the introduction on the next page. Both capture attention and provide background information. The first introduction, however, fails to focus the reader's attention on the main idea.

UNFOCUSED
INTRODUCTION

The bald eagle has been the symbol of the United States since 1792. Some early Americans, including Benjamin Franklin, did not like that choice. However, since the eagle is found only in North America, it was voted to receive the high honor of representing the United States. Two hundred years later, President Ronald Reagan declared 1982 "the Year of the Eagle." The eagle is indeed a magnificent bird of prey.

For more than 200 years, the bald eagle
has been the symbol of the United States.
At the time it was chosen as the national
emblem, bald eagles numbered about 50,000
in 48 states. By the early 1970s, however,
only about 3,000 remained. The last great
refuge for bald eagles is Alaska, where an
estimated 30,000 still live. Fear for the
dwindling population has led to laws
protecting eagles in all states, including

MAIN IDEA

Alaska. Perhaps even more important,
scientists are finding creative ways to increase
the eagle population.

Notice that all of the sentences in the second introduction build up to the main idea. No unrelated ideas are included. This introduction provides a clear promise to the readers.

Drafting the Body

With your outline as a guide, drafting the body of your report is a matter of developing your ideas into smoothly connected sentences and paragraphs. You will use transitions to help guide your readers from idea to idea.

Notice how the following report body follows the outline on page C382.

MODEL: Body of the Report

**FROM ROMAN
NUMERAL I
IN OUTLINE**

One of the most effective ways of increasing the eagle population is by controlling
the hatching of eggs. At a research center
in Maryland, eggs laid by captive eagles are
taken away from the nest. They are then in-
cubated under chickens. Meanwhile, the
mother soon lays more eggs. If she had her

original brood to watch, she would not lay more eggs. In this way more eaglets can be born from each mother. In some cases the eggs laid by captive eagles are taken into the wild and placed in the nests of other eagles. Most wild eagles seem willing to adopt and care for the new eggs.

FROM ROMAN NUMERAL II

Another technique for increasing the population is called hacking. *Hacking* means "moving young birds to a new, safe habitat." In most cases eaglets are taken from their birthplace and moved to a caged tower in the new location. There they are fed by workers. To prevent these wild birds from becoming dependent on humans, the workers never get close enough to the birds to be seen. When they are old enough to survive on their own, the eagles are released.

FROM ROMAN NUMERAL III

Although these measures have helped the eagle population, they are not enough. The wilderness homes of the eagles must also be protected, especially in Alaska. Many of the birds taken captive for breeding and hacking are taken from Alaska. If water pollution and the use of insecticides become too widespread, Alaska's stock of bald eagles may also become threatened. Some researchers believe that developers should not be allowed to work in the 48,000-acre preserve in southeast Alaska where most bald eagles live.

Drafting the Conclusion

A strong conclusion provides a wrap-up of the details in the body of a report. Use the following guidelines whenever you write a conclusion to a report.

- Restate your main idea in new words.
- Include a comment that shows the importance of your subject.
- Round out the report by referring to an idea in the introduction without repeating it exactly.
- Avoid simply repeating the ideas in the body.
- Avoid adding a completely new idea.
- Avoid such phrases as "Now you have seen . . . " or "I have just told you . . . "

Notice how the following conclusion follows these guidelines.

MODEL: Conclusion of a Report

In recent years the eagles have found many friends to help them survive. Since 1979, a bald eagle conference has been held every year in the Klamath Basin on the Oregon–California border. The purpose of the conference is to study the eagle and discuss more ways to protect it. In 1982, President Ronald Reagan focused attention on the eagle by declaring the 200th birthday of the national symbol as "the Year of the Eagle." The hatching and hacking programs in many states are also critical to the birds' survival. The more people learn about the needs of the eagle and how to protect it, the greater are the chances that this majestic national symbol will celebrate its 300th birthday next century.

Including Visuals

Many reports can be enhanced with the use of visuals. Visuals can include illustrations, photos, graphs, and charts. In the case of a report that is to be published on a Web page, movie clips may also be included. If you are using a word processing program to prepare your report, and you have a scanner, you can scan the images directly into your document. With some programs, you can also enter data and the program will prepare a graph or table of your choosing.

The most important thing to remember when deciding whether to include a visual in your report is that it must clarify or extend the meaning of your text. In other words, all visuals must be relevant to your topic and be included for a reason. Visuals can help deepen your reader's understanding if used and placed properly.

Writing a Title

Once you have finished your first draft, give your report an interesting title. Your title should catch your reader's interest and indicate what your report is about.

Communicate Your Ideas

DRAFTING *Introduction, Body, Conclusion, Title*

Use your outline to draft your report. Then reread your report, add any visuals, and give it a title. Save your draft for later use.

Listing Sources

As a final step in preparing your report, you need to list your sources of information. This list will be the final page of your completed report. You can build this list from your source cards. *(page C376)* Arrange your source cards in alphabetical order according to the author's last name. If no name is given, use the first word in the title for alphabetizing. Write the word *Sources* centered at the top of the page. Then list your sources in the order in which you arranged your cards.

The following examples show the correct order of information and punctuation for different types of sources. Notice that page numbers are given only for magazine articles.

MAGAZINE ARTICLES	Blake, Tupper Ansel. "In Celebration of Eagles." <u>Sierra</u>. March–April: 68-69.
BOOKS	Callahan, Philip S. <u>The Magnificent Birds of Prey</u>. New York: Holiday House, 1974.
ENCYCLOPEDIA	Drury, William H. "Eagle." <u>World Book Encyclopedia</u>. 1982 ed.
CD-ROMS	"Bald Eagles." <u>Encarta 98 Deluxe Encyclopedia</u>. CD-ROM. Redmond: Microsoft Corporation, 1999.
WEBSITES	"All About Eagles." <u>National Foundation to Protect American Eagles</u>. 26 March 1999. 23 Sept. 1999 <u><http://www.eagles.org></u>

PRACTICE YOUR SKILLS

● *Preparing a Sources Page*

The following sources are on the subject of careers in writing and journalism. Prepare a sources page in correct form. Remember, if you cannot find certain information, include all the information you have.

1. *Extraordinary Women Journalists,* a book by Claire Price-Groff, published in New York by Childrens Press, in 1998.

2. "Journalism" in *Merriam-Webster's Vocabulary.* 1998 edition.

3. a magazine article titled "100 Best Writers of the 20th Century," published in *Writers Digest* in the November 1999 issue on pages 7–20.

4. an article on *Alice in Wonderland* on CD-ROM, *Merriam-Webster's Encyclopedia of Literature,* by Merriam-Webster, Incorporated.

5. an article on an Internet Web page called *The Write Site* **www.writesite.org**, titled "Creating Human Interest: Famous Journalists and Photojournalists" that you found today. It was updated three days ago.

Communicate Your Ideas

DRAFTING *Sources Page*

Prepare a sources page for your report. Be sure you list your sources in the correct form. Save your work.

Revising   Writing Process

In the process of writing your report, you may not have been able to concentrate on all the elements of clear writing. During the revising stage, you can stand back from your report and try to read it with a fresh eye.

> ## Evaluation Checklist for Revising
> **Checking Your Report**
> ✓ Does your introduction contain a sentence expressing the main idea of the report? *(pages C385–C386)*
> ✓ Does the body of your report support the main idea with specific information and examples? *(pages C267–C268)*
> ✓ Did you use your own words? *(page C380)*
> ✓ Did you use transitions? *(pages C274–C278)*
> ✓ Does your report have unity? *(pages C171–C172)*

✓ Does your report have coherence? *(pages C172–C173)*

✓ Does your conclusion add a strong ending? *(pages C387–C388)*

✓ Does your report have a title? *(page C389)*

✓ Does your report have a sources page? *(pages C389–C390)*

Checking Your Paragraphs

✓ Does each paragraph of the body have a topic sentence? *(pages C97–C98)*

✓ Is each paragraph unified and coherent? *(pages C171–C173)*

Checking Your Sentences and Words

✓ Are your sentences varied? *(pages C67–C76)*

✓ Are your sentences concise? *(pages C78–C82)*

✓ Did you use specific, vivid words? *(pages C40–C41)*

Writing Tip

Revise your writing to combine simple sentences into compound sentences, improving the flow of the piece.

Communicate Your Ideas

REVISING *Conferencing*

Using the **Evaluation Checklist for Revising** and the **Revising Workshop** on the next page, revise the report you wrote. Then exchange work with a classmate and give each other suggestions for further revision. Listen to all suggestions and revise your work as you feel necessary. Save your work for further revising and for editing and publishing later.

Prewriting Workshop
Drafting Workshop
Revising Workshop ▶
Editing Workshop
Publishing Workshop

Combining Simple Sentences

When you revise your report, read your sentences aloud. Do they sound short and choppy? Simple sentences can be combined to form longer, more varied sentences. If two simple sentences have related ideas, they can be joined to form a sentence with a compound subject or verb. The following examples show different ways to combine sentences.

TWO SIMPLE SENTENCES	The priests mummified Tutankhamun. They placed a mask over his head.
ONE SENTENCE WITH A COMPOUND VERB	The priests mummified Tutankhamun and placed a mask over his head.

You can combine sentences using the conjunctions *but, and,* or *or.*

SIMILAR IDEAS	They wrapped his body in cloth. They buried him with all his treasures.
	They wrapped his body in cloth **and** buried him with all his treasures.
CONTRASTING IDEAS	Scientists do not identify mummies with the naked eye. They use X rays.
	Scientists do not identify mummies with the naked eye **but** with X rays.
CHOICE BETWEEN IDEAS	The pharaohs hunted on horseback. Sometimes pharaohs hunted from chariots.
	The pharaohs hunted on horseback **or** from chariots.

One of the final stages in writing a research report is to edit your work for proper grammar, mechanics, spelling, and usage.

> ### Editing Checklist
>
> ✓ Are your sentences free of errors in grammar and usage?
>
> ✓ Did you spell each word correctly?
>
> ✓ Did you capitalize and punctuate correctly?
>
> ✓ Does your list of sources match the form given on page C390?
>
> ✓ Did you use correct manuscript form? *(page C31–C32)*
>
> ✓ Did you make a neat final copy of your report?

PRACTICE YOUR SKILLS

● *Editing a Concluding Paragraph*

Use the Editing Checklist **to polish this final paragraph from a research report about the repairing of the Statue of Liberty. There are ten errors.**

Restoring and repairing the Statue of Liberty cost millions of dollars, and involved many years of hard work. The results, however, was well worth the expense. Miss Liberty is not just an ordinary statue standing in new york harbor. She is a cymbal of the United States of america and a sign of freedom for the rest of the world. Because of the recent alterations, the statue of Liberty is stronger and beautifuller than ever. The contributions made by people across the United States will help keep the famus torch burning brightly. For many years into the future.

Communicate Your Ideas

EDITING

Use the **Editing Checklist** on the preceding page to edit your report.

Publishing ▸ Writing Process

Publishing is an important part of report writing—the purpose of writing in this form is to present information. During the process of writing a research report, the writer learns about his or her subject in order to pass the information on to an interested reader. When deciding how to publish a research report, keep in mind the subject and who might benefit from reading about it.

Communicate Your Ideas

PUBLISHING

Present a final copy of your research report to an interested reader. You and your classmates might display your reports on a table in your school library or media center.

PORTFOLIO

Time Out to Reflect

In what ways have your skills in researching and writing reports improved after going through this chapter? Find a report that you wrote earlier in the year. Is it different from the one you just wrote? How? What did you do differently in this recent report? What report-writing skills would you like to improve upon? Record your thoughts in the Learning Log section of your **journal.**

▶ Process of Writing a Report

Remember you can move back and forth among the stages of the process to achieve your purpose. For example, during editing, you may wish to return to the revising stage to add details that have occurred to you while editing. The numbers in parentheses refer to pages where you can get help with your writing.

PREWRITING

- Choose a subject requiring research and limit it. *(pages C373–C374)*
- Prepare a source card for each of your sources. *(page C376)*
- Gather information from varied print and electronic sources. *(pages C375–C376)*
- Take notes on note cards. *(pages C379–C380)*
- Organize your notes into categories and use them to outline the body. *(pages C380–C384)*

DRAFTING

- Write an introduction that includes a sentence expressing your main idea. *(pages C385–C386)*
- Use your outline to write the body in your own words. *(pages C386–C387)*
- Add a concluding paragraph. *(pages C387–C388)*
- Add a title. *(pages C389)*
- Prepare a list of sources as your final page. *(pages C389–C391)*

REVISING

- Use the **Evaluation Checklist for Revising** on pages C391–392 to improve your first draft.

EDITING

- Use the **Editing Checklist** on page C394 to polish your work.

PUBLISHING

- Make a neat final copy to present to interested readers.

▷ A Writer Writes
An I-Search Report

Purpose: to inform and explain
Audience: your classmates

Research reports for school can be rather formal and impersonal. There is a type of report, however, that takes a more personal approach—the I-search report. An I-search report is based on a topic of personal interest or importance to you. It is a search for a deeper personal knowledge of a subject. An I-search report is usually written in the first person and is less formal than a research report. Like other reports, an I-search report contains facts, but they are not presented in the same way as a typical research report.

Prewriting

The first thing to do when writing an I-search report is to choose a topic that interests you—something that you want to know more about. Use your **journal** entries and notes to help you find a topic. Next, make a list of possible sources of information. You can use traditional sources but you can also use interviews with people who know about your topic. People you interview can be people you know personally—family, friends, neighbors, or people you are not as familiar with, such as experts you contact via E-mail, telephone, or mail.

Drafting

As with a research report, your I-search report will have an introduction, a body, and a conclusion. Your introduction might state why you chose the topic you are writing about. In the body of your report, you can describe your research and what you have learned. Your conclusion might state how your research helped you discover more about your topic than you previously knew.

Although an I-search report has a less formal tone than a traditional research report, you should still avoid personal stories and reflections that do not relate to the topic you are covering.

Just as with a research report, your I-search report should have a list of sources. Review the guidelines for recording sources on page C380 before you prepare your list.

Revising

Revise your I-search report using the **Evaluation Checklist for Revising** on pages C391–C392. Share your paper with a classmate and ask for any suggestions he or she may have on how to improve it. A classmate who is interested in your topic will be most helpful in suggesting other aspects of the topic for you to explore in more detail.

Editing

Use the **Editing Checklist** on page C394 to edit your report.

Publishing

Prepare a final copy of your report and share it with interested readers. You may wish to send copies of your report to specialists on your topic or publish your paper on a Website devoted to your topic.

Connection Collection

Representing in Different Ways

From Visuals . . .

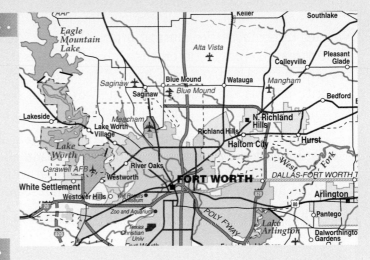

From Print . . .

The legendary Island of Bismuth is shaped roughly like an outline of a fish—its western end like the fish's tail and the eastern end like the fish's body. The western end is dominated by the tallest point, Mt. Mooselip. Bismuth is 8 miles long and 4 miles at its widest point. Off the eastern end there is another tiny island, called Orson's Crag, where islanders harvest wild lavender.

. . . to Print

Write a paragraph that describes the area pictured on the map. Use the compass points (the top is north) to help you describe where things are in relation to each other.

- Which strategies can be used for creating both written and visual representations? Which strategies apply to one, not both? Which type of representation is more effective?
- Draw a conclusion and write briefly about the differences between written ideas and visual representations.

. . . to Visuals

Draw a map of Bismuth Island. Label all of its significant features (like Mt. Mooselip), and give the island's dimensions (its length and width). Also, label the compass points.

Writing in Everyday Life
Note to Your Brother

For your birthday your parents are allowing you to attend the concert of your choice—but only if you bring your little brother and you let him choose the musical group that you are going to see. Unfortunately your little brother has his heart set on seeing his favorite band, the Lip Synch Boys. You want to tell him that your favorite band is the best band in the world, but he will not stop watching music videos long enough to listen.

Write a note to your brother explaining why your favorite band is the best choice. Research your favorite band on the World Wide Web and collect information about them that will persuade your little brother. Use this information to compose your note.

What strategies did you use to inform your brother?

Writing for Oral Communication
Speech to the Library Planning Board

You think the time has come for your local library to buy new books for the reference collection because there is hardly a single new book in it. You plan to attend a Library Planning Board meeting and convince them to order new books. Current highlights of their outdated collection include the following books: *Hovercrafts 2000: Vehicles of the Future* (1969); *The Totally Far-Out History of Rock Music* (1974); *Lost Forever: The Titanic Story* (1975); and *Operation of the Mimeograph Machine* (1978).

Prepare notes for a short speech to the Library Planning Board. Recommend new books for the library to buy, evaluate the current collection, and suggest a plan for staying up-to-date in the future. You may wish to interview a local or school librarian to investigate how libraries acquire new books.

You can find information on preparing speeches on pages C433–C439.

What strategies did you use to convince the Library Planning Board?

Assess Your Learning

Mayor Donny Chance wants a new professional football team, the Turf Monsters, to make his city its home. The Turf Monsters say that they will move to the city if it builds a new $8 million stadium downtown. The mayor believes the team will bring a new sense of civic pride to the city. He also believes it will encourage economic growth by drawing people to the city who will eat at local restaurants and shop at the city's stores.

▶ **Write a report for the mayor providing him with information that he can use in presenting his plan to the people of the city.**

▶ **In your report include information you gather by interviewing some of the city's "citizens" (your classmates). Combine the information you gather from "the citizens" with information you gather from other sources about the cost of the stadium versus the revenues it will create.**

Before You Write Consider the following questions:
What is the *subject?*
What is the *occasion?*
Who is the *audience?*
What is the *purpose?*

After You Write Evaluate your work using the following criteria:
- Does your introduction contain a sentence expressing the main idea of your report?
- Does the body of the report support the main idea with specific information and examples?
- Did you use your own words?
- Did you use transitions?
- Did your conclusion have a strong ending?
- Did you use your sources correctly?

Write briefly on how well you did. Point out your strengths and areas for improvement.

Letters

Everyone likes to receive a letter in the mail. When you receive a letter, an exciting feeling grabs hold of you. You feel good that someone has written especially to you. Maybe you feel important or just simply remembered.

Writing letters is just as important as receiving them. With a letter you can stay in touch with friends or family members who live in other places, thank someone for doing something for you, or explain why you have to turn down an invitation. Today you can also keep in touch with E-mail.

With a letter you can request information for a report or research project for school. Often you will need to write a letter to order merchandise, or to request a form to join a club or to sign up for a service.

In this chapter you will learn the correct form for different kinds of letters. You will also practice shaping your written message to suit both the purpose of the letter and the receiver.

Reading with a Writer's Eye

In the letter below, the author Laura Ingalls Wilder writes to her husband, Manly, as she travels across the country by train on her way to San Francisco. Notice that the letter is dated 1915. Remember that this was before people could keep in touch by telephone or E-mail. As you read, think about how vivid and detailed Wilder's descriptions are. Try to picture her journey and the landscape she describes.

FROM

WEST FROM HOME

Letters of
Laura Ingalls Wilder
San Francisco, 1915

On train somewhere in Nevada
Thursday, August 26, 1915

Manly Dear,

Well I'm safely on the last lap of the journey. Was so very lucky as to get a lower tourist berth at Salt Lake and did not have to change at Ogden. Our car was just attached to the San Francisco train, but the ugly D.&R.G. [Denver & Rio Grande] being so late hooked us on to a slow train through Arkansas and we are three hours late. Just sent a telegram to Rose when to meet me.

I crossed Great Salt Lake in the moonlight last night and it was the most beautiful sight I've seen yet. Miles and miles of it on each side of the train, the track so narrow that it could not be seen from the window. It looked as though the train was running on the water. I undressed and lay in my berth and watched it, the moonlight making a path of silver across the water and the farther shore so dim and indistinct and melting away into the desert as though there was no end to the lake. I thought I would watch until we came to the end of the lake, but I was so tired my eyes shut and when I opened them again it was morning and we were away out on the Nevada deserts.

I saw the sun rise on the desert as I lay in my berth and it was lovely. The bare, perfectly bare, rocky mountains in all kinds of heaps and piles us though the winds had drifted them into heaps and they had turned to rock, were purple in the hollows and rose and gold and pink on the higher places. There were yellows and browns and grays and the whole softly blended together. At the feet of the mountains lay the flat gray plain covered with sage brush, with patches of sand and alkali[1] showing. Such a desolate dreary country even though beautiful in its way. All morning we have been going through the desert and now we are where there are piles of loose sand. All the way wherever there is a little spot of green someone is living, or perhaps I should say wherever someone is living there is a spot of green, but not always. I saw two houses and a windmill and one green bush between them. There was a river bottom for a little ways and corrals and cattle and a cowboy in red chaps driving a bunch of horses. We thought we were seeing water off at one side and I asked the porter what water it was. He laughed and said it looked like alkali beds. Then we saw them later close by, miles of perfectly white ground. In places it looked like water and then it looked like snow. There was a little house and corral right out in the middle of one big bed. Not a living creature or a green thing in sight. There was a road out and it looked like a road made in about three inches of snow with dry dirt underneath. Oh, this awful, awful country we have come to now.

This is the desert proper we have read of where people get lost in sand storms and perish of thirst. There are

---

[1] **alkali:** A salt or mixture of salts that is found in arid soils.

scattered clumps of what I think is sage brush and they are nearly buried in drifts and mounds of sand. The ground between is perfectly bare and covered with loose sand and alkali. The car and my eyes and nose are full of sand and alkali dust and everything and everyone is so dirty. We are all making a joke of it. There is a nice crowd in our car and we all talk to each other and have a good time getting acquainted. One woman talking to me this morning said they live in Kansas City and they are thinking of getting a farm. Want to trade city property. She was very much interested to know all about the Ozarks and says they will come down and see them.

We will get to San Francisco about eleven tonight. I think I have brought you up to date so will quit.

Love,
Bessie[2]

---

[2] **"Bessie"** was the name Wilder was known by within her family.

Thinking as a Writer

Evaluating Style in Context

Wilder wrote letters almost daily to her husband. Letter writing was the main way of communicating in that time.

- Find the passages in her writing that are particularly vivid for you.
- Imagine seeing the West for the first time. Would you describe your impressions in the same way as she does? If not, how would your description be different?

Interpreting Tone

Oral Expression
- Choose a passage that you especially like from Wilder's letter. Think about the tone of the passage. What feelings or emotions does she express?
- Read the passage aloud. Do the same feelings come through when you read aloud? Can you express the tone of the writing when you read aloud?

Describing a Landscape

Viewing
- In a small group, take turns describing the landscape in the photograph below. Take notes on each person's comments. Notice whether different people notice different details, and what language each person uses to describe his or her impressions.
- Go back to the notes you took. With the group, brainstorm additional words to enrich and extend the descriptions.

Developing Your Everyday Writing Skills

Even in the current age of E-mail, there may be times when you need to write a letter.

Friendly Letters

When you write a friendly letter, you can take time to think and make changes before you send it out.

A **friendly letter** is an informal letter that you write to a friend or relative.

PARTS OF A FRIENDLY LETTER	
HEADING	This includes your full address with the zip code. Use the full name of your state or the abbreviation. *(page C418)* Always include the date after your address. Follow the rules for capitalizing proper nouns and using commas.
SALUTATION	This is your friendly greeting and is followed by a comma. Use the name you would call the person if you were talking with him or her. Capitalize the first word and any proper nouns. **D**ear **U**ncle **H**ugh, **D**ear **M**om,
BODY	This is your conversational message. Remember to indent the first word in each paragraph.
CLOSING	End your letter with a brief personal closing followed by a comma. Capitalize the first word of the closing. **L**ove always,
SIGNATURE	Sign your name below the closing.

Friendly Letter Form

The model below shows the correct form for a friendly letter. All friendly letters have five main parts: a heading, salutation, body, closing, and signature.

MODEL: Friendly Letter

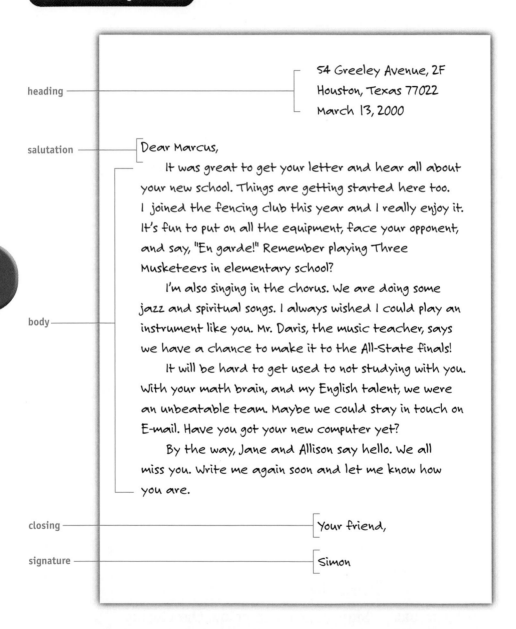

heading

54 Greeley Avenue, 2F
Houston, Texas 77022
March 13, 2000

salutation

Dear Marcus,

body

It was great to get your letter and hear all about your new school. Things are getting started here too. I joined the fencing club this year and I really enjoy it. It's fun to put on all the equipment, face your opponent, and say, "En garde!" Remember playing Three Musketeers in elementary school?

I'm also singing in the chorus. We are doing some jazz and spiritual songs. I always wished I could play an instrument like you. Mr. Davis, the music teacher, says we have a chance to make it to the All-State finals!

It will be hard to get used to not studying with you. With your math brain, and my English talent, we were an unbeatable team. Maybe we could stay in touch on E-mail. Have you got your new computer yet?

By the way, Jane and Allison say hello. We all miss you. Write me again soon and let me know how you are.

closing

Your friend,

signature

Simon

▶ Social Letters

Social letters usually have a specific purpose, such as to thank someone for something, to invite someone to an event, or to express your regret for being unable to do something. Social letters have a more formal tone than personal letters. However, social letters follow the same form as personal letters.

Thank-You Letters   A thank-you letter lets someone know how much you appreciate what that person has done for you. It carries more weight than a verbal thank-you, because it shows you took the time to sit down and write out your thoughts.

Invitations   An invitation informs someone about an occasion you would like that person to attend. It includes the time and place and any other special details your guests might need to know. Special details might include how to get to the event by car or public transportation, or how to dress (formally or informally). Sometimes invitations tell the receivers whether they may bring a friend or whether they are expected to bring food.

Letters of Regret   When you are unable to attend an event to which you have been invited, you write a letter of regret. In it, you explain why you will be unable to attend, and you express your regret. Invitations that include an **RSVP** (an abbreviation for "please respond") often require a written response. You should always respond in a timely fashion to an invitation, allowing the person planning the event to know how many people he or she can expect.

Letters to the Editor

One very common use of letter writing is the **letter to the editor.** Most newspapers and magazines have a section for letters that readers have written. Usually these letters have to do with a story or editorial the newspaper or magazine has published. Other letters may be on subjects that are of concern to the community.

The letters to the editor that are published are brief and to the point. The editors of the newspaper or magazine may edit the letter so that it does not contain unnecessary information. Very often letters to the editor are now sent as E-mail messages. E-mail messages arrive almost immediately, which means the letter can be printed the day after a story is published.

Media Activity

- Look through local newspapers and national newsmagazines for the letters to the editor section.
- Study the formats in which these letters are published. Then plan a class newspaper devoted to hearing the opinions of your classmates.
- Send classmates an E-mail message asking for their opinions on a subject they are interested in, such as keeping the classroom neat, or how to behave during recess.
- When several classmates have responded, publish the letters by using a word processor.

● Business Letters

Most business letters do more than simply report news. They usually call for the receiver of the letter to take some kind of action. Two examples of business letters are letters of request and order letters. To make sure your point is understood, keep your business letters clear and simple.

A **business letter** is a formal letter that asks for some action on the part of the receiver.

Business Letter Form   Most of the business letters you write will be sent to a company. When a business letter arrives at a company, it is usually taken out of the envelope before it reaches the person receiving the letter. For this reason, a business letter has one more part than a friendly letter. This part is called the inside address.

The **inside address** contains the name and address of the person to whom you are writing. The parts of a business letter are the *heading, inside address, salutation, body, closing,* and *signature.*

Before you begin drafting a business letter, be sure you know the purpose of your letter, as well as the complete mailing address of the person who will receive your letter. The model on page C414 shows the correct form for a business letter. Use the guidelines below to help you understand the parts of a business letter.

THINGS TO REMEMBER
WHEN WRITING A BUSINESS LETTER

- Use white stationery, preferably $8\frac{1}{2}$ by 11 inches.

- Leave margins at least 1 inch wide on all sides.

- Keep a copy of each business letter you write.

PARTS OF A BUSINESS LETTER

HEADING	The heading is the same as the heading of a friendly letter. Include your full address followed by the date. Follow the rules for capitalizing proper nouns and using commas. Use the full name of your state or the abbreviation. *(page C418)* If you use the abbreviation, be sure to abbreviate the state in the inside address, too.
INSIDE ADDRESS	Start the inside address two to four lines below the heading. Write the name of the person if you know it. Use *Mr., Ms., Mrs., Dr.,* and so on before the name. If the person has a title, such as *General Manager,* write it on the next line. Then write the receiver's address.
SALUTATION	Start the salutation, or greeting, one line below the inside address. In a business letter, use a colon after the salutation. Dear Ms. Morley: Dear Mr. Adams:
BODY	One line below the salutation, begin the body of the letter. Indent each new paragraph.
CLOSING	Use a formal closing. Start the closing one or two lines below the body. Line it up with the left-hand edge of the heading. Capitalize the first letter only and use a comma. Sincerely, Yours truly, Sincerely yours, Very truly yours,
SIGNATURE	In the signature of a business letter, your name appears twice. First type or print your name four or five lines below the closing. Then sign your name in the space between the closing and your typed name. Do not refer to yourself as Mr. or Ms.

Prewriting Workshop
Drafting Workshop
Revising Workshop
Editing Workshop ▶
Publishing Workshop

Commas

When you write letters, you must be aware of certain rules and conventions. One of these rules is to present your letter in proper form, with correct punctuation. Pay special attention when editing your letters to make sure you have used commas correctly in dates and address.

In the date, use commas to separate the day of the month from the year.

> COMMAS SEPARATING
> DAY FROM YEAR
> (IN HEADING)
>
> March 31, 2000
> April 25, 2000

In addresses, use commas to separate most parts of addresses that appear on the same line. Do not use a comma to separate the state from the ZIP code.

> COMMAS SEPARATING
> PARTS OF ADDRESS ON
> SAME LINE (IN HEADING)
>
> 1612 Maple Avenue, Apt. 16
> Grace, MS 38745

If you use the abbreviation of the state in the inside address, use it again on the envelope. Do not mix using abbreviations and full state names.

> EXAMPLE
>
> 1612 Maple Avenue, Apt. 16
> Grace, Mississippi 38745
> **or**
> 1612 Maple Avenue, Apt. 16
> Grace, MS 38745

Editing Checklist

✔ Have you used commas correctly in dates an addresses?
✔ Have you not mixed abbreviations and full state names?

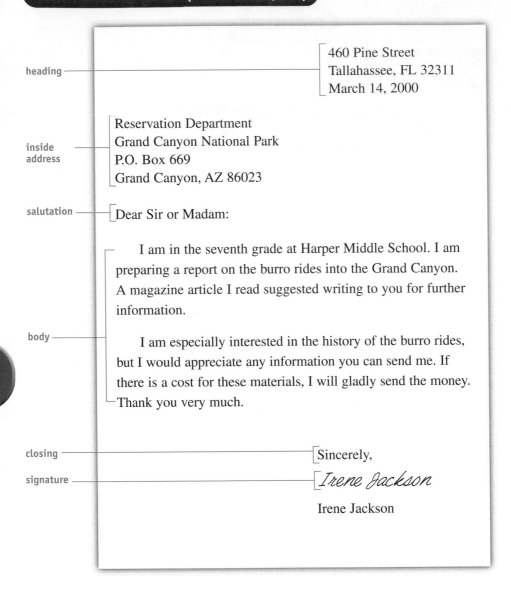

heading
460 Pine Street
Tallahassee, FL 32311
March 14, 2000

inside address
Reservation Department
Grand Canyon National Park
P.O. Box 669
Grand Canyon, AZ 86023

salutation
Dear Sir or Madam:

body
I am in the seventh grade at Harper Middle School. I am preparing a report on the burro rides into the Grand Canyon. A magazine article I read suggested writing to you for further information.

I am especially interested in the history of the burro rides, but I would appreciate any information you can send me. If there is a cost for these materials, I will gladly send the money. Thank you very much.

closing
Sincerely,

signature
Irene Jackson

Irene Jackson

There are many styles for writing business letters. The **block form** puts each part of the letter at the left margin of the page. A blank line is left between each paragraph in the body of the letter. The paragraphs are not indented.

In the **modified block style,** the heading, closing, and signature are on the right. The inside address, salutation, and body all start at the left margin. Paragraphs are indented. The models in this chapter are in the modified block style.

COMPUTER TIP

Before you print a letter, you can check to see what it will look like on the page. Go to Print Preview under File to check the page layout.

Envelopes

The envelope should be clearly addressed. If you type the letter, also type the envelope. If you handwrite the envelope, it should be very neat. Place your own name and address in the upper left-hand corner. The receiver's address, which is the same as the inside address in a business letter, is centered on the envelope. Use the postal abbreviation for the state and always include the zip code.

How you fold your letter to place it in the envelope depends on the size of your stationery. If you use business-sized envelopes that are the same width as your stationery, fold the letter in thirds, as shown below.

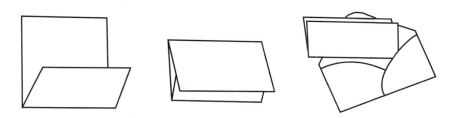

If your envelopes are narrower than your stationery, fold the letter in sixths.

your name	Irene Jackson
your address	460 Pine Street
state abbreviation	Tallahassee, FL 32311
receiver's address	Reservation Department
	Grand Canyon National Park
	P.O. Box 669
	Grand Canyon, AZ 86023

Setting Goals

When writing a letter of request, you will be most likely to receive the information you require if you have planned your letter carefully. An important part of that planning is setting goals. Setting goals means stating what result you expect.

Look back to the letter Irene Jackson wrote to the Reservation Department at Grand Canyon National Park. Before writing, she thought carefully about what she wanted her letter to accomplish. She wrote out a goal for her effort.

> Goal for Letter of Request: to get as much information as possible about the burro rides into the canyon, with special emphasis on the history of the rides, so I can use the information in my report

After she set the goals for her letter, Irene could then made sure she included all the necessary information in her letter to make sure she got back the information she requested. She made her needs very clear to guarantee that the receiver of the letter would know how to respond.

THINKING PRACTICE

The following body of a letter of request was written to Bowman Publishing Company to achieve several goals. Read the excerpt and identify the goals.

> I recently enjoyed the book *Outerspace Outings* by Julia Knowles, published by your company. I would like to tell the author how much I liked it. Please send me an address where I can write to her.
>
> I would also like to know what other books your company has about spaceships. If possible, please send me a list.

STATE ABBREVIATIONS

Alabama	AL	Montana	MT
Alaska	AK	Nebraska	NE
Arizona	AZ	New Hampshire	NH
Arkansas	AR	New Jersey	NJ
California	CA	New Mexico	NM
Colorado	CO	New York	NY
Connecticut	CT	Nevada	NV
Delaware	DE	North Carolina	NC
Dist. of Columbia	DC	North Dakota	ND
Florida	FL	Ohio	OH
Georgia	GA	Oklahoma	OK
Hawaii	HI	Oregon	OR
Idaho	ID	Pennsylvania	PA
Illinois	IL	Rhode Island	RI
Indiana	IN	South Carolina	SC
Iowa	IA	South Dakota	SD
Kansas	KS	Tennessee	TN
Kentucky	KY	Texas	TX
Louisiana	LA	Utah	UT
Maine	ME	Vermont	VT
Maryland	MD	Virginia	VA
Massachusetts	MA	Washington	WA
Minnesota	MN	West Virginia	WV
Mississippi	MS	Wisconsin	WI
Missouri	MO	Wyoming	WY

Letters of Request

Requesting information is one common purpose of a business letter. When requesting information, be as specific as you can about what information you need.

Order Letters

You can also use a business letter to order merchandise from catalogs or advertisements. Your order letter should give complete information. Be sure to include a description of the item, size, order number, price, and the quantity you want. If you enclose payment for your purchase, your letter should state the amount you have enclosed. Check over your arithmetic to be sure you have enclosed the proper amount.

Model: Order Letter

333 Westmont Drive
Ramer, TN 38367
July 15, 2000

Stowaway Supplies
42 Ridge Avenue
Agoura Hills, CA 91301

Dear Sir or Madam:
    Please send me the following items from your 2000 fall catalogue.

2 student book bags— 1 green, 1 red, Order # 356—AZ5, $9.99 each	$19.98
1 navy blue sweatshirt, size medium, Order # 455—AM2, $17.50	$17.50
Total:	$37.48

    I have enclosed a check for $39.48 to cover the cost of the merchandise plus $2.50 for shipping and handling.

Sincerely,

Martin J. Conway

Martin J. Conway

Business Forms

You will need to fill out business forms for a variety of reasons. Applying for a library card, sending a money order, or registering for an online service are just a few instances. Following are some guidelines for filling out business forms.

Completing Business Forms

- Read all of the directions carefully before you begin to fill out the form.
- Check both sides of the form to make sure you do not miss any questions written on the back.
- Do not leave blanks. If a question does not apply to you, write N/A (not applicable) in the space provided.
- Always use blue or black pen.
- Be sure to print neatly and clearly.
- Remember to sign the form.

If the form you are filling out is long, you may want to write the answers on a separate sheet of paper first. Then copy the answers onto the form in pen.

The form on the following page shows an application for a savings account.

COMPUTER TIP

Most word-processing programs contain standard document styles to choose from. Many programs also allow you to create a custom style that you can store and use again.

Savings Account Application Form

Tri-Town Savings Bank

Type of Account: _Savings_

Customer's Name: _Karen Kelly_

Home Address (Street): _16 River Drive_

(City): _Hanover_ (State): _NH_ (Zip): _03755_

Phone: _646-1212_ Date of Birth: _4/24/88_

Social Security: _184-45-4380_

Initial Deposit: _$10.00_ Branch: _Hanover_

Signature: _Karen Kelly_ Date: _2/28/00_

When you want to put money into your account, you will need to fill out a savings deposit slip.

Deposit Slip

Tri-Town Savings Bank   Date _3/17/00_

Karen Kelly

NAME ON ACCOUNT (PLEASE PRINT)

ACCOUNT NUMBER | 1 | 2 | 3 | 4 | 5

CASH	$50	00
CHECKS (LIST SEPARATELY)	$25	00
TOTAL	$75	00

Writing Different Kinds of Letters

The following exercises will give you practice in writing various kinds of letters, with different purposes. Remember to use the proper form for each letter you write.

Writing Friendly Letters

Sending someone a handwritten letter can be great way to be in touch, even in today's world of E-mail messages, fax machines, and voice mailboxes. The following exercise will give you practice in writing a friendly letter to someone you know. The person who receives a friendly letter from you may even send you a handwritten response!

Writing a Friendly Letter   Draft a letter to a friend or relative about something happening in your life. Think of a way to encourage an answer from the person to whom you are writing. Send your letter to your friend or relative. Remember to respond in a timely fashion when you get a response.

Writing Social Letters

Whether you are writing to invite someone to a party, to decline an invitation, or to express thanks, you can use the form for social letters to achieve your purpose. The following exercises will give you practice in writing all three kinds of social letters.

Writing an Invitation   Imagine you are giving a party. Answer the following questions: What is the occasion of the party? Where and when will it be given? What special details might your guests need to know? Then draft the invitation to your party using the personal letter form.

Writing a Letter of Regret   Imagine you have received an invitation to a birthday party for a friend. Write a letter of regret explaining why you will be unable to attend.

Writing a Thank-You Letter   Write a letter to someone who took the time, energy, or expense to do something for you. Be specific in explaining why his or her action means so much to you.

Writing Business Letters

Use the skills you learned about business letters to practice writing a request letter and an order letter. The following exercises will help you. Remember to use a proper heading, an inside address, and a signature after your closing. The body of each letter will depend on your purpose for writing.

Writing a Letter of Request   Imagine you are researching life on the ocean floor. Write a letter to a museum requesting information. You may want to find the name and address of a museum in your area. Be specific in requesting the kind of information you wish to receive.

Writing an Order Letter   Imagine that you are living one hundred years ago. Write a letter to a company, ordering merchandise. Use your knowledge of the past to create the company and the merchandise that might have been available. You may choose to do research in the library, on the Internet, or by interviewing a family member.

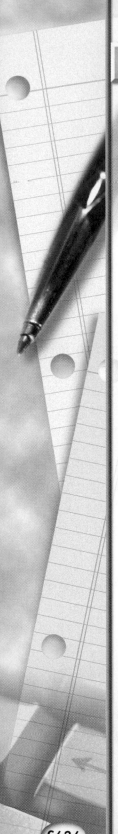

A Writer Writes
A Personal Letter

Purpose: to express admiration

Audience: a person from history

Choose one person you admire from the following list of famous people from the past, or choose someone else you prefer. Then in your **journal**, write down questions you might want to ask this person.

Write a personal letter to the person you chose. Before you write, consider what would be the appropriate tone for your purpose.

Think about the following ideas. What would you like to be able to communicate to this person? Brainstorm with someone, freewrite, or cluster to develop reasons why these topics would be important to convey to your reader.

- what effect the person has on your life
- how the person is remembered today
- what effect the person has had on the world
- how the world is different today
- what things are happening now that would be of interest to the receiver of your letter

Famous People from History
1. Martha Graham: dancer
2. Crazy Horse: Dakota Sioux Chief
3. Jackie Robinson: baseball player
4. Amelia Earhart: aviator
5. Martin Luther King, Jr.: civil rights leader
6. Alfred Hitchcock: film director
7. Susan B. Anthony: women's rights leader

A Business Letter

Purpose: to order stage props

Audience: order filler at Theater Supplies

Imagine that you are the set director for a play called **The Haunted Castle.** You have only one hundred dollars to spend for props. Choose from the following items advertised in the Theater Supplies fall catalog and order the things you need. The address of Theater Supplies is 45 Highland Avenue, Lexington, Massachusetts 02173. Add $7.50 for shipping and handling.

Item	Number	Price
creaking stairway	#368-B	$65.00
bushel of cobwebs	46-9z	9.00
drawbridge	55-C	82.00
dungeon cell	116-V	47.50
black curtains	99-D	24.00
ghoulish-laughter tape	20-A	3.75 each
torches	67-A	7.50 each
portrait with moving eyes	21-B	35.00
motorized rats	56-X	12.00 each
puffs of smoke	77-221	34.00 each

do not hold with the tenet, which has been popular during the last decade, "It's not enough that I succeed; my best friend must fail." With this everyone loses. With this ritual today you are officially part of the struggle. "Which struggle?" you say. In the end there is only one struggle: The struggle is to survive on the planet. The human race is struggling for survival every day, and our only weapon is knowledge. It is the shell on our backs, the poison in our fangs, and the camouflage that covers our bodies. Gaining knowledge is our only hope for survival. Passing that knowledge on to future generations is our most important challenge. Our society needs a good educational system. You have graduated, so you may now start to learn. You must learn so that you will teach. We have a long way to go before we are living in a symbiotic relationship with this planet. Symbiosis is two dissimilar organisms living together—especially when the association is mutually beneficial. It is the most important thing that I learned from my friend here at the film school. It is the most important thing we must learn if we are to survive as a society. Thank you very much.

Thinking as a Writer

Evaluating the Effectiveness of a Speech

- What was George Lucas's purpose in delivering this speech? To whom do you think he was speaking?
- What impact do you think the speech had on the audience? Do you think the speech achieved its purpose?
- How did you feel at the end of the speech? What things did the speaker say to make you feel that way?

Matching the Tone to the Content

Oral Expression
- Take turns with a partner reading aloud and listening to different parts of the speech. Discuss the ways the speaker uses language to engage the listener. Are there any special words or phrases that stand out?
- Try to match your style of reading to the tone of the speech. Do you think the speech invites a special tone to come through? What is it?

Evaluating a Visual Image

Viewing Visuals are often used during speeches to reinforce the ideas of the presentation.

At the right is a poster for the movie *Star Wars,* directed by George Lucas.

- Would this have been an effective visual for Lucas's speech? Why or why not?
- How does this image relate to the ideas presented in the speech?
- What other visuals might have been appropriate?

Developing Your Informal Speaking Skills

In your day-to-day life, there is not much time for formal speeches. For example, if you are on a brief phone call with a friend, or if someone asks you for directions, you will not have a chance to prepare a formal speech. That is why informal speeches are useful ways to communicate—they require little or no advance preparation. However, before you speak informally, you can still organize your ideas to make sure your message is clear and easy to understand.

Informal speaking is a form of speech that is suitable for everyday use or for casual occasions.

Giving Directions

If you have ever been lost, you know how important a clear set of directions can be. Read the two sets of directions that follow.

UNCLEAR   The concert hall? That's not too far from here. Just go down the main street for a while. Turn at the traffic light, go down that street a short way, and it is on your right.

CLEAR   To get to the concert hall, continue on Central Street for two blocks. At the second traffic light, take a right onto Grove Avenue. Follow Grove Avenue for one-half mile. You will cross a small bridge, and the concert hall will be on your right.

Notice that the second set of directions gives specific details, such as exact distances, street names, and landmarks. The first set of directions does not provide enough information. When you give directions, remember that you may know exactly where a place is located, but the other person does not.

The following strategies will help you give clear, concise directions.

Giving Directions

- Use *right, left,* and *straight* rather than *north, south, east,* or *west.*
- Use names of streets if you know them.
- Mention landmarks whenever possible.
- Include the approximate number of miles if you know this information.
- If possible, draw a map.
- Do not give directions for a difficult shortcut.
- If you are unsure of the correct directions, do not guess at them. Direct the person to someone who might know.
- Speak clearly.
- Repeat the directions or have the other person repeat the directions to you.
- Look at the person who asks you for directions.
- Pay attention to nonverbal clues that may indicate he or she does not understand.

When you give directions, keep in mind that most people cannot easily remember more than three to five steps of directions. If the directions are long and complicated, sometimes the best thing to do is give directions to a halfway point. Then tell the person to ask for additional directions from there. Whatever directions you give, make sure they are clear and accurate.

Practice Your Skills

● *Improving Directions*

List five errors in the directions below. Then rewrite the directions using specific details of your own choice.

Oh, the Crown Building! Go south on the main street through the town for a while. Turn at the streetlight and go for another mile or so. After you cross a bridge, go north. The Crown Building should be on your left.

● *Giving and Following Directions*

Write directions from your classroom to the following places in your school. Include as many specific details as possible. Then take turns with a partner reading your directions. Try to follow the directions you are given. If anything is unclear about the instructions, ask questions to clarify. Discuss ways the directions could be improved.

1. cafeteria   **4.** library

2. gymnasium   **5.** playground

3. auditorium   **6.** principal's office

Developing Your Formal Speaking Skills

Have you ever given an oral book report or made a nomination speech during a school assembly? Situations such as these are called formal speeches. A **formal speech** is usually longer than an informal speech, and it requires careful preparation.

Preparing Your Speech

The steps that you follow when you prepare a formal speech are much the same as those that you follow when you prepare a written report. *(page C396)* The main difference is that you will practice your speech and deliver it orally rather than write it.

Choosing and Limiting a Subject

To choose an appropriate subject, first make a list of subjects that you know well. Then choose one that both you and your audience will enjoy. For example, if you were speaking to younger students about your school, you might tell them about the courses your school offers. If you were speaking to your classmates, however, this subject would not interest them. A better subject for your classmates might be new courses the school should offer in the coming year.

Once you have decided on a subject, think about how much time you have to deliver your speech. If you have only ten minutes, you cannot give a speech on all the courses you would like to see your school offer. Instead, you might talk about the importance of offering computer courses.

Is Thinking

Evaluating Your Audience

Before choosing a subject for a speech, think about who your audience will be. Throughout your school years, most of your speeches will be delivered to your class. Once in a while, however, you may be asked to give a short speech before teachers or give a talk to a group of younger students. You need to be sure that the speech you give is right for your audience.

Answering the following questions will help you decide what subject will be suitable for your audience. This will also help you decide what information you should include in your speech.

KNOWING YOUR AUDIENCE

1. What are the interests of my audience? Are they similar to mine?

2. What will my audience already know about the subject I have chosen for my speech?

3. What point of view will my audience have?

4. Is my audience there to learn, to be persuaded, or to be entertained?

THINKING PRACTICE

Choose one of the following occasions, and use the questions above to evaluate your audience. How do your answers affect the way you would prepare your speech?

1. Your little sister asks you to speak in front of her class about middle school.

2. You just won a cooking contest, and a reporter asks you for a statement.

3. You are asked to read a story to a group of first graders and talk about it.

PRACTICE YOUR SKILLS

● *Choosing and Limiting a Subject*

Write the subject of a speech for each item below. Then limit each subject so that it is suitable for a ten-minute speech.

EXAMPLE   food
POSSIBLE ANSWERS   food rich in vitamins
                       citrus foods rich in Vitamin C

1. great musicians   **6.** snakes

2. heroines   **7.** oceans

3. movies   **8.** great books

4. Olympic events   **9.** world leaders

5. environmental issues   **10.** American history

Communicate Your Ideas

PREWRITING *Subject*

You will be presenting a ten-minute speech to your class. The topic will be "Someone I Admire". Brainstorm, cluster or freewrite to choose a subject that is appropriate to the length and audience of your speech. Jot down the subject, as well as any initial ideas you may have about it. Save your work for later use.

SAVE YOUR WORK

Understanding Your Purpose

Before you gather information about your speech, you should think about your purpose. Most speeches have one of the following three purposes.

PURPOSES OF A SPEECH

Purpose	Examples
To Inform	• to explain how the Special Olympics began
	• to explain how the Egyptian pyramids were built
	• to explain how electricity works
To Persuade	• to encourage people to vote for a certain person for president
	• to encourage others to try out for the school musical
	• to convince others to visit Canada
To Entertain	• to tell about the time you played the lead in a play and forgot your lines
	• to tell about the time you went sailing without a sail
	• to tell about the first time you went ice-skating

PRACTICE YOUR SKILLS

● *Determining a Purpose for a Speech*

Label the purpose of each speech: to inform, to persuade, or to entertain.

1. to explain how exercise and diet affect people's health

2. to give information about the life of an athlete

3. to encourage students to attend school events

4. to tell about the time you went fishing and ended up going swimming instead

5. to encourage your listeners to buy Wam-o running shoes

6. to explain how to make a flying machine from a milk carton

7. to explain the plot of Steven Spielberg's science fiction movie *ET*

8. to tell about the day you spent with a movie star

9. to encourage your teachers to make a computer available in every classroom

10. to tell about your first dance class

Communicate Your Ideas

PREWRITING *Purpose*

Look back at the subject you chose for your speech. Decide on the purpose for your speech. Note your purpose. Save your work for later use.

Gathering and Organizing Your Information

The next steps in preparing your speech are to gather information and then organize it. These steps are similar to those you follow when writing a report. *(pages C375–C383)* Following are some helpful reminders to help you gather and organize your information.

Gathering Information
- List what you already know about your subject.
- Gather more information in the library or through an interview.
- Find interesting examples and quotations to include.
- Take notes on the information you find.

Organizing Information
- Make an outline of your speech.

- The **introduction** of your speech should capture the attention of your audience. It should also include the main idea of your speech.
- The **body** of your speech should include your supporting points. Arrange your points in a logical order. Use transitions to connect your ideas.
- The **conclusion** of your speech should summarize your main idea.

PRACTICE YOUR SKILLS

● *Gathering Information with Note Cards*

The following paragraph about George Lucas is from *Encyclopedia Britannica Online.* **Take index card notes on the paragraph as if you were preparing a speech about Lucas's life. An example card has been filled out for you.**

Lucas became interested in filmmaking while in high school. He received encouragement from the cinematographer Haskell Wexler and gained admission to the film department of the University of Southern California (B.A., 1966). Lucas's first full-length film was *THX 1138* (1971), a grim fantasy about a robotized, dehumanized society in the distant future. His second film, *American Graffiti* (1973), a sympathetic recollection of adolescent American life in the early 1960s, was a surprise success at the box office.

Source: Encyclopedia Britannica Online
—first full-length film: THX 1138
—1971
—about future robot society
par. 5

PREWRITING, DRAFTING *Research, Outline*

Look back at the subject and purpose you chose for your speech. Write what you know about it on note cards. Next, go to the library and find information for at least four more note cards. Then organize your cards and write an outline of your speech. Save your work for later use.

Practicing Your Speech

Practicing your speech aloud is a very important step in delivering a successful speech. Following are some helpful suggestions to think about as you practice.

> ### Practicing Your Speech
>
> - Read your complete outline several times until you are familiar with all the information.
> - Make a few notes to use as you practice.
> - Practice in front of a long mirror so that you will be aware of your facial expressions and gestures.
> - Practice looking around the room as you talk.
> - Time the length of your speech. If it is too long, decide what information you can omit. If it is too short, you should find more information.
> - Practice over a period of several days.

After practicing your speech several times, try it before members of your family or some friends and ask for suggestions. If possible, tape-record your speech. Listen especially for how often you say "um" or "ah." The more you practice your speech aloud, the more self-confident you will become.

Prewriting Workshop
Drafting Workshop
Revising Workshop
Editing Workshop ▶
Publishing Workshop

Run-on Sentences

Often when preparing speeches, people try to put too much information into one sentence. This kind of sentence error is called a run-on sentence. A **run-on sentence** is two or more sentences that are written or spoken as one sentence. They are separated by a comma or no punctuation mark at all. Run-on sentences may confuse your audience or cause them to become bored with your speech. Correct run-on sentences using the following strategies.

- Turn a run-on sentence into two separate sentences.

RUN-ON SENTENCE	Gaining knowledge is our only hope for survival passing that knowledge on to future generations is our most important challenge.
SEPARATE SENTENCES	Gaining knowledge is our only hope for survival. Passing that knowledge on to future generations is our most important challenge.

- Create a compound sentence by adding a comma and a conjunction such as *and*, *but*, *or,* or *yet*.

RUN-ON SENTENCE	We recommended each other for jobs we helped each other with our projects, we worked on each other's scripts.
COMPOUND SENTENCE	We recommended each other for jobs, we helped each other with our projects, and we worked on each other's scripts.

Communicate Your Ideas

REVISING, EDITING *Practice*

Practice your speech several times. Choose a partner and take turns practicing your speech in front of each other. Listen to your classmate's speech and discuss how the speech might be improved. If needed, revise and edit your speech. Save your work.

Delivering Your Speech

If you are well prepared, you are less likely to feel nervous. Following are some suggestions for delivering your speech.

Guidelines for Delivering Your Speech

- Be well prepared and have all the necessary materials.
- Wait until your audience is quiet and settled.
- Take a deep breath and begin.
- Stand with your weight evenly divided between both feet. Avoid swaying back and forth.
- Speak slowly, clearly, and loudly enough to be heard.
- Use rehearsed gestures and facial expressions to emphasize your main points.
- Look directly at the people in your audience, not over their heads. Try to make eye contact.
- Use pictures and other audiovisual aids to increase the attention of your audience.

The size of the letters that your computer prints is called the font size. You can print out your speech in a slightly larger than usual font size. This way, you can more easily read your outline as you give your speech. You can find the font controls on your tool bar under Font or Format. Try 14 or 15 point type.

Communicate Your Ideas

PUBLISHING

Present the speech you've been practicing before a group of classmates. In your **journal**, list things that you think you did well and things you would like to improve in your next speech. Save your speech for future reference.

PORTFOLIO

Time Out to Reflect

Join with your classmates to compare and contrast the different speeches. What makes one speech stand out in your mind? In the minds of your classmates? What skills do each of the students have to work on? You may want to use the Oral Presentation Assessment Form on page C453. Record this information in the Learning Log section of your **journal**.

▶ Process of Presenting a Speech

Remember that while preparing a speech you can move back and forth among the stages of the process. For example, during editing you may wish to return to the revising stage to add details that you have thought of. The numbers in parentheses in the list below refer to pages where you can get help with your preparation.

PREWRITING

- Identify a subject that suits the purpose and audience for your speech. *(pages C433–C436)*
- Limit your subject to fit the purpose, audience, and length of your speech. *(pages C433–C434)*
- Make a list of what you know about your subject along the lines of a general speech structure. *(page C437)*
- Research your material and write it on note cards. *(pages C437– C438)*
- Organize your note cards so that your ideas follow a logical order. *(pages C274–C278)*

DRAFTING

- Make an outline from your note cards. *(page C438)*

REVISING, EDITING

- Practice your speech and make notes. *(page C439)*
- Practice your speech in front of others and listen to their suggestions. *(page C439)*
- Make changes as needed.

PUBLISHING

- Remember that you are presenting your speech orally, not in writing.
- Use the **Guidelines for Delivering a Speech** to make your presentation as effective as possible. *(page C441)*
- Use the **Oral Presentation Assessment Form** for you and others to assess your speech so that you can improve your skills. *(page C453)*

Developing Your Listening Skills

Most people spend over 50 percent of each day just listening. Surprisingly, however, most people remember only about one-fourth of what they hear. This section will help you improve your listening skills.

> ## Guidelines for Listening to an Oral Presentation
>
> **During the Presentation:**
> - Pay attention.
> - Don't interrupt, shuffle, or make unneccessary noise.
> - Listen for comprehension and enjoyment.
> - Be alert to the expressive power of pause.
> - Observe the use of gesture, voice, and facial expression to enhance the message.
> - Listen for changes of volume, intonation, and pitch to emphasize important ideas.
>
> **After the Presentation:**
> - If possible, ask for an explanation of anything you didn't understand.
> - If the speaker is available, respond with appropriate remarks or questions and thank him or her for the presentation.

PRACTICE YOUR SKILLS

● *Listening Carefully*

Stop all classroom activity for several minutes and listen. Then describe each sound you hear. Compare your descriptions with those of your classmates.

▶ Listening to Enjoy and Appreciate

One of the most important aspects of listening is enjoying and appreciating what you are listening to. You will remember more about a presentation you enjoyed than one you were not interested in. Many times, speakers will use humor or descriptions to solidify their points and keep their speech interesting. Paying attention and listening carefully will help you to enjoy the speech more. You will also better appreciate what the speaker is trying to say.

PRACTICE YOUR SKILLS

● *Listening to Enjoy and Appreciate*

Take turns with a partner reading the following poem aloud. Close your eyes if that helps you focus. Take the time to enjoy and appreciate what you are hearing. When you have each heard the poem, answer the following questions:

> "*I am the creativity*" —Alexis De Veaux
>
> I am the dance step
> of the paintbrush singing
> I am the sculpture
> of the song
> the flame breath
> of words
> giving new life to paper
> yes, I am the creativity
> that never dies
> I am the creativity
> keeping my people
> alive

- Did you enjoy the poem? Why or why not?
- Even if you didn't enjoy the poem, did you appreciate what the author was trying to convey?

● Listening for Information and Taking Notes

To improve your ability to receive and understand a speaker's message, focus your attention on the main idea and supporting ideas of the speech.

Listening for the Main Idea

In a well-planned speech, the main idea, along with the speaker's purpose, will be in the introduction. Often both will be stated directly in a single sentence. For example, if you heard the sentence *Using a computer makes writing easier than using a typewriter,* you would know that the speech would be about the advantages of using a computer for writing. You would also know that the speaker's purpose would be to persuade you to use a computer rather than a typewriter.

Be alert during the introduction, however, because the main idea is not always stated directly. Instead, it may be expressed in a question, a quotation, or a personal example.

Listening for Supporting Ideas

Once you have identified a speaker's main idea and purpose, concentrate on finding the major supporting ideas in the speech. Listen for clues such as *There are three reasons why* or *I will explain the four main causes of,* since such phrases often introduce major supporting ideas. As the speech progresses, a speaker may also signal major supporting ideas by using transitional expressions like *first, second, third, moreover, most important,* or *finally.*

As each major supporting idea is introduced, listen for supporting details that the speaker offers to clarify or drive home the major idea. These supporting details often take the form of facts and examples, such as statistics, quotations from experts, or anecdotes. In some cases a speaker will alert you to an important supporting point by introducing it with a phrase such as *for example, studies show that,* or *according to one expert.*

Keep in mind that not all details are important. As you listen to the speech, focus on major supporting ideas and supporting points that help you understand and evaluate the speaker's main idea. If anything is unclear and the speaker is available after the presentation, ask questions that may clarify the speech for you.

Taking Notes While Listening

Taking notes on speeches helps you to listen more carefully. In order to write down the information, you need to listen for important points and organize the information clearly. Following are some guidelines for taking notes.

> **Taking Notes on Speeches**
> - Write the main ideas presented in the introduction.
> - Write the main topics, using Roman numerals (I, II, III) in an outline form.
> - Under each main topic, write the subtopics or supporting points, using capital letters (A, B, C).
> - In the conclusion of the speech, write the restatement of the main idea.

On the following page is an outline of a speech on the subject of how video games are designed.

Main Idea

Designing video games is a complex, carefully planned procedure.

Main Topic
Subtopics

I. Games developed around one theme
   A. Ideas from books, magazines, movies, dreams, life experience
   B. Ideas suggested by other popular games
II. Idea or theme developed on paper
   A. Sequence of sketches or drawings called storyboards
   B. Flow charts or block diagrams showing a game in words and boxes
III. Game programmed into computer
   A. Game coded in *assembly* or *machine* computer language
   B. *Assembly* languages give game its speed and exactness
IV. Game tested and marketed
   A. Children play new games, and their reactions are studied
   B. Games put in arcades and records kept on use
   C. If popular, game produced in large quantities and sold for home use

Summary statement: Designing video games includes several steps. They are (1) developing a theme, (2) putting it down on paper, (3) programming the game into the computer, and (4) testing and marketing the game.

When you take notes, do not try to write everything down. If you do, you might miss important points. Write only the information that it is necessary to remember accurately. Your notes will then help you remember the other details.

PRACTICE YOUR SKILLS

● *Listening, Taking Notes and Following Directions*

Prepare a brief explanation of how to do something, such as how to do a certain dance step or how to make an omelet.

- Take notes as each student presents an explanation to the class.

- When the explanation is complete, summarize it in one complete sentence.

- Clarify with the speaker any points about which you are unclear.

- If you didn't know how to do something before, use what you heard to try to do it. Were the directions clear enough for you to follow?

- Compare notes with your classmates to see if you have included the same topics.

● *Listening to Information and Taking Notes*

Work with a classmate who attends the same science or social studies class as you do. Working separately, listen carefully during the next discussion period and take notes.

- Try to restate the main ideas of the discussion in a few sentences.

- Compare your notes with your classmate's. Did you miss any important ideas?

Listening Critically

When listening to a speech, always evaluate what is being said. One way to do this is to consider the perspective of the speaker. What point of view does the speaker have on the subject? Does the speaker have any reason to mislead the audience in any way? One way a listening audience can avoid being misled is by differentiating misleading information from actual facts. The following sections will help you do just that.

Hasty Generalizations

A **hasty generalization** is a misleading statement. It is a broad judgement based on only a few examples. A hasty generalization does not consider individual differences.

HASTY GENERALIZATIONS	All football games are boring.
	The buses never leave on time.
	Taxes are unfair for everyone.

Such words as *all, always, never, none, everyone,* and *only* often signal a hasty generalization. Although *some* football games may be boring, *all* are not. Although buses may *sometimes* be late, it is unlikely that they *never* leave on schedule. In the same way, the tax system may treat *some* people unfairly, but not *everyone*. Since a hasty generalization may contain some truth, it can sound entirely true—if you are not listening carefully.

PRACTICE YOUR SKILLS

● *Rewriting Hasty Generalizations*

Rewrite the following hasty generalizations so that they are not misleading.

EXAMPLE   The city is always noisy.
POSSIBLE ANSWER Sometimes the city is noisy.

1. That rock group never sings songs I like.

2. The service at Bob's Grill is always slow.

3. Only people who read the newspaper are informed.

4. All teenagers are irresponsible.

5. Everyone in our neighborhood likes dogs.

Fact and Opinion

A **fact** is a statement that can be proved, but an **opinion** is a personal feeling or judgment.

FACT   Albany is the capital of New York.
OPINION Albany is a wonderful city.

FACT   The rock group the Mobots will tour the United States this summer.
OPINION The Mobots is the best rock group in the world.

Very often *opinions* are stated as facts. Sometimes it is only a careful listener who can tell them apart.

PRACTICE YOUR SKILLS

● *Understanding Fact and Opinion*

Label each statement *fact* or *opinion*.

1. Our school has a girls' basketball team.

2. Christopher Hamilton is a poor actor.

3. Our school is the oldest school in the city.

4. Maria won the state spelling contest.

5. Everyone should go to college.

6. Our cafeteria serves terrible food.

7. California is the best state to live in.

8. Water expands when it is frozen.

9. My mother and father were born in Oklahoma.

10. Everyone today wants something for nothing.

Political Debate

Among the many uses of public speaking is the political debate. Such debates, between supporters and opponents of a proposed idea, or between candidates for elective office, have been an important part of American politics since the country began. In 1960, however, millions of people watched presidential candidates Senator John F. Kennedy and Vice President Richard M. Nixon in the first-ever televised political debates. Suddenly Americans were able to see for themselves how the candidates looked and sounded, instead of just reading a description in a newspaper. In fact, because of close-ups and editing, how the candidates looked and sounded suddenly seemed more important than their political beliefs.

Nixon did not appear relaxed. Under the hot television lights, he began to perspire visibly. In contrast, Kennedy appeared poised and confident. Naturally more comfortable, younger, and better-looking than Nixon, Kennedy—through the medium of television—won the hearts of millions of Americans during those debates.

Media Activity

Using the Internet or your school library, research the Kennedy-Nixon debates. One place to read a transcript and hear a recording of one of the debates is at http://www.cs.umb.edu/jfklib/60-2nd.htm. What does the transcript tell you about what Americans saw on their televisions that night? What does the recording tell you? Should the qualities the debate revealed be important in selecting a president? How do you think this debate affected how politicians campaign today? Write a paragraph that discusses your findings.

Listening to Evaluate

After you have listened to a speech in class, you can assess the speech for its effectiveness. Through self-assessment and sharing others' assessments, you can improve your listening and speaking skills and help your classmates to improve theirs. You may want to use the Oral Presentation Assessment Form.

ORAL PRESENTATION ASSESSMENT FORM

SUBJECT _____

Speaker _____ Date _____

Content
Was the subject appropriate for the audience?
Was the subject appropriate for the length of the speech?
Was the main point clear?
Was the purpose clear?
Did all the ideas clearly relate to the subject?

Organization
Was the introduction clear and interesting?
Did the introduction include the main idea?
Did the ideas in the body follow a logical order?
Were transitions used between ideas?
Did the conclusion summarize the main idea?

Presentation
Was the speaker well prepared?
Did the speaker speak loudly and clearly enough?
Did the speaker speak at a good speed?
Did the speaker make eye contact with the audience?
Did the speaker speak at a good pitch and tone of voice?
Did the speaker use gestures and pauses well?
If there were audiovisual aids or other props, were they used well?
Were cue cards or an outline used well?
Comments/Added Criteria _____

A Speaker Speaks

Purpose: to share information about your cultural traditions

Audience: your classmates

Prewriting

In his speech *(page C427)*, George Lucas talks about the culture he grew up in and how it affected him in later life. He explains that growing up in the sixties led him to feel a responsibility for his fellow human beings. Reread the speech, noticing how Lucas shares his knowledge of the times in which he grew up.

Your own culture is a big part of who you are. One side of your cultural heritage is your family traditions. Think about your family's origins. Are there any traditions or holidays your family celebrates because of your background? Choose one of these events to share with your class in a ten-minute speech. Keep in mind the length of the speech, the audience, and your purpose in sharing. Make notes on anything you already know about your subject. Do additional research if necessary: use reference materials and talk to older family members. When you have enough information, organize it into a logical order.

Drafting

Use your organized notes to outline your speech. Be sure to include an introduction, a body, and a conclusion. If necessary, transfer the outline to index cards that you will use during the speech. As you prepare your speech, keep in mind that certain words you choose may be directly related to your background.

Your audience may not understand these phrases unless you explain their meaning.

Practicing

Practice your speech for a few days. Observe yourself in a mirror and use body language and gestures to reinforce important ideas. Experiment with pauses. Time your speech, then add or remove material as necessary. When you are comfortable, practice your speech in front of a friend who can give you advice. Use suggestions to revise. If needed, edit your outline. Prepare any visuals you plan to use.

Speaking

When it is time to deliver your speech to your class, relax and take your time. Deliver the speech as you practiced it, using rehearsed gestures and pauses. Remember to display any visuals you have prepared. When you are finished, remember to thank your audience.

Listening

- Listen carefully while your classmates give their speeches.
- See if any of your ideas on cultural customs are similar to those expressed in the speeches. Perhaps you share some element of culture, or maybe your cultural background is very different from theirs.
- Enjoy and appreciate what your classmates are sharing with you. Be attentive!
- Listen for the main and supporting ideas.
- If you have questions or comments on something, wait until the speaker is done and then you can speak.
- Speak with the rest of the audience about what you heard, comparing your perceptions of the speeches.

Connection Collection

Representing in Different Ways

From Visuals . . .

BIG TOP CIRCUS

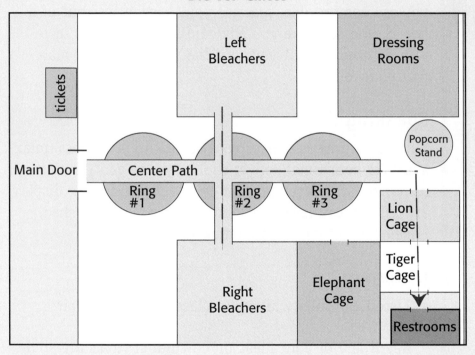

. . . to Print

Using the map above, prepare a short announcement giving directions to the restroom to the circus audience. Be sure your directions are clear and concise.

Welcome to Big Top Circus. If you need to use the telephones anytime during the performance please follow these directions:

- Exit the bleachers down the center path and head toward the main door.
- Once outside you will see a ladder to your left.
- Proceed up the ladder for 50 feet and then across the high wire to the far platform.
- From there, descend the ladder.
- The telephones will be directly in front of you, next to the giant cannon. Please do not speak to the man in the cannon as he is preparing for his act. Thank you and enjoy the show.

. . . to Visuals

From the information in the above instructions, draw a map showing the circus audience how to get to the public telephones.

- **Which strategies can be used for creating both written and visual representations? Which strategies apply to one, not both? Which type of representation is more effective?**
- **Draw a conclusion and write briefly about the differences between written ideas and visual representations.**

Writing for Oral Communication
Descriptive Speech

Your co-workers at Sitstill Inc. have decided to start a basket-weaving club. While you appreciate the beauty of finely woven crafts, you would rather participate in a more lively activity. You think it would be good for the employees to get outside and get some exercise.

> **Prepare a speech for your co-workers about some of the activities you think they might enjoy. Be sure your speech has an introduction, body, and conclusion. Describe the activities using vivid language and details. Use colorful verbs to grab and hold their interest. Deliver your speech to classmates who will act as co-workers.**
>
> **What strategies did you use to make your description interesting to your co-workers?**

You can find more information on preparing speeches on pages C433–C439.

Writing for Oral Communication
Directions for Your Dog

As you were eating breakfast this morning your dog, Chat, stood up on his hind legs and spoke to you in perfect English. As shocking as this was, you were also surprised to hear him say that he disliked the food that you have been feeding him for the past two years. He would like to go to the store to pick out his own food.

> **Prepare directions for Chat to the store closest to your home. Be certain to tell him the distances he will have to go and specific directions like right and left. Mention any landmarks. Read your directions to a classmate who will listen as Chat. Speak slowly and clearly so he doesn't get lost.**
>
> **What strategies did you use to give Chat directions?**

You can find information on giving directions on pages C430–C432.

Assess Your Learning

Your theories on the many uses for bubble gum are revolutionary. In fact, you were recently nominated for the No-tell Peace Prize for your book, *Chew Our Way to a Brand New World*.

▶ Prepare an informative speech about the many uses of gum to present at a worldwide press conference.

▶ As you prepare remember that the style of your speech should suit the occasion and audience of the speech. Be sure your speech contains an introduction, body, and conclusion. Try to capture the audience's attention in the introduction. Arrange the supporting points in the body of your speech in a logical order to ensure coherence. Practice your speech, paying attention to body language that can emphasize your main points. Deliver your speech to your classmates who will listen as reporters at the press conference.

▶ *Before You Write* Consider the following questions:
What is the *subject?*
What is the *occasion?*
Who is the *audience?*
What is the *purpose?*

▶ *After You Write* Evaluate your work using the following criteria:
- Does the speech suit the occasion and audience?
- Does the speech contain an introduction, body and conclusion?
- Does the introduction seek to capture the audience's attention?
- Are ideas organized to ensure coherence, logical progression and support?
- Does the conclusion of the speech summarize the main ideas?
- Is the work free of run-on sentences?
- When presented, was the speech well delivered?

Write briefly on how well you did. Point out your strengths and areas for improvement.

CHAPTER 15

Vocabulary

Words are powerful. They give you control over your surroundings. When you were a baby, for example, you learned the word *water*. Suddenly you had the power to request exactly what you wanted when you were thirsty. The more words you know, the more "word power" you have.

In this chapter, you will learn about the origins, varieties, and structure of the English language. This will be helpful to you as a writer—giving you a deeper understanding of the tools you use to shape your ideas into written form. You will be better able to choose what types of language are appropriate for different occasions and audiences.

Reading with a Writer's Eye

There are many theories about how human language first came about. The following selection describes some of the most popular theories. Read the selection a few times. First, read through it to get a general understanding. Then read it again. Try making a mental list of the ways language may have first been used. Is language still used for the same purposes?

FROM

NATIVE TONGUES

Charles Berlitz

There are a variety of theories concerning the first words uttered by emerging humankind. Perhaps language started with a warning to others, such as "Look out!" "Run!" "Over here!" or "Help!" as a swiftly moving or lumbering beast was approaching. Other "first words" may have been hunting instructions during a group effort or—later—orders from the leader of a war party. On a more personal level, perhaps the first words expressed a warning of a threat to stay away from one's food, or mate, or possession, or warned someone away from a cave or—as animals still do—challenged a rival to combat.

Linguists[1] call another explanation about the beginning of language the "pooh-pooh" theory. It suggests that our first words came as an exclamation of dislike, hunger, pain, or pleasure, eventually leading to the expression of more developed ideas and emotions. In this case the first word would have been an involuntary "Ow!" which, in most languages, still exists as some form of "ow" or "ai."

The "bow-wow" theory postulates[2] that emergent human beings established a beginning vocabulary based on the sounds that certain animals made, as a means of identifying them. This type of naming is still noticeable in childish references to

---

[1] **linguists:** (lĭng′ gwĭsts): *n.* People who study languages.
[2] **postulates:** (pŏs′ chə lāts): *v.* Claims.

a "moo-cow," a "bow-wow" for a dog, a "quack-quack" for a duck, and the expression "baa-baa black sheep." A cat in Chinese is a *mao,* spoken in a tone exactly parodying the "meow" of any cat. A striking example for the "bow-wow" theory that has come down through the ages is the word "barbarian," from *barbaros,* originally used by ancient Greek travelers to designate foreigners who did not speak Greek, the language of culture, but who sounded, as they spoke their outlandish tongues, like sheep bleating "baa-baa."

Still another explanation of the beginnings of language is offered by the "ding-dong" theory, which suggests that humans began their ascent to language by naming objects, actions, and phenomena with a recognizable sound, such as "boom" for thunder, "splash" for water, "swish" for a cutting weapon, or "crackle" for a fire. The Japanese *pika-pika* is a good descriptive word for a flash of lightning, as is the English "boom!" for any explosion, including the atom bomb. The word for coining words to echo a sound (or to give a verbal impression of a sight) is *onomatopoeia*,[3] which comes from the Greek and means "to make a name."

In the language of the Chinook Indians of Oregon the word for "heart" is *tun-tun,* an apt description of the noise the heart makes if you listen to it.

The "yo-he-ho" concept of initial language development is based on a belief in human cooperation, certainly an idealistic explanation of the purpose of language. This theory proposes that the earliest language was chanting to stimulate collective effort, whether moving great stones to block off cave entrances from roving carnivores, carrying or dragging large game back to the tribal compound, or repeating warlike phrases to inflame

---

[3] **onomatopoeia** (ŏ′ nə măt′ ə pē′ ə): *n.* The forming of a word that imitates the sound of the thing it refers to.

the fighting spirit. It is fairly certain that poetry and song came from this aspect of beginning speech. Songs of this nature are still with us, such as the song of the Volga boatman and the sea chanties of clipper-ship days.

It is probable that humans started their speech patterns in small family groups and then, as their circles of communication spread, adopted new words from other groups. This went on until a common vocabulary or basic language was formed and proved its worth for cooperative hunting or raids.

Words that have come down from Neolithic[4] times can sometimes be recognized in languages spoken today. In Basque, the word for "knife" is a compound which translates as "the-stone-that-cuts," and "ceiling" literally means "roof-of-the-cave."

While theories of basic language origin refer to emergencies, the hunt, and combat, words for emotions and spiritual feelings probably derive from applying sounds to emotion—the "pooh-pooh" theory. "Love" and "hate" are good examples. In almost all languages the word for "love" is a pleasant, mellifluous[5] sound, while the word equivalent for "hate" is harsh and rasping. The same match of a sound and meaning is found in other word pairs ("beautiful" and "ugly," for example) in many languages.

Language probably derived not from one but from a combination of the various sources proposed by theorists. Max Müller, the famous archaeologist and linguist, suggested that the increasing development and intricacy of language followed the development of the human brain over a period of thousands of years.

---

[4] **Neolithic** (nē′ ə lĭth′ ĭk): *adj.* Of or relating to the period of human culture that began around 10,000 B.C. in the Middle East.
[5] **mellifluous** (mə lĭf′ loo əs): *adj.* Smooth and sweet.

Thinking as a Writer

Exploring the Purpose of Language

- According to the theories explained in the article, what did early humans probably first use language for? List the purposes.
- As a writer, do you use language for the same purposes as early humans?
- When certain writers, especially poets, cannot find the exact word they need to say something, they make one up. Look over the theories given in the selection. Which of these theories could you use to make up a word for a poem you were writing? Using the theory, explain the steps you would take to go about creating your "new word."

Using Onomatopoeia

- Oral Expression • Reread the section of the selection on page C462 regarding onomatopoeia. Read the examples given aloud. Listen to hear how the sounds of the words mimic the sounds of the things they name.
- Make a list of other words you know that are examples of onomatopoeia. Choose a partner and take turns reading your lists aloud. When your partner is reading, listen carefully. Can you hear why each word is an example of onomatopoeia?
- Choose a familiar object or animal that makes noise. Listen to it carefully. Pretend you have just invented or discovered this thing. Name it using onomatopoeia— make up a word (or words) that mimics the sound your invention or discovery makes.
- Explain to a partner why you chose the name you did. Ask that person if he or she agrees that you have chosen a suitable name.

Naming Objects by Sight

Viewing Often, simply the way something looks will bring to mind feelings, sounds, and words. Think of a kitten. Doesn't the word *fur* sound exactly like the softness of the cuddly creature?

- Look at the objects shown below. Name them according to the feelings and sounds that come to mind when you see them. Why did you choose the names you chose?

Growth of the English Language

Just like people, languages are born and they develop. Many different factors can influence the development of a language. Immigration, technology, and popular culture are some examples of things that have greatly influenced our own language. To better understand the vocabulary we use, we need to understand where our language comes from and how it has changed.

● Origins

The English language and all other languages come from a single language that was spoken thousands of years ago. At some point in history, a form of English branched off as a separate language. If you were to hear this early English spoken, it would probably sound like a foreign language and not at all like the English we speak today. This is because English has developed over the centuries. Words were added, and spellings, meanings, and pronunciations changed.

● Spelling

Although some words have stayed the same, many English words have changed spellings over the years. Even today, there are alternate spellings of the same word. Dictionaries call these the *preferred spelling* and the *variant spelling*. You should always use the preferred spelling when you write.

CHANGES IN SPELLING				
MODERN	center	music	plow	three
ORIGINAL	centre	musik	plough	threo

VARIATIONS IN SPELLING				
PREFERRED	ax	lovable	raccoon	theater
VARIANT	axe	loveable	racoon	theatre

 Pronunciation

Just as the spellings of English words have changed over centuries, so too have pronunciations. These changes in pronunciations can sometimes help explain what might otherwise seem like odd spellings of words. For example, the silent *k* in many modern English words is left over from the time when those words used to be pronounced with hard *c* or strong *k* sounds at their beginnings. In other words, at one time, in the words *knife, knight,* and *knee,* the *k* was pronounced and not a silent letter. Eventually, the pronunciations of the words changed, but the spellings remained, reflecting the words' history.

Meaning

The meanings of words have also changed over the years. For example, the word *fear* today usually means "to be afraid of" but at one time it also meant "to respect." The word *surf* had always referred to a water sport until the Internet came along. Now *surf* can also refer to exploring different Websites.

PRACTICE YOUR SKILLS

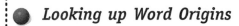

Looking up Word Origins

Look up the following words in the dictionary to find each of their origins. You can find more information on how to use the dictionary to find word origins in Chapter 16.

1. prop   **4.** trunk   **7.** approve

2. ski   **5.** jelly   **8.** alight

3. tuck   **6.** captain   **9.** oak

Varieties of the English Language

Although English is one language, there are many varieties of it. There are variations in the way it is spoken, differences in the way it is used, in varieties of sayings, and in meanings of the same words.

● American Dialects

The English language is made up of almost one million words, and it is spoken in many different countries around the world. Not all English-speaking people speak the language in the same way; even across our own country there are differences in the way different regions pronounce certain words. These different ways of speaking are called **dialects.** For example, New Englanders are said to speak with a twang and Southerners with a drawl.

American English varies among three main regional dialects: Eastern, Southern, and Standard American. Each of these dialects may contain many subdialects. Dialects can be different from one another in vocabulary, pronunciation, and even grammar. In Philadelphia, Pennsylvania, for instance, a large sandwich may be called a *hoagie,* and in Boston, Massachusetts, that same sandwich may be called a *submarine.* A similar sandwich in the South is called a *po'boy.* Dialects add color and richness to the English language.

● Standard American English

Standard American English is the most widely used and accepted form of English in our country. While it is not any more or less correct than other forms, using Standard American English helps people of different regions to be able to communicate clearly with one another. While dialects and other variations of American English may be appropriate in informal conversation and creative writing, Standard English should be used in formal speeches and informative writing. Standard English is the English taught in school and used in newspapers, on radios, and in scholarly works.

Writing Tip

Use Standard English when writing for school and for a large general audience.

PRACTICE YOUR SKILLS

● *Identifying Dialects*

Different people use different words for the same thing. With a small group of classmates, discuss the words you use for items in your home and how you pronounce them. For example, do you say *sofa, lounge, davenport, couch,* or *settee*? Do you say *soda, pop,* or *tonic*? Do you carry a *pail* or a *bucket*? Do you use the same words and pronunciations that you hear spoken on television?

● Nonstandard American English

Nonstandard American English is English that does not follow the rules and guidelines of Standard American English. It is not incorrect, but simply language that is inappropriate in situations, with audiences, or on occasions where Standard English is expected.

Colloquialisms

A **colloquialism** is an informal phrase or colorful expression that is not to be taken literally, but is understood to have a particular meaning. Colloquialisms are appropriate for conversation and informal writing but not for formal writing.

| COLLOQUIALISMS | As soon as Dan and Luis met, they **hit it off**. (got along well together) |
| | For dinner the Hendersons certainly **put out a spread**. (served a generous amount of food) |

Slang

Slang consists of nonstandard English expressions that are developed and used by particular groups. Such expressions are highly colorful, exaggerated, and often humorous. Although most slang goes out of fashion quickly, a few slang expressions—such as those that follow—have become a permanent part of the language. Slang is not appropriate for formal writing.

| SLANG EXPRESSIONS | Simone earned ten **bucks** (dollars) by mowing the Henshaws' lawn. |
| | Sitting and waiting for someone in an airport can be **a real drag.** (tiresome) |

PRACTICE YOUR SKILLS

● *Identifying Informal Language*

Each sentence below contains informal language. Rewrite each sentence using Standard English.

1. You should get a load of Jane's new bicycle.

2. James would leap at the chance to earn extra money.

3. My mom keeps bugging me to clean out the garage.

4. The library has tons of books on dinosaurs.

5. I ain't gonna go to the zoo with them on Saturday.

6. There are lots of things to do at the park.

7. It can be difficult and time-consuming to score a part-time summer job.

8. A rainy summer day can be a bummer.

9. I am going to have to power through my homework tonight in order to get it all done.

10. The band's last song brought the house down.

Tired Words

A **tired word** is a word that has been so overused that it has been drained of meaning. Take, for example, the word *wonderful*. This word literally means "full of wonder." Now, through overuse, the word means "good."

We often use tired words when we speak. We call sunsets "pretty," movies "fabulous," and sweaters "cute." None of these words conveys precise information, however.

> **Writing Tip**
>
> Avoid tired words and your writing will be fresher, more precise, and more interesting to read.

Denotations and Connotations

When you look up a word in a dictionary, you will find its denotative meaning. The **denotation** of a word means the *specific* definition of a word. However, sometimes through usage a word takes on additional meanings; this is the **connotation** of a word. For example, although *lazy* and *idle* have similar denotative meaning, they have a very different connotative meaning. *Lazy* has come to mean "not willing to work," while *idle* means "not working." The difference in connotative meanings of these words is important to consider when choosing which one to use in writing.

PRACTICE YOUR SKILLS

● *Identifying Denotations and Connotations*

Read the following list of words. Each pair shares a denotative meaning. Which word in each pair do you think also has a connotative meaning? Why?

1. smart; brainy
2. nosy; curious
3. tall; lanky
4. childish; youthful
5. mature; aged
6. boss; leader
7. economical; cheap
8. picky; selective
9. dark; unlit
10. clown; fool

COMPUTER TIP

E-mail users often use emoticons as a form of shorthand to transmit emotion to an unseeing correspondent. For example, you can convey sarcasm with a winking smiley face constructed with a semicolon and a single parenthesis: ;) Or, if you are having a bad day, you may construct a sad face: : (Emoticons are easy ways to add a connotation to an E-mail message, but they are poor substitutes for language. To convey emotion and ideas, use precise vocabulary.

Word Meaning

What do you do when you come across words that are new to you? Suppose you came across this sentence.

The short story took place in a bucolic setting.

Perhaps you know that *bucolic* means "rural" or "country-like," but more likely it is a new word to you. One way to learn its meaning is to look it up in a dictionary. In this chapter you will learn several other ways to unlock the meaning of a new word.

● Context Clues

Often you can pick up clues about a word's meaning from its context. The **context** of a word is the sentence, the surrounding words, or the situation in which a word is used. Use the surrounding words to determine the meaning of *automaton* in the following sentence.

CONTEXT CLUES	Dr. Sawyer's mechanical servant Robbie is the ideal **automaton.**

Mechanical servant tells you that an automaton is a robot.

There are several kinds of context clues. You have probably seen the following types often in your reading.

EXAMPLE	The **conifers**, such as cone-bearing pine and spruce trees, are found in cooler climates.
DEFINITION	Animals that feed on plants are **herbivores.**
SYNONYM	The **Isle** of Wight lies off the coast of England. The island is famous for its scenery and mild climate.

In the first item, examples of conifers appear in the sentence. In the second item, the word *herbivores* is defined in the sentence. In the third item, a synonym for the word *isle* is used in the following sentence. All of these examples show how the surrounding words can be used to determine the meaning of new words.

PRACTICE YOUR SKILLS

● *Using Sentence Context Clues*

Write the letter of the answer that is closest in meaning to the underlined word.

1. Kathleen is reading the <u>biography</u> of Thomas Edison because she is interested in his life as well as in his inventions.
(A) book   (B) life story   (C) encyclopedia
(D) paperback   (E) journal

2. Be sure to save your <u>receipt</u>; it will show when you bought your sweater and how much you paid for it.
(A) credit card   (B) money   (C) package
(D) sales slip   (E) price tag

3. James was nicknamed "Stretch" because he was so lean and <u>lanky</u>.
(A) handsome   (B) smart   (C) irritable
(D) handy   (E) tall

4. "I cannot <u>predict</u> the outcome of the game," the coach said, "but I can tell you that our players are ready to put up a good fight."
(A) foretell   (B) explain   (C) justify
(D) forgive   (E) undo

5. Superman didn't even <u>flinch</u> when the boulder came tumbling down on him; he just stood there, hands on hips, unmoved.
(A) cry out   (B) fly   (C) duck
(D) moan   (E) stare

6. While all the other members of the jury thought the man was guilty, a single <u>juror</u> held on to her "not guilty" vote.
(A) witness   (B) judge   (C) jury member
(D) officer   (E) defense lawyer

7. After several accidents, a new school law was passed that <u>prohibits</u> skateboards on school grounds.
(A) encourages   (B) forbids   (C) requires
(D) produces   (E) permits

8. In areas of high <u>elevation</u>, such as the Rocky Mountains, the air is thin and breathing is difficult.
(A) scenery   (B) height above sea level (C) trees
(D) rainfall   (E) temperature changes

9. When you fill out the order form, <u>specify</u> the size and color of the T-shirt you want so your order can be filled accurately.
(A) name exactly   (B) leave out   (C) cross out
(D) reduce   (E) pick out

10. The train sat <u>stationary</u> out in the middle of nowhere, while the anxious passengers wondered if it would ever move again.
(A) heavy   (B) unmoving   (C) loaded
(D) sliding   (E) rotating

● *Using Paragraph Context Clues*

Write each underlined word and its meaning. Use the context of the paragraph to help you. Then check your answers in a dictionary.

The aging <u>monarch</u> sat on his throne with his head bowed. Outside, the thunder of distant armies carried an <u>ominous</u> warning. The king knew that soon he would have to <u>yield</u> his throne to his enemies, who were now strong enough to overpower him. His only hope was the band of loyal, brave soldiers who had been <u>summoned</u> from fighting in a distant land. Would they <u>materialize</u> in time?

Suddenly the quiet of the throne room was shattered by a great <u>commotion</u> outside the palace. Were the cheers and hoofbeats those of his <u>valiant</u> troops, or were they the victory sounds of his <u>treacherous</u> enemies? <u>Rousing</u> himself from despair, the king raced toward the palace gate to <u>discern</u> his fate.

● Prefixes and Suffixes

Another way to discover the meanings of unfamiliar words is to break the words down into their parts. Suppose, for example, that you come across the word *disobey*. Chances are you recognized one part of this word, *obey*. This part is called the *root*.

A **root** is the part of the word that carries the basic meaning.

The roots in the following words are in **bold** type.

Roots	mis**trust**	un**drink**able
	dis**agree**ment	**joy**ful

PRACTICE YOUR SKILLS

● *Finding Roots*

Write each word and underline the root.

1. distasteful	**6.** unhappy	**11.** misfire
2. unreachable	**7.** visualize	**12.** subtopic
3. unwise	**8.** debtor	**13.** displease
4. prerecorded	**9.** unbearable	**14.** prepayment
5. truthful	**10.** dishonest	**15.** dependence

Prefixes

The part of the word that comes before the root is called a **prefix.** In the word *disobey,* the prefix is *dis-*. If you know that *dis-* means "not," then you can figure out that *disobey* means "not obey." Following are some common prefixes and their meanings.

PREFIX	MEANING	EXAMPLE
anti-	against	anti + freeze = antifreeze
dis-	not	dis + agree = disagree
in-	not	in + human = inhuman
mis-	incorrect	mis + spell = misspell
pre-	before	pre + school = preschool
re-	again	re + appear = reappear
sub-	under	sub + way = subway
un-	not	un + healthy = unhealthy

PRACTICE YOUR SKILLS

● *Combining Prefixes and Roots*

Write the prefix that has the same meaning as the underlined word. Then write the complete word defined after the equal sign.

EXAMPLE <u>again</u> + copy = copy again
ANSWER re-, recopy

1. <u>before</u> + view = to see something ahead of time

2. <u>against</u> + war = opposed to war

3. <u>incorrect</u> + pronounce = to use the wrong pronunciation

4. <u>again</u> + freeze = to freeze a second or third time

5. <u>not</u> + approve = to judge unfavorably

6. <u>incorrect</u> + print = an error in a published work

7. <u>not</u> + popular = not pleasing to most people

8. <u>under</u> + average = lower than average

9. <u>not</u> + direct = roundabout

10. <u>again</u> + capture = to seize again

● *Using Prefixes to Form Words*

Write as many words as you can by combining each prefix with as many roots as possible. Use a dictionary to be sure you have made real words.

Prefixes	anti-, re-, mis-, sub-, pre-, un-		
Roots	view	treat	place
	connect	take	divide
	organize	do	judge
	group	develop	freeze

Suffixes

The part of the word that comes after the root is called a **suffix.** Like prefixes, suffixes can have one or more syllables. Unlike prefixes, many suffixes can change a word from one part of speech to another. In the following chart, notice how suffixes can create different parts of speech.

NOUN SUFFIXES	MEANING	EXAMPLES
-ance, -ence	state of	depend + ence
-er, -or	one who or that	debt + or
-ment	state of	resent + ment
-ness	state of	kind + ness

VERB SUFFIXES	MEANING	EXAMPLES
-ize	make or cause to be	final + ize
-en	make or become	sharp + en

ADJECTIVE SUFFIXES	MEANING	EXAMPLES
-able	capable of	break + able
-ful	full of	care + ful

ADVERB SUFFIXES	MEANING	EXAMPLES
-ly	in a certain way	slow + ly

PRACTICE YOUR SKILLS

● **Combining Suffixes and Roots**

Write the suffix that has the same meaning as the underlined words. Then write the complete word defined after the equal sign.

EXAMPLE   bold + <u>state of</u> = daring

ANSWER   -ness, boldness

1. train + <u>capable of</u> = able to be taught

2. catch + <u>one who</u> = ball player behind batter

3. strength + <u>make or become</u> = to make stronger

4. rapid + <u>in a certain way</u> = quickly

5. hospital + <u>make or cause</u> = to place in a hospital

6. develop + <u>state of</u> = growth

7. soul + <u>full of</u> = filled with feeling

8. confine + <u>state of</u> = the state of being restricted

9. resist + <u>state of</u> = efforts to fight back

10. sick + <u>state of</u> = disease

● **Using Suffixes to Form Words**

Add two different suffixes to each word to create different parts of speech. After each word, write its part of speech. Use the list of suffixes on pages C478–C479 to help you.

Example	bright
Possible Answers	brighten—verb, brightly—adverb

1. fair	**11.** like
2. employ	**12.** treat
3. light	**13.** flat
4. visual	**14.** legal
5. deep	**15.** dark
6. collect	**16.** sad
7. rude	**17.** natural
8. read	**18.** teach
9. moral	**19.** quiet
10. personal	**20.** kind

● *Using Prefixes and Suffixes*

Write the letter of the answer that is closest in meaning to the word in capital letters. The prefixes and suffixes you have learned in this chapter will help you figure out the meanings of the capitalized words.

1. INFREQUENT (A) again and again (B) often (C) not often

2. REFRESH (A) not fresh (B) to become fresh again (C) to become fresh before

3. SUBMARINE (A) under water (B) across water (C) above water

4. PREPAID (A) paid late (B) paid in advance (C) not paid

5. DISPLEASE (A) not please (B) please again (C) please after

6. AVIATOR (A) state of flying (B) one who pilots (C) to cause to fly

7. HASTEN (A) to make haste (B) one who hurries (C) state of hurrying

8. CHANGEABLE   (A) state of changing
(B) to make a change   (C) capable of change

9. CHEERINESS   (A) capable of being cheery
(B) state of cheer   (C) one who is cheery

10. SORROWFUL   (A) against sorrow
(B) to cause sorrow   (C) full of sorrow

▶ Synonyms

Because English has so many words, you can choose words that express your meaning exactly. Sometimes two or more words will have similar meanings. A word that has nearly the same meaning as another word is called a **synonym.**

In the following sentences, the words *tall* and *towering* are synonyms. Although they have similar meanings, *towering* paints a more precise picture.

The shade from the **tall** tree kept us cool.
The shade from the **towering** tree kept us cool.

In these sentences *sat* and *perched* are synonyms. Which word gives you a clearer picture of the bird's position?

The bird **sat** on the ledge of my windowsill.
The bird **perched** on the ledge of my windowsill.

Dictionaries often include synonyms for words. Some also explain the slight differences in the meanings of synonyms. A thesaurus is a special type of dictionary that gives you many synonyms for a word.

Writing Tip

When you write, search for the word that conveys your meaning exactly. Use a dictionary or thesaurus to help you, but avoid using words that you do not fully understand. You should write in your own voice and style, and with your own words.

PRACTICE YOUR SKILLS

● *Recognizing Synonyms*

Write the letter of the answer that is closest in meaning to the word in capital letters. Then check your answers in a dictionary.

1. CONVICTION (A) infection (B) prison
   (C) belief (D) offering (E) revenue

2. NEUTRAL (A) electric (B) indifferent
   (C) sharp (D) lifeless (E) hardy

3. FATAL (A) deadly (B) earnest
   (C) pale (D) wishful (E) empty

4. SANITIZE (A) wrap (B) mock
   (C) worship (D) sterilize (E) wax

5. MOBILE (A) energetic (B) movable
   (C) graceful (D) sturdy (E) relaxed

6. FEAT (A) deed (B) game
   (C) hunt (D) cheer (E) gossip

7. ABSOLUTELY (A) carelessly (B) quickly
   (C) totally (D) possibly (E) doubtfully

8. ALTOGETHER (A) wholly (B) solely
   (C) tightly (D) separately (E) partly

9. CONCLUSION (A) continuation (B) ending
   (C) secret (D) promise (E) injury

10. DECOY (A) sticker (B) warning (C) flash
    (D) sacrifice (E) lure

● *Choosing the Better Word*

Write the synonym in parentheses that better fits the meaning of each sentence. Use a dictionary for help.

1. Our friends were so deep in (conversation, discourse) that they barely noticed us.

2. Lara has a (shiny, brilliant) mind.

3. Samuel (spotted, detected) a hint of disapproval in his father's voice.

4. The glass figurines were very (flimsy, fragile).

5. For his report Ian prepared a (graph, picture) showing the average monthly temperatures in Mexico City.

6. Marissa hoped a (lullaby, song) would calm her baby sister.

7. The speaker bored everyone with his (repetitious, monotonous) voice.

8. The decorator chose (neutral, indifferent) colors for the living room.

9. Kim's library books are (expected, overdue).

10. The baby (scribbled, wrote) all over the mural.

● *Using Synonyms*

Write as many synonyms as you can for the underlined word in each phrase.

1. a <u>nice</u> person

2. a <u>big</u> boat

3. a <u>great</u> day

4. a <u>good</u> movie

5. a <u>little</u> fish

6. a <u>tall</u> building

7. a <u>bad</u> time

8. a <u>hot</u> sun

9. a <u>sad</u> story

10. a <u>super</u> game

● Antonyms

An **antonym** is a word that means the opposite of another word. Dictionaries list antonyms for many words. All of the following pairs of words are antonyms.

amateur: professional

discard: save

stationary: movable

continuous: interrupted

vanity: modesty

routine: unusual

resident: visitor   resemble: differ

resistance: willingness   reduce: increase

Antonyms show a contrast between extremes. Often, however, there are words in between that show a smaller degree of contrast. Between *wet* and *dry,* for example, we can find such words as *damp, moist,* and *humid.* Knowing the whole range of words between antonyms will help you choose exactly the right word when you write.

COMPUTER TIP

Many word-processing programs have a Thesaurus feature. It can sometimes be found on the Tools menu, or combined with the Spell Check feature. This feature can be a valuable tool while writing. It will give you a list of synonyms (and sometimes antonyms) for any word with just a click of the mouse.

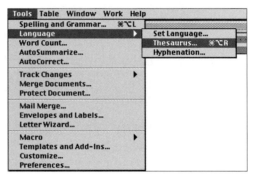

PRACTICE YOUR SKILLS

● *Recognizing Antonyms*

Write the letter of the answer that is most nearly opposite in meaning to the word in capital letters. Then check your answers in a dictionary.

1. SUSPICION   (A) crime   (B) trust   (C) worry
   (D) suspense   (E) kindness

2. TRIUMPHANT   (A) victorious   (B) disappointed
   (C) musical   (D) defeated   (E) loud

3. VILLAIN   (A) character   (B) joker   (C) hero
   (D) criminal   (E) resident

4. THOROUGH   (A) total   (B) narrow
(C) straight   (D) lasting   (E) incomplete

5. STRICT   (A) tight   (B) old
(C) permissive   (D) striped   (E) rigid

6. MATURE   (A) wise   (B) eager
(C) childish   (D) ripe   (E) respected

7. GALLANT   (A) courteous   (B) friendly
(C) daring   (D) cowardly   (E) similar

8. CHANGEABLE   (A) steady   (B) unreliable
(C) nervous   (D) cranky   (E) upset

9. BLUNT   (A) dull   (B) rude   (C) wide
(D) heavy   (E) sharp

10. EXHALE   (A) relax   (B) snore
(C) inhale   (D) greet   (E) decline

● Analogies

Some vocabulary tests will ask you to identify relationships between pairs of words. These relationships are called **analogies.** Following is an item from a test of analogies.

EXAMPLE   KIND:CRUEL :: (A) tired:sleepy
(B) late:tardy (C) top:bottom

The first step in answering this question is to identify the relationship between the two capitalized words. In this case the words are antonyms, since the meaning of *cruel* is nearly opposite the meaning of *kind.*

The next step is to find another pair of words with the same relationship. The words *tired* and *sleepy* mean about the same thing, so they are synonyms. The words *late* and *tardy* are also synonyms. Letter C, *top* and *bottom,* is the correct answer. *Top* and *bottom* are antonyms, just as *kind* and *cruel* are.

The capitalized words may also be synonyms.

EXAMPLE   RAPID:SWIFT :: (A) shallow:deep
(B) simple:difficult (C) polite:courteous

The first two pairs of words are antonyms, so they cannot be correct. The correct answer is C, since *polite* and *courteous,* like *rapid* and *swift,* are synonyms.

PRACTICE YOUR SKILLS

● *Recognizing Analogies*

Write *synonyms* or *antonyms* to tell how the words in capital letters are related. Then write *A, B,* or *C* to tell which pair of words is related in the same way.

EXAMPLE   NIGHT:DAY ::　(A) violin:fiddle
                    (B) health:illness　(C) dish:plate

ANSWER   antonyms—B

1. TREACHEROUS:DANGEROUS ::　(A) brave:afraid
(B) shaky:unsteady　(C) hungry:full

2. DAZE:STUN ::　(A) walk:stroll　(B) work:play
(C) come:go

3. PROHIBIT:ALLOW ::　(A) guard:protect
(B) save:keep　(C) wash:soil

4. STATIONARY:IMMOVABLE ::　(A) hard:difficult
(B) chilly:warm　(C) dark:light

5. YIELD:RESIST ::　(A) sew:stitch
(B) listen:hear　(C) sink:float

6. HASTEN:HURRY ::　(A) succeed:fail
(B) sit:stand　(C) cry:sob

7. RESEMBLE:DIFFER ::　(A) arrive:leave
(B) eat:dine　(C) grow:mature

8. GALLANT:BRAVE ::　(A) soft:hard
(B) easy:simple　(C) many:few

9. REDUCE:INCREASE ::　(A) spend:save
(B) win:triumph　(C) recollect:remember

10. STRICT:PERMISSIVE ::　(A) sad:sorrowful
(B) quick:slow　(C) distant:far

Across the Media: Implied Messages

Have you ever noticed that in television news programs, the older male anchor is usually seated to the left of the younger female anchor? This is because we perceive things on the right to be "friendly" and those on the left to be "distant." The younger female anchor is on the right because the producers want her to be perceived as warm and kindly, somebody with whom the audience wants to spend time. The man usually wears dark colors and business suits, which make us think that he is somber and serious. The woman may have on warm colors, lipstick and jewelry, maybe a silk scarf, which make her seem soft and approachable. All these perceptions take place within seconds, as soon as we see the two of them on television. A whole set of signals has been sent and received, often without our being aware of it.

This is the vocabulary of the media, made up of images, sounds, physical relationships, shapes, texture, lighting, and camera angles, as well as words.

Media Activity

Working in groups of three, watch a local news program. Also examine the covers of two weekly newsmagazines. Then answer the following questions.

- What is the lead story in each broadcast and publication?

- What subtle details are used, such as lighting or camera angles on television, and layout or word choice in newsmagazines?

- What is the implied or underlying message in these details?

Share your findings with your class.

CHAPTER 16

Dictionary

Words are obviously essential to any kind of writing. As an author, you need to use and spell words correctly in order to uphold the credibility of your writing. No matter how good a piece of writing may be, misspelled or improperly used words can cause a reader to judge the writing to be poor. One aid in avoiding this writing pitfall is a dictionary. Dictionaries not only help you to define and spell words, but also provide you with pronunciation and the ways in which a word may be used.

Dictionaries come in many types and forms. Although some dictionaries are in book form, and others are electronic, all dictionaries are organized in the same general manner and they can be valuable research and reference tools if you know how to use them. This chapter will review the information available in dictionaries, their organization, and how to use a dictionary efficiently.

Reading with a Writer's Eye

In our quick-moving world, language is always changing. One way to track changes in our ever-evolving language is to look at a dictionary. This selection explains how one very popular dictionary goes about selecting words and definitions for entry into its publication. As you read the selection, think about why the process is so involved. How might the dictionary editing process affect you as a writer?

How Does a WORD Get into the DICTIONARY?

from *The Merriam-Webster Homepage* www.m-w.com

"How does a word get into the dictionary?" That's one of the questions Merriam-Webster editors are most often asked.

The answer is simple: usage.

To decide which words to include in the dictionary and to determine what they mean, Merriam-Webster editors study the language to determine which words people use most often and how they use them.

Each day most Merriam-Webster editors devote an hour or two to reading books, newspapers, magazines, electronic publications—in fact a cross section of all kinds of published materials; in our office this activity is called "reading and marking." The editors are looking for new words, new meanings of existing words, evidence of variant spellings or inflected forms—in short, anything that might help in deciding if a word belongs in the dictionary, understanding what it means, and determining typical usage. Any word of interest is marked, along with surrounding context that offers insight into its form and use.

The marked passages are then input into a computer system and stored both in machine-readable form and on 3" x 5" slips of paper to create ***citations.***

Each citation has the following elements:

1. the word itself
2. an example of the word used in context
3. bibliographic information about the source from which the word and example were taken

Merriam-Webster's citation files, which were begun in the 1880s, now contain nearly 15 million examples of words used in context and cover all aspects of the English vocabulary. Citations are also available to editors in a searchable text database (linguists call it a **corpus**) that includes 50,000,000 words drawn from a great variety of sources.

How does a word make the jump from the citation file to the dictionary?

The process begins with dictionary editors reviewing groups of citations. Definers start by looking at citations covering a relatively small segment of the alphabet—for example **gri–** to **gro–**—along with the entries from the dictionary being reedited that are included within that alphabetical section. It is the definer's job to determine which existing entries can remain essentially unchanged, which entries need to be revised, which entries can be dropped, and which new entries should be added. In each case, the definer decides on the best course of action by reading through the citations and using the evidence in them to adjust entries or create new ones.

Before a new word can be added to the dictionary, it must have enough citations to show that it is widely used. But having a lot of citations is not enough; in fact, a large number of citations might even make a word more difficult to define, because many citations show too little about the meaning of a word to be helpful. A word may be rejected for entry into a general dictionary if all of its citations come from a single source or if they are all from highly specialized publications that reflect the jargon of experts within a single field.

To be included in a Merriam-Webster dictionary, a word must be used in a substantial number of citations that come from a wide range of publications over a considerable period of time. Specifically, the word must have enough citations to allow accurate judgments about its establishment, currency, and meaning.

The number and range of citations needed to add a word to the dictionary varies. In rare cases, a word jumps onto the scene and is both instantly prevalent and likely to last, as was the case in the 1980s with **AIDS.** In such a situation, the editors determine that the word has become firmly established in a relatively short time and should be entered in the dictionary, even though its citations may not span the wide range of years exhibited by other words.

The size and type of dictionary also affects how many citations a word needs to gain admission. Because an abridged dictionary, such as **Merriam-Webster's Collegiate® Dictionary, Tenth Edition,** has fairly limited space, only the most commonly used words can be entered; to get into that type of dictionary, a word must be supported by a significant number of citations. But a large unabridged dictionary, such as **Webster's Third New International Dictionary,** has room for many more words, so terms with fewer citations can still be included.

Change and variation are as natural in language as they are in other areas of human life and Merriam-Webster reference works must reflect that fact. By relying on citational evidence, we hope to keep our publications grounded in the details of current usage so they can calmly and dispassionately offer information about modern English. That way, our references can speak with **authority**, without being **authoritarian**.

Thinking as a Writer

Evaluating the Dictionary Editing Process
- What are the steps involved in editing a dictionary?
- Do you think the process described is the best way to go about writing a dictionary? Why or why not?
- "Words have power." How does this statement apply to the process of dictionary writing?

Evaluating a Dictionary Illustration

Viewing Many people say that "a picture is worth a thousand words." This is sometimes true in a dictionary where an illustration is given to clarify a definition. The picture shown below is a dictionary illustration for the word *platypus*.
- Without knowing the definition of *platypus*, what information can you gather from the illustration alone?
- Is there any vital information that you cannot gather from the illustration? Would reading the written definition answer those questions? Keep in mind that dictionaries should give you the basics about the meaning of a word, not necessarily detailed information.

platypus
Ornithorhynchus anatinus

Developing Your Dictionary Skills

When, in the course of your writing, you need to confirm the spelling, meaning, or pronunciation of a word, you look that word up in a dictionary. You can also use a dictionary to research the origin or history of a word as well as to find out what part of speech the word is. Some dictionaries will also provide you with synonyms (words with similar meanings).

A **dictionary** is a resource that provides the pronunciations, definitions, parts of speech, and other information about the words of a particular language.

Dictionary Structure

Most dictionaries are organized similarly. The structure of a dictionary is meant to help you quickly find the information you need. All the words in a dictionary are listed in alphabetical order.

As you look over the following dictionary entries, notice how the information is organized. Especially notice that the entries are listed in alphabetical order.

MODEL: Dictionary Entries

Ne The symbol for the element **neon**.

abbreviation — **NE** *abbr.* An abbreviation of: **1.** Northeast. **2.** Nebraska. **3.** New England.

Ne·an·der·thal (nē·ǎn'dər·thôl') *n.* Neanderthal

capitalization

Near East (nîr). A region of southwest Asia generally thought to include Turkey, Lebanon, Israel, Iraq, Jordan, Saudi Arabia, the other countries of the Arabian Peninsula, and sometimes Egypt and Sudan.

spelling · definitions · pronunciation · related forms · part of speech · word origin · synonyms · antonyms

near•ly (nîr′lē) *adv*. **1**. Almost but not quite: *That coat nearly fits.* **2**. Closely or intimately: *The two girls are nearly related.*

near•sight•ed (nîr′sī′tĭd) *adj*. Unable to see distant objects clearly; myopic. —**near′sight′ed•ly** *adv*. —**near′sight′ed•ness** *n*.

neat (nēt) *adj*. **neat•er, neat•est. 1**. Orderly and clean; tidy: *a neat room; neat handwriting.* **2**. Orderly, as in appearance; not careless or messy: *a neat person.* **3**. Performed with precision and skill: *a neat, graceful takeoff.* **4**. *Slang*. Wonderful; fine: *a neat party.* [First written down in 1542 in Modern English, from Latin *nitidus*, elegant, gleaming.] —**neat′ly** *adv*. —**neat′ness** *n*.

Synonyms: neat, tidy, trim, shipshape. These adjectives mean marked by good order and cleanliness. **Neat** means pleasingly clean and orderly: *Marcia pulled back her hair into a neat ponytail.* **Tidy** suggests precise arrangement and order: *Even their closets and drawers were kept tidy.* **Trim** stresses a smart appearance because of neatness, tidiness, and pleasing proportions: *The trim little boat was all ready to set sail.* **Shipshape** means both neat and tidy: *We'll have the kitchen shipshape in no time.* **Antonyms: messy, sloppy.**

Word Location

A dictionary is organized in alphabetical order to help you find the information you need quickly. Guide words tell you at a glance which words can be found on each page.

Guide Words

The two words printed in heavy type at the top of each dictionary page are called **guide words**. Each pair of guide words shows the first and last words defined on the page. The guide words *pinch/pioneer*, for example, show you that *pine* and *pinto bean* are listed on that page. The words *pistachio* and *pit*, however, would appear on a later page.

Practice Your Skills

● *Using Guide Words*

Make two columns on your paper. Write the guide words *babble/badminton* at the top of the first column and *baffle/balloon* at the top of the second column. Then write each of the following words in the proper column.

baboon	Bahamas	babysit
bachelor	baggage	backyard
backgammon	balance	bagpipe
bacteria	balcony	ballerina
badly	backpack	ballet
Badlands	bald eagle	ballad
bakery	badger	bacon

Alphabetical Order

Once you have located the right page, you can find the word you need by following a strict, letter-by-letter alphabetical order. Compound words are alphabetized as if there were no space or hyphen.

SINGLE WORD	space
ONE-WORD COMPOUND	spacecraft
TWO-WORD COMPOUND	space station
HYPHENATED COMPOUND	space-time

The dictionary also lists proper nouns, prefixes, suffixes, phrases, and abbreviations. Abbreviations are alphabetized letter by letter and not by the word they stand for. The abbreviation *rd.* for *road* would fall between the words *razor* and *read*. It would not be placed next to *road*.

PRACTICE YOUR SKILLS

● *Alphabetizing Words*

Arrange the underlined words in each phrase in alphabetical order.

EXAMPLE   as <u>wild</u> as a <u>winter</u> <u>wind</u>
ANSWER   wild, wind, winter

1. the <u>mystery</u> of the <u>missing</u> <u>meatball</u>
2. <u>millions</u> of <u>mighty</u> <u>mice</u>
3. the <u>wicked</u> <u>witch</u> of the <u>West</u>
4. the <u>case</u> of the <u>cagey</u> <u>canary</u>
5. a <u>band</u> of <u>baboons</u> playing <u>banjos</u>
6. <u>eleven</u> <u>elephants</u> in an <u>elevator</u>
7. <u>selling</u> <u>seashells</u> by the <u>seashore</u>
8. a <u>gaggle</u> of <u>gawky</u> <u>geese</u>
9. <u>buggy</u> <u>bumpers</u> for <u>bouncing</u> <u>baby</u> <u>buggies</u>
10. <u>Peter</u> <u>Piper</u> <u>picked</u> a <u>peck</u> of <u>pickled</u> <u>peppers</u>

● *Alphabetizing Words*

Write the words in each column in alphabetical order.

1.	**2.**	**3.**
seafloor	moonstruck	snowball
sea legs	moonrise	snow job
seamanship	moonlit	snow-white
seabed	moonbeam	snow leopard
seagoing	moonstone	snow tire
seafowl	moonlight	SNOBOL
seascape	moonward	snowshoe
seasick	moon shot	snow-blind
sea dog	moonflower	Sno-Cat
seawall	moonquake	snowcap

⬤ Information in an Entry

All of the information given for a word is called an **entry**. The entry is made up of four main parts: (1) the entry word, (2) the pronunciation, (3) the definitions, and (4) the word origin. The following entry for the word *disk* shows these four main parts.

pronunciation

entry word— **disk** also **disc** (dĭsk) *n.* **1.** A thin, flat, circular object, such as a plate or coin. **2.** Something that resembles such an object: *the moon's disk reflected in the pond.* **3.** Often **disc. a.** A phonograph record. **b.** A round flat plate coated with a magnetic substance on which computer data is stored. **c.** An optical disk, especially a compact disk. [First written down in 1664 in Modern English, from Greek *diskos,* quoit, from *dikein,* to throw.]

definitions—

word origins—

The Entry Word

The **entry word** provides three kinds of information. It shows (1) how to spell a word, (2) whether a word should be capitalized, and (3) where a word breaks into syllables.

Spelling   The entry word shows how to spell a word correctly. Some words have more than one correct spelling. The most common spelling, called the **preferred spelling,** is given first. The second spelling is called the **variant spelling.** Always use the preferred spelling of a word in your writing.

preferred spelling   variant spelling
   the·a·ter   or   **the·a·tre**

A dictionary entry also shows how to spell the plurals of nouns, the principal parts of verbs, and the comparative and superlative degrees of adjectives and adverbs. These are only given if the form or spelling is irregular.

PRINCIPAL PARTS	**com•mute** (kə **myoot′**) v. **com•mut•ed, com•mut•ing, com•mutes.**
NOUN PLURAL	**mouse** (mous) n., pl. **mice**
ADJECTIVE FORMS	**rust•y** (rŭs′tē) adj. **rust•i•er, rust•i•est.**

Words formed by adding a prefix or suffix to the entry words are often shown at the end of the entry. These related forms are called **derived words**.

nois•y(noi′zē) *adj.* **nois•i•er, nois•i•est. 1.** Making a lot of noise: *a noisy engine.* **2.** Full of, character-

derived words ized by, or accompanied by noise: *noisy streets.* —**nois′i•ly** *adv.* —**nois′i•ness** *n.*

PRACTICE YOUR SKILLS

● *Checking Spelling*

Write each word with the ending given in parentheses. Use a dictionary to check your spelling.

EXAMPLE drive (ing)
ANSWER driving

1. spy (s)
2. wolf (s)
3. tomato (s)
4. quiz (s)
5. cloudy (ness)
6. bus (s)
7. charity (s)
8. busy (er)
9. compass (s)
10. lonely (ness)

11. satisfy (ed)
12. refer (ed)
13. continue (ing)
14. bury (ing)
15. omit (ing)
16. lovely (est)
17. lazy (ness)
18. monkey (s)
19. crispy (est)
20. precede (ed)

Capitalization   If a word should be capitalized, the entry word will be printed with a capital letter. If a word should only be capitalized sometimes, the word will be shown with a capital letter near the appropriate definition.

> **web** (wĕb) *n.* **1.** A woven fabric, especially one on or just removed from a loom. **2.** A latticed or woven structure: *A web of palm branches formed the roof of the hut.* **3.** A structure of fine silky strands woven by spiders or by certain insect larvae. **4.** Something that traps or snares by or as if by entangling: *a web of deceit.* **5.** A fold of skin or thin tissue connecting the toes of certain water birds or other animals. **6.** **Web.** World Wide Web. —*tr.v.* **webbed, web·bing, webs.** To provide with a web or webs. [First written down about 725 in Old English and spelled *webb.*]

capital letter

Syllables   When you write your final copy of a report or composition, you will sometimes need to divide a word at the end of a line. When you do this, you cannot divide the word in the middle of a syllable. The dictionary shows you how a word breaks into syllables.

as • tro • naut   I • tal • ian   pri • va • cy

PRACTICE YOUR SKILLS

● *Dividing Words into Syllables*

Using a dictionary, write each word with a small dot between syllables.

EXAMPLE   resourceful
ANSWER   re • source • ful

1. majestic   6. assistant
2. discolor   7. usually
3. justify   8. lawmaker
4. coincide   9. article
5. immunity   10. exhibit

Pronunciation

If you are not sure how to pronounce a word, you can look it up in the dictionary. A phonetic spelling is shown in parentheses after each entry word. The phonetic spelling shows how to pronounce the word correctly.

knee (nē)   **ra • di • o** (rā′dē ō)

At the front of the dictionary is a complete pronunciation key to help you understand the letters and symbols used in the phonetic spellings. Many dictionaries also provide a shortened form of the key on every other page for easy reference.

PARTIAL PRONUNCIATION KEY

Symbols	Examples	Symbols	Examples
ă	pat	o͞o	boot
ā	pay	th	this
âr	care	ŭ	cut
ä	father	ûr	urge, term, firm,
ĕ	pet		word, heard
ē	bee	zh	vision, pleasure,
hw	whoop		garage
ĭ	pit	ə	about, item, edible,
ī	pie, by		gallop, circus
îr	dear, deer, pier	ər	butter
ŏ	pot		
ō	toe	**Foreign Symbols**	
ô	caught, paw, for	œ	French feu
o͝o	took	ü	French tu
		KH	Scottish loch
		N	French bon

Diacritical Marks In the pronunciation key on the previous page, there are marks over some of the vowels. These are called **diacritical marks** and show the different sounds a vowel can make. For example, the different sounds of the vowel *a* are shown in the following ways.

DIACRITICAL **a** as in hat **ā** as in **age** **ä** as in far
MARKS

The Schwa Sometimes vowels are pronounced like the sound *uh*. Dictionaries use the symbol ə to represent this sound. This symbol is called a **schwa**.

a • bove (ə bŭv′) **lem • on** (lĕm′ən) **to • ken** (tō′kən)

PRACTICE YOUR SKILLS

● *Marking Pronunciation*

Using a dictionary, write the pronunciation of each word. Be sure that you include all diacritical marks.

EXAMPLE   adrift
ANSWER   (ə drift′)

1. rate **3.** dust **5.** final **7.** provide **9.** canteen
2. film **4.** mild **6.** strike **8.** benefit **10.** feline

Accent Marks An **accent mark** shows which syllable should be stressed in the pronunciation. Accent marks appear in the phonetic spelling of a word.

fa • mous (fā′məs) in • jus • tice (ĭn jŭs′tĭs)

Some words will have two accent marks. The darker one, called the **primary accent**, tells you which syllable receives more stress. The lighter one, called the **secondary accent**, receives slightly less stress.

PRIMARY ACCENT
SECONDARY ACCENT

in • ex • pen • sive (ĭn′ĭk spĕn′ sĭv)

PRACTICE YOUR SKILLS

● *Placing Accent Marks*

Using a dictionary, write the pronunciation of each word. Leave space between syllables and mark both primary and secondary stresses.

EXAMPLE   hydrochloride
ANSWER   hī′drə klôr′īd

1. composition

2. vegetarian

3. navigation

4. scientific

5. desperation

6. territory

7. dictionary

8. interstate

9. afternoon

10. helicopter

Definitions

Most words have more than one meaning. The following entry for *program* gives eight definitions.

pro•gram (prō′grăm′ *or* prō′grəm) *n.* 1. A list of the order of events and other information for a public presentation or entertainment: *a printed program of the concert.* 2. A public performance, presentation, or entertainment: *We presented a program of folk music.* 3. A radio or television show. 4. An ordered list of activities, courses, or procedures; a schedule: *arranged her program so that she could have Mondays off.* 5. A course of academic study or extracurricular activities: *an excellent African studies program.* 6. A system of services or projects designed to achieve a goal: *the space pro-gram.* **7.a.** The set of steps necessary for a computer to solve a problem, including the collection and processing of data and the presentation of results. **b.** The set of instructions that a computer must ex-ecute in carrying o~~ut~~ these steps *—tr.v.* **pro·** ~~gramme~~ ~~~~ ~~~~ **q, pr** ~~~~ **s or**

To find the definition that fits the sentence you have in mind, read all of the definitions and examples carefully. Then decide which meaning makes sense in your sentence.

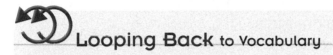 **Looping Back** to Vocabulary

Expanding Your Vocabulary

In Chapter 15, you learned about vocabulary. The larger your vocabulary, the more precisely you will be able to express yourself as a writer. Leafing through a dictionary is an excellent way to expand your vocabulary. Try opening the dictionary and learning the meaning of a random new word. Do this daily, and challenge yourself to use the word in a sentence sometime during the day.

PRACTICE YOUR SKILLS

● *Choosing an Appropriate Meaning*

Using the entry for *program* given on page C502, write the definition that tells what *program* means in each sentence.

EXAMPLE   We watched a comedy <u>program</u> last night.
ANSWER   a radio or television show

1. I completed the scuba diving <u>program</u> in three weeks.

2. I used a word-processing <u>program</u> to do my homework.

3. I read the <u>program</u> until the lights went down.

4. The recycling <u>program</u> was a success.

5. Stopping at the playground was not a part of the <u>program</u>.

6. My old school has an excellent art <u>program</u>.

7. I used an accounting <u>program</u> to add up the numbers.

8. The state's conservation <u>program</u> is going very well.

9. I enjoy watching nature <u>programs</u> on television.

10. The museum presented a <u>program</u> on the history of stringed instruments.

Parts of Speech Labels

Dictionaries use the following abbreviations to tell what **part of speech** a word is.

n.	noun	*pron.*	pronoun
v.	verb	*prep.*	preposition
adj.	adjective	*conj.*	conjunction
adv.	adverb	*interj.*	interjection

tug (tŭg) *v.* **tugged, tug·ging, tugs.** —*tr.* **1.** To pull at vigorously; strain at: *The puppy was tugging the leash.* **2.** To move by pulling with great effort or exertion; drag: *I tugged a chair across the room.* See Synonyms at **pull. 3.** To tow by a tugboat. —*intr.* To pull hard: *kept tugging until the boot came off.* —*n.* **1.** A strong pull or pulling force. **2.** A tugboat. [First written down before 1200 in Middle English and spelled *toggen,* from Old English *tēon.*]

Since many words can be more than one part of speech, two or more abbreviations may appear in a single entry.

Be sure to find the right part of speech when searching for the definition of a word.

PRACTICE YOUR SKILLS

● *Finding Different Meanings of Words*

Look up the word *back* in a dictionary and write the part of speech of each underlined word. If the word is a noun or a verb, also write the number of the definition that tells what *back* means in the sentence.

EXAMPLE   The cat arches its back.
Answer   noun, 2

1. The line curled all the way around the <u>back</u> of the movie theater.

2. The firefighters told the crowd to stand <u>back</u>.

3. On the <u>back</u> of the letter, the spy wrote a message in code.

4. The lawyer tried to <u>back</u> the case with solid evidence.

5. The ball soared over the <u>back</u> fence.

Synonyms

Words with almost the same meaning are called **synonyms**. Dictionaries often list synonyms at the end of an entry and explain the special meaning of each.

Aside from the synonyms that are sometimes provided in a regular dictionary, there is another type of dictionary that features synonyms. It is called a thesaurus.

glad (glăd) *adj.* **glad·der, glad·dest. 1.** Experiencing or showing joy and pleasure: *We were so glad to get your letter.* **2.** Providing joy and pleasure: *The wedding was a glad occasion.* **3.** Pleased; willing: *I would be glad to help.* **—glad′ly** *adv.* **—glad′ness** *n.*

Synonyms: glad, happy, cheerful, lighthearted, joyful. These adjectives mean being in or showing good spirits. **Glad** often means satisfied with immediate circumstances: *I am so glad we finally met.* **Happy** can mean feeling pleasurable contentment, as from a sense of fulfillment: *Jane is happy with her new job.* **Cheerful** means having good spirits, as distinct from being pleased: *Leroy tried to remain cheerful while he was in the hospital.* **Lighthearted** means free of cares and worries: *Summertime always puts you in a lighthearted mood.* **Joyful** means having great happiness and liveliness: *Their wedding was a joyful occasion.*

Word Origins

The English language is constantly changing and growing. The dictionary provides information about the history of words that have long been part of our language. It also gives the sources of new words. The following entry shows that the word *compute* comes from two Latin words meaning "to reckon together."

com·pute (kəm pyo͞ot′) *v.* **com·put·ed, com·put·ing, com·putes. —***tr.* **1.** To work out (a result, an answer, or a solution) by mathematics; calculate: *The bank computes the interest on savings accounts.* **2.** To determine by use of a computer: *compute the most efficient design of a sailboat.* —*intr.* **1.** To determine an amount or a number. **2.** To use a computer. [First written down in 1631 in Modern English, from Latin *computāre : com-*, together + *putāre*, to reckon.]

Many of the words we use come from Latin and Greek. The English language, however, also contains words from many other languages.

WORDS FROM OTHER LANGUAGES/CULTURES			
AMERICAN INDIAN	chipmunk opossum	hickory raccoon	moccasin skunk
DUTCH	cookie slim	cruise waffle	iceberg wagon
FRENCH	garage parachute	menu picnic	liter souvenir
GERMAN	hamster noodle	nickel pretzel	zinc waltz
ITALIAN	confetti pizza	lagoon stanza	opera volcano
SPANISH	burrito guacamole alligator tornado	cafeteria stampede fiesta rodeo	canyon taco mosquito tuna

Words with Unusual Origins

Borrowing words from other languages is only one way our language grows. New words come into our language in a variety of other ways. Some words, called **compound words**, are formed by combining two words.

weekend birthday sunglasses moonlight

Some words are a blend of two words.

breakfast + lunch = brunch   twist + whirl = twirl
guess + estimate = guesstimate smoke + fog = smog

Some words are shortened forms of longer words.

SHORTENED FORM	LONGER FORM
plane	airplane
super	superior
fan	fanatic
sub	submarine

Some words imitate sounds.

Ping-Pong   hiss   sizzle   swish   pitter-patter

Some names of people have also become words.

Levi Strauss—maker of **Levi's** blue jeans
George Ferris—inventor of the **Ferris** wheel
Louis Pasteur—first to **pasteurize** milk

Some words are acronyms. Acronyms are words that are formed from the first letter or syllables of other words.

NASA   National Aeronautics and Space Administration
VISTA   Volunteers in Service to America
radar   radio detecting and ranging

The word origin is usually listed at the end of an entry. Keep in mind, however, that all dictionaries do not arrange information in exactly the same way. All dictionaries provide an explanation of their arrangement at the front of the book.

PRACTICE YOUR SKILLS

● *Finding Word Origins*

Use the dictionary to write the origin of each of the following words.

1. walrus   **3.** piano

2. vanity   **4.** helicopter

5. chocolate　　　**8.** trampoline

6. technique　　　**9.** patio

7. kindergarten　**10.** toboggan

● *Finding Unusual Origins*

Tell how each of the following words came into the English language by writing *compound, blend, shortened form, sounds, person's name,* or *acronym*. Use the dictionary and the examples on pages C507–C508 to help you.

1. splash	**6.** newspaper	**11.** deli	**16.** chuckle
2. moped	**7.** lab	**12.** motel	**17.** shoelace
3. raincoat	**8.** squiggle	**13.** SAT	**18.** sandwich
4. scuba	**9.** saxophone	**14.** whoosh	**19.** limo
5. tangelo	**10.** diesel	**15.** chortle	**20.** ZIP code

Time Out to Reflect

You have used the dictionary to transform words that were unfamiliar to you into words for which you know spelling, syllables, pronunciation, meanings, and perhaps even origins. Do you have a different understanding now of the sentences you originally heard the words in? Did you learn anything new about the dictionary? Is there information in the dictionary that you didn't know was there? Are there any dictionary skills that you feel you need to sharpen in order to make better use of this valuable tool? Record your thoughts in the Learning Log section of your **journal.**

Advertising

The meaning of the words we use is very important. Nowhere is this more true than in the media. Whether you are watching television, reading a magazine, or surfing the Web, the words that you read were carefully chosen to catch your attention. When used with precision by advertising agencies, words can have a meaning that goes far beyond their dictionary definition. The language in ads often make no sense grammatically but we still understand what it means. "Got Milk?" is not a complete sentence, but when it is paired with a picture of chocolate cake, the meaning ("You should have milk if you are really going to enjoy this piece of cake to the fullest.") becomes clear.

Advertisers often try to sell their product by associating them with ideals we care about such as happiness or social status. Advertisers may also target a buyer's fears, telling them that their product will give them confidence. All ads want to reach their audience quickly, usually by creating an immediate emotional reaction in the viewer. In all cases, the words ads use were chosen specifically to create a desired response.

Media Activity

Working in a group, brainstorm a list of five advertising slogans for existing products. What promises do they make? Do they target any insecurities? Do the slogans apply to adults? children? men? women? Why? Now, look up each word of the slogan in a dictionary. Then use a thesaurus to rewrite the slogan using different words. Do the new slogans work as well? What made the original slogan work in the first place? Share your work with the rest of the class in a group discussion of words in advertising.

Assess Your Learning

Your local word-collector club is preparing to launch a Website dedicated to finding new words and understanding the origins of words. The president of the club, Nora Webster, has asked you to contribute a paragraph to be placed on the Website telling how to get this information from a dictionary.

▶ **Look over your work from this chapter and study a dictionary to brainstorm ideas for what you will write. Be sure to include information on pronunciation, guide words, alphabetical order, parts of speech, and word origins. Use several dictionaries and ask your librarian or media center specialist for help. Also be sure to check some dictionaries on the Internet to see how these topics are handled in those dictionaries, since your audience is likely to be people who use the Web. Then organize your information into a paragraph with a topic sentence, supporting details, and a conclusion.**

▶ *Before You Write* Consider the following questions:
What is the *subject?*
What is the *occasion?*
Who is the *audience?*
What is the *purpose?*

▶ *After You Write* Evaluate your work using the following criteria:
- Have you organized your ideas to ensure coherence and logical progression in your paragraph?
- Have you used several dictionaries and thesauruses to find information for your paragraph?
- Have you enlisted the help of your librarian or media specialist?
- Is your writing accurate, informative, and meaningful?
- Does your paragraph show accurate spelling and correct use of conventions of punctuation and capitalization?

Write briefly on how well you did. Point out your strengths and areas for improvement.

CHAPTER 17

Library and Media Center

When you walk into a library or media center, you are entering a place where centuries of knowledge are gathered under one roof. These places are storehouses of information and ideas—invaluable resources for any writer. Libraries answer your questions and help you figure out what questions to ask next. They entertain and inspire.

As a writer, you will often have to do research. This will not only be true when you write research reports, but in other cases as well. Suppose you wanted to write a short story that takes place in Venice, Italy, but you have never been there. Perhaps you are working on a fairy tale that involves a shoemaker, but you know nothing about the craft. In these cases, you would research your topic.

Libraries and media centers are arranged so that you can find what you need quickly and easily. If you know the system, the door to knowledge is open.

Reading with a Writer's Eye

As you read the following selection about how the Library of Congress came into being, think about what libraries mean to you. What would the Library of Congress have been like if it had been based on the books *you* own?

Thomas Jefferson's Library

from the **American Treasures of the Library of Congress Website**

http://lcweb.loc.gov/exhibits/treasures

Thomas Jefferson (1743–1826), who had one of the finest libraries in America, intended that his collection should benefit the nation. All through his years of public service—as minister to France, as vice president, and as president—he used every opportunity to add to his collection of documents about America and its past, as well as volumes in many languages about philosophy and history, science and technology, agriculture and horticulture, architecture and painting, poetry and rhetoric. He shared the vision of the nation's Founders that liberty and learning are inseparable and that a free democratic people must have free access to information in order to carry out their civic responsibilities.

After the War of 1812, during which the British burned the Capitol and with it all the volumes of the Library of Congress, Jefferson offered his own collection to Congress, which they purchased in 1815. The former president, then living in retirement in Monticello, was paid $23,950 for nearly 6,500 books, almost twice the number lost in the fire. Thus, the Library of Congress has grown from the seed of Jefferson's own library, universal in subject matter and format, into a library that serves as Congress's working research collection, as the nation's library, and as a symbol of the central role that free access to information plays in our knowledge-based democracy.

Thinking as a Writer

Evaluating the Role of Libraries

- Think of all the different ways you have used the library or media center. Which of those uses might help you as a writer? How?
- Think of projects you are currently working on that you could research in the library. What kinds of sources would be helpful to you?
- Make a list of areas you would like to research for yourself such as music, summer internship programs, or specialized high schools. How would you begin your research?

Telling Formal from Informal Tone

- Oral Expression • What is the tone of the article on libraries? Does the piece seek to inform and explain? Is it formal or informal? What words give you a clue to the tone?
- Read the article aloud, trying to match your style of reading to the tone of the written word. Listen carefully when others do the same, and evaluate whether their reading expresses the tone that comes through in the writing.

Evaluating Visual Images

Viewing Study the picture of the entrance to the main branch of the New York City Public Library. The two lion statues in front of the library are historic landmarks.

- What does the design of this entrance tell you about the way its creators thought about libraries?
- When the library was planned and designed, what might have been the purpose for choosing this particular style and design?
- Does the design of the library match its function? Why or why not?

New York Public Library Main Branch

Developing Your Reference Skills

Samuel Johnson wrote, "A man will turn over half a library to make one book." You may never have to write a whole book or turn over half a library, but developing your library and media center skills will certainly help you—whether you are writing a novel or a page.

This chapter will introduce you to the materials available in most libraries and media centers and tell you how to use them. Remember that different establishments may have different materials available. Not every library has everything. Some libraries are specialized. For example, there are law libraries— libraries that deal exclusively in law-related materials; and performing arts libraries—full of information on the performing arts as well as archived performances, like a videotape of a play. There are also general libraries and media centers that give a broad range of materials. For almost all of the research you will do for school, you will be able to use a general community or school library or media center. Keep in mind, however, that other materials may be available elsewhere.

● Library Arrangement

A library arranges books on the shelves so you can find them easily. Books of fiction are organized in alphabetical order. Nonfiction books are arranged by numbers and filed in a separate section.

Fiction

Books of **fiction** include novels and stories that are partly or totally imaginary. These books are put on the shelves in alphabetical order by the author's last name. The following rules will help you find books of fiction.

> **Library Arrangement**
- Two-part names are alphabetized by the first part of the name.

  DaRosa   **Mac**Mahon   **O'**Leary   **Van** Dam
- Names beginning with *Mc* or *St.* are alphabetized as if they began with *Mac* or *Saint*.
- Books by the same author are alphabetized by title, skipping *a, an* and *the* at the beginning.

PRACTICE YOUR SKILLS

● *Arranging Fiction*

Write this list of novels in the order that they should be placed on the shelves.

M. C. Higgins, the Great, Virginia Hamilton

Across Five Aprils, Irene Hunt

Little Women, Louisa May Alcott

Dr. Doom: Superstar, T. Ernesto Bethancourt

Tina Gogo, Judie Angell

Arilla Sun Down, Virginia Hamilton

The Wolves of Willoughby Chase, Joan Aiken

The Empire Strikes Back, Donald F. Glut

The Wonderful Wizard of Oz, L. Frank Baum

The Blind Colt, Glen Rounds

● *Solving Shelving Problems*

Write the following list of fiction authors in the order that their books would appear on the shelves.

Mary O'Hara	Madeleine L'Engle
J. K. Rowling	Robert O'Brien
Scott O'Dell	Helen MacInnis
Patricia A. McKillip	Scott O'Neill
Jean Van Leeuwen	Betty MacDonald
Walter Dean Meyers	Virginia Hamilton
Lawrence Yep	Gary Soto

Nonfiction

Nonfiction books contain factual information and document events. Most libraries use the Dewey decimal system to arrange nonfiction books on the shelves. In this system each book is assigned a call number according to its subject.

A **call number** is a number and letter code used to identify a book by subject and category.

There are ten general categories in the Dewey decimal system. This system makes it easy to find a book about a certain subject. For example, a subject that falls under science—such as astronomy—is assigned a number between 500 and 599. A book about robots would be listed under technology. It would be assigned a number between 600 and 699. This number is written on the **spine**—the part of the book that faces you when it is on the shelf. The books are then arranged on the shelves in numerical order.

DEWEY DECIMAL SYSTEM	
000–099	General Works (reference books)
100–199	Philosophy
200–299	Religion
300–399	Social Science (law, education, economics)
400–499	Language
500–599	Science (mathematics, biology, chemistry)
600–699	Technology (medicine, inventions)
700–799	Fine Arts (painting, music, theater)
800–899	Literature
900–999	History (biography, geography, travel)

Biographies and Autobiographies

Biographies and autobiographies are usually kept in a separate section. Most libraries label each book with a *B* for biography or with the Dewey decimal number 920. Biographies and autobiographies are arranged in alphabetical order by the last name of the subject, not the author.

PRACTICE YOUR SKILLS

● *Understanding the Dewey Decimal System*

For each of the following nonfiction books, write the range of numbers and the category each falls under in the Dewey decimal system. Use the chart above.

EXAMPLE   *The History of Rock 'n' Roll*
ANSWER   700–799   Fine Arts

1. *Laws, Courts, and Lawyers*
2. *The Life of John F. Kennedy*
3. *The Philosophy of Plato*
4. *The Invention of Ordinary Things*
5. *Religions of the World*
6. *Math and Logic Games*
7. *Heart Transplants*
8. *Hit Broadway Plays*
9. *You Can Speak French*
10. *Famous American Poets*

Solving Shelving Problems

Write the following Dewey decimal numbers and book titles in the order that the books would appear on the shelves. Remember that nonfiction books are arranged in numerical order, not in alphabetical order.

590.7   *A Zoo for All Seasons*
581.4   *The Life of a Forest*
598.2   *Birds of the Ocean*
594.5   *Kingdom of the Octopus*
582.3   *What's in the Names of Flowers*
591.9   *Animals of the Antarctic*
595.7   *Familiar Insects of America*
586   *Plants without Leaves*
597.3   *The Natural History of Sharks*
593.9   *The Living Wilderness*

● Types of Catalogs

In order to find a book on the shelves of the library, you need to know the book's call number. You can find the call number of a book in the library or media center's catalog. There are two types of catalogs: the traditional card catalog and the online catalog.

Traditional Card Catalog

The traditional card catalog is a cabinet of small drawers. The drawers contain file cards for every book in the library. The drawers also contain cards for other types of materials, such as filmstrips, tapes, and records. Each drawer is labeled to show what part of the alphabet it covers.

There are three cards for each book in the catalog. You can look up an author card, a title card, or a subject card to find the book you need.

Author Cards   Sometimes you know the author of a book but not the title. You can look in the card catalog under the author's last name. To find a book by James Muirden, for example, you look in the drawer that covers the letter *M*.

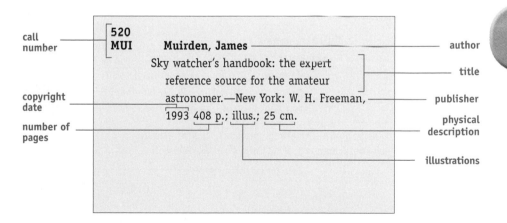

call number — 520 MUI

author — Muirden, James

title — Sky watcher's handbook: the expert reference source for the amateur

copyright date — astronomer.—New York: W. H. Freeman,

publisher

number of pages — 1993 408 p.; illus.; 25 cm.

physical description

illustrations

Title Cards Sometimes you know the title of a book but not the author. You can find the book by looking up the first word in the title (except *a, an,* and *the*). To find *Sky Watcher's Handbook,* for example, look in the drawer containing the letter *S.*

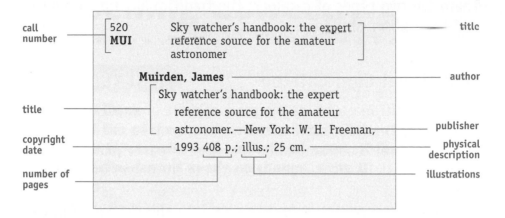

Subject Cards When you are looking for books for a report, you will use subject cards more than title or author cards. If your subject were astronomy, you would look in the drawer that covers the letter *A.* There you would find cards for all of the books about astronomy available in that library.

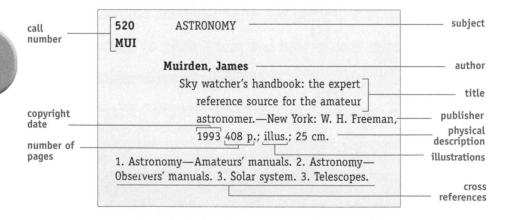

Guide Cards   Guide cards are blank cards with a word or a letter printed at the top. These cards are arranged in alphabetical order in each file drawer of the card catalog. They are slightly larger than the other cards and usually tabbed. Using guide cards will help you find title, author, and subject cards quickly.

Online Catalog

The online catalog is a computerized card catalog. While the traditional card catalog is usually limited to providing information on books and only a few other types of materials, most online catalogs usually catalog all the materials available in a library or media center. You use it by entering the title, author, or subject of the book you are looking for. The computer will then display the results of your search. Some online catalogs can also tell if the material you are looking for is held by the library or media center you are in, whether it is currently available to check out, and whether other libraries have it.

SEARCH RESULTS FROM ONLINE CATALOG	
Author:	Muirden, James
Title:	Sky watcher's handbook: the expert reference source for the amateur astronomer/ James Muirden.
Edition:	1st ed.
Published:	New York: W. H. Freeman, c1993
Description:	viii, 408 p.: illus.; 25 cm.
Call Number:	520 MUI
Notes:	Basic guide to searching the night sky. Star charts.
Subjects:	Astronomy—Amateurs' manuals. Astronomy—Observers' manuals.

When the library's online catalog displays the results of a search, instead of taking notes by hand, you can print out the information you need using the Print command. This will save you time and ensure that the information you are using to find a book is accurate.

Strategies for Finding Books

1. Find out if the library has the book you want by finding the author card, the title card, or the subject card in the card catalog or by looking it up in the online catalog.

2. Read the card or screen to see if the book is likely to contain the information you need. Check the copyright date to see how current the information is.

3. On a slip of paper, copy the call number, the title, and the name of the author for each book you want to find, or print out the information.

4. Use the call number to find each book. The first line of the call number tells which section of the library or media center to look in.

F or FIC	fiction section
B or 920	biography section
call number	nonfiction section

Then find each book on the shelves by looking for its call number, located on the spine.

PRACTICE YOUR SKILLS

● *Using the Traditional Card Catalog*

Write the letter or letters of the drawer in which you would find cards for each of the following topics in the card catalog.

EXAMPLE   *The Hobbit*

ANSWER   He–I

1. *The Mysterious Planet*

2. Kristin Hunter

3. photography

4. computers

5. the Internet

6. Isaac Asimov

7. *Search for Bigfoot*

8. Rudyard Kipling

9. scuba diving

10. Italy

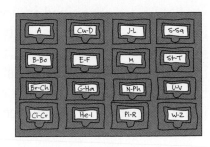

Writing Catalog Cards

Write an author card, a title card, and a subject card using the following information.

Football, 23 centimeters, published in New York by Childrens Press, Dewey decimal number 796.33, copyright date 1995, written by Ray Broekel, 48 pages with illustrations.

Searching Online Catalogs

Using the online catalog in your local or school library, find call numbers for the following books.

1. a nonfiction book about flowers

2. a book by Margaret Miller

3. *The Diary of Anne Frank*

 Parts of a Book

Books are organized in a way that will allow you to find the information you need quickly and easily. In order to find information in a book, you need to know how to use the parts of a book. The following chart lists the different parts of a book and the information available in each. As you review the chart, keep in mind that not all books contain all these different parts.

INFORMATION FOUND IN PARTS OF A BOOK	
PART	**INFORMATION**
TITLE PAGE	gives the full title, the name of the author or authors, the publisher, and the place of publication
COPYRIGHT PAGE	gives the date of the first copyright and of any revisions
TABLE OF CONTENTS	lists titles of chapters and sections and their starting page numbers
APPENDIX	provides additional information about the book's subjects; sometimes contains maps and charts
GLOSSARY	defines difficult words or terms used in the book (in alphabetical order)
BIBLIOGRAPHY	lists sources used in writing the book; sometimes provides titles of materials on related topics
INDEX	lists topics mentioned in the book and the page numbers where they can be found; sometimes lists in alphabetical order the page where a certain illustration can be found

PRACTICE YOUR SKILLS

● *Using the Parts of a Book*

Use this book, along with the chart on the previous page, to answer the following questions.

1. Who is the publisher of this book?

2. In what year was this book copyrighted?

3. How many chapters does this book include?

4. What does the word *brainstorming* mean?

5. Where can you find information about writing business letters?

● Print and Nonprint Reference Materials

Reference books, such as encyclopedias, dictionaries, atlases, and almanacs, are kept in a separate section of the library. Usually, these books cannot be checked out, and you must use them while you are in the library.

Most libraries also have a section for nonprint materials such as audiotapes, CDs, videos, and software. These can be found either in the reference section or in their own separate section.

Readers' Guide to Periodical Literature

Magazines can give you information on most subjects. They are especially useful for providing the most recent information available. The *Readers' Guide to Periodical Literature* is an index that can tell you which magazines have articles on your subject. Bound volumes of the *Readers' Guide* are published every year, and paperback volumes are issued during the year. A list of all the magazines covered is in the front of each volume.

Entries in the *Readers' Guide* are listed by subject and author. Following are several entries from one issue.

Following are some results from a search of the online version of the *Readers' Guide* for the subject of electronic mail.

TITLE
   E-mail addiction
PERSONAL AUTHOR
   Kawasaki,-Guy, 1954-
SOURCE
   Forbes. v. 162 no14 Dec. 28 1998 p. 128

TITLE
   E-mail: write protection?
OTHER TITLES
   Augmented title: Wesley College case
PERSONAL AUTHOR
   Zirkel,-Perry-A
SOURCE
   Phi-Delta-Kappan. v. 79 no8 Apr. 1998 p. 631-2

TITLE
   E-phones connect
PERSONAL AUTHOR
   Kirschner,-Suzanne-Kantra
SOURCE
   Popular-Science. v. 253 no2 Aug. 1998 p. 62-5

TITLE
   Going online: America Onlines's new E-mail tools
PERSONAL AUTHOR
Phelps,-Alan
SOURCE
   Smart-Computing. v. 9 no11 Nov. 1998 p. 50

TITLE
   Grandparenting by E-mail
PERSONAL AUTHOR
   Estess,-Patricia-Schiff
SOURCE
   New-Choices. v. 38 no8 Oct. 1998 p. 67

Each entry in the *Readers' Guide* provides all the information you need to locate articles on a particular subject. Notice how the information is listed in the following print and online entries on electronic mail.

PRINT EXAMPLE

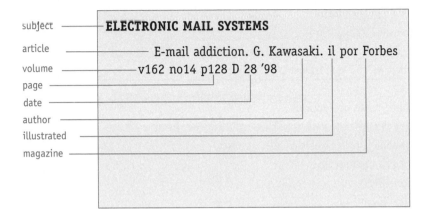

subject — ELECTRONIC MAIL SYSTEMS
article — E-mail addiction. G. Kawasaki. il por Forbes
volume — v162 no14 p128 D 28 '98
page —
date —
author —
illustrated —
magazine —

ONLINE EXAMPLE

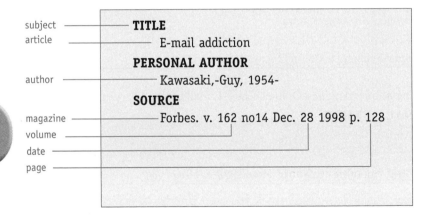

subject — TITLE
article — E-mail addiction
PERSONAL AUTHOR
author — Kawasaki,-Guy, 1954-
SOURCE
magazine — Forbes. v. 162 no14 Dec. 28 1998 p. 128
volume —
date —
page —

PRACTICE YOUR SKILLS

● *Using the Readers' Guide*

Use the entries from the print version of the *Readers' Guide (page C528)* to answer the following questions.

1. What are the titles of two articles on the subject of electronic mail?

2. What are the names of the two magazines that published these stories?

3. What are the titles of two articles published in *Smart Computing*?

4. In what volume of *Forbes* does the article about E-mail addiction appear?

5. On what pages in *Popular Science* magazine does the article "E-phones connect" appear?

6. What subject heading would you look under if you wanted information on electronic journals?

7. Who is the author of the article about America Online's new features?

8. On what page in *Smart Computing* magazine can this article be found?

9. What two cross-references are listed under electronic mail systems?

10. How many of the articles listed under electronic mail systems are illustrated?

Encyclopedias

When you are gathering information for a report, encyclopedias are a good place to start. These works contain general information on a wide variety of subjects.

The information in most encyclopedias is arranged alphabetically by subject. Guide letters on the spine show which letter or letters are covered in each volume. Guide words at the top of each page help you find your subject.

When looking for information in an encyclopedia, be sure to check the index. It will tell you if your subject is discussed in more than one volume or if it is listed under another name.

Online and CD-ROM encyclopedias are arranged in the same manner as printed encyclopedias—alphabetically, but there are no guide words or indexes. Instead, in order to find information on a particular subject, you enter the subject in a search box. The program will then show you the results of your search. Some programs will also give you short movies, a list of related topics, and links to Internet sites about your subject. Following are some popular encyclopedias.

PRINT	*Collier's Encyclopedia* *Encyclopedia Americana* *Encyclopaedia Britannica* *The World Book Encyclopedia*
CD-ROM	*Encarta Encyclopedia Deluxe Edition* *The World Book Multimedia* *Encyclopedia Deluxe Edition* *Compton's Interactive Encyclopedia*
ONLINE	The Concise Columbia Electronic Encyclopedia, http://www.encyclopedia.com Encyclopedia Britannica Online, http://www.britannica.com

Some CD-ROM encyclopedias provide not only information but also a tutorial on the research itself. They include tips about finding a research topic, collecting information, taking notes, organizing information, creating an outline, drafting the report, revising the text, and identifying sources.

Specialized Encyclopedias

Specialized encyclopedias have the same organization as general encyclopedias. Specialized encyclopedias, however, concentrate on one specific subject. They provide more extensive information than general encyclopedias do. Just like general encyclopedias, specialized encyclopedias come in print, online, and CD-ROM versions.

Following are some specialized encyclopedias.

PRINT   *The Baseball Encyclopedia*
Encyclopedia of Animal Care
International Wildlife Encyclopedia
*Encyclopedia for American Facts and
    Dates*
Encyclopedia of Comic Book Heroes
The Encyclopedia of Dance and Ballet
*The Illustrated Encyclopedia of World
    Coins*
*The McGraw-Hill Encyclopedia of Science
    and Technology*

ONLINE   Encyclopedia Smithsonian,
http://www.si.edu/resource/faq/start.htm
The World eText Library,
http://www.netlibrary.net/WorldReferenceE.
html

General Biographical References

Biographical reference works give you information about the lives of famous people. Check your library or media center to see which of the following biographical references it has.

PRINT   *Current Biography*
Who's Who in America
Webster's Biographical Dictionary
Dictionary of American Biography
*American Men and Women of
    Science*

CD-ROM   *Her Heritage: A Biographical
    Encyclopedia of Famous American
    Women*

ONLINE   Biography, http://www.biography.com

PRACTICE YOUR SKILLS

● *Using General Biographical References*

Each of the following Americans was the first at what he or she did. Using a biographical reference, briefly explain what this famous first was.

1. Jackie Robinson
2. Sally Ride
3. Guion Bluford
4. Geraldine Ferraro
5. Robert E. Peary

6. George Washington
7. Sandra Day O'Connor
8. Neil Armstrong
9. Amelia Earhart
10. Charles Lindbergh

Atlases

An **atlas** is a collection of maps. Atlases also contain facts about oceans, deserts, mountains, climate, population, and natural resources. They do not all contain the same maps and information. The pages at the front of each printed atlas and the introduction section of each electronic atlas will tell you what the atlas contains and how the information is presented. Following is a list of commonly used atlases.

PRINT	*Collier's World Atlas and Gazetteer*
	Hammond's Medallion World Atlas
	Rand McNally International World Atlas
	Goode's World Atlas
	The National Geographic Atlas of the World
ONLINE	U.S. Geological Survey, http://www.nationalatlas.gov/mapit.html

Almanacs and Yearbooks

Almanacs and yearbooks include facts about many subjects. They contain world records, noteworthy achievements, facts about famous people, and much more. Since almanacs and yearbooks are published every year, they usually contain up-to-date information. Following are the names of some well-known almanacs and yearbooks.

PRINT	*Information Please Almanac*
	World Almanac and Book of Facts
	Hammond's Almanac
CD-ROM	*Guinness Book of World Records*
ONLINE	*The Old Farmer's Almanac,* http://www.almanac.com

Specialized Dictionaries

Specialized dictionaries contain entries related to one specific subject. Some, for example, list only synonyms. Some list only those terms that are used in mathematics, or computers, or even sports. Following are a few of the many specialized dictionaries available.

PRINT	*The New Roget's Thesaurus in Dictionary Form*
	Webster's New Dictionary of Synonyms
	Abbreviations Dictionary
	Compton's Illustrated Science Dictionary
	Dictionary of American History
CD-ROM	*Oxford English Dictionary*
ONLINE	*English and foreign language dictionaries,* http://www.dictionary.com
	Roget's Thesaurus, http://www.thesaurus.com

PRACTICE YOUR SKILLS

● *Using Specialized Reference Materials*

Following is a list of library resources. Write the name of the best source for answering each question.

specialized encyclopedia   atlas
specialized dictionary   almanac or yearbook
biographical reference

1. For which president's inauguration did Maya Angelou write a poem?

2. Who is the subject of Andrew Wyeth's famous painting *Christina's World*?

3. How many people can the Rose Bowl in Pasadena, California, seat when it is filled to capacity?

4. Lorraine Vivian Hansberry was the first black woman to have a play produced on Broadway. What was the name of the play?

5. In tennis, what is a foot fault?

6. During what years was the American buffalo nickel made?

7. Name the countries partly covered by the Alps.

8. What cities were sites of the Olympic Games in 1968 and 1984?

9. In what state is Kalamazoo, and what large city is directly north of it?

10. In music, what does the term *rockabilly* mean?

● *Finding Facts in Reference Materials*

Use appropriate reference materials to find answers to the ten questions listed above.

Vertical Files

Libraries keep pamphlets, catalogs, newspaper clippings, and other kinds of leaflets. These are usually kept in a filing cabinet called the **vertical file.** The items are placed in folders and arranged alphabetically by subject.

Microforms

Another useful reference source that can be found in many libraries is newspapers. Your library will probably have the most recent editions of local papers as well as major national ones. Because they take up so much space and are delicate, older editions of papers are usually stored in microform: either **microfilm** (a reel of film) or **microfiche** (a sheet of film). You can view these types of film by using a special projection machine. The films are usually cataloged in books similar to the *Reader's Guide to Periodical Literature (page C527)*. Once you have found a film with information on your topic in the guide, you can use a projection machine to view the appropriate pages of the archived newspaper.

Recorded Materials

Most libraries have a section where the recorded materials are kept. These usually include audio tapes, CDs and records, videos and DVDs, CD-ROMs and other software. If your library has an online catalog, you will find these materials indexed there. If your library uses a card catalog, you will find these materials indexed there or in a separate, smaller card catalog near where the materials are stored.

Some of the recorded materials may be borrowed and others can be used only in the library. Many libraries and media centers have listening, viewing, and computer rooms where these types of materials can be used.

Internet Search Engines

Trying to do research on the Internet can be like looking for a needle in a haystack! You know the information is there, but how do you go about finding it? Typing a few words into a search engine can take you all over the world as it matches your request. It can also give you a message like: *2,300 pages were found that match your search criteria.* How are you ever going to dig through all of those pages?

As with all tools—and the Internet is a very useful research tool—you need to know how to get the best results with the least effort. Use the following tips to help improve your use of this tool.

- Enclose your keywords in quotation marks.

- Put a + before a word or phrase that must appear; use a - before terms not needed.

- Use Boolean search techniques. In a Boolean search (named after English mathematician George Boole), an *and* is added between two words if they must both appear in the results; an *or* is added if either term will do.

Media Activity

Select a subject and go online to try these different search techniques. Keep a log of your original search words, the variations you added, where your search took you, and record the time you spent online trying to research a topic. Make your log specific, so you can learn from the mistakes and corrections. Then try researching another subject. Keep a log of that experience as well. See if your last experience improves your use of this powerful tool.

You have seen that some information in a library or media center is in print form, while other information is in electronic form. Each format has its own advantages. What advantages did you find in using the Internet to gather information instead of going to print or bound materials? Were there any advantages to looking in books instead of going online? In what situations would each form of information be more useful? Record your reflections in your **journal.**

A Writer's Guide to Electronic Publishing

The Internet offers many ways to do research, including the World Wide Web, E-mail, and much more. Together with the resources in your local library or media center, you can gather a large amount of data to help you create a well-developed project or report.

Once you've organized your material, ask yourself: What's the best way to present this information?

Years ago, your choices might have been limited to using text from a typewriter, photos and glue, and construction paper. But now electronic publishing offers choices such as desktop publishing (creating printed documents on your computer), audio and video recordings, and even online publishing on the World Wide Web (creating your own Website).

Not every type of electronic publishing is right for every project. Each method has advantages and disadvantages. You will need to choose the method that best suits your topic and project. Ask yourself:

- Is my project **visual?** For example, perhaps you're doing a report on backyard insects. Video would be a good choice for this topic.

- Is **sound** an important part of this project? Suppose you're putting together an opinion poll, and you plan to interview many people. An audio recording could work very well in this situation.

- Could my project **branch off** into many sections? Perhaps you're preparing a presentation that addresses different aspects of your community service club. This topic could make an effective Website.

Once you decide which publishing method is right for your project, let your imagination go!

Desktop Publishing

The computer is a powerful tool that gives you the ability to create everything from party invitations and banners to newsletters and illustrated reports. Many software programs deliver word-processing and graphic arts capabilities that once belonged only to professional printers and designers. Armed with the knowledge of how to operate your software, you simply need to add some sound research and a healthy helping of creativity to create an exciting paper.

Word-Processing Magic

The written word is the basis of almost every project. Using a standard word-processing program, such as Microsoft Word, makes all aspects of the writing process easier. Use a word-processing program to:

- create an outline;
- create charts and graphs;
- save multiple versions of your work;
- revise your manuscript;
- proof your spelling, grammar, and punctuation;
- produce a polished final draft document.

Fascinating Fonts

Once your written material is revised and proofed, it's fun to experiment with type as a way to enhance the content of your written message. Different styles of type are called **fonts** or **typefaces.** Most word-processing programs feature more than 30 different choices. You'll find them listed in the Format menu under Font.

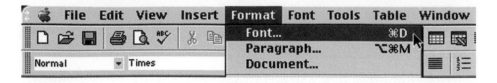

Or they may be located on the toolbar at the top left of your screen.

Although each typeface has its own distinguishing characteristics, most fonts fall into one of two categories: serif typefaces or sans serif typefaces. A serif is a small curve or line added to the end of some of the letter strokes. A typeface that includes these small added curves is called a **serif** typeface. A font without them is referred to as **sans serif,** or in other words, without serifs.

> Times New Roman is a serif typeface.
> Arial is a sans serif typeface.

In general, sans serif fonts have a sharp look and are better for shorter pieces of writing, such as headings and titles. Serif typefaces work well as body copy.

Of all the typefaces, whether serif or sans serif, which is best? In many cases, that decision depends on your project. Each font has a personality of its own and makes a different impression on the reader. For example:

> *This is French Script MT and might be fun to use in an invitation to a special birthday party.*
>
> **This is Playbill and would look great on a poster advertising a performance by the Drama Club.**
>
> **This is Stencil and would be a great way to say "Top Secret" on a letter to a friend.**

As fun as they are, these three typefaces are probably inappropriate for a school report or term paper. Specialized fonts are great for unique projects (posters, invitations, and personal correspondence) but less appropriate for writing assignments for school.

Since most school writing is considered formal, good font choices include Times New Roman, Arial, Helvetica, or Bookman Antiqua. These type styles are fairly plain and straightforward. They allow the reader to focus on the meaning of your words instead of being distracted by the way they appear on the page.

One last word about fonts: With so many to choose from, you may be tempted to include a dozen or so in your document. Be careful! Text **printed** *in* **multiple** fonts *can* be extremely *confusing* **to read**. The whole idea of different typefaces is to enhance and clarify your message, not the other way around!

A Sizable Choice

Another way to add emphasis to your writing is to adjust the size of the type. Type size is measured in points. One inch is equal to 72 points. Therefore, 72-point type would have letters that measure one inch high. To change the point size of your type, open the Format menu and click Font.

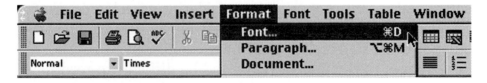

Or use the small number box on the toolbar at the top left side of your screen.

For most school and business writing projects, 10 or 12 points is the best size type for the main body copy of your text. However, it's very effective to change the type size for titles, headings, and subheadings to give the reader a clear understanding of how your information is organized. For example, look at how the type in the subheading "A Sizable Choice" on page C543 is different from the rest of the type on that page, indicating the beginning of a new section.

Another way to add emphasis is to apply a style to the type, such as **bold**, *italics,* or <u>underline</u>. Styles are also found in the Format menu under Font.

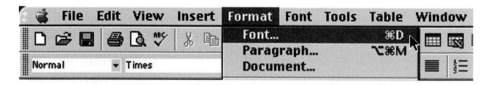

You can also look for them in the top center section of the toolbar on your screen abbreviated as **B** for bold, *I* for italics, and <u>U</u> for underline.

Here's one more suggestion—**color.** If you have access to a color printer, you may want to consider using colored type to set your headings apart from the rest of the body copy. Red, blue, or other dark colors work best. Avoid yellow or other light shades that might fade out and be difficult to read.

Like choosing fonts, the trick with applying type sizes, styles, and colors is to use them sparingly and consistently throughout your work. In other words, all the body copy should be in one style of type, all the headings should be in another, and so on. If you pepper your copy with too many fonts, type sizes, styles, and colors, your final product could end up looking more like a patchwork quilt than a polished report.

Layout Help from Your Computer

One way to organize the information in your document is to use one of the preset page layouts provided by your word-processing program. All you have to do is write your document using capital letters for main headings, and uppercase and lowercase letters for subheadings. Set the headings apart from the body copy with returns. Then open the Format menu and click the Autoformat heading. Your copy will probably look like this:

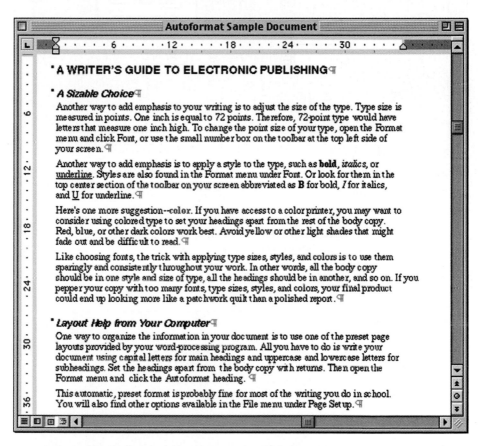

This automatic, preset format is probably fine for most of the writing you do in school. You'll also find other options available in the File menu under Page Setup. For example, you can create a document in the size of large or small index cards for note-taking.

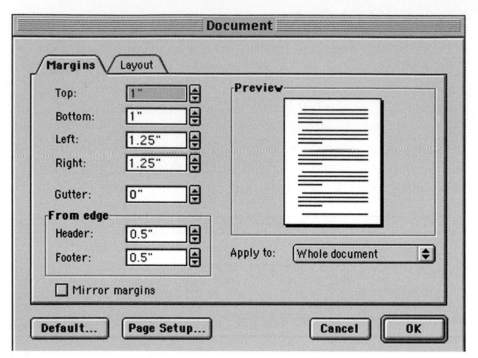

Here you can change the margins and add headers, footers, and page numbers. **Headers** and **footers** are descriptive titles that automatically appear at the top or bottom of each page without your having to retype them each time. For example, you may wish to add the title of your project and the date as a header or footer to each page.

```
Header
Project Title Here ¶
Date Here ¶
```

Let's Get Graphic

The old saying, "A picture is worth a thousand words" is particularly true when it comes to spicing up papers and reports. Desktop publishing programs (such as Adobe PhotoDeluxe Home Edition, Macromedia FreeHand, Microsoft PhotoDraw, and Microsoft PowerPoint) give you the ability to include photographs, illustrations, and charts in your work that can express your ideas more clearly and concisely than words alone.

The key to using graphics effectively is to make sure each one conveys a message of importance. Don't use graphics just for decoration. Be sure they add something meaningful, or you'll actually take away from your written message.

Drawings   Many paint and draw programs allow you to create or import (bring in from another program) an illustration for your document. Drawings can help illustrate concepts that are difficult to describe, such as mechanical parts or procedures. Cartoons can also add a nice touch. If you use them sparingly, they can lighten up an otherwise dry, technical report.

Clip Art   Another kind of drawing is called clip art. These simple, black-and-white or color line pictures are often included in desktop publishing or word-processing programs. Pre-drawn clip art usually is not very good for illustrative purposes, but it does work well as graphic icons that can help guide your reader through various parts of a long report.

For example, suppose you are writing a report on the top arts programs in the United States. You might choose the following clip art for each of the sections:

When you introduce the section of your report that deals with music, you might use the music icon at the large size pictured above. Then, in the headers of all the following sections that deal with music, you might use a smaller version of the icon that looks like this:

 **Music Groups**

Using clip art as icons in this way lets your readers know at a glance which part of the report they are reading.

Charts and Graphs   If your project, or part of your project, deals with comparing numbers and statistics, one of the best ways to communicate this information is by using charts and graphs. Programs such as Microsoft PowerPoint allow you to create bar graphs, pie charts, and line graphs that can communicate fractions, figures, and measurements much more powerfully than written descriptions.

Photographs   When you flip quickly through a book or a magazine, what catches your eye? Probably photographs. Most of us are naturally curious and want to see what we are reading about. Photos are the perfect companions to written work. With the widespread availability of digital cameras and scanners, adding photos to your project is an easy and effective way to enhance your content.

Using a digital camera or a scanner, you can load photos directly into your computer. Another option is to shoot photographs with a regular camera, but when you have them developed, request that they be returned to you as "pictures on disc," which you can open on your computer screen.

Photographic images are stored as bits of data in an electronic file. Once you have the photos in your computer, you can use a graphics program such as Adobe PhotoDeluxe Home Edition to manipulate the images in a variety of ways and create amazing visual effects. You can crop elements out of the photo, add special filters and colors, combine elements of two different pictures into one—the possibilities are endless.

After you have inserted the edited photo into your document, be careful when you print out your final draft. Standard printers often don't reproduce photographs well. You may want to take your document on disk to a professional printing company and have it printed out on a high-resolution printer to make sure you get the best quality.

Captions and Titles   While it's true that a single photo can say a great deal, some pictures still need a little explanation in order to have the strongest impact on your reader. Whenever you include an illustration or photograph in a document, also include a simple caption or title for each image.

Add captions in a slightly smaller type size than the body copy and preferably in a sans serif typeface. Use the caption to add information that isn't immediately apparent in the photo. If there are people in the picture, tell us who they are. If the photo features an odd-looking structure, tell us what it is. Be smart with your captions. Don't tell the reader the obvious. Give him or her a reason to read your caption.

For example, suppose you are doing a report about Mt. Everest and you include a dramatic photograph of its snowy peak.

WEAK CAPTION   The summit of Mt. Everest is very high and treacherous.

STRONG CAPTION   At its summit, Mt. Everest soars to 29,028 feet, making it the tallest mountain in the world.

Stand-Alone Graphics   Occasionally you may include well-known graphics or logos in a story or report. These graphics convey powerful messages on their own and don't require captions. Examples of these logos or symbols include:

You may also want to design your own logos and scan them into your work.

Nonprint Media—Audio and Video

The world we live in is becoming increasingly more multimedia-savvy. The power of the spoken word and the visual image is widely recognized for the impact it carries. Many businesses rely on multimedia presentations to market their products or convey messages to consumers and employees. Exciting opportunities exist for people who can produce clear, concise messages in audio and visual formats.

Pre-Production—Put It on Paper First

Although the final presentation of your subject material may be an audiotape or a video, your project needs to begin on paper first. When you write down your ideas, you do four things:

- Organize your thoughts.
- Narrow your focus.
- Isolate the main messages.
- Identify possible production problems.

Grabbing a tape recorder or camcorder and then running off to record your project is a sure-fire way to create an unorganized mess. This helter-skelter collection of shots and sound bites probably takes hours longer to unravel and fix than if you had taken the time to plan your production in the first place. Resist the urge to record immediately! You will be glad you did.

Concept Outline   The first task in the writing process is a short, one-page document that describes the basic idea of the project. Ideally this should be three paragraphs—one paragraph each describing the beginning, the middle, and the end. Do not go forward until you have clearly identified these three important parts of your project.

Brief   Next ask yourself, What is the purpose of this video or audiotape? Who is the audience? What is the result you hope to achieve when this group of people sees or hears your presentation? Do you want them to be informed about something? Motivated to do something? Excited about something? Write three paragraphs that describe the point of your project: how it will be used, who the intended audience is, and what you hope to achieve with the presentation.

Treatment   The next phase of the writing process fleshes out the ideas you expressed in your outline and brief. The treatment is several pages long. It contains descriptions of the characters, dialogue, and settings, and describes the presentation, scene by scene, in order of how it will appear. Include in your treatment descriptions of the mood and the tone of your piece. Is it upbeat and whimsical, or dark and scary? If your project is a video, set the stage by describing the overall look and feel of the production.

Script   Now you are ready to go to script. The script is the blueprint for your production, similar to a blueprint for a house. Everything that is mentioned in the script is what will wind up in the audio recording or on the screen. On the other hand, anything that is left out of the script will likely be overlooked and omitted from the final production.

For an audio recording, the script contains all narration, dialogue, music, and sound effects. For a videotape, it contains all of these elements plus descriptions of the characters, any sets, props, or costumes, plus all camera shots and movements, special visual effects, and onscreen titles or graphic elements. In short the audio script includes everything that is heard, and the video script covers everything that is seen and heard.

Storyboard   Last, for video productions, it's also helpful
to create storyboards—simple frame-by-frame sketches with
explanatory notes jotted underneath—that paint a visual
picture of what the video will look like from start to finish.

The final stages of pre-production include putting together
all of the elements you will need before you begin recording
your audiotape or shooting your video. Here's a general
checklist.

> **Pre-Production Checklist**

Audiotape Tasks

✓ Arrange for audio
  recording equipment

✓ Cast narrator/actors

✓ Find music (secure
  permission)

✓ Arrange for sound effects

✓ Set up recording schedule

✓ Coordinate all cast and
  crew

✓ Arrange for transportation
  if needed

✓ Rehearse all voice talent

Videotape Tasks

✓ Arrange for video
  equipment (including
  lighting and sound
  recording equipment)

✓ Cast narrator/host/actors

✓ Find music (secure
  permission)

✓ Arrange for sound/visual
  effects

✓ Set up shooting schedule

✓ Coordinate all cast and
  crew

✓ Arrange for transportation
  if needed

✓ Set up shooting locations
  (secure permission)

✓ Arrange for costumes,
  props, sets

✓ Arrange for makeup if
  needed

✓ Rehearse all on-camera
  talent

Video Production Schedule   Tucked into the list of pre-production tasks is "Set up recording/shooting schedule." For videotaping, this means much more than just deciding what day and time you will begin shooting.

During the video production phase of your project, the idea is to shoot everything that your script calls for in the final production. Often the most efficient way to do this is what is called "out-of-sequence" filming. This means that, rather than shoot scenes sequentially (in the order that they appear in the script), you shoot them in the order that is most convenient. Later you will edit them together in the correct order in post-production.

For example, your video might begin and end in the main character's office. Rather than shoot the first office scene, then move the cast and crew to the next location, then later at the end of the day return to the office, it might be easier to shoot both office scenes back-to-back. This will save a great deal of time and effort of moving people, lights, and props back and forth.

Lighting may be a factor in the order in which you shoot your scenes. For example, scenes 3, 4, and 7 may take place in the daytime, and scenes 1, 2, 5, and 6 may take place at night.

To take into account all of these factors, you will need to plan your shooting schedule very carefully. The difference between a smooth shoot day and chaos is a well thought-out shooting schedule.

Last, for video or audio recording, it's also a good idea to bring your team together for a pre-production meeting before you begin. This is your chance to have everyone read through the script, go over time schedules, review responsibilities of each person involved, plus answer any questions or discuss possible problems before you begin rolling tape. Pre-production meetings are worth their weight in gold for reducing stress levels and headaches during production!

Production—We're Rolling!

At last, you've completed all your preparation. Now it's time to roll tape!

Audio Production   The better the recording equipment, the higher-quality sound recording you will be able to achieve. The most convenient format for student audio recording is the audiocassette—a high-quality tape in a plastic case that you simply drop inside your cassette recorder.

If you are using an audiocassette recorder, use an external microphone rather than the built-in microphone on the tape recorder for best results. To increase the quality of your production, consider the following suggestions:

- Select a high-quality, low-noise tape stock.

- Choose a quiet place to do your recording. Look for a quiet room with carpeting, soft furniture, and a door you can close firmly. Hang a sign outside the door that says, "Quiet Please— Recording in Progress" so you will not be disturbed in the middle of your session.

- Do a voice check before you begin recording so you know whether the sound level on the recorder is set correctly.

- Lay the script pages out side-by-side to eliminate the rustling sound of turning pages.

- If music is part of your production, cue up the correct cut and practice turning it on and fading the volume up and down at the appropriate parts. Do a sound check on the music volume before you start. Do the same with any sound effects.

Video Production   As with audio recording, there are a number of different formats to choose from for video recording.

Here are some common video formats.

Video 8	A format sometimes referred to as a camcorder. The Video 8 shoots 8-millimeter videotape. It produces a good quality picture and hi-fi sound. With special cable attachments, you can play the tape back through your VCR or television.
High 8	A compact and lightweight format. High 8 is much more expensive than Video 8, but the quality of sound and picture is excellent. High 8 video can be played back on a TV or VCR using special cable attachments.
Betacam	A professional standard video that delivers top-quality sound and pictures. Most news crews shoot Betacam video. Betacam tape can only be played back on a Betacam tape deck.

Ideally you will have ironed out issues regarding shooting when you wrote your production schedule, back in the pre-production phase. This will leave you free during production to focus on your production value, your camera shots, and your actors' performances.

Production value is another way of saying how polished and professional your project turns out. There are many ways to increase the production value of your presentation. Some of the easiest include the following:

- Use a tripod to keep the camera steady. Nothing screams "Amateur!" louder than shaky, hand-held camera shots. If you can't get your hands on a tripod, lean against something sturdy, such as a tree or the side of a car, to keep your subjects from bouncing around in the frame.

- Use sufficient light. If your audience can't see what's happening, they will quickly lose interest in your show. The best way to light a subject is from one side at a 45-degree angle with the light shining in a downward direction. Supplement this with a slightly less powerful light from the other side and even from behind your subject to avoid unsightly shadows.

- Check your focus frequently. Don't wait until your entire production is nearly finished to check whether the shots are clear. Sometimes the manual focus on some cameras is more reliable than the auto-focus feature. Experiment with your camera using both methods *before* your shoot day to see which gives you the better result.

- Use an external microphone. The built-in microphone on the camera will only pick up sounds that are very close by. If you want to record sounds that are farther off, try using an external microphone that can plug into the video recorder. Poor sound quality can greatly lessen the production value of your video.

Next think about *how* you shoot your video. One way to keep your production lively and interesting is to vary your camera shots. The next time you watch a television show or movie, keep a little notepad handy. Every time you notice a different camera move or cut, make a hash mark on your notepad. At the end of 15 minutes, count the hash marks. You may be amazed to find out how many shots were used!

To hold the interest of your audience, use a variety of camera shots, angles, and moves. Check your local library or media center for good books on camera techniques that describe when and how to use various shots—from long shots to close-ups, from low angles to overhead shots. As a rule, every time you change camera shots, change your angle slightly as well. This way, when the shots are edited together, you can avoid accidentally putting two nearly identical shots side-by-side, which creates an upsetting jarring motion called a "jump cut."

Do some research on framing techniques as well to make sure you frame your subjects properly and avoid cutting people's heads off on the screen. Also, try to learn about ways to move the camera in order to keep your audience eager and interested.

For example, three common, but effective camera moves include panning, tracking, and zooming. **Panning** means moving the camera smoothly from one side of the scene to another. Panning works well in an establishing shot to help direct your audience to the setting where the action takes place.

Tracking means moving the camera from one place to another in a smooth action as well, but in tracking, the camera parallels the action, such as moving alongside a character as he or she walks down the street. It's called tracking because in professional filmmaking, the camera and the operator are rolled forward or backward on a small set of train tracks alongside the actor or actress.

Zooming means moving the camera forward or back, but zooming actually involves moving the lens, rather than the camera. By touching the zoom button, you can push in on a small detail that you'd like to emphasize, or you can pull out to reveal something.

The important factor in any kind of camera move is to keep the action moving and, in most cases, slow and steady. Also, use camera movement sparingly. You want to keep your audience eager and interested, not dizzy and sick!

Another good way to keep your presentation moving is to use frequent cuts. While the actual cuts will be done during post-production, you need to plan for them in production. Professional filmmakers use the word *coverage* for making sure they have enough choices for shots. You can create "coverage" for your production by planning shots such as the following:

establishing shot	This shot sets up where the action of the story will take place. For example, if your story takes place inside a classroom, you may want to begin with an establishing shot of the outside of the school.

reaction shot	It's a good idea to get shots of all on-camera talent even if that person does not have any dialogue but is listening to, or reacting to, another character. This gives you the chance to break away from the character who is speaking to show how his or her words are affecting other people in the scene.
cutaway shot	The cutaway shot is a shot of something that is not included in the original scene, but is somehow related to it. Cutaways are used to connect two subjects. For example, the first shot may be of a person falling off a boat. The second shot could be a cutaway of a shark swimming deep below the water.

If you are adventurous, you might also want to try some simple special effects. Dry ice can create smoke effects. You can also have your actors freeze; then stop the camera, remove an object from the set, and restart the camera. This technique will make objects seem to disappear as if by magic. Other effects can be achieved using false backdrops, colored lights, and filters. Just use your imagination!

Post-Production—The Magic of Editing

Without access to a sound mixing board, it's difficult to do post-production on audio recordings. However, there's a great amount of creative control you can have over your video project in post-production using your camera and your VCR.

Once all of your videotaping is complete, it's time to create the **final cut**—that is, your choice of the shots you wish to keep and the shots you wish to discard. The idea, of course, is to keep only your very best shots in the final production. Be choosy and select the footage with only the best composition, lighting, focus, and performance to tell your story.

There are three basic editing techniques.

in-camera editing　This process means you edit as you shoot. In other words, you need to shoot all your scenes in the correct sequence in the proper length that you want them to appear. This is the most difficult editing process because it leaves no room for error.

insert editing　In insert editing you transfer all your footage to a new video. Then, on your VCR, you record over any scenes that you don't want with scenes that you do want in the final version.

assemble editing　This process involves electronically copying your shots from the original source tape in your camera onto a new blank tape, called the edited master, in the order that you want the shots to appear. This method provides the most creative control.

In the best scenario, it's ideal to have three machines available—the camera, a recording VCR for transferring images, and a post-production machine or computer program for adding effects. These effects might include a dissolve from one shot to another instead of an abrupt cut. A **dissolve** is the soft fading of one shot into another. Dissolves are useful when you wish to give the impression that time has passed between two scenes. A long, slow dissolve that comes up from black into a shot, or from a shot down to black, is called a **fade** and is used to open or close a show.

In addition to assembling the program, post-production is the time to add titles to the opening of your program and credits to the end of the show. Computer programs, such as Adobe Premiere, can help you do this. Some cameras are equipped to generate titles too. If you don't have any electronic means to produce titles, you can always mount your camera on a high tripod and focus it downward on well-lit pages of text and graphics placed on the floor. Then edit the text frames into the program.

Post-production is also the time to add voice-over narration and music. Voice-overs and background music should be recorded separately and then edited into the program on a separate sound track once the entire show is edited together. Video editing programs for your computer, such as Adobe Premiere, allow you to mix music and voices with your edited video. Some VCRs will also allow you to add sound tracks.

Publishing on the World Wide Web

The World Wide Web is an exciting part of the Internet where you can visit thousands of Websites and communicate with other people all over the world via E-mail. You can also become a part of the exciting Web community by building and publishing a Website of your own.

Scoping out Your Site

There are no hard-and-fast rules on how to build a Website. However, the Web is a unique medium with distinctive features that make it different from any other form of communication. The Web offers:

- universal access to everyone;
- interactive communication;
- the ability to use photos, illustrations, animation, sound, and video;
- unlimited space;
- unlimited branching capabilities;
- the ability to link your site with other Websites.

If you are going to publish on the Web, it makes sense to take advantage of all of these features. In other words, it's possible to take any written composition, save it in a format that can be displayed in a Web browser, upload it to a server, and leave it at that. But how interesting is it to look at a solid page of text on your computer screen?

Just as you plan a video, you need to plan your Website. Don't just throw text and graphics together up on a screen. The idea is to make your site interesting enough that visitors will want to stay, explore, and come back to your site again—and that takes thought and planning.

Back to the Drawing Board

Again, you need to capture your thoughts and ideas on paper before you publish anything. Start with a summary that states the purpose of your Website and the audience you hope to attract. Describe in a paragraph the look and feel you think your site will need in order to accomplish this purpose and hold your audience's attention.

Make a list of the content you plan to include in your Website. Don't forget to consider any graphics, animations, video, or sound you may want to include. Next go on a World Wide Web field trip.

Ask your friends and teachers for the URLs of their favorite Websites. Visit these sites and bookmark the ones you like. Then click around these sites and ask yourself, Do I like this site? Why or why not? Determine which sites are visually appealing to you and why. Which sites are easy to navigate and why? Print out the pages you like best, and write notes on your reactions.

On the other hand, which sites are boring and why? Print out a few of these pages too, and keep notes on how you feel about them. Chances are the sites you like best will have clean, easy-to-read layouts, be well written, contain visually stimulating graphic elements, and have understandable **interfaces** that make it simple to find your way around.

One sure kiss of death in any Website is long, continuous blocks of text. Scrolling through page after page of text is extremely boring. Plan to break up long passages of information into manageable sections. What will be the various sections of your site? Will there be separate sections for editorial content? News? Humor? Feedback? What sections will be updated periodically and how often?

Pick up your drawing pencil and make a few rough sketches. How do you picture the "home" page of your site? What will the icons and buttons look like? Then give careful thought to how the pages will connect to each other starting with the home page. Your plan for connecting the pages is called a **site map.**

Because the Web is an interactive medium, navigation is critical. Decide how users will get from one page to another. Will you put in a navigation bar across the top of the page or down the side? Will there be a top or home page at the beginning of each section?

Once you have planned the content, organized your material into sections, and designed your navigation system, you are ready to begin creating Web pages.

Planning Your Pages

To turn text into Web pages, you need to translate the text into a special language that Web browsers can read.

- You can use the Save as HTML feature in the File menu of most word-processing programs.

- You can import your text into a Web-building software program and add the code yourself if you know how.

- You can use a software program such as Adobe PageMill that does the work for you. Web-building software programs are referred to as WYSIWYG (pronounced "Wiz-E-Wig"), which stands for What You See Is What You Get.

Web-building software also allows you to create links to other Web pages using a simple process called **drag and drop.** Be sure to read the directions that come with your software package for complete instructions.

Putting It All Together

Writing for the Web is different from writing for print. The Web is a fast medium. It's about experiences, not study time, so write accordingly. Keep your messages concise and to the point. Use short, punchy sentences. Break up your copy with clever subheads. Try not to exceed 500 to 600 words in any single article on any one page.

Compose your Web copy on a standard word-processing program. This will give you access to your formatting tools and spell-check features. Following the directions of your Web-building software, you can then import the completed text into the software program for placement on your Web page.

Next you will want to lay out your Web page and flow the text around some interesting graphics. Be sure to include blank space on the page as well. Blank space lets your page "breathe" and makes for a much more inviting experience.

You can use a variety of images on your Website, including charts, graphs, photos, clip art, and original illustrations. Collect graphics for the Web in exactly the same way you would get graphics for any desktop publishing project—scan in images, use a digital camera, or create your own graphics using a graphics software program.

You can also add audio files and video files (referred to as QuickTime Video) to your Website. These are fun and interesting additions. However, there are two drawbacks—audio and video files are time-consuming to prepare and take a long time for the user to load. Also, audio quality can be quite good on the Web, but full-motion video is still not at the broadcast-quality level most people have come to expect.

As an alternative to video, consider animated graphics. Animated graphics are much easier to create using graphics software programs. These programs also allow you to compress the animations so that they load much faster than video files and still run smoothly on screen.

If you'd like to learn more about adding audio and video features, as well as graphics, to your Web pages, visit http://msc.pangea.org/tutorials/www/cap_5-eng.htm.

Going Live

Once all your pages are put together you are ready to go live on the World Wide Web, right? Not quite.

Before you upload your new Website, it's a good idea to test all your pages first, using common Web browsers such as Netscape's Navigator or Microsoft's Internet Explorer—browsers your visitors are likely to use. Open your pages on these browsers and look at them closely. Do the text and graphics appear the way you had designed them? Are all the page elements fitting neatly into the screen space, or do you need to tweak the copy or graphics a little to make them fit better?

Test all links on your page. Click on every page and be sure that it takes you to the site you originally intended. Click on all your navigation elements and buttons. Is everything working the way it's supposed to work? Make any corrections on your home or classroom computer before uploading your Website to a host server and going live to the world.

Your Web-building software program has built-in features that make uploading and adding files to your Website a snap. In fact, some of this software is even available free on the Internet and is easy to download right onto your home or classroom computer.

For more information on how to build and launch your own Website, check the Web. You'll find some great tips at http://www.hotwired.com/webmonkey/kids.

This Website even features a guided lesson plan called "Webmonkey for Kids" with step-by-step directions on how to create your own site. It also has information about useful software programs that schools and other educational institutions can download free.

Here's one more shortcut to building a Website. If you or your school already has an Internet Service Provider (ISP), you may be entitled to a free Website as part of your service package. In fact, if you already have an E-mail address for correspondence, this address can be changed slightly to serve as the URL address of your Website. Call your ISP and ask about Website services included in your sign-up.

Last beware of small errors that can occur when you transmit your Website material to the Web. As soon as you have finished uploading your Website, open your browser, enter the URL address, and take your new site out for a test drive. Click on all your navigational buttons, links, animations, or any other multimedia features. Check to make sure all the pages are there and everything looks the way you planned it.

Does everything check out? Great. Now all you have to do is send an E-mail to everyone you know and invite each person to visit your brand new Website!

A Writer's Guide to Using the Internet

Have you heard people use the word *cyberspace* or the phrase *Information Superhighway?* These terms refer to the Internet—an intricate communication system made up of hundreds of thousands of computers all over the world that can "talk" to one another.

The Internet has been around for several decades. It started as a government project in 1969 when a group of scientists and engineers connected the computers of four universities together. This connection gave them the ability to share research information by sending it back and forth to each other using their computers.

There was only one problem—the information was not organized in any way! Imagine if you went to the library to do some research for a school report and all the books were just piled together in the middle of the floor. How would you find anything?

The next step was to find a way that people could search through the Internet to find specific information. Over the next few years, several different methods were developed. One of the best is still the most popular search system used today. It's called the World Wide Web.

The Web is a network of computers *within* all of the computers that make up the Internet. This special network can deliver all kinds of information that you would find in books right to your computer screen— text, photographs, and illustrations. The Web can also deliver multimedia content—sound clips (music and voice), animation (cartoons), and video.

Best of all, like the Internet, the World Wide Web comes over the same communication lines into personal computers all over the globe—including yours!

How Does the Internet Work?

The Internet is made up of literally thousands of networks all linked together around the globe. Each network consists of a group of computers that are connected to one another to exchange information. If one of these computers or networks fails, the information simply bypasses the disabled system and takes another route through a different network.

No one "owns" the Internet, nor is it managed in a central place. No agency regulates or censors the information on the Internet. Anyone can publish information on the Internet as he or she wishes.

In fact, the Internet offers such a vast wealth of information and experiences that sometimes it's described as the "Information Superhighway." So how do you "get on" this highway? It's easy. Once you have a computer, a modem, and a telephone or cable line, all you need is a connection to the Internet.

The Cyberspace Connection

A company called an Internet Service Provider (ISP) connects your computer to the Internet. Examples of ISPs that provide direct access are AT&T, Microsoft Network, MediaOne, and Netcom. You can also get on the Internet indirectly through companies such as America Online (AOL), Prodigy, and CompuServe.

ISPs charge a flat monthly fee for their service. Unlike the telephone company, once you pay the monthly ISP fee, there are no long-distance charges for sending or receiving information on the Internet—no matter where your information is coming from, or going to, around the world! Once you are connected to the Information Superhighway, all you have to do is learn how to navigate it.

Alphabet Soup—Making Sense of All Those Letters!

Like physical highways, the Information Super Highway has road signs that help you find your way around. These road signs are expressed in a series of letters that can seem confusing at first. You've already seen some of these different abbreviations—ISP and AOL. How do you make sense out of all these letters? Relax. It's not as complicated as it looks.

Each specific group of information on the World Wide Web is called a **Website** and has its own unique address. Think of it as a separate street address of a house in your neighborhood. This address is called the URL, which stands for Uniform Resource Locator. It's a kind of shorthand for where the information is located on the Web.

Here's a typical URL: **http://www.bkschoolhouse.com.**

All addresses, or URLs, for the World Wide Web begin with **http://**. This stands for HyperText Transfer Protocol and is a programming description of how the information is being exchanged.

The next three letters are easy—**www.** They let you know that you're on the World Wide Web. The next part of the URL—**bkschoolhouse**—is the name of the site you want to visit. And the last three letters, in this case **com**, indicate that this Website is sponsored by a commercial company. Here are other common endings of URLs you will find:

- "org" is short for organization, such as in http://www.ipl.org, which is the URL of the Website for the Internet Public Library.

- "edu" stands for education, as in the Web address for the Virtual Reference Desk, http://thorplus.lib.purdue.edu/reference/index.html, featuring online dictionaries, telephone books, and other reference guides.

- "gov" represents government-sponsored Websites, such as http://www.whitehouse.gov, the Website for the White House in Washington, D.C.

To get to a Website, you use an interface called a **browser**. Two popular browsers are Netscape's Navigator and Microsoft's Internet Explorer. A browser is like a blank form where you fill in the information you are looking for. If you know the URL of the Website you want to explore, all you have to do is type it in the area marked Location, click Enter on your keyboard, and wait for the information to be delivered to your computer screen.

There are many other ways to find information on the Web. We'll talk more about these methods later in this guide.

☐ Basic Internet Terminology

Here are some of the most frequently used words you will hear associated with the Internet.

address
The unique code given to information on the Internet. This may also refer to an E-mail address.

bookmark
A tool that lets you store your favorite URL addresses, allowing you one-click access to your favorite Web pages without retyping the URL each time.

browser
Application software that supplies a graphic, interactive way to search, find, view, and manage information on the Internet.

cyberspace
The collective realm of computer-aided communication.

download
The transfer of programs or data stored on a remote computer to a storage device on your personal computer.

E-mail
Electronic mail that can be sent all over the world from one computer to another. May also be short for Earth-mail because no paper (and no rainforest acreage) is involved.

FAQs	The abbreviation for Frequently Asked Questions. This is a great resource to get information when visiting a new Website.
flaming	Using mean or abusive language in cyberspace. Flaming is considered to be in extremely poor taste and may be reported to your ISP.
home page	The start-up page of a Website.
keyword	A simplified term that serves as subject reference when doing a search.
link	Short for *Hyperlink*. A link is a connection between one piece of information and another.
Net	Short for *Internet*.
netiquette	The responsible and considerate way for a user to conduct himself or herself on the Internet.
network	A system of interconnected computers.
online	To "be online" means to be connected to the Internet via a live modem connection.
real time	Information received and processed (or displayed) as it happens.
search engine	A computer program that locates documents based on keywords that the user enters.
spam	Electronic junk mail.
surf	A casual reference to browsing on the Internet. To "surf the Web" means to spend time discovering and exploring new Websites.
Website	A page of information or a collection of pages that is being electronically published from one of the computers in the World Wide Web.

Why Use the Internet?

By the end of the 1990s, the Internet had experienced incredible growth. An estimated 196 million people were using the Internet worldwide, spending an average of 8.8 hours a week online. By 2003, this number is estimated to increase to more than 500 million people who will be surfing the Web. Why? What does the Internet offer that makes so many people want to go online? And what are the advantages of using the Internet for writers in particular?

The World at Your Fingertips

The answer is, the Internet offers an amazing amount of knowledge and experiences at the touch of your computer keyboard. For writers, it's a great way to get ideas and do in-depth research. You'll find thousands upon thousands of Websites offering a mind-boggling array of subjects. You can explore the Web as a way to jumpstart your creativity or tap into unlimited information.

The Internet also lets you communicate with experts whom you might not otherwise have access to. Plus, you can connect with other people all over the world who have the same interests you do—maybe even find a new writing partner!

In short, the Internet is an invaluable tool for creating great writing. In this section, we'll explore just some of these exciting advantages.

Just an E Away

One of the most popular features of the Internet is electronic mail, or E-mail for short. Unlike traditional mail (nicknamed "snail mail" by tech-savvy people), E-mail messages are practically instantaneous. It's so convenient that, by 1999, 46 percent of Americans were sending or receiving E-mail every day.

E-mail is a fun and easy way to keep in touch with friends and relatives. You can send anything from a lengthy family newsletter to a quick question or "news flash." E-mail is also appropriate for formal correspondence, such as requesting information from a museum. In this case, it's a good idea to follow up with a hard copy in the traditional mail.

Have you ever teamed up with another student or maybe a group of students in your class to work on a project together? With E-mail, you can collaborate with other students in other states or even other countries! Many schools are taking advantage of E-mail to pair a class in say, Houston, Texas, to work on a cooperative project with a class in Seattle, Washington, or maybe as far away as Sydney, Australia.

For writers, E-mail is an especially valuable tool. It's a great way to communicate with people who are experts in their fields. Many times well-known authorities, who are difficult to reach by phone or in person, will respond to questions and requests for information via E-mail. E-mail comes in particularly handy when the person you would like to communicate with lives in another part of the world. It eliminates the expense of long-distance phone calls plus awkward problems due to different time zones.

An easy way to locate experts in a particular area is to visit Websites about that subject. Many times these Websites will list an E-mail address where you can send questions.

Another way writers can use E-mail is to gather information and make contacts. E-mail queries can be sent out to many people in a single click by simply adding multiple addresses to the same message.

For example, suppose you are writing a paper about raising exotic fish. With one click, you can send out an E-mail to 30 friends and associates that asks, Do you know anyone who has exotic fish? Chances are at least a few of the people you ask will have one or two contacts they can provide—and think how much faster corresponding by E-mail is than making 30 phone calls!

You can learn more about sending E-mail on pages C578–C582.

Picture This

Whatever you write will probably have more impact if it's accompanied with some sort of visual. Many sites on the World Wide Web offer photos, illustrations, and clip art that can be downloaded and integrated into your work. Sometimes there are fees for using this artwork, but many times it's free.

Another way to illustrate your writing is to take your own photos, turn them into electronic images, and integrate them into your work. One way to do this is to use a digital camera and download the images directly into your computer. If you don't have a digital camera, you can also take pictures using a regular camera. When you have the photos developed, ask the developer if you can have them returned to you either on disc or via E-mail.

Another option is to use a scanner, a device that looks somewhat like a copy machine. You place the photo on the glass, and the image is scanned into your computer.

Once you have an image in your computer, you can add it to a report or article in a number of ways—for example, on the cover page as a graphic or border design. There are even a number of photo-editing programs available that give you the ability to manipulate images in all sorts of creative ways.

Sometimes a graph or chart can help you illustrate your point more clearly. Using a program such as Microsoft PowerPoint, you can create all kinds of graphs and tables that you can incorporate into your writing project for extra emphasis.

One of the best advantages of photos, graphs, and artwork that are stored as electronic images is that you can also send them as E-mail attachments. Imagine—with a click of a button, you have numerous options.

- Share photos of your last soccer game instantly with friends and relatives anywhere in the world.

- Take your pen pals on a "virtual" tour of your home, school, or neighborhood.

- Swap pictures and graphs with writing partners across the globe and double your resources.

Online Help

Hundreds of Websites can help you with specific subjects you are probably studying right now. These sites cover a variety of topics in English, social studies, math, science, foreign languages, and more. Here's just a tiny sample of some of the sites waiting to help you:

- The Guide to Grammar and Writing (http://webster.commnet.edu/HP/pages/darling/grammar.htm)

- The Looney Bin—a light-hearted look at how to improve your study skills (http://www.geocities.com/Athens/3843/index.html)

- The Math Forum—interesting math challenges, featuring the whimsical "Ask Dr. Math" (http://forum.swarthmore.edu/students)

- The Guide to Experimental Science Projects (http://www.isd77.k12.mn.us/resources/cf/SciProjInter.html)

- The Smithsonian Institution—links to sites ranging from Aeronautics to Zoology (http://www.si.edu)

 One cautionary note when surfing the Web:

- No matter how tempting, do not give out your name, address, telephone number, or school name to any site that may ask for this information.

- If you sense any inappropriate requests for information, notify your teacher and/or a parent.

Don't Believe Everything You Read

Wow, all this terrific information—just a click away. There's only one problem. Not all of it is credible or accurate.

When you check out a book from the library, a librarian or a committee of educators has already evaluated the book to make sure it's a reliable source of information, but remember, no one owns or regulates the Internet. Just because you read something online, doesn't mean it's true. How can you tell the difference? Here are a few guidelines on how to evaluate an online source.

- **Play the name game**
  First, find out who publishes the site. Does the URL end in ".com" (which means it's a commercial company)? If so, is it a large, reputable company, or one you've never heard of that might just be trying to sell you something? An educational site in which the URL ends in ".edu," such as a college or university, might be a more reliable choice. Or a site sponsored by a well-known organization (with a URL that ends in ".org"), such as the American Red Cross (http://www.crossnet .org), would also probably be a credible source.

- **Scope it out**
  Click around the site and get a feel for what it's like. Is the design clean and appealing? Is it easy to get around the site and find information? Are the sections clearly labeled? Does the site accept advertising? If you think the site seems disjointed or disorganized, or you just have a negative opinion of it, listen to your instincts and move on to another one.

- **Says who?**
  Suppose you find an article on the Web that seems chock-full of great information. The next question you need to ask yourself is, Who is the author? Is the person an acknowledged expert on the subject? If you don't recognize the author's name, you can do a search on the

Web, using the author's name as the keyword to get more information about him or her.

In some cases, an article won't list any author at all. If you don't find an author's name, be skeptical. A credible site clearly identifies its authors and usually lists the person's professional background and credentials.

- **Is this old news?**
If you are doing research on the pyramids, it's probably all right if the information wasn't posted yesterday. But if you're looking for information in quickly changing fields, such as science and politics, be sure to check the publish date before you accept the data as true.

- **Ask around**
Reliable Websites frequently provide E-mail addresses or links to authors and organizations connected to the content on the site. Send off a quick E-mail to a few of these sources, tell them what you are writing, and ask them: Is this material accurate?

Perhaps the best way to find out if the information on any Website or the information in any article (signed or unsigned) is accurate is to check it against another source—and the best source is your local library or media center.

Internet + Media Center = Information Powerhouse!

Although the Internet is a limitless treasure chest of information, remember that it's not catalogued. It can be tricky to locate the information you need, and sometimes that information is not reliable. The library is a well-organized storehouse of knowledge, but it has limited resources. If you use the Internet *and* your local media center, you've got everything you need to create well-researched articles, reports, and papers.

> ## Use the Internet to

- get great ideas for topics to write about;
- gather information about your topic from companies, colleges and universities, and professional organizations;
- connect with recognized experts in your field of interest;
- connect with other people who are interested in the same subject and who can put you in touch with other sources.

> ## Use the Media Center to

- find additional sources of information either in print or online;
- get background information on your topic;
- cross-check the accuracy and credibility of online information and authors.

I Don't Own a Computer

You can still access the Internet even if you don't have your own computer. Many schools have computer labs that are open after school and on weekends. Some schools will even allow students to use these labs even though they are not enrolled at that particular school. Many libraries are also equipped with computers and Internet connections.

Consider taking a computer course after school or even attending a computer camp. You'll find information about these programs listed at the library, the YMCA, and in parenting magazines.

Last, maybe you have a friend or neighbor with a computer that you can use in exchange for a service you might provide, such as babysitting or yard work.

How to Communicate on the Internet

E-mail is a great way of exchanging information with other people on the Internet. Here's how to use this useful form of communication, step-by-step.

Keep in Touch with E-mail

Any writer who has ever used E-mail in his or her work will agree that sending and receiving electronic messages is one of the most useful ways of gathering information and contacts for writing projects. It's fast, inexpensive, and fun!

Once you open your E-mail program, click on the command that says, Compose Mail. This will open a new blank E-mail similar to the one pictured below. Next, fill in the blanks.

Type the person's E-mail address here. There is no central listing of E-mail addresses. If you don't have the person's address, the easiest way to get it is to call and ask them for it. You can address an E-mail to one or several people, depending on the number of addresses you type in this space.

CC stands for courtesy copy. If you type additional E-mail addresses in this area, you can send a copy of the message to other people.

BCC stands for blind courtesy copy. By typing one or more E-mail addresses here, you can send a copy of the message to others without the original recipient knowing that other people have received the same message. Not all E-mail programs have this feature.

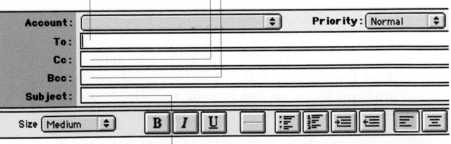

This is where you type your message.

This is called the subject line. Write a few brief words that best describe what your E-mail message is about.

Say It with Style

Like regular letters, E-mail can have a different tone and style depending on to whom you are writing. Usually informal E-mails, such as instant messages (IMs) to close friends, are light, brief, and to the point. In the case of more formal E-mails, such as a request for information from an expert or a museum, it's important to keep the following guidelines in mind:

- Make sure your message is clear and concise.
- Use proper grammar and punctuation.
- Check your spelling. (Some E-mail programs have their own spell-check function—use it!)
- Double-check the person's E-mail address to be sure you've typed it correctly.

Because E-mail is a fast medium designed for quick communication, E-mail users have developed a kind of shorthand that helps them write their messages even faster. Here are a few commonly used abbreviations that you may find in informal E-mail:

COMMON E-MAIL ABBREVIATIONS

BRB	be right back	BTW	by the way
FYI	for your information	F2F	face-to-face
IMHO	in my humble opinion	IOW	in other words
LOL	laughing out loud	L8R	later
OIC	oh, I see	ROFL	rolling on the floor laughing

Are you sending the E-mail to a friend or relative? If so, would you like to add a touch of fun? Then you may want to explore **emoticons** (also known as "smileys")—little faces made out of keyboard symbols that you add to your messages to express how you feel about something.

COMMON EMOTICONS

:)	happy	:(	sad
:-D	laughing	:`-(	crying
;-)	winking	:-}	smirking
:-0	shocked	:-/	skeptical
:-<>	bored	^<|:-)	Santa Claus
:-#	my lips are sealed	8-)	I'm wearing glasses

Attach a Little Something Extra

When you send E-mail, you can send other information along with your message. These are called **attachments.** Depending on your E-mail program's capabilities, you can attach documents, photos, illustrations—even sound and video files. Click Attach, and then double-click on the document or file on your computer that you wish to send.

After you have composed your message and added any attachments you want to include, click the Send button. Presto! Your message arrives in the other person's mailbox seconds later, regardless if that person lives right next door or on the other side of the world. Because there is usually no charge to send E-mail, it's a great way to save money on postage and long-distance telephone calls.

Follow Up

It's important to note, however, that just because you've sent a message, you shouldn't automatically assume that the other person has received it. Internet Service Providers (ISPs) keep all messages that are sent until the recipient requests them. The person you sent your E-mail to might be away from his or her computer or may not check messages regularly.

Also, the Internet is still imperfect. From time to time, servers go down or other "hiccups" in electronic transmissions can occur, leaving your message stranded somewhere in cyberspace. If you don't get a reply in a reasonable amount of time, either resend your original E-mail message or call the person and let him or her know that your message is waiting.

You've Got Mail

When someone sends *you* an E-mail message, you have several options:

Reply: Click Reply, and you can automatically send back a new message without having to retype the person's E-mail address. (Be sure you keep a copy of the sender's E-mail address in your address book for future use.)

Forward: Suppose you receive a message that you would like to share with someone else. Click Forward, and you can send a copy of the message, plus include a few of your own comments, to another person.

Print: In some instances, you may need to have a paper copy of the E-mail message. For example, if someone E-mails you directions to a party, click Print to take a hard copy of the instructions with you.

Store: Do you want to keep a message to refer to later? Some E-mail programs allow you to create folders to organize stored messages.

Delete: You can discard a message you no longer need just by clicking Delete. It's a good idea to throw messages away regularly to keep them from accumulating in your mailbox.

Mind Your Manners!

As in any social setting, there are a few guidelines to follow when you're talking to people online. These suggestions will help you be considerate of others in cyberspace. This conduct is called **netiquette.**

- Never use harsh or insulting language. This is called **flaming** and is considered rude. Derogatory terms swapped back and forth in a continuing argument is called a **flamewar.** Avoid this situation.

- Type your messages using uppercase and lowercase letters. WRITING IN ALL CAPITAL LETTERS IS DIFFICULT TO READ AND IS REFERRED TO AS "SHOUTING."

- Respect other people's ideas and work. Don't forward a message or attach documents written by someone else without first asking the author's permission.

- Don't send spam. **Spamming** refers to sending messages to entire lists of people in your E-mail addresses for the purpose of selling something. Don't use the Internet to spread rumors or gossip.

- Respect other people's privacy. The Internet is an enormous public forum, so be careful about what you write and post on the Internet that hundreds or thousands of people might see.

How to Do Research on the Internet

The Information Superhighway could be the best research partner you've ever had. It's fast, vast, and always available. But like any other highway, if you don't know your way around, it can also be confusing. It takes time to learn how to navigate the Net and zero in on the information you need. The best thing to do is practice early and often. Don't wait until the night before your paper is due to learn how to do research on the Internet!

Getting Started

Just as there are several different ways to get to your home or school, there are many different ways to arrive at the information you're looking for on the Internet.

CD-ROM Encyclopedia One way to begin is not on the Web at all. You might want to start your search by using a CD-ROM encyclopedia. These CD-ROMs start with an Internet directory. Click the topic that is closest to your subject. This will link you to a site that's likely to be a good starting point. From there, you can link to other resources suggested in the site.

Search Page Another good first step is your browser's search page. Type a word or short phrase that describes what you're searching for. Then select the search tool you wish to use. Some of these tools, sometimes referred to as **search engines,** include:

> Excite—http://www.excite.com
> HotBot—http://www.hotbot.com
> InfoSeek—http://www.infoseek.com
> Lycos—http://www.lycos.com
> WebCrawler—http://www.webcrawler.com
> Yahoo!—http://www.yahoo.com

Search services usually list broad categories of subjects, plus they may offer other features such as "Random Links" or "Top 25 Sites," and customization options. Each one also has a search field. Type in a word or short phrase, called a **keyword,** which describes your area of interest. Then click Search or press the Enter key on your keyboard. Seconds later a list of Websites known as "hits" will be displayed containing the word you specified in the search field. Scroll through the list and click the page you wish to view.

So far this sounds simple, doesn't it? The tricky part about doing a search on the Internet is that a single keyword may yield a hundred or more sites. Plus, you may find many topics you don't need.

For example, suppose you are writing a science paper about the planet Saturn. If you type the word *Saturn* into the search field, you'll turn up some articles about the planet, but you'll also get articles about NASA's Saturn rockets and Saturn, the automobile company.

Search Smart!

Listed below are a few pointers on how to narrow your search, save time, and search *smart* on the Net.

1. The keyword or words that you enter have a lot to do with the accuracy of your search. Focus your search by adding the word "and" or the + sign followed by another descriptive word. For example, try "Saturn" again, but this time, add "Saturn + space." Adding a third word, "Saturn + space + rings" will narrow the field even more.

2. On the other hand, you can limit unwanted results by specifying information that you do *not* want the search engine to find. If you type "dolphins not football," you will get Websites about the animal that lives in the ocean rather than the football team that uses Miami as its home base.

3. Specify geographical areas using the word "near" between keywords as in "islands near Florida." This lets you focus on specific regions.

4. To broaden your search, add the word "or" between keywords. For example, "sailboats or catamarans."

5. Help the search engine recognize familiar phrases by putting words that go together in quotes such as "Tom and Jerry" or "bacon and eggs."

6. Sometimes the site you come up with is in the ballpark of what you are searching for, but it is not exactly what you need. Skim the text quickly anyway. It may give you ideas for more accurate keywords. There might also be links listed to other sites that are just the right resource you need.

7. Try out different search engines. Each service uses slightly different methods of searching, so you may get different results using the same keywords.

Last, check the spelling of the keywords you are using. A misspelled word can send a search engine in completely the wrong direction. Also, be careful how you use capital letters. If you type the word *Gold,* some search services will only bring up articles that include the word with a capital *G.*

Saving a Site for Later

You may want to keep a list handy of favorite Websites or sites you are currently using in a project. This will save you time because you can just click on the name of the site in your list and return to that page without having to retype the URL.

Different browsers have different names for this feature. For example, Netscape calls it a **bookmark**, while Microsoft's Internet Explorer calls it **favorites.**

Searching out a Subject

Suppose you are writing a paper about dinosaurs, specifically Velociraptors—the really smart, agile dinosaurs depicted in the original film *Jurassic Park*. Here's an idea of one way to research this topic.

First, we'll select a search engine. We'll start with InfoSeek—at http://infoseek.go.com/. The first keyword we'll enter is "dinosaurs." The search engine found these sites:

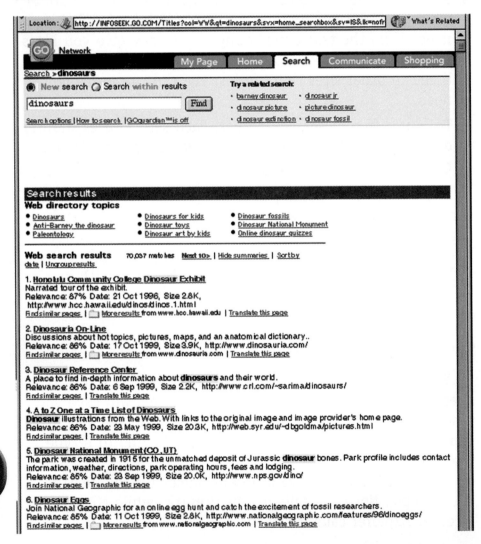

Copyright ©1998–2000 Infoseek Corporation

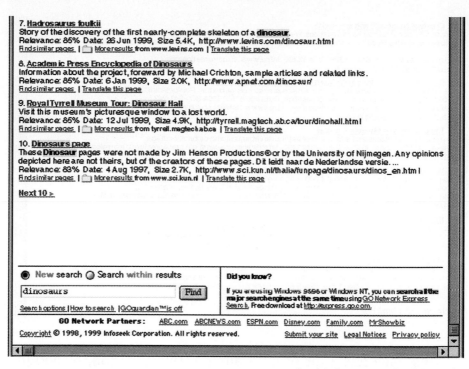

Wow! Look at all these sites about dinosaurs, but there aren't any specific topics related to Velociraptors. By clicking on the words "next 10" at the bottom of the page, we can get another page of topics to look at.

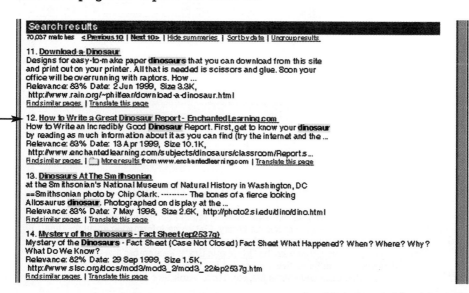

15. Creation, Dinosaurs and the Flood
Creation Explanation You have questions We have answers Ask your questions about Creation, Evolution, **Dinosaurs**, Noah's Flood here. Creation Science Workshops Seminars, Books and Videos November 11, 1999
...
Relevance: 82% Date: 6 Oct 1999, Size 13.5K, http://www.sixdaycreation.com/
Find similar pages | Translate this page

16. Guide to Dinosaur Sites in Western Colorado and Eastern Utah
has moved to its new home at http://www.dinosaurweb.com/guide.htm Rocky Mountain West Electronic Publishing 739 Belford Avenue Grand Junction, Colorado 81501 USA 970-243-2431 ...
Relevance: 82% Date: 4 Jun 1999, Size 1.0K, http://www.rmwest.com/dinosaur/guide.htm
Find similar pages | Translate this page

17. The Queensland Museum Explorer
A virtual visit to Queensland's Museum of natural environment and cultural heritage.
Relevance: 82% Date: 26 Dec 1998, Size 1.3K, http://www.qmuseum.qld.gov.au/nature/dinowelcome.html
Find similar pages | Translate this page

18. Dinosaurs
The planet earth is VERY old, about 4,600 million years. (thats a lot of birthday candles!!!). * There was no life at all on earth for millions of years. * The first living things lived in the sea, they were so ...
Relevance: 82% Date: 23 May 1997, Size 6.7K, http://www.oink.demon.co.uk/topics/dinosaur.htm
Find similar pages | Translate this page

19. NMNH Dinosaur Homepage
Click "Welcome" to enter. Scientific illustrations by Frederick Berger
Relevance: 82% Date: 30 Sep 1998, Size 1.2K, http://www.nmnh.si.edu/paleo/dino/
Find similar pages | ☐ More results from www.nmnh.si.edu | Translate this page

20. MY DINOSAUR PAGE
Table of Contents General **Dinosaur** Information Specific **Dinosaurs** Museums and Parks Fossils Education General **Dinosaur** Information Barrett's Web Pointers Dino Russ's Lair **Dinosaur** Extinction: The Volcano ...
Relevance: 82% Date: 21 Sep 1999, Size 9.6K, http://www.eagle.ca/~matink/dinosaur.html
Find similar pages | ☐ More results from www.eagle.ca | Translate this page

< Previous 10 | Next 10 >

This page has a lot of dinosaur information, too, although there isn't anything specific about Velociraptors here either. But since you are writing a report about dinosaurs, this site about "How to Write a Great Dinosaur Report" seems worth checking out.

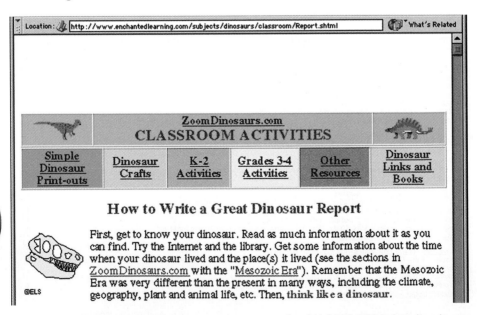

Location: http://www.enchantedlearning.com/subjects/dinosaurs/classroom/Report.shtml   What's Related

ZoomDinosaurs.com
CLASSROOM ACTIVITIES

| Simple Dinosaur Print-outs | Dinosaur Crafts | K-2 Activities | Grades 3-4 Activities | Other Resources | Dinosaur Links and Books |

How to Write a Great Dinosaur Report

First, get to know your dinosaur. Read as much information about it as you can find. Try the Internet and the library. Get some information about the time when your dinosaur lived and the place(s) it lived (see the sections in ZoomDinosaurs.com with the "Mesozoic Era"). Remember that the Mesozoic Era was very different than the present in many ways, including the climate, geography, plant and animal life, etc. Then, think like a dinosaur.

@ELS

For information on particular dinosaurs, try the Dinosaur Information Sheets and the Dinosaur and Paleontoloy Dictionary.

When you write your report, try to answer as many of the following questions as you can (not all of these things are known for all dinosaurs):

- What does its name mean? Often this will tell you something important or interesting about the dinosaur.
- What did your dinosaur look like? For example, how big was it, what shape was its body, were its legs long or short, did it have horns, plates, crests or claws, describe the teeth, head, neck, tail, etc. Draw a picture if you can. Remember that dinosaur weights are very hard to estimate and can vary widely from one reference to another.
- How did its anatomy affect its life? For example: a giant sauropod had to eat a lot but didn't have to worry much about protecting itself, a tiny dinosaur probably had to be fast to escape being eaten for dinner, an armored dinosaur didn't have to be fast, but did have to avoid being flipped over, etc.
- What did it eat and how did it get its food? Where was this dinosaur in the food chain?
- How did it walk (2 or 4 legs - slow or fast locomotion)?
- Is there anything special about this dinosaur? This can often be the best part of the report, taking you off on interesting topics. For example, how did blood get to a Brachiosaurus' head, what were Stegosaurus' plates used for, what was Parasaurolophus' unusual crest probably used for, or how did Spinosaurus use its sailback?
- What is known about your dinosaur's behavior, if anything? For example: Is there evidence of herding? Did it nurture its young? Have any nests or eggs been found? How did your dinosaur rate in terms of intelligence?
- How did it defend itself (and/or attack other animals)?
- What animals might have attacked it? Or what animals might it have preyed upon? (See the section on when your dinosaur lived during the Mesozoic Era to find some of its contemporaries.)
- What type of dinosaur was it (how is it classified and what dinosaurs is it closely related to)?
- When did it live? Was it an early dinosaur or one of the last before the K-T extinction.
- What was the Earth like at that time? What was your dinosaur's environment like and what other dinosaurs (and other interesting animals) lived in that environment? What did the Earth's continents look like at that time? (This information is available in the section called "Mesozoic Era.")
- Where have fossils been found? When were they first found? Are there just a few fragments or are there almost complete specimens?
- Who named the dinosaur? Is there anything interesting about that scientist?

Use your own words. Check your spelling and grammar. Define any technical terms (look them up in the Dinosaur Dictionary). And remember to think like a dinosaur.

References: When you write your bibliography, list all of your references. A format for each type of publication follows (there are different formats):

- **Web Site:** Author(s). *Title of Site or web page* . URL of site, copyright year listed.
- **Book:** Author(s). *Title of book* . Edition. Location of publisher: Name of Publisher, year of publication.
- **Encyclopedia:** *Title of encyclopedia* , volume of encyclopedia used. Location of publisher: Name of Publisher, year of publication, pages where the article is located.
- **Magazine or Journal:** Author(s). "Title of article." *Name of magazine* , Volume.issue (date): pages where the article is located.

Author(s) are listed last name first, first name or initials (as cited in the publication)

For example: Zoom Dinosaurs would be cited as follows:

Col, Jeananda. Zoom Dinosaurs. http://www.ZoomDinosaurs.com 1999.

We've found a number of good ideas for writing a report. This might be a page worth copying into a file on your computer or printing out.

Obviously we could go on and on. The important thing to remember is to use your imagination plus a little common sense. Just imagine you are a paleontologist yourself and doing your very own *Internet* dinosaur search!

A **Abbreviation** shortened form of a word.

Action verb word that tells what action a subject is performing.

Adjective word that modifies a noun or a pronoun.

Adverb word that modifies a verb, an adjective, or another adverb.

Analogy logical relationship between a pair of words.

Antecedent word to which a pronoun refers.

Antonym word that means the opposite of another word.

Appositive noun or pronoun that identifies or explains another noun or pronoun in a sentence.

Audience person or persons who will read your work or hear your speech.

B **Body** one or more paragraphs composed of details, facts, and examples that support the main idea.

Brainstorming prewriting technique of writing down ideas that come to mind about a given subject.

Business letter formal letter that asks for action on the part of the receiver and includes an inside address, heading, salutation, body, closing, and signature.

C **Case** form of a noun or a pronoun that indicates its use in a sentence. In English there are three cases: the nominative case, the objective case, and the possessive case.

Chronological order the order in which events occur.

Clarity the quality of being clear.

Clause group of words that has a subject and verb and is used as part of a sentence.

Close reading reading carefully to locate specific information, follow an argument's logic, or comprehend the meaning of information.

Coherence logical and smooth flow of ideas connected with clear transitions.

Collective noun noun that names a group of people or things.

Colloquialism informal phrase or colorful expression that is not taken literally, but is understood to have a particular meaning.

Complement word or group of words used to complete a predicate.

Complex sentence sentence that consists of a dependent and an independent clause.

Composition writing form that presents and develops one main idea.

Compound sentence sentence made up of two simple sentences, usually joined by a comma and the coordinating conjunction *and, but, or,* or *yet.*

Compound subject two or more subjects in a sentence that have the same verb and are joined by a conjunction.

Compound verb two or more verbs in one sentence that have the same subject and are joined by a conjunction.

Concluding sentence a strong ending added to a paragraph that summarizes the major points, refers to the main idea, or adds an insight.

Conclusion paragraph that completes an essay and reinforces the main idea.

Conjunction word that connects words or groups of words.

Connotation meaning that comes from attitudes attached to a word.

Contraction word that combines two words into one. It uses an apostrophe to replace one or more missing letters.

Coordinating conjunction single connecting word used to join words or groups of words.

Creative writing writing style in which the writer creates characters, events, and images within stories, plays, or poems to express feelings, perceptions, and points of view.

D | **Declarative sentence** statement or expression of an opinion. It ends with a period.

Demonstrative pronoun word that substitutes for a noun and points out a person or thing.

Denotation literal meaning of a word.

Descriptive writing writing that creates a vivid picture of a person, an object, or a scene by stimulating the reader's senses.

Dialogue conversation between two or more persons.

Direct object noun or a pronoun that answers the question *What?* or *Whom?* after an action verb.

Direct quotation passage, sentence, or words stated exactly as a person wrote or said them.

Documentary images, interviews, and narration put together to create a powerful report.

Double negative use of two negative words to express an idea when only one is needed.

Drafting stage of the writing process in which the writer draws ideas together on paper forming a beginning, a middle, and an ending in a composition.

E | **Editing** stage of a writer's process in which the writer polishes his or her work by correcting errors in grammar, usage, mechanics, and spelling.

Elaboration addition of explanatory or descriptive information to a piece of writing, such as supporting details, examples, facts, and descriptions.

Electronic publishing various ways to present information through the use of technology. It includes desktop publishing (creating printed documents on a computer), audio and video recordings, and online publishing (creating a Website).

E-mail electronic mail that can be sent from one computer to another.

Essay composition of three or more paragraphs that presents and develops one main idea.

Exclamatory sentence expression of strong feeling that ends with an exclamation point.

F **Fact** statement that can be proven.

Fiction prose work that is partly or totally imaginary.

Freewriting prewriting technique of writing freely about ideas as they come to mind.

Friendly letter writing form that may use informal English and includes six parts: heading, salutation, body, closing, and signature.

G **Generalizing** forming an overall idea that explains something specific.

Glittering generality word or phrase that most people associate with virtue and goodness that is used to trick people into feeling positively about a subject.

H **Helping verb** auxiliary verb that combines with the main verb to make up a verb phrase.

I **Imperative sentence** a request or command that ends with either a period or an exclamation point.

Indefinite pronoun word that substitutes for an unnamed person or thing.

Indirect object noun or a pronoun that answers the question *To or for whom?* or *To or for what?* after an action verb.

Infinitive verb form that usually begins with *to* and is used as a noun, adjective, or adverb.

Informative writing writing that explains with facts and examples, gives directions, or lists steps in a process.

Interjection word that expresses strong feeling.

Internet global network of computers that are connected to one another with high speed data lines and telephone lines. (See also *Basic Internet Terminology* in *A Writer's Guide to Using the Internet.*)

Interrogative pronoun pronoun used to ask a question.

Interrogative sentence a question. It ends with a question mark.

Introduction first paragraph of a composition that catches the reader's attention and states the main idea.

Irregular verb verb that does not form its past and past participle by adding *-ed* to the present participle.

L **Linking verb** verb that links the subject with another word that renames or describes the subject.

M **Modifier** word that makes the meaning of another word more precise.

N **Narrative writing** writing that tells a real or an imaginary story with a clear beginning, middle, and ending.

Network a system of interconnected computers.

Nonessential phrase phrase or clause that can be removed from a sentence and the sentence will still make sense.

Nonfiction prose work that contains facts about real people or events.

Nonstandard English less formal language used by people of varying regions and dialects. Not appropriate for use in writing.

Noun word that names a person, place, thing, or idea. A common noun gives a general name. A proper noun names a specific person, place, or thing and always begins with a capital letter. Concrete nouns can be seen or touched; abstract nouns can not.

O | **Occasion** cause or purpose for writing; an event which prompts a writer to take action.

Online connected to the Internet via a line modem connection.

Opinion judgment or belief that cannot be absolutely proven.

Order of importance or size way of organizing information by arranging details in the order of least to most (or most to least) pertinent.

Outline information about a subject organized into main topics and subtopics.

P | **Paragraph** group of related sentences that present and develop one main idea.

Participle verb form used as an adjective.

Parts of speech eight categories into which all words can be placed: noun, pronoun, verb, adjective, adverb, preposition, conjunction, and interjection.

Personal writing writing that tells a real or imaginary story from the writer's point of view.

Persuasive writing writing that expresses an opinion and uses facts, examples, and reasons in order to convince the reader of the writer's viewpoint.

Play piece of writing to be performed on a stage by actors.

Plot sequence of events leading to the outcome or point of the story; contains a climax or high point, a resolution, and an outcome or ending.

Plural form of a noun used to indicate two or more.

Poetry form of writing that uses rhythm, rhyme, and vivid imagery to express feelings and ideas.

Possessive pronouns pronouns used to show ownership or possession.

Predicate part of a sentence that tells what a subject is or does.

Predicate adjective adjective that follows a linking verb and modifies the subject.

Predicate nominative noun or a pronoun that follows a linking verb and identifies, renames, or explains the subject.

Prefix one or more syllables placed in front of a base word to form a new word.

Preposition word that shows the relationship between a noun or a pronoun and another word in the sentence.

Prepositional phrase group of words made up of a preposition, its object, and its modifiers.

Prewriting stage of the writing process in which the writer plans for drafting based on the subject, occasion, audience, and purpose for writing.

Principal parts of a verb the *present*, the *past*, and the *past participle*. The principal parts are used to form the tenses of verbs.

Proofreading carefully rereading and making corrections in grammar, usage, spelling, and mechanics in a piece of writing.

Pronoun word that takes the place of one or more nouns. Three types of pronouns are personal, reflexive, and intensive.

Publishing stage of writing process in which the writer may choose to share the work with an audience.

Purpose reason for writing or speaking on a given subject.

R | **Regular verb** verb that forms the past and past participle by adding *–ed* or *–d* to the present.

Relative pronoun pronoun that begins most adjective clauses and relates the adjective clause to the noun or pronoun it describes.

Report composition that documents specific information from books, magazines, and other sources to support the thesis of the report.

Revising stage of the writing process in which the writer rethinks what is written and reworks it to increase its clarity, smoothness and power.

Root part of a word that carries the basic meaning.

Run-on sentence two or more sentences that are written as one sentence and are separated by a comma or have no mark of punctuation at all.

S | **Sentence** group of words that expresses a complete thought.

Sentence fragment group of words that does not express a complete thought.

Sequential order the order in which details are arranged according to when they take place or where they are done.

Setting environment (location and time) in which the action takes place.

Short story well-developed story about characters facing a conflict or problem.

Simple sentence sentence that has one subject and one verb.

Slang nonstandard English expressions that are developed and used by particular groups.

Spatial order the order in which details are arranged according to their physical location.

Standard English proper form of the language that follows a set pattern of rules and conventions.

Style visual or verbal expression that is distinctive to an artist or writer.

Subject names the person, place, thing or idea that a sentence is about; the topic of a composition or essay.

Subordinating conjunction single connecting word used to introduce a dependent clause.

Suffix one or more syllables placed after a base word to change its part of speech and possibly its meaning.

Supporting sentences specific details, facts, examples, or reasons that explain or prove a topic sentence.

Synonym word that has nearly the same meaning as another word.

T

Tense form a verb takes to show time. The six tenses are the *present, past, future, present perfect, past perfect,* and *future perfect.*

Thesaurus online or print reference that gives synonyms for words.

Topic sentence sentence that states the main idea of the paragraph.

Transitions words and phrases that show how ideas are related

U

Understood subject unstated subject that is understood.

Unity combination or ordering of parts in a composition so that all the sentences or paragraphs work together as a whole to support one main idea.

V

Verb word used to express an action or state of being.

Verb phrase main verb plus one or more helping verbs.

Voice the particular sound and rhythm of the language the writer uses (closely related to *tone*).

W

World Wide Web network of computers within the Internet capable of delivering multimedia content and text over communication lines into personal computers all over the globe.

Writing process recursive stages that a writer proceeds through in his or her own way when developing ideas and discovering the best way to express them.

Note: Italic page numbers indicate skill sets.

Note: Italic page numbers indicate skill sets.

INDEX

Note: Italic page numbers indicate skill sets.

INDEX

Note: Italic page numbers indicate skill sets.

Note: Italic page numbers indicate skill sets.

Note: Italic page numbers indicate skill sets.

Note: Italic page numbers indicate skill sets.

Note: Italic page numbers indicate skill sets.

Note: Italic page numbers indicate skill sets.

INDEX

Note: Italic page numbers indicate skill sets.

Barrett Kendall Publishing has made every effort to trace the ownership of all copyrighted selections in this book and to make full acknowledgment of their use. Grateful acknowledgment is made to the following authors, publishers, agents, and individuals for their permission to reprint copyrighted material.

C3: From *Eighth Book of Junior Authors and Illustrators* by Graham Salisbury. **C35:** Copyright © 1993 by Julia Alvarez. Published in *Newsday,* February 1993. Reprinted by permission of Susan Bergholz Literary Services, New York. All rights reserved. **C63:** Reprinted with the permission of Simon & Schuster Books for Young Readers, an imprint of Simon & Schuster Children's Publishing Division from *Hatchet* by Gary Paulsen. © 1987 Gary Paulsen. **C91:** From *When I was a Puerto Rican* by Esmeralda Santiago. Copyright © 1993 by Esmeralda Santiago. Reprinted by permission of Perseus Books Publishers, a member of Perseus Books, L.L.C. **C119:** "The Siren Who Won Anthony and Caesar: Cleopatra," from *Illustrated Minute Biographies* by William A. DeWitt, illustrated by Samuel Nisenson, copyright 1949, 1953, renewed © 1977 by Samuel Nisenson, renewed © 1981 by Rebecca Nisenson. Used by permission of Grosset & Dunlap, Inc., a division of Penguin Putnam Inc. **C153:** Text copyright © 1999 by Paula W. Graham from *Speaking of Journals* by Paula W. Graham. Published by Boyd Mills Press, Inc. Reprinted by permission. **C183:** From *Julie of the Wolves,* by Jean Craighead George, HarperCollins Publishers. **C213:** From *Pauses: Autobiographical Reflections of 101 Creators of Children's Books,* by Lee Bennett Hopkins. Copyright 1995 by Lee Bennett Hopkins. HarperCollins Publishers. **C217:** "Stray" from *Every Living Thing* by Cynthia Rylant. Bradbury Press, Macmillan Publishing. © 1985 by Cynthia Rylant. **C257:** Austin American-Statesman, September 26, 1999. **C325:** Reprinted by permission of Don Congdon Associated, Inc. Copyright © 1960 by the Curtis Publishing Co., renewed 1988 by Ray Bradbury. **C367:** NGI/NGS Image Collection. **C403:** Copyright © 1974 by Roger Lea MacBride. Used by permission of HarperCollins Publishers. **C427:** © George Lucas. **C438:** From *Encyclopedia Britannica Online,* http://members.eb.com/bol/topic?eu=50415&sctn=1. C445: "I am the creativity" by Alexis De Veaux, copyright © 1993 by Alexis De Veaux, from *Soul Looks Back In Wonder* by Tom Feelings. Used by permission of Dial Books for Young Readers, a division of Penguin Putnam Inc. **C461:** "How Languages Started" from *Native Tongues* by Charles Berlitz. © 1982 by Charles Berlitz. Grosset & Dunlap, NY. **C489:** By permission from Merriam-Webster Online © 1999 at Web site http://www.m-w.com by Merriam-Webster, Incorporated. **C493, C494, C497-C499, C502, C504, C506:** Copyright © 1998 by Houghton Mifflin Company. Reproduced by permission from *The American Heritage Student Dictionary.* **C528:** *Readers' Guide to Periodical Literature,* February 1999, Volume 98, No. 12, "Electronic Journals" through "Grandparenting by email." Copyright © 1999 by the H.W. Wilson Company. Material reproduced with permission of the publisher. **C529:** *http://webspirs3.silverplatter.com-Readers' Guide to Periodical Literature-Online* "E-mail addiction" through "E-mail: write protection." Copyright © 1999 by the H.W. Wilson Company. Material reproduced with permission of the publisher.

PHOTO CREDITS

Key: (t) top, (c) center, (b) bottom, (l) left, (r) right.

C5: (b) © Robert Holmes/Corbis. **C38:** © Gail Mooney/Corbis. **C42:** © Jennie Woodcock/Reflections Photolibrary/Corbis. **C45:** © George Lepp/Corbis. **C47:** © Jan Butchofsky-Houser. **C49:** © Kevin Schafer/Corbis. **C50:** © Layne Kennedy/Corbis. **C91:** © Corbis. **C119:** © PictureQuest. **C121:** © Yann Arthus-Bertand/Corbis. **C147:** © Karl Weatherly/Corbis. **C154:** PhotoLink/PhotoDisc. **C183:** © David A. Northcott/Corbis. **C188:** © Kelly-Mooney Photography/Corbis. **C197:** The Art Institute of Chicago. Mr. and Mrs. Frank G. Logan Prize Fund. Photograph © The Art Institute of Chicago. All rights reserved. 1935.313. **C199:** © Joe McDonald/Corbis. **C200:** © Shepard Sherbell/Stock Boston/PNI. **C202:** © SuperStock. **C215:** © 1993 Vietnam Women's Memorial Project, Inc., 1993. Photo by Gregory Staley, courtesy of Goodacre Studio, Santa Fe. **C253:** The Museum of Modern Art, New York, acquired through the Lillie P. Bliss Bequest. Photograph © 1996 The Museum of Modern Art, New York. © 2001 Artists Rights Society (ARS), New York/ADAGP, Paris. **C258-C263:** Fossil illustrations and topography map by Susan D. Hovorka and John Andrews, Bureau of Economic Geology, The University of Texas at Austin. **C286:** ©Joseph Sohm; ChromoSohm Inc./Corbis. **C289:** © Jeff Maloney/PhotoDisc. **C292:** © Bettmann/Corbis. **C299: (l)** © Stock Trek/PhotoDisc; **(r)** © PhotoDisc. **C325:** Corbis. **C333:** © Medford Historical Society/Corbis. **C367: (t)** Kenneth Garrett/NGS Image Collection; **(b)** Photograph © The Metropolitan Museum of Art. **C368: (t)** Kenneth Garrett/NGS Image Collection; **(b)** John Buxton/NGS Image Collection. **C377:** © Fran Antmann. **C403:** © Bettmann/Corbis. **C406:** © Scott T. Smith/Corbis. **C427:** © AFP/Corbis. **C429:** © Neal Preston/Corbis. **C465: (t)** © PhotoDisc; **(b)** © Fran Antmann. **C513:** © Bettmann/Corbis. **C515:** © Bernard Boutrit/Woodfin Camp/PictureQuest.